The United States and the Americas

Lester D. Langley, General Editor

This series is dedicated to a broader understanding of the political, economic, and especially cultural forces and issues that have shaped the Western hemispheric experience — its governments and its peoples. Individual volumes assess relations between the United States and its neighbors to the south and north: Mexico, Central America, Cuba, the Dominican Republic, Haiti, Panama, Colombia, Venezuela, Peru, Ecuador, Bolivia, Brazil, Paraguay, Argentina, Chile, and Canada.

The United States and the Americas

America and the Americas

OTHER BOOKS BY LESTER D. LANGLEY (partial list)

The United States and the Caribbean in the Twentieth Century (1989)

Mexico and the United States: The Fragile Relationship (1991)

The Americas in the Age of Revolution, 1750–1850 (1996)

The Americas in the Modern Age (2003)

Simón Bolívar: Venezuelan Rebel, American Revolutionary (2009)

Lester D. Langley

America and the Americas: The United States in the Western Hemisphere

SECOND EDITION

The University of Georgia Press
Athens & London

© 1989, 2010 by the University of Georgia Press
Athens, Georgia 30602
www.ugapress.org
All rights reserved
Set in 10/14 Minion Pro

Printed digitally in the United States of America

Library of Congress Cataloging-in-Publication Data

Langley, Lester D.
America and the Americas : the United States in the
western hemisphere / Lester D. Langley. — 2nd ed.
    p.   cm. — (The United States and the Americas)
Includes bibliographical references and index.
ISBN-13: 978-0-8203-2888-1 (hardcover)
ISBN-10: 0-8203-2888-x (hardcover)
ISBN-13: 978-0-8203-2889-8 (pbk.)
ISBN-10: 0-8203-2889-8 (pbk.)
1. Latin America — Relations — United States. 2. United
States — Relations — Latin America. I. Title.
F1418.L27 2010
303.48'27308 — dc22   2009032868

British Library Cataloging-in-Publication Data available

For

Arthur Preston Whitaker (1895–1979)

Fredrick B. Pike

John Gentili, my junior high school history teacher

And the authors of the volumes in this series

Contents

Acknowledgments

My first acknowledgment goes to the authors of the books in this series, who, more than I, have sustained it. They are listed in the order in which their respective volumes appear.

Louis A. Pérez Jr., Cuba
William F. Sater, Chile
Thomas M. Leonard, Central America
Michael L. Conniff, Panama
Stephen J. Randall, Colombia
Brenda Gayle Plummer, Haiti
W. Dirk Raat, Mexico
John Herd Thompson and Stephen J. Randall, Canada
Judith Ewell, Venezuela
G. Pope Atkins and Larman C. Wilson, Dominican Republic
Lawrence A. Clayton, Peru
Kenneth D. Lehman, Bolivia
David M. K. Sheinin, Argentina
Frank O. Mora and Jerry W. Cooney, Paraguay
Ronn Pineo, Ecuador
Joseph Smith, Brazil (forthcoming)

Sadly, some of those who contributed so much to the founding of the series or a reading of the original manuscript in 1988 have died: Malcolm Call of the University of Georgia Press, who as director of the Press guided it to national prominence; Stan Lindberg, who made the *Georgia Review* into an elite national literary voice; and David Pletcher, a pioneer in the history of inter-American relations.

In addition, I am particularly grateful to Fredrick Pike, who read the original manuscript; to Karen Orchard, formerly executive editor and director of the University of Georgia Press, who assumed initial responsibility for overseeing the series; and to Nancy Grayson, who now handles that responsibility.

Thom Whigham, a distinguished Latin American scholar and a former colleague in the History Department of the University of Georgia, alertly pointed out my errors. Michael Conniff, who authored the volume on Panama in the series, provided me with a most helpful reading of the 1989 volume and has reprised that role for this volume.

No author has been better served.

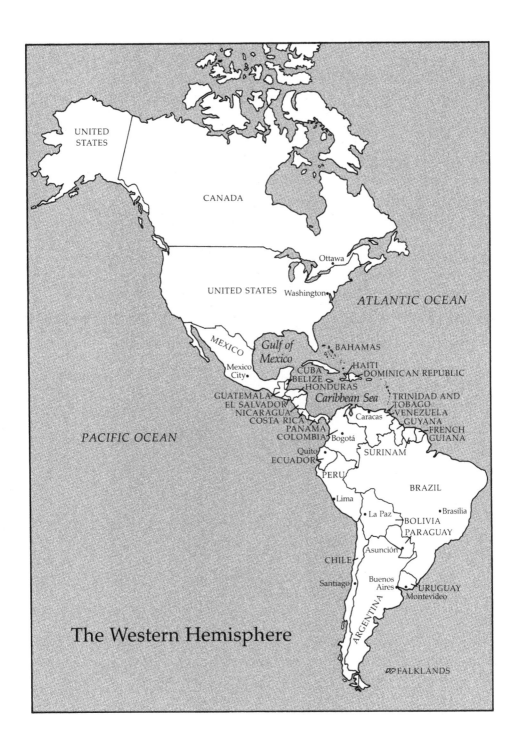

The Western Hemisphere

Introduction to
the Second Edition

America and the Americas was published in 1989 as the first volume in what has become a successful series on the relations between the United States and the other countries of the Western Hemisphere. That series — The United States and the Americas — has achieved widespread recognition from U.S., Canadian, and Latin American historians and other social scientists for its efforts to incorporate social and especially cultural dynamics into the history of inter-American relations. Several of the volumes have gone into new editions. The approach of the 2010 bicentennial of the Latin American wars of independence (1810–25) provides ample reason for a thorough reassessment of several of the major themes I explored in the 1989 volume.

Since 1989, there have been fundamental changes in the relationship between the United States and the other nations and regions of the Western Hemisphere: Canada became a full-fledged member of the inter-American system; the United States, Canada, and Mexico have crafted the North American Free Trade Agreement (NAFTA), which some advocates believe will become the foundation for a North American Union; the United States launched a major diplomatic effort to create a hemispheric free trade area; and in 1994 the first of several Summits of the Americas convened in Miami. These and similar undertakings reinforced older economic, political, and cultural bonds. In different ways, each precipitated widespread and sometimes harsh outcries against U.S. domination, thus muting President George W. Bush's affirmation — announced before the calamitous 11 September 2001, attack on the World Trade Center and the Pentagon — that the twenty-first century will be the "century of the Americas."

People — especially people on the move — have begun to transform the hemisphere and especially the United States in ways and to degrees that governments, including the most powerful government in history, could not have anticipated. Early in the twenty-first century, Hispanics (60 percent of whom are of Mexican heritage) surpassed African Americans in number and have rapidly begun to alter the political dynamics of several states. Immigration, especially from Latin America (principally although not exclusively from Mexico, Central America, and the Caribbean), has become an explosive political and social issue, thus resurrecting old fears about "broken borders" and outcries against "illegal aliens" for taking jobs from Americans and exerting heavy demands on an already overburdened social service system. In a curious although not unexpected way, the United States now sees itself as "victim" in the inter-American story. Some believe this is the inevitable legacy of decades of U.S. domination of hemispheric governments and peoples who have no other way to live the "American dream" save by going to the United States. Indeed, the "Latin Americanization" of the United States is a dramatization of a befuddling although believable example of cultural transfer. For example, Cubans, undeniably anti-American, are in some ways more "Americanized" in their cultural preferences than Puerto Ricans, who have been de facto "colonials" for more than a century.

Too often forgotten or slighted in these accounts are the myriad ways in which the ties between the United States and the other countries of the hemisphere (especially Mexico, Central America, and the Caribbean) have actually been strengthened, often in underappreciated ways, through music, literature, food, and other cultural exchanges. On the most basic level, remittances of Latin Americans working in the United States back to their home countries reached $56 billion, almost half of which went to Mexico. Several U.S. labor unions are beginning to organize these workers. Familial ties have become more important, even as the United States has made more difficult the once traditional back-and-forth migration, especially between Mexico and this country. Less visible but critical to the story are the ways in which Latin Americans are altering the cultural, artistic, and literary landscape and even the cuisine of this country. In brief, the challenge of this book and the other volumes in the series is to frame the history of the Western Hemisphere, which is an integral part of global history as well as the emerging field of Atlantic world history.

As was my purpose in the first volume, my goal in this revised study is something other than a traditional text on inter-American relations, U.S. policy toward Latin America, or the history of the Americas. In this edition, I have given more attention to the U.S. relationship with Canada — a subject virtually ignored in the 1989 volume — a change that places the narrative more closely in a North American context. We Americans look north and see people who appear to value and imitate our cultural preferences and political values, and from such superficial observations we incorrectly assume that Canadians share little of the anti-American sentiments of other countries in this hemisphere. In their feelings if not always in their behavior, Canadians have deep-seated grievances against the United States. We understand better the lingering animosities of Mexico, which lost half its national domain in the 1846–48 war with the United States. The "Canadian connection" takes on a special meaning in part 1 of this volume ("Genesis"). Too often, we in the United States forget or slight the ways in which Canada has influenced U.S. history from our pre-Revolutionary experience to the Civil War of 1861–65. In the same decade, Mexico experienced an equally fratricidal conflict (which precipitated foreign intervention), and Canadians, fearful of U.S. absorption, united in forming a more cohesive federation with the British North America Act.

In the years after the French and Indian War (1754–63), Great Britain, British America, and the U.S. government assumed differing postures toward the other places and peoples of the Americas. At the same time, the American people acquired their basic attitudes, beliefs, prejudices, and fears about their hemispheric neighbors. These fundamental attitudes were shaped largely against the backdrop of three revolutions in the fifty-year span from 1775 to 1825. The first, in British North America, culminated in the creation of the first independent state in the Western Hemisphere. The second, in French Saint-Domingue, was a sanguinary struggle that resulted in the only successful slave revolt in history and the declaration of an independent Haiti. In 1810 a generation of Spanish American Creoles, reacting to the French usurpation of the Spanish throne, began a war initially seeking not independence but autonomy. Fifteen years later, however, mainland Latin America was largely independent.

Traditionally, Latin Americans and Canadians and most U.S. historians look upon this era as one in which an expansionist United States largely disdained the professed "good neighborliness" expressed by the early revolutionary generation and, using as excuse issues of national security and the expansion of slavery, shamelessly tarried in its support of Spanish American independence movements. Some students also indict the United States for its ambivalent posture toward any formal commitment to a collective hemispheric pact and, later, its drive to achieve continental dominion in North America, largely at the expense of Mexico. Many Latin Americans, Caribbean peoples, and even Canadians remember that era — lauded as the age of Manifest Destiny in U.S. history — as representative of unbridled expansionism by an aggressive U.S. government. The parallel drive of the American Democracy to assert U.S. dominion and control into the Caribbean, especially Cuba, and into Central America coupled with the fratricidal debate over the extension of slavery into the territories would plunge the nation into civil war.

As I make clear, the story is more complicated than relating an account of a seemingly relentless U.S. drive to dominate the North American continent. Questions of governance, national security, and especially the incorporation of people of color into an emerging democratic society rent by conflicting political and social passions proliferate during this era. Each of these issues made more problematic the linkages between the emerging United States and its hemispheric neighbors. In his classic study of the 1830s, *Democracy in America*, Alexis de Tocqueville portrayed the young republic in largely positive terms and in the process contrasted U.S. society with that which had emerged in the Old World in the aftermath of the French Revolution. In so doing, often brilliantly so, he glossed over several important hemispheric bonds and blinded a generation to the often subtle ways in which the (first) American Revolution and the first century of the United States were intertwined with other revolutions and new governments of the Western Hemisphere, particularly greater North America and the Caribbean.

These were years in which both U.S. national leaders and the American public acquired their fundamental views and opinions about the lands and peoples of the other Americas. Theirs was an understandable but infuriatingly convoluted judgment that ranged from general prejudices that Latin Americans suffered from an incurably debilitating colonial heritage (and Canadians from an incapacity to wean themselves from their monarchical past) to beliefs that the United States, despite the deepening political tensions and divisions within the republic that led to a devastating civil war, offered a political, economic, and social model to emulate. In this century, the American perception of the other Americas took shape, a perception shaped as much by the fears and insecurity identified with the presumed weakness and instability of neighboring lands as a drive to dominate and expand the national domain. At the same time, in this formative era, the people as much as those who governed proved to be a driving force in the course of U.S. expansion in North America.

In part 2 ("Empire"), I survey the years from about 1876 — the year of the centennial, the triumph of economic liberalism, and the ignominious defeat of Custer at the Little Big Horn — until the mid-1930s, an era in which the dynamic U.S. industrial growth with its presumptive role as policeman of the New World would transform — in both positive and negative ways — the image of the United States in the hemisphere.

In the forty-year span from about 1880, immigration (principally although not exclusively from Europe) would alter not only the political culture but also the economies and societies of four countries in the Americas — the United States, Canada, Argentina, and Brazil. In this era, it has been argued, a generation of U.S. political and economic leaders confronting domestic labor strife and a parallel threat of radical unionism concluded that a policy of "social imperialism" — defined as the extension of informal U.S. economic and political controls into Latin America — was necessary to ease domestic labor discord, a parallel to the older British argument that the working classes of the homeland were better off than the laborers of the far-flung places of the empire. Not surprisingly, the U.S. military drew on its experience in the Indian wars to guide its "pacification" of its insular empire acquired after the victory over Spain in the Cuban-Spanish-American War of 1898. Coincidentally, in this era the United States became a driving force in the creation of a Pan-American system, inspired largely out of economic and political self-interest but as well from a general belief that the independent governments of the Americas shared basic goals about hemispheric trade and what U.S. leaders defined as the European challenge to economic independence. After the beginning of the twentieth century, when U.S. intervention in the circum-Caribbean became increasingly controversial, many Latin Americans became increasingly distrustful of the U.S. commitment to such concepts as self-determination and non-intervention, but in these years American leaders did acknowledge the need for an American public law and the strengthening of the Pan-American system.

The benchmark dates/events for this era are the 1876 centennial and its symbolic importance for the U.S. image in the hemisphere (and especially in

North America) and the dramatic turn in U.S. thinking about its strategy in the hemisphere in the mid-1930s. The latter date is selected because the liberal economic model undergirding the U.S. economy had collapsed in the Great Depression. Beginning about 1935, the U.S. military concluded that it could no longer defend the Panama Canal under existing plans and that its ability to safeguard the hemisphere from external attack was severely limited. That conclusion, reinforced by the determination of the Roosevelt administration to expand U.S. trade in the hemisphere (and a parallel cultural movement to improve U.S.–Latin American relations) signaled yet another shift in hemispheric affairs.

In part 3 ("The Global Crisis"), I assess a quarter-century era when U.S. concerns about the hemisphere shifted dramatically to security issues, commencing with the mid-1930s debate over the impact of the European crisis on the hemisphere and culminating with the Cuban Missile Crisis of October 1962. In the academic literature, judgments about U.S. policy in this era are generally critical: U.S. leaders, it is argued, sacrificed the Good Neighbor policy in the interest of, first, its global commitment against the Axis powers and, second, its confrontation with the Soviet Union. The consequence of such an approach, this argument follows, was the effective denial of self-determination to those hemispheric countries or dependencies striving not only to assert their political independence but also to gain control of their economic future and cultural identity, and, in effect, the justification for the Guatemalan and, especially, Cuban revolutions. U.S. efforts to quash the Cuban Revolution would lead directly to the Missile Crisis, the most dangerous event of the Cold War.

In this revised volume, I expand on these themes by incorporating the account of President Roosevelt's extraordinary commitments to Canada after 1 September 1939. In addition I have added new material on U.S. pursuit of Nazi sympathizers in Latin America and the role of U.S. cultural and educational endeavors in Latin America during and after the war. Too often neglected in accounts of these years are the significance of the country-to-city migration in Latin America (and in the United States) and its political significance for those organizing new political bases, and the impact of World War II on U.S. thinking about the hemisphere, especially in North America.

In covering the Cold War years, I expand on themes introduced in the first edition in order to provide more detail about the impact of the Cold War on the U.S.-Mexico-Canada relationship, the development debate of the 1950s, and the notion of an emergent middle-class "convergence of interest" in the Americas, an appealing notion to those who believed in a nonviolent path to economic and social change. I also give more attention to the "Americanization" of the hemisphere, which found expression in numerous ways, from the social and cultural impact of U.S. developers in the hemisphere to the emergence of the shopping mall. Perhaps too often we in the United States forget that much of the popular enthusiasm in Latin America for revolution after World War II may be attributed *less* to the appeal of Marxism or the example of the Soviet Union than to the American exaltation of materialism and progress and its impact on the ever-growing numbers of consumers. As the late Frank Tannenbaum observed in a seminal 1950s work: "A peasant with a transistor radio does not think like a peasant."

In part 4 ("The Modern Era"), the book addresses four decades of dramatic and profound changes in the relationship between the United States and the other nations and cultures of the Americas — the transformation of the inter-American system; the fashioning of a North American economic bloc and projected "union"; ambitious plans for a free trade area of the Americas; a succession of hemispheric summits since 1994, which have resulted in not only economic agreements but also a highly praised democratic charter of human rights; an exponential leap in cultural exchanges; the migration of Latin Americans, especially Mexicans, Central Americans, and Caribbean peoples, to the United States and with them dramatic changes in the labor market and U.S. society and culture.

Yet, not surprisingly, older, often contentious, issues punctuate this era: concerns over national security; trafficking in drugs and people; the resurgence of anti-Americanism and an anti-U.S. bloc; the survival of the Cuban Revolution; the continuing appeal of military solutions to political problems, among others. In these final chapters, I focus on hemispheric impulses for political, economic, and social change but with greater emphasis on North America than was the case in the original volume. To the original commentary on the tumultuous changes in hemispheric affairs in the 1960s — perhaps best exemplified by the battle over Cuba, the Alliance for Progress, and the 1965 Dominican Intervention — I have added more commentary on the Peace Corps; the Partners of the Americas Program, a people-to-people endeavor that began as Partners of the Alliance; and the political responses to social, cultural, and economic changes, particularly in North America, but also in such key countries as Chile, Argentina, and Brazil. In addition, in this revised edition I have assessed the 1965 U.S. immigration law more so in the context of the civil rights movement. And I have also added much-needed material on the Canadian-U.S.-Mexican relationship of the decade. This chapter concludes with accounts of the Rockefeller mission of 1969, the rise and fall of the socialist government of Salvador Allende in Chile, and its impact on hemispheric affairs.

In the final chapter ("The Defiant Hemisphere"), I recapitulate the hemispheric drama from the mid-1970s to the end of the century, years in which governments of the Americas often proved defiant in their relationship with Washington, D.C., but also years in which the American people fashioned new links with the other peoples and cultures of the Americas. Among the topics are 1) the triumphs and frustrations of President Jimmy Carter's Latin American policies; 2) the Central American crisis; 3) the immigration debate and the Mexican connection; 4) the resurgence of democracy in Latin America; and 5) neoliberalism and new hemispheric initiatives (NAFTA, the Enterprise of the Americas, Summits of the Americas).

The epilogue revisits several issues explored in the first edition, but its main themes assess how and why the place of the United States in the Americas has fundamentally changed in the early twenty-first century. The issues of drug and arms trafficking, immigration, and the impact of the terrorist attack of 11 September 2001, remind us that security concerns continue to dominate the U.S. hemispheric agenda. At the same time, the United States, Canada, and Mexico are more closely integrated economically, despite continuing political conflict. Although subsumed in other issues, the Puerto Rico status question has again resurfaced with a peculiar twist: the U.S. government has now had to accept that "perfecting" the commonwealth arrangement — what Puerto Ricans have persistently called de facto colonialism — is not feasible without a constitutional amendment. In other words, there is no "British way" for the U.S. system. This debate speaks (tangentially, I admit) to some of the larger questions I am addressing in this book: What is Americanization? Who are Americans? The Library of Congress Authorities lists 150 definitions — in effect, Theodore Roosevelt's hyphenate America. How do we Americanize

America? as Randolph Bourne asked in a famous 1916 essay, "Transnational America."

I have retained several fundamental and overarching themes from the first volume. The first is my continuing belief that the United States has had, undeniably, an often conflictual history with the other nations of the hemisphere, but, contrarily, it also has a shared history with those nations and especially their peoples. The central issue here is not a "common history" but what may be better described as an "uncommon" history — that is, linkages between peoples whose histories and cultures have intersected over the course of more than two centuries. Those cultural, informal, and familial linkages, as I make clear, are more clear-cut in the U.S. relationship with its North American and Caribbean neighbors, but they often resonate in seemingly remote hemispheric nations as well.

A second, related theme of the 1989 volume is the distinction I make — and the other peoples of the Americas continue to make — between the "United States" and "America." Although the issue may seem trivial, the United States is the only country in the world without a name, for the reason that the first leaders of the republic could not agree on one. There is no American army, navy, or air force. No one has an American passport. By the end of the nineteenth century, except for formal discourse (such as the "American republics"), the words *American* and *America* became increasingly synonymous with the United States and its people. Too often, we in the United States fail to understand or certainly appreciate the emotional and psychological impact the word *America* evokes in continental discourse. Over more than two centuries, the differing images and sentiments prompted by the mention of the *United States* and *America* in the world and especially in the Western Hemisphere can be striking. The first is a political entity crafted by the American Revolution, an expansionist and, undeniably, imperial presence in the Americas and especially on the North American continent and in the Caribbean and Central America. But *America* evokes differing, less strident and threatening images, that of improvement and liberation. Put differently, the United States is *in* the Americas, but America is *of* the Americas.

In our time, undeniably, the once apparently stronger formal bonds crafted by hemispheric governments — and, certainly, the U.S.-dominated hemispheric entities — have weakened. The reasons are numerous — a U.S. preoccupation with more immediate political and strategic priorities in other parts of the world; the rise of formidable hemispheric blocs challenging an apparently weakening U.S. power; and the restoration of a European presence and the dramatic rise of an equally formidable Asian, especially Chinese, influence in the hemisphere. But, as I make clear in the epilogue, the human and cultural bonds between the United States and the Americas, between America and the Americas, have proved more lasting.

America and the Americas

Prelude:
The Birth of the Second America

As one of the founders, John Adams, often remarked, the revolution that brought forth the first independent state in the Western Hemisphere began in the hearts and minds of the people before the first shot was fired.

It had begun as protest — a welling up of emotions and outrage over the determination of a generation of British leaders to impose order on the vast domain of inland North America that had been the empire's reward for its victory over France in the last colonial war. That conflict, remembered in the Atlantic colonies as the French and Indian War, had begun in 1754 not in Europe but in the Ohio country, and the instigators had been a British governor in cahoots with opportunistic Virginia land speculators. To reconnoiter the region they had dispatched an equally ambitious young second lieutenant in the militia, George Washington. It was his first command, and the effort resulted in a humiliating defeat. But in that embarrassment to his pride he acquired a healthy respect for the nature of war in the backcountry. The following year, a much larger British force under General Edward Braddock would suffer an even more resounding loss to a much smaller force. From that experience, the British vowed to finish off the French empire in North America and in victory to guarantee the security of its Atlantic seaboard colonies and, they naively believed, gain the unending gratitude and loyalty of their peoples.

Within five years the British avenged those setbacks in the trans-Appalachian region, and when the Spanish foolishly entered the war on the side of their French enemy, London exacted yet another stupendous victory with the seizure of the port of Havana in 1762. During the ten-month occupation, the British opened the port to merchants and traders, who dazzled the Cubans with consumer goods, staples, and tools. British traders brought in ten thousand slaves. A fourth of the occupation force consisted of North Americans. The encounter between Cubans and North Americans in this occupation promoted ties that persisted into the nineteenth century and inspired successive generations of rebellious Cubans with beliefs that North Americans were kindred spirits.

At the settling up of territorial rewards, however, the losers appeared to benefit more than the victor. France willingly conceded its North American territory east of the Mississippi but regained the infinitely more valuable sugar islands of St. Lucia, Guadeloupe, and Martinique. Spain in turn gave up the Floridas to the British in order to recover its vital port of Havana, and to repay their commitment the French turned over to Spain the port of New Orleans and most of Louisiana west of the Mississippi.

What occurred in the aftermath of the British triumph proved to be a turning point in the history of North America and the future of the Western hemisphere. Indians of the Ohio country — a people accustomed to dealing with Europeans as equals — correctly sensed that the defeat of their French ally would only worsen their condition. Loosely united under the leadership of Pontiac, they rebelled. In London, British officials now faced a quandary. To avoid yet another costly campaign, they attempted to mollify the Indians with a stopgap measure — the Proclamation of 1763 — aimed at restoring the profitable Indian trade and at the same time stemming the veritable flood of white settlers pouring through the Appalachian passes into the Ohio country.

It proved to be a rational but costly calculation. These presumably loyal Britons had been enthusiastic participants in the war against the French enemy, but they viewed the barriers posed by the Proclamation as a denial of their claims to Ohio country lands. Some of them were newcomers, part of the migration of ethnically diverse Britons and Europeans who left the motherland to "make" America. In an era when European philosophers of the Enlightenment largely disdained their countrymen in the New World as inferior and were beginning to praise its native inhabitants as "noble savages," these newcomers clung instinctively to notions of "natural liberty." They wanted land, and in their frustration they spoke more and more of Indians in starkly harsh terms. They understood abstractions such as freedom, liberty, progress, and nation in racial terms. And guarantee of their security conditioned their loyalty to government.

British imperial policy had run afoul of sentiments and passions far more formidable than any momentary sense of pride in the colonial contribution to the victory over France. Once united to the motherland by a common enemy — France — Atlantic seaboard colonials began to defy the increasing efforts of metropolitan Britain to pacify and then subdue them. Over the next dozen years after the victory over France, as Crown and Parliament demanded colonial subservience to imperial policy, their efforts would precipitate a parallel debate among other European peoples in the New World about their relationships to the motherland. Sparsely populated Nova Scotia and Newfoundland were too vulnerable to protest. In French Quebec, the British elected to preserve French civil law and the Catholic religion, and British West Indian sugar planters were too dependent on the home market and too fearful of the black and colored majorities in their midst to defy the motherland.

The French and Indian War, more so than the American Revolution that came in its wake, was the seedtime of the second America. For Britain and France, the conflict in North America figured as only one of several theaters in a world war. To Atlantic seaboard Britons, however, the victory over France not only meant the removal of the Indian-French threat in the interior but also validated claims to the Ohio country by ambitious Virginia speculators and their land-hungry compatriots. In this debate over the spoils of war and two visions of empire, the determination of British leaders to deny Atlantic seaboard Britons equal rights within the British empire and to use force to quell their protests would precipitate the first American Revolution.

For the first America, however, conflict with the motherland followed a different course. American-born Spaniards (Creoles) of overseas Spain, privileged descendants of the conquerors, had become equally resentful of metropolitan controls, and some rebellious British American leaders presumed that Spanish American protests essentially replicated their own. For three centuries, Spanish American Creoles had ensured the domination of the Spanish king in his American "kingdoms," and a succession of Spanish monarchs had rewarded them with land and Indian labor. As much as Britons of the Atlantic seaboard, they viewed new administrative controls emanating from the Spanish Crown after 1763 as a challenge to their historic privileged position. They lacked the representative assemblies North Americans identify with their own revolution, but they had their literary voices of protest and shared with British Americans a belief that they had earned a place of equality with European Spaniards. A Hispanophile society — forerunner of the American Philosophical Society — flourished among a small but influential number of North Americans.

To their dismay and bitterness, a reformist Spanish monarch, Charles III, and his successor would compound the presumed betrayal of their social compact with the Crown by broadening the definition of "Creole nation" to include peoples from the social margins and to erode the caste laws by granting "certificates of whiteness" to permit people of color to enter professions or gain access to privileges once reserved solely for whites. Most of these decisions would come in the aftermath of the first American Revolution, but Creole resentments over their treatment by the Crown paralleled those taking place in British America.

But there was a fundamental difference between the two elites, and its legacy for the role of the United States in the Americas would survive the era of revolution and reach well into the nineteenth century. British American Whigs seized on independence as the only sure means of gaining equality with the motherland and, at the same time, containing the democratic social forces from below and preserving slavery. British Americans could define *nation*, *unity*, *freedom*, *liberty*, and *equality* in racial terms and yet gain their independence by relying not on farmers and militia but on an army of social marginals. And they would benefit by the cumulative hatred of Britain in France and Spain to transform the revolution at home into a world war. When Spanish American Creoles threw down the gauntlet of defiance in 1810, as discussed shortly, some did so to protest the French usurpation of the Spanish throne. Others, such as the Mexican Miguel Hidalgo and the Venezuelans Francisco de Miranda and Simón Bolívar, were unambiguously pro-independence from the beginning. The bitterness between the two groups would plunge Spanish Americans into civil war. More ominously, their entry into the revolutionary age occurred in the aftermath of the unexpected "revolution from below," the slave revolt in French Saint-Domingue, which culminated in the creation of Haiti in January 1804. The birth of the second independent nation in the Americas would dramatically alter the meaning and dynamics of the revolutionary age.

These three upheavals, distinctive and different in so many ways, were formative events in the often troublesome development of the Western Hemisphere in its first century of independence and the U.S. role in that history. How and why that was the case is the central issue explored in the first part of this book.

PART 1
Genesis

1   The Revolutionary Age

In the half-century span after 1775 there occurred not one but three revolutions in the Americas. The one most familiar is the first, the American Revolution, what the British general Sir Henry Clinton called the American rebellion. But there were two other revolutions in this era — in French Saint-Domingue, the richest colony in the Americas; and in the vast American kingdoms of the Spanish monarch. Each sprang from different causes. Each had its own ideology. Each had its immediate origins in the politics and rivalries of three European powers — Great Britain, the presumptive heir to Rome; France, its implacable enemy and benefactor of the first American Revolution; and Spain, the parent of the First America. In this fifty-year epoch, the distinctive political cultures of America would take root.

In the beginning, at least, British Americans viewed their cause as defensive. At the onset, almost a year before they proclaimed their independence to a "candid world," delegates to the second Continental Congress called for an army of twenty thousand and named as its commander George Washington, the only member to attend dressed in military uniform. The delegates resolved to take their rebellion into Nova Scotia and Quebec. They justified the invasion as a necessary measure against a projected British strike against New England with the intention of severing the region from any assistance from other colonies. Volunteers from the newly created Continental Army gathered in churches in Newburyport, Massachusetts, to receive blessings for their arduous march northward. There was an ideological urgency to the strike. As one New England firebrand, John Hancock, proudly declared, the purpose was to "open a way for the Blessing of Liberty, and the Happiness of well-ordered Government to visit that vast Dominion."[1]

Defiant British Americans looked on the invasion both as a defensive measure to discourage a British invasion and as a means of spreading their protest against London's "tyranny" among presumably kindred spirits. Nova Scotia's inhabitants shared not only an ethnic bond but also religious and linguistic bonds with New Englanders. The more numerous Quebecois were another matter. A year before, as part of its punitive legislation against the colonials, the British had incorporated the Ohio country into the Quebec province. Its hundred thousand French-speaking residents were overwhelmingly Roman Catholic, and their political and landholding traditions were alien to everything New Englanders held dear. Nonetheless, the outspoken members of the Second Continental Congress were persuaded that the "oppressed" people of Quebec would rally to the revolutionary banner and join the American union.

By implication, the rebellious Americans also made clear that their appeal was conditional: If French Canadians did not join up, they would suffer reprisals in the event they elected to assist the British in resisting the invasion. In the course of the campaign, then, the French remained neutral if not indifferent to their presumed liberators. In their options, they chose the lesser of two evils, a British master who at least tolerated their religion and traditions. Some English merchants with personal ties to the American rebels expressed a tentative sympathy.

There were two separate invasions. One succeeded in capturing Montreal; the second laid siege to Quebec City. British reinforcements retook both the following spring. The British counteroffensive in 1777 proved no more successful, as General Edward Burgoyne's disastrous collapse at Saratoga in October and, more important, the ability of a generation of American diplomats to exploit French-British jealousies, made possible the alliance that brought France into the war and transformed the American Revolution into a world war.[2]

The Caribbean was also a critical theater in the war. American patriots received aid, particularly vital military supplies, from the French, Spanish, Dutch, and even the British Isles. Indeed, the Caribbean phase of the war played a decisive role in how the American Revolution ended. The British naval commander in the West Indies, Admiral Sir George Rodney, grew so angry over aid to the rebels from Dutch St. Eustatius that he subjected the island to a prolonged siege. His preoccupation with punishing the island in part explained his inability to intercept the French fleet that played a decisive role in ensuring the American victory at Yorktown. Afterward, Rodney redeemed his reputation with a tremendous victory over that same French fleet at the Battle of the Saintes (12 April 1782), and thus preserved British rule over Jamaica. But in different ways the American Revolution had an impact on the British

West Indies. Free coloreds, inspired in part by republican ideology from the north, challenged the white planter class, as did the abolitionists in the motherland. Ironically, the slaveholding West Indian planters looked more and more to Southern slaveholding elites as kindred spirits and became increasingly unhappy with their place in the empire. But they were too fearful of slave rebellion to imitate the course chosen by a generation of Atlantic seaboard revolutionaries.[3]

Spain and the American Revolution

The French alliance proved critical to the winning of independence. It gave the American cause money and a navy and made possible Spain's involvement in the war, in both moneys and military action.

The difference, of course, was that the French were true believers. Their hatred of Britain ran deeper. The Spanish made a political but not an ideological commitment to the American cause. An independent United States would be troublesome, but assisting their revolution would be one way of retaliating against the British for more than two decades of humiliation. And they were beguiled by their French mentors, who had once again implicated them in a direct way in the age-old French struggle against Britain. To the American rebels they sent supplies and moneys, usually via Havana or New Orleans. Unwilling to act merely as a supplier, the Spanish undertook an invasion of Spanish Florida, effectively destroying British power on the Lower Mississippi, and dispatched a naval expedition against Mobile. Two thousand miles to the west, Spanish soldiers and priests pushed up the California coast, building presidios and missions, twin symbols of Spain's North American imperial frontier.

There were other battles, and the Spanish emerged from the American Revolution believing they had strengthened their presence in North America. But they came away from the peace conference with a sense of betrayal by their French friend. In the arcane diplomatic intrigues of the settlement of this war, the British had agreed that the northern boundary of west Florida would be marked not at Vicksburg but farther south. More than that, most Americans now viewed them as duplicitous and untrustworthy. And, as they regained the

Floridas and ensconced themselves in New Orleans, they were seen as a threat. Spanish governors permitted a British company — Panton, Leslie — to oversee the Indian trade of the Southeast from a Florida base.

With the continued British presence in the old Northwest, the informal Anglo-Spanish alliance indirectly controlled the western country. Among leaders of the young republic, there was a palpable sense that the Revolution and the progress it promised might be reversed. The Spanish representative at the peace negotiations in Paris, the Conde de Aranda, confirmed American fears when he asserted that the lands between the Appalachian Mountains and the Mississippi River rightfully belonged to the Indian nations who lived there. U.S. delegates summarily rejected that idea, of course, but in the ensuing years it became clear that the authority of the young republic in the trans-Appalachian territory would have to be maintained by force of arms.[4]

Already, the Spanish began to view themselves as victims of an expansionist republic in the Mississippi Valley, and they were alert to the debilitated state of the new republic. In 1785 they offered a liberal commercial treaty in exchange for U.S. concessions on Mississippi River navigation, but pressure from western interests killed the measure. In the aftermath, Spanish governors in New Orleans began to intrigue among disaffected Americans in the trans-Appalachian country. One, the Baron de Carondelet, allegedly bribed a U.S. general, James Wilkinson, who was apparently persuaded that a Spanish protectorate might provide the security the sparsely settled western settlements coveted.

But as had occurred during the Revolution, European rivalries benefitted the young republic. In 1793 Spain joined the first coalition against Revolutionary France, suffered a humiliating defeat, and in the settlement two years later was compelled to cede the eastern portion of Hispaniola to French control. Already the administration of George Washington had knuckled under to British pressure and agreed to a neutral position in the European war in return for the withdrawal of British forces from key northwest forts. When the Spanish Crown got wind of the arrangement, the Spanish minister of foreign relations summoned the U.S. minister, Thomas Pinckney, and to the U.S. diplomat's consternation the Spanish conceded virtually every major issue among the list of frontier grievances. The most important was the right to navigate the Mississippi to New Orleans with the even more beneficial privilege of shipping goods from the port.

Thus ended the first phase of the battle for the interior of North America. For more than three decades, the British and then Americans had tried to deal with the uncertainties of a relentless migration of people into the western country. In the years after independence, frontier politics became even more complicated, with states vying for control and an inept federal administration trying to assert its authority. One solution lay in a master plan for the Ohio country — the Northwest Ordinances — an admittedly imperfect formula for transforming the region into territories and then into states. As Washington astutely observed, the survival of the young nation — indeed, the affirmation of national sovereignty — depended on retaining the western country, the locale of a "long war" that had commenced with Pontiac's rebellion in 1763 and continued for another half century after the American Revolution. Access to New Orleans was one vital element in this scheme. The second was defeat of the Indian tribes that had historically looked to France and then Great Britain and Spain to protect their lands from these migrants from the east.[5]

But there was a feature to the story of the Old Northwest that has always complicated the traditional account of the history of the American Revolution as ideological conflict between republican and liberal theorists or the denial of legitimate democratic urgings of ordinary people by calculating elites. It was one thing for a revolution to enlist the loyalty of people in the cause of independence. Maintaining their loyalty was a different matter, and equally problematical. In the uncertainties of the time, those who governed would draw a color line, and in the process they would redefine revolutionary words such as *freedom* and *liberty* and *nation* in ways that would reassure white people but effectively exclude others from full participation in the political culture. After all, the first naturalization act of 1790 had limited citizenship to "free white persons," thus excluding not only slaves but indentures and free colored. On the frontier, then, white elite and white settler entered into a variation of the social compact — a denial of the claims of squatters and other newcomers and a parallel commitment against the Indians to safeguard the property and lives of both large and small property holders. In return for this security, they pledged their loyalty to the state. In this fashion, then, Thomas Jefferson's "empire of liberty" took root, a continental domain conceived in the ambitions of Washington and dominated by people who defined the fundamental ideals of the young republic in the rhetoric of liberty and color.

What Spain had given up, both Americans and Spaniards knew, could just as readily be withdrawn. The more restricted right of deposit at New Orleans, which had accompanied the vital concession of free navigation for American vessels on the lower Mississippi, became in these years a symbolic test of Spanish intentions. For eight years after Pinckney's diplomatic victory in Europe, the "western question" was unresolved. Two successive presidents — John Adams and Thomas Jefferson — correctly perceived that national unity depended on placating the continuous western demands for access to New Orleans, yet they were alert to the potential dangers of provoking a frontier conflict with Spain that could very well escalate into a confrontation with the French.

Sensing the American dilemma — how to push Spain out of the lower Mississippi without giving their French ally a convenient excuse to intrude — the Spanish followed their traditional diplomatic strategy of pretending to pursue one course when their goal was another. Though recognizing Louisiana's inevitable loss — as the Conde de Godoy had observed, "We can't lock up an open field," a sardonic reference to the impossibility of defending the lower Mississippi Valley — Spanish governors in New Orleans continued their generous immigration policies.[6] They tried to lure European settlers into Louisiana and the Floridas. That failing, they revived their intrigues with the Americans they had occasionally befriended or suborned. Wilkinson, who became U.S. Army commander in the West after the death of Anthony Wayne, continued to receive a subsidy from them, and he encouraged other Americans in madcap schemes to detach the western country and make it into a Spanish protectorate. In 1797 yet another Spanish conspiracy — this one involving Senator William Blount of Tennessee — collapsed under a torrent of anti-Spanish sentiment. A year later, when an undeclared naval war with France erupted on the high seas, Alexander Hamilton and other Federalists schemed to unite east and west by declaring war on Spain and invading the lower Mississippi.

The resolute Adams would not hear of it. His cautious diplomacy avoided a war with two European empires but did not immediately bring Louisiana into the American snare. When the United States and France ended their naval war in 1800, the Americans rid themselves of the Revolutionary War alliance, but Spain had already secretly ceded Louisiana to France. The Spanish policy of maneuver and, to Americans, deception appeared vindicated. In five years of debilitating European conflict and frontier intrigue, the Spanish had sustained a weak but symbolically authoritative presence in the lower Mississippi Valley and the Floridas. A small invading force of Americans, they believed, could have taken New Orleans. But the United States had not taken advantage of Spanish military weakness in its Louisiana outpost. Adams had restrained the more aggressive instincts of his countrymen, and perhaps more important, the Spanish court had recognized that Louisiana would never be the bastion of imperial defense. Accepting that reality, the Spanish had followed a time-honored strategy of yielding but not breaking before the more powerful winds from the north.[7]

The Haitian Revolution

In the aftermath came Napoleon and Talleyrand's imperial design to revive New France in Louisiana and Saint-Domingue, an expanse rivaling in economic productivity the British Empire before the American Revolution. The outbreak of the French Revolution in 1789 threw the island into turmoil, commencing with political battles between powerful white slaveholders and lower-class whites and then escalating into an even bloodier conflict by coloreds claiming equality under the new revolutionary decrees. A slave revolt had erupted in Saint-Domingue in 1791 and found a leader in a former slave, Toussaint Louverture, who skillfully took advantage of French international distress. In 1798, when the undeclared naval war broke out with the United States, he confronted a powerful British army in Haiti, invited in by fearful white planters in 1793. Toussaint struck a deal with the British: he would not export his slave rebellion to Jamaica, and the British and the Americans could share in the lucrative trade. By the end of the decade he had established control over the western third of the island. Toussaint abolished slavery but retained the plantation economy and imposed a severe labor code to ensure the retention of workers. All the while, he professed loyalty to France and the inherited rights of revolutionary France.

In the twilight of his presidency Adams ended the naval war with France and with it the Revolutionary War alliance. He had not reckoned on the revived French ambitions in the Western Hemisphere. He dutifully sent orders to American naval officers to cease dealing with Toussaint, who was then mounting a campaign to subdue the eastern portion of the island. Simultaneously, Napoleon compelled the Spanish to retrocede Louisiana and began planning to deal with the "Black Napoleon" in the Queen of the Antilles.

Thomas Jefferson's affections for French culture led Napoleon and his foreign minister, Talleyrand, to believe the new U.S. president would support the French cause in the Caribbean. They presumed, correctly, that the Americans feared Toussaint's autonomous Saint-Domingue as much as the British and that there would be no British naval interception of a French invasion force dispatched to subdue Toussaint. American officials made ambiguous statements about the ambitious French design, coupled inextricably with rumors of Louisiana's retrocession. Secretary of State James Madison told the new French chargé d'affaires of American concerns. The French diplomat, alert to the nuances of American politics, asked for U.S. cooperation in keeping Toussaint from shifting into the British embrace by keeping open a small part of the American trade with the black leader. Madison then strongly hinted that if France made peace with Britain the French navy could starve the Haitians into submission. When these words reached Talleyrand, they were interpreted as a pledge of American cooperation in the French venture. In October 1801 Napoleon ceased hostilities against Britain. Then he named his brother-in-law, Joseph LeClerc, commander of a powerful French invasion force dispatched to restore his authority over the defiant Haitians. In LeClerc's instructions, Napoleon wrote, "Jefferson has promised that from the moment the French army arrives, every measure shall be taken to starve Toussaint and to aid the army."[8]

Jefferson the Francophile and slaveholder was then in his first year as president. He was a montage of contradictions, but where Louisiana was concerned he was a strategist and opportunist, mindful of the primacy of the western question in the country's dealings with the European powers. He shared Napoleon's fears about a free or even an autonomous Saint-Domingue. When he found out about the retrocession of Louisiana, his admiration for France slackened. His policy became fundamentally expedient, even to daring talk about allying with the British to keep the French out of Louisiana. Earlier, the more socially conservative Adams had evinced some concern for Toussaint's cause, if for no other reason than to serve American national interests, and had initiated trade with the black leader. But Jefferson, then the presidential aspirant, had opposed even this limited contact. He told Madison in 1799, when Congress was debating the issue, "We may therefore expect black crews, and supercargoes and missionaries thence into the Southern states. . . . If this combustion can be introduced among us under any veil whatever, we have to fear it."[9]

Jefferson was more prophetic than he knew about the fears the Haitian rebellion would provoke in the United States. With an unappreciated guile and determination, Jefferson pressed the Louisiana issue. Unexpectedly, the French invasion of Haiti in late 1801 abetted his cause. The French commander, Joseph LeClerc, tricked Toussaint into surrendering and then sent him in chains to France. He died two years later in an Alpine prison. Across the ocean, the momentary order he had imposed lapsed into racial and class warfare, bringing with it forty thousand French casualties. Jefferson had already dispatched a special emissary, James Monroe, to negotiate with the French. By the time Monroe arrived, Napoleon had decided to abandon Louisiana — even before the French had formally taken possession — and in the process break his pledge to his Spanish ally not to transfer the province to a third power. Jefferson wanted New Orleans and the Floridas. Monroe bought the Isle of Orleans and the French added Louisiana to the purchase. By the end of 1802 American newspapers had picked up the rumor of the transfer. When the Spanish learned of it, they were furious and immediately restored the right of deposit they had earlier canceled.

The withdrawal of that right by Spain and, by implication, France roused the westerners into a war fever. If Spain could not deal with the Americans on that and related matters, neither could France. In a few years the Spanish had unintentionally furthered the American cause in New Orleans by opening the city and the frontier to American commerce and Americans. When France eventually took possession of the city in early December 1803, its Americanization had already begun. Rumors of Spanish efforts to prevent the U.S. takeover had inspired volunteers from the West to invade the city and, if necessary, to seize it. The story was one of several widely held views of Spanish perfidy. The most notorious was the "Black Legend" about the rapacity of the Spanish conquest that William Hickling Prescott used as a literary theme in his histories and that

Americans too often believed. When the U.S. flag was unfurled a few weeks later, the volunteers were scattered about the city. But their menacing presence was unnecessary. The Spanish had no intention of fighting for a province and a city that they had already determined to relinquish.

Within a year after the Louisiana Purchase, the Haitian Revolution ended. Out of its carnage emerged the second independent state of the Americas. The upheaval dampened the spirits of even the most committed revolutionaries of Jefferson's generation. Its destructiveness, its symbolic horror of class and racial conflict, and its lasting imagery of violence deeply affected those who shaped U.S. policy toward the hemisphere and the precursors of Latin American independence. Even the effusive Francisco de Miranda — a transatlantic crusader — confessed to an English friend in 1798: "As much as I desire the liberty and independence of the New World, I fear the anarchy of a revolutionary system. God forbid that these beautiful countries become . . . a theatre of blood and of crime under the pretext of establishing liberty. Let them rather remain if necessary one century more under the barbarous and imbecilic oppression of Spain."[10]

In most accounts of the acquisition of the Louisiana territory, the slave revolt in Saint-Domingue and the Haitian Revolution assume a secondary importance in explaining Jefferson's triumph — an episode in the storied history of U.S. advantage over Europe's distresses and rivalries. For contemporaries, however, the impact of that upheaval on U.S. slave culture and politics and the debate over the use of slave soldiers in the Spanish-American wars of independence was considerable. Before Washington's first term had ended, French planters had already begun fleeing Saint-Domingue with their slaves for other islands in the Caribbean and, ultimately, to the United States. Southern governors were often outspoken in their opposition to what they considered a dangerous presence of Saint-Domingue's slaves in the South. Years before Louisiana became a state the influence of these Europeans from the Caribbean in New Orleans offered a sharp contrast in attitudes about the role of free coloreds in the territory.[11]

Without the Haitian slave victory over the French, however, the history of the Caribbean and the character of pre–Civil War politics would have taken a different course. Ironically, the early leaders of independent Haiti (which split into two entities in 1807 and remained divided for fifteen years) vowed to preserve the plantation system with former slaves working under a strict labor code. They encouraged immigration of slaves from Africa, from other islands in the Caribbean, and even from the United States, pledging to offer the newcomers their freedom in return for their work on the plantations. But the former slaves would not submit, and the immigrants, especially those from the United States, had little interest in the harsh work in the countryside. In the end, Haiti's masters did learn how to control the Haitian peasant, but the former slaves had proved to the world and especially to the Americas that they were the avengers of the New World and would forever be remembered as having triumphed over slavery. Their persistence in fighting to end slavery and (to the dismay of their leaders) their continuing opposition to the plantation economy would instill pride in successive generations of African Americans and fear among their masters. Yet, ironically, their struggle had a profound legacy for the United States in the nineteenth century. As Henry Adams noted in his monumental *History of the United States*, their defeat would have meant that "the wave of French empire would roll on to Louisiana and sweep far up the Mississippi," but their resistance assured that "America would be left to pursue her democratic destiny in peace."[12]

The Hemispheric Crisis

For years the fears that accompanied Haitian independence reinforced Americans' notions about the cataclysmic finality of any rebellion in the slave Caribbean, although that belief only moderately lessened their enthusiasm for the cause of independence on the mainland of Spanish America. They were captivated with the notion of liberation of an America that transcended national domain and encompassed the entire hemisphere. Thomas Jefferson described it as "one hemisphere . . . having a different system of interest" yet suffering from the "passions and wars" of European tyranny. Even his later doubts that "priest-ridden people" could sustain "free civil government" did not diminish his faith that "America has a hemisphere to itself."[13]

The star-crossed plotter Francisco de Miranda was perhaps the first Creole liberator Americans knew. For a generation he conspired with British ministers and U.S. political leaders in schemes for the liberation of Spanish America. The

American revolutionary triumph inspired him, and he found kindred spirits and, he believed, support for his own liberating cause among American leaders. Preparing for an assault on Venezuela in 1806 he obtained vital provisions and converts in the United States. Jefferson and Madison, then warily charting American policy toward Spanish America, did not commit themselves directly, but they were assured that others would support the charismatic Creole who admired British and American political culture. When he launched the ill-fated assault on Venezuela in 1807, American money, men, and matériel abetted his cause. This liberating expedition failed, but Miranda never lost the determination to press on. He went back to London and was rewarded with a comfortable country house, a library, and a coterie of friends. Still he plotted to free his Venezuelan homeland from Spanish rule.[14]

Over the preceding decade American interest in Spanish America had sharpened considerably. The first missions to the Spanish colonies after the liberalization of trade policies in 1797 were largely commercial. A U.S. consulate opened in Santiago de Cuba a year later and another in 1800 at La Guaira, Venezuela. Neither was officially recognized, but according to local custom, they were tolerated. A few prominent Americans were later implicated in Miranda's ill-fated scheme to liberate Venezuela, and no less a vocal patriot than Andrew Jackson was mesmerized by former vice president Aaron Burr's bizarre plot to liberate Florida, Texas, and Mexico. A few Americans had become students of Hispanic culture and were sufficiently aware of the empire's cultural achievements to offer a demurral to the more popular view of "barbarous, Popish" Spanish America.[15]

What ultimately became a continental war for independence began as a struggle for autonomy and equality within a Hispanic nation under assault from France. In 1807 Napoleon removed Ferdinand VII from the Spanish throne and replaced him with his brother Joseph. For the Creoles who gained a political foothold in local Spanish government throughout the empire, Napoleon's act confirmed Spanish debility and in 1808 provoked some *cabildos* (town councils) to denounce the French and reaffirm their loyalty to Ferdinand, *el deseado*, the "desired one." In the following years, the protests escalated into violence in a dozen cities. Everywhere the rallying cry was reaffirmation of loyalty to Ferdinand, but in some places, notably Mexico, the conflict portended social upheaval. In Spanish South America, it was the defiance of an alienated and opportunistic Creole elite who hearkened to the constitutional monarchism of Britain and the chorus of commercial freedom sung by Americans.[16]

These events brought hints of more daring policies from Washington. For a year Jefferson had watched his political reputation wither before a storm of criticism over his economic policies, especially the hated embargo, which had shut down American shipping and plunged New England into a depression. What he perceived as the impending collapse of Spanish authority in the New World offered yet another opportunity to take advantage of Old World distresses. Spain confronted not only civil war in Spanish America but conflict at home between the *afrancesados* (those who went along with the French takeover because they believed Spain would progress under French guidance) and the patriots loyal to the deposed Ferdinand. The latter had new-found friends among the British.

For Jefferson the tumult in Spain and its fractious colonies offered the prospect for extending American commercial interests without parallel political commitments. Anti-Jeffersonian historians have described his Latin American policies as either vacillating or self-serving. His defenders have exalted his strategic vision and even credited him with laying the groundwork for the Monroe Doctrine. He told U.S. agents hastily dispatched to South America to make no political obligations to the rebels but to express American friendship and warn them against British or French manipulation. Sometime later, he expressed the view that American and Hispanic American revolutionaries agreed that "European influence" must be excluded from the Western Hemisphere. Despite American hesitation, the Spanish American revolutionaries did benefit from even the limited concessions they received.[17]

As had Jefferson, Madison avoided making political commitments, but to his credit he permitted patriot emissaries to purchase munitions. Agents from Buenos Aires, Venezuela, Mexico, Colombia, and even Cuba descended on Baltimore and Philadelphia, the two commercial entrepôts for the arms trade. A similar privilege was accorded de Onís when Ferdinand was restored to the throne and launched his counterrevolution. But these limited commitments to revolutionary governments supposedly fighting for the same reasons Americans themselves had struggled in their own war of independence did not provide lasting reassurances. The United States favored Latin American independence but would not recognize the fledgling revolutionary governments, nor would the private American businessmen who sold to them (such as John

Jacob Astor) assume unnecessary risks. Furthermore, the American emissaries sent to negotiate with the rebels often found themselves outmaneuvered by British agents, who were winning commercial agreements from rebel governments even while maintaining an alliance with the Spanish Crown.

Great Britain had already surpassed the United States in the quest for Latin American commerce. Exploiting the free ports system in the Caribbean and skillfully using its naval power, Britain overcame blockades and opened revolutionary ports to merchants who had lost their markets in Europe and the United States. In Portuguese Brazil the British advance was political as well as economic. Until 1808 British ships had to sail by way of Lisbon to trade with the colony. But Napoleon's entry into Iberia had sent the Braganza royal house to safety in Brazil under the guard of British warships. A commercial treaty drawn up by the British minister in 1810 virtually assured British commercial domination for a generation.

Through these years of vacillation and undisguised opportunism, American leaders continued to believe that alienated Spanish American Creoles would find in the United States a political model to emulate and would, as had the United States, identify Britain as the transatlantic economic menace. The reality was infuriatingly more complicated. What British Americans had accomplished in defying the mother country was commendable, as Bolívar himself acknowledged, but in looking for an ally or a mediator the British proved the far stronger party. True, Miranda had expressly preferred the U.S. to the French model of revolution, and the first Venezuelan republic exhibited some of the federalist character identified with the Articles of Confederation government of the United States. But neither Miranda nor the federalist system survived the collapse of the first republic in 1812, the year the United States went to war with Great Britain, and a band of Spanish liberals hammered out a constitution that, save for peoples of African origin, professed to treat both European and American Spaniards as equals.

Clearly, then, the United States in these months before the onset of the War of 1812 proved to be in a weak position in trying to insinuate itself much further in the Spanish-American conflicts. Nonetheless, its government professed a hemispheric defiance, albeit one focused on the troublesome issue of Florida. In 1811 Congress resolved that Spanish Florida must not be transferred to another non–Western Hemispheric power. In the same year it created the

Committee on the Spanish American Colonies, expressing its sympathy for the patriot cause and hesitantly advancing a commitment to hemispheric unity. By 1814 the wars for independence had reached a stalemate. Bolívar fled into exile for the second time. Ferdinand VII returned to power and peremptorily revoked the liberal 1812 constitution. In Venezuela the royalist counterrevolution had apparently triumphed. In Mexico the social upheaval launched by Father Hidalgo's army had been checked, and in faraway Buenos Aires a cabal of rebellious Creoles had become noticeably hesitant in denouncing Spanish authority. If U.S. policies reflected international political and economic realities and, at bottom, furthered the national interest, a generation of Latin American revolutionaries shrewdly chose British over American friendship for similar reasons of statecraft, not ideological affinity.[18]

American determination to acquire the Floridas had figured prominently in the congressional debate over hostilities. Even before the "no-transfer" resolution prohibiting the transfer of Florida from one European power to another, the United States had begun a piecemeal absorption by occupying extreme west Florida (from the Mississippi to the Pearl River) in 1810. A year later, using as pretext the collapse of adequate Spanish jurisdiction over the province and an impending British invasion, President James Madison secretly encouraged an anti-Hispanic former governor of Georgia to rouse ruffians in the border towns for an invasion of the province. The invaders took Fernandina Island and prepared for an assault on St. Augustine, but the Spanish protested, and Madison backed down. U.S. troops remained for the duration of the war, and to the west the United States occupied the remainder of the peninsula from the Pearl to the Perdido rivers. At war's end, the Spanish had a choice: they could hold Florida with British support or they would eventually lose it to the persistent Americans.

There were similar sentiments about pushing the British out of Canada. On the eve of the war a few western congressmen, notably the Kentuckian Henry Clay, called for an invasion of Upper Canada (essentially Ontario), as did southerner John C. Calhoun. Their arguments echoed familiar conspiratorial themes — British merchants were arming warriors of the Algonquin Confederation who threatened white settlers — and inspired those who believed those Americans who had fled north during the Revolution might be induced to rejoin the republic. Others, such as the irascible John Randolph of Virginia, scoffed at such notions, but a few of the "War Hawks" from the western districts argued that seizing Canada as "hostage" offered the surest means of defeating the Indian confederacies, advancing westward expansion, and countering British supremacy on the high seas.

As Canadian historians routinely observe, Thomas Jefferson's boast that U.S. victory in any northward invasion would be little more than a "mere matter of marching" ended in a series of humiliating defeats. As they had shown in 1775 and 1776, Canadians evinced little sympathy for the invaders, and with Indian allies they repulsed every U.S. strike. U.S. naval forces did surprisingly well against the Royal Navy on the Great Lakes, and its land forces successfully repulsed a British invasion from the north. British troops were able to land in the Chesapeake region and march on Washington, D.C., where they torched the Executive Building in retaliation for the burning of government buildings in Canada. But the war ended in a territorial stalemate, and the British also made other concessions to their former colonials. A few weeks after the Christmas 1814 peace settlement at Ghent, Andrew Jackson commanded a ragtag army of westerners, free coloreds, and Indians in a stunning victory over a superior British force in the Battle of New Orleans.

Jefferson and Madison had touted the war as a vindication of maritime rights and the Revolution, but the conflict had deeply divided New Englanders from the South and the West. The biggest losers were Britain's Indian allies, who has staked much on their support for the Royal cause but at war's end found themselves either dependent on the Crown's good intentions or facing increasingly vindictive westerners. Two years later, British and U.S. diplomats followed with a fundamental agreement providing for the neutrality of the Great Lakes, thus putting to rest a potential naval arms race, and in 1818 thrashed out a territorial settlement along the forty-ninth parallel from the Lake of the Woods to the crest of the Rocky Mountains.[19]

A Decade of Crisis

In 1815, when the United States was finally assured that its independence would not be revoked, the Latin American independence movements appeared doomed. Their leaders were exiled, jailed, or dead. The restored Spanish monarch Ferdinand had repudiated the liberal 1812 constitution and dispatched an army of pacification into the heartland of revolutionary Venezuela and New Granada. Simón Bolívar was exiled a second time from his homeland. A refugee in Jamaica, he crafted a fundamental statement about patriot cause and his prognosis for the future of South America. In the Southern Cone, the Argentine José de San Martín began to equip and mobilize his Army of the Andes for the liberation of Chile and, ultimately, Peru. Throughout Europe, the defeat of Napoleon appeared to validate monarchy and, more ominously, the restoration of the Spanish kingdom in America.

Yet, a decade after the end of the Napoleonic war, most of mainland Latin America was independent and, with the notable exception of monarchical Brazil, republican, but the explanation for this achievement had less to do with what later generations of North Americans would attribute to their own government and, particularly, to the December 1823 statement of President James Monroe accepting the irrevocability of Latin American independence than to other factors — the critical decision of the British government to oppose any effort by friendly European governments to assist Spain, a lessening enthusiasm for the war among Spanish liberals, and, most important, the transformation of the patriot war into a continental struggle. The ever cynical Spanish minister in Washington, Luis de Onís, predicted that the British decision was an ominous portent for the hemisphere: "Now the United States is going to become a great nation, full of pride, presumption and the ambition to conquer."[20]

Had Onís been privy to some of the ruminations of some of the nation's leaders about the future of the nation, he might not have written these words. Undeniably, the nationalist rhetoric accompanying the end of the war with Britain and, particularly, celebrations of Jackson's victory at New Orleans indicated that the republic had put aside much of the political bickering and sectional hatreds of the years before the war. Fourth of July oratory and the cult of George Washington resonated throughout the political culture, and the press wrote of an "era of good feelings" between political adversaries and consensus about the national purpose. That phrase was a domestic variation of a "spirit of good neighborliness," words that some enthusiasts used to describe the country's support for the cause of Spanish American independence and the belief that the survival of the federal republic depended, indirectly at least, on the creation of similar federated governments throughout Spanish America.

Indeed, in newspapers and in the halls of Congress, the name of Simón Bolívar, who with assistance from Haitian president Alexandre Pétion revived the patriot war in Venezuela, evoked praise. Henry Clay was particularly outspoken in his support of the independence movement. At a critical moment in the congressional debate over recognition of the Venezuelan republic in early 1818, when several of his colleagues voiced concern about Bolívar's dictatorial rule during the second republic of 1813–14, the infamous "war to the death" decree (which applied even to those Spaniards who were neutral), and particularly to Bolívar's decision to liberate those slaves who fought in the patriot army, Clay pointed to the situation Bolívar confronted, and especially to the royalists' decision to use slaves as soldiers and the atrocities they had committed against the patriots. He asked rhetorically: "Could it be believed if the slaves had been let loose upon us in the south . . . that General Washington would not have resorted to retribution?"[21]

For every voice urging a stronger commitment to the Spanish American patriot cause, others expressed doubts about plunging into making any further commitments. President James Monroe, an early enthusiast, became noticeably more cautious about altering U.S. neutrality policy after receiving a report of a special fact-finding commission to several revolutionary governments. Among other things, the secretary of the commission, Henry Marie Brackenridge, suggested that overturning the neutrality policy might very well damage the patriot cause, especially if the decision provoked European governments. In an effort to be fair, Brackenridge acknowledged that European and U.S. criticisms about the capabilities of Spanish Americans for self-government echoed those made about Americans during the revolution. Those who expressed concern about Bolívar's political ambitions about dominating a hemispheric alliance were mistaken. The United States, Brackenridge concluded, repeating what other U.S. leaders had prophesied, was destined to be the "natural head of the New World."[22]

John Quincy Adams remained doubtful about this prospect. From the day he took office as secretary of state — a post that by tradition led directly to the presidency — he had been consumed with doubts about how the Spanish American conflicts directly and indirectly affected the interests of the country and particularly the security of the union. Adams was steeped in the transatlantic diplomatic tradition, understood power politics, and, despite his father's doubts, believed in the republican revolutionary tradition. From the onset of his tenure as secretary of state, he fretted endlessly over the challenges presented by the president's goals of acquiring the Floridas (East and West), securing the cession of Texas, and determining a transcontinental boundary that would secure the U.S. claim to the Oregon country.

Not surprisingly, Spanish minister Luis de Onís calculated that Florida's loss was inevitable but that Adams would restrain the president and especially the Congress on the issue of recognition of Spanish American patriot governments and, further, would enforce the neutrality laws more aggressively. What neither Onís nor Adams anticipated was the volatility of these issues in the increasingly combative political debates in the Congress and, particularly, in the firestorm developing in the wake of the meteoric surge of popularity of Andrew Jackson, the hero of New Orleans.

When tensions between the two governments worsened over alleged Indian raids from Florida against American settlements—a violation of the Treaty of 1795—Jackson received what he later swore were orders to deal with the matter. In his invasion of the Spanish province, he burned Indian villages and created an international incident by executing two British subjects for allegedly supplying the Indians with arms. Several in the cabinet wanted Jackson reprimanded, but the Tennessean had an improbable defender in Adams, for whom the incident was yet another example of the breakdown of Spanish authority. In late November 1818, Adams wrote the U.S. minister to Spain that "Spain must immediately . . . place a force in Florida adequate at once to the protection of the territory . . . or cede to the United States a province . . . which is . . . a derelict open to the occupancy of every enemy, civilized or savage, of the United States."[23]

Three months later, Onís signed the Transcontinental Treaty, which validated four decades of U.S. expansion at Spain's expense. At any other time, Adams would have exulted, but over the next two years, as the Spanish intentionally tarried in approving the treaty, he suffered the ignominy of continuing political assaults from the westerners in the Congress who decried his "giveaway" of U.S. claims to Texas and his reluctance in pushing the administration to recognize the new republics in Spanish America. Some of the more outspoken, including Clay, called for sending troops into Texas. A prominent westerner, Thomas Hart Benton, editorialized in his Saint Louis newspaper that Texas was twenty times more valuable to the future of the country than Florida. What Adams perceived as a diplomatic triumph, both for the nation and his political future, threatened to alienate westerners and southerners from the fragile union crafted by the country's founders.

But there were deeper issues at stake. Old-line Federalists, who had grumbled about the incorporation of "Gallic" Louisiana with its Franco-Spanish civic culture into the union, now became more outspoken as the Congress plunged into the debate over the admission of Missouri as the next state. The relevant matter, most agreed, was whether or not Missouri would be a slave state, but for republican old-timers, there was a more fundamental issue: the place of freed slaves and free people of color in the young nation. In this debate, some pointed to the creation of the republic of Colombia, the unification of Venezuela, New Granada, and Quito, which symbolized the hazards of incorporating mixed-race peoples into a republican civic culture. For some, including Clay and even Jackson (who had defended the place of free colored in the civic culture to Louisiana slaveholders during his New Orleans campaign), the solution for the United States lay in the American Colonization Society. Founded in 1817, the society provided a means for manumitted slaves to be resettled in Africa or even in Haiti. Although the process would later come under assault from abolitionists, the project of resettlement of African Americans would remain an option for successive generations of ambitious political leaders (including, at least for a time, Abraham Lincoln) trying to reconcile not only sectional interests but the ever-growing numbers of "free white" laborers who believed themselves threatened by the free colored population.

Adams was slow to recognize what this democratic surge could mean for his political future or that it might be necessary for him to articulate international goals and strategies to respond to it. For a few years, as the Spanish became more intransigent in ratifying the Transcontinental Treaty, he doggedly persisted in his plan to pursue a neutral course toward the Spanish American revolts. When a counterrevolutionary European alliance stifled revolts in Italy and Austria, there were rumors about a similar effort on Spain's behalf against the Spanish American patriots. The British government quickly made it clear that it would not countenance such a move. British merchants, frankly, did not wish to endanger the lucrative trade that had begun to develop with Spanish American cities. Fear of European meddling in the Spanish American wars, however, prompted Adams to suppress his instinctive Anglophilia to inquire about cooperation in recognizing the inevitability of Spanish American independence. The British prime minister, Lord Castlereagh, demurred at that suggestion, but in the course of events it became more and more evident to Adams that if he wanted to be president he would have to find a means of responding to the Holy Alliance without relying on the British and at the same time to distance himself from the more militant voices of his political adversaries.

Even after the Transcontinental Treaty was signed and Adams wrote effusive self-praise in his diary for settling a territorial issue that had persisted since the Revolution, the Spanish American patriots doubted American commitment. The settlement with Spain reinforced their suspicion that Washington had tarried on the issue of recognition so as to gain territorial concessions from the Spanish and now intended to continue its policy of "watchful waiting." This was inaccurate. The Spanish delayed (until 1821) in ratifying the Florida treaty because the United States had refused to pledge not to recognize the rebellious juntas. There is evidence that had Adams received more positive assurances from Castlereagh, he might have pushed the issue of Anglo-American cooperation. And until 1821, when Mexican Creoles signed their pact of peace with the royalists, and the following year, when the young Brazilian monarch declared his independence of Portuguese rule, the United States would have been hard-pressed to identify a Latin American rebel government that merited recognition.

Yet, subtly but unmistakably, Adam's thinking about a course for the nation to follow in the hemisphere had begun to change. In actuality, he was as much motivated by political expediency as any obligation he felt as secretary of state. He retained his instinctive New Englander's doubts about Latin Americans. As his kindred spirit Edward Everett, editor of the influential *North American Review*, expressed it: "We have no concern with South America . . . we can have no well-founded sympathy with them [the South Americans]," nor could the United States hope their leaders would become "George Washingtons."[24]

Adams had begun to change his mind about some form of Anglo-American cooperation to guarantee against any threat of the Holy Alliance against the Spanish American cause. In an Independence day 1821 response to Clay's suggestion that the United States should take the lead in crafting an "American system" for the hemisphere as a counterthrust against the menace of the Holy Alliance, a move that mandated immediate recognition of the new republics, Adams expressed doubts about trying to unite the two Americas if that required military involvement and even greater apprehension about embroiling the nation in European difficulties.

Liberty, he professed, would triumph over despotism. Colonialism was incompatible with U.S. political institutions. The United States had already defied European tradition by extending recognition to a belligerent, but there were deeper issues at stake, among them the belief that the American Revolution was more than an anti-colonial struggle and that if the two Americas did not share cultural or political traditions, they were united by ideological bonds, which justified recognition of the new independent states. But he was adamant about any greater involvement in any foreign conflict. In one stroke, he had applied Washington's warning about "foreign entanglements" in the affairs of Europe to the Western Hemisphere.[25]

What made the case for Anglo-American cooperation appealing to others in Monroe's cabinet were stories of French political intrigue in the La Plata region of South America. In 1820 a Spanish army poised at Cádiz for an expedition against Buenos Aires revolted. Within a few months the rebellious officers and Spanish liberals had decreed the restoration of the constitution of 1812 and a limited monarchy. News of the events heartened the U.S. government, but just as quickly there came rumors that the Buenos Aires Creole rebels (who were disdainful of rival independence leaders in the interior) were plotting with the French to create a Bourbon empire in the La Plata. The French intrigue, coupled with a rapid lessening of Spanish resolve for a reconquista, confused both the British and U.S. governments. Though Mexican and Central American independence in 1821, followed by the Brazilian declaration and Bolívar's liberation of Venezuela, New Granada (Colombia), and Ecuador in 1822, reinforced the belief that a Spanish reconquest was unlikely, the nagging French threat remained. It was strengthened in April 1823 when the French dispatched an army south to restore Bourbon absolutism on the Spanish throne.

That summer, George Canning, now British foreign minister, made his famous proposal to Richard Rush, the U.S. minister, for a joint statement on the Latin American question. The offer threw the cabinet into months of wrangling and debate. There were strategic and philosophical issues at stake. The president was alert to the expansion of Russian commercial influence in the Northwest and, presumably, responsive to congressional urging for a forthright statement on the Greek struggle for independence. Until the final weeks, those who favored joining with the British in a collective statement were, according to Adams, in the majority. But he persisted with his pleas for a unilateral course. More than his colleagues — most of them contenders with him for the 1824 presidential nomination — he grasped the political benefits of a unilateral declaration, especially in an era when the public image of political leaders was becoming a feature of U.S. electoral campaigns.[26]

There is little evidence (save Adams's own claim) that he persuaded the others with his analysis of the British proposal; they may have intuitively sensed that a statement of national purpose would diminish the political appeal of their common opponent, Andrew Jackson. In any event, when Monroe announced U.S. policy in December, Adams's in-house campaign for a unilateral statement won out. The message had a dual purpose: to prevent the restoration of the Spanish Empire on the Latin American mainland and to express American conviction about the future of the Western Hemisphere. The first was Adams's contribution, but its effective guarantee was Canning's earlier reminder to the French that the British navy would intercept any French fleet convoying a Spanish army to the New World.

Hemispheric Priorities

One year after Monroe's promulgation of the "destiny" of the Western Hemisphere, His Excellency, Simón Bolívar, the Liberator of Colombia and supreme commander of the republic of Peru, dispatched a momentous circular to the new governments of Spain's former colonies, calling for a meeting at Panama. The purpose was to form a defensive alliance, a compact to shield against the expected assault from the Old World empires. In their labors, he solemnly observed, "will be found the plant of the first alliances that will have marked the beginning of our relations with the universe."[27]

The Liberator made no mention of Monroe's message, for good reason. Although Americans had sold arms to the rebels, issued hortatory proclamations of goodwill, and even served in their cause, the United States, in Bolívar's estimation, had contributed little to their victory. True, the United States had been the first to recognize a revolutionary government (Colombia in 1822), but it could not protect the new republics with Monroe's declaration. Rather, in Bolívar's sometimes curious logic, the United States professed to deny Britain the opportunity to safeguard Latin America's independence. In these days he was preoccupied with European intentions, believing correctly that the Spanish would require a supportive French fleet to retake their colonies. Everything thus depended on British action. If the British did not intervene against the continental allies and the Spanish landed from French warships, he would abandon the coastal cities and fight his war in the mountainous interior. A defensive alliance of the Spanish-speaking republics, with a contemplated army of one hundred thousand, posed a formidable deterrent.

To invite the United States, Bolívar argued, would only antagonize London. So he employed a convenient excuse — the official U.S. neutrality during the long wars of liberation — to exclude them. But his putative allies, the Central Americans, who had peacefully declared their independence in 1821 and three years later had bound themselves into the United Provinces, believed the United States deserved a seat at the first great conference of the Americas. It was the beginning of a long tradition among the *centroamericanos* of inviting outsiders to sit at the Hispanic family table.[28]

By now even the outspoken Clay had become a convert to Adams's hemispheric priorities. In the election the presidential aspirants, Clay among them, had watched as Adams infused the nationalistic rhetoric of Monroe's message into his campaign against the most popular figure of his generation, Andrew Jackson. When the election was thrown into the House of Representatives, Clay had turned against Jackson, throwing his lot (and his political future) with Adams. The reward was the secretaryship of state, pathway to the executive mansion. But there is some evidence that Clay, like other Americans, had substantially altered his views about hemispheric revolution and American identification with the new republics. He certainly required little convincing about rebellion in the insular Caribbean, with its incendiary Haitian symbol. In 1823, when a band of Cuban conspirators descended on Washington looking for assistance, Adams had shunted them aside, observing later that Cuba better served the United States as a weak vassal in the Spanish Empire until the day arrived when it would fall into America's outstretched hands.

Clay still professed his commitment to the revolutionary tradition, but his views were moderating. At one time, he had believed that the best assurance of preserving the union lay in the forming of a spirit of unity — a true American system — among the independent states of the hemisphere. Recognition, once a volatile issue, was now a secondary matter. There were more fundamental issues at stake. In the Congress, a "Hellenic bloc" led by Daniel Webster, avowed that Monroe's statements applied as much to the Greek as the Spanish American cause, but those voices paled before more powerful arguments that the twin issues of security and ideology destined the United States to look more closely at what was happening in the Western Hemisphere. The president's great worry was the rumor of a wild scheme, bandied between the Mexicans and Colombians, calling for the liberation of Cuba. Adams surmised that such folly would, at least, provoke the British into occupying the island and, at worst, unleash the racial horrors of "another Haiti." Canning sensed the American unease, and in 1825 he proposed a tripartite guarantee of Spanish Cuba between Britain, the United States, and Spain. It was a weakly disguised maneuver to prevent American annexation. Adams rejected the plan but carefully instructed U.S. representatives to the Panama Conference to block the Mexican-Colombian scheme.

In truth, Bolívar knew that what he was proposing would have little appeal to U.S. leaders. His conception of hemispheric unity sharply contrasted with what North Americans had in mind. When Adams finally named the two U.S. representatives (Richard Anderson, then minister to Colombia, and John Sergeant, a Kentucky congressman), the House of Representatives (which funded their mission) plunged into a four-month debate about virtually everything but the central issues of American participation — what Monroe *really* meant, what the constitutional issues *really* were, and even the delicate matter of white Americans sitting at the conference table with black Haitians. The voice of western opinion, Senator Thomas Hart Benton of Missouri, had put the issue in unequivocally racial terms when he protested against sending any U.S. delegates to a meeting where antislavery issues might be discussed or deal with governments "who have already put the black man upon an equality with the white, not only in their constitutions but in real life . . . [or] who have . . . black generals in their armies and mulatto senators in their congresses!"[29]

Clay exhausted sixty-four pages of instructions ventilating these issues. As matters turned out, one of the commissioners died en route to the meeting, and the other arrived too late, after the fretful delegates had fled the pestilential lowlands of Panama for the more salubrious climate of the Mexican highlands. Several of the new governments remained indifferent. Bolívar's emissary was able to push through a strongly worded defensive alliance. Three of his colleagues joined him in signing it. But only the Colombians, under Bolívar's prodding, ratified the pact. (In fairness to Bolívar's project, it must be noted that the four states represented at the conference eventually divided into twelve independent countries.) The conference not only revealed the differing views of the Americans and the Latin Americans but demonstrated that the new republics were less committed to alliance than Bolívar had believed. Perhaps a European combination (with British acquiescence) offering a more realistic threat might have prompted them to create the defensive league Bolívar argued was vital to their survival. Clearly, U.S. determination to remain aloof from such political commitments jeopardized but was not decisive in the failure of the Liberator's grand design.

In a sense, both Bolívar and Adams had abandoned the earlier faith in an "America" of differing cultures and differing politics but a common purpose. That misfortune ultimately lay in the U.S. decision to identify the Monroe Doctrine as its own and in Latin Americans' mutual suspicions and jealousies. The Creole liberators who guided their peoples to independence became, in triumph, leaders who turned inward to consolidate their power in societies where republican government took form but could not flourish. Such was the judgment of U.S. leaders. It was an unfair assessment, it can be argued, and the judgment too often reflected frankly racist sentiments. Some, like Bolívar himself, despaired of the continent's future. Others fell before a rising generation of men on horseback who appeared to have little concern for hemispheric solidarity or representative government. Except for his choice of monarchy as the preferred model of governance, the Brazilian "patriarch of independence," José Bonifácio, concurred in such a judgment. "What a picture unhappy [Spanish] America shows us," Bonifácio wrote in 1823. "For fourteen years its peoples have torn themselves to pieces, because . . . they aspire to establish a licentious liberty. And, after having swum in blood, they are no more than the victims of disorder, poverty, and misery."[30]

Not a few U.S. political leaders expressed the sentiment that the twin realities of their Spanish (and Portuguese) political and cultural heritage and the racial makeup of their population made Latin Americans poor candidates for a republican future. At the same time, the bitter political debates that had ensued over the admission of Louisiana and especially Missouri as states offered a reminder of the fragility of the U.S. republic and the political compromises necessary to preserve the union. More disturbingly, these and related issues offered reminders to the first post-revolutionary generation that the undermining of a monarchical and hierarchical society and the emergence of a republican political culture made more problematic the reconciliation of the ideology and ideals of independence with slavery and the fundamentally related matter of the place of free colored and free black persons in the society. Measured by the ideological postulates of the French experience and Enlightenment thought, the social fault line of class ideally blurred into insignificance, but in the Americas (including Haiti), the experience of revolution sharpened racial and ethnic divisions and reminded those political aspirants who spoke eloquently about the "blessings of liberty and freedom" that the republican variation of the social compact mandated the drawing of a color line.

Not to do so, as Bolívar often commented (and Thomas Jefferson concurred), might mean rule not by "mobocracy," a disparaging word often heard in Boston, New York, and Philadelphia in pre-revolutionary days, but *pardocracia*, rule by people of color and persistent social discord. At the same time, the Spanish American "George Washington" continually reminded his white comrades that the liberating army he had amassed in 1817 depended heavily on *libertos* (slaves offered their freedom) and other mixed-race peoples and that the Spanish Americans were neither European nor North American in their racial makeup. In such a society, governance and the preservation of liberty depended on a firm hand. As much as he had once admired the success of the United States with its federal system of governance, Bolívar remained doubtful that the North American political experience could be used by Venezuelans and other Spanish Americans as a model for the new republics. He traced many of the debilities of Spanish America to three centuries of Spanish misrule.[31]

One of the persistent anomalies in the U.S. assessment of the Latin American wars of independence is the parallel belief in contradictory judgments: first, those who believed that the commitment to independence accurately reflected those passionate sentiments about liberty that North Americans had voiced in 1776 and, second, those who doggedly argued that Latin Americans were by both racial and cultural heritage ill-prepared for the task of self-government and for that reason seemed destined for a future of discord or rule by strong men. Not surprisingly, Bolívar became a symbol to both groups—the Spanish American "George Washington" in the eyes of the first; the Napoleonic pretender, to the second. Bolívar himself expressed an ambivalence about the United States that his modern admirers too often gloss over in their determination to portray the man as the embodiment of an anti-imperialist warning against the U.S. threat to the hemisphere and the leader committed to racial equality and democracy who believed that Latin Americans must look to their own traditions and customs for their laws and reject alien models of governance.

Viewed from the geopolitical calculations that continued to guide European thinking, the notion that "America was a hemisphere unto itself" and thus must be spared from the travail of the Old World reflected more naïveté than anything else. No utterance from the president of a country as militarily weak as the United States would be the decisive factor in the decision of the European powers to look differently at the "western question"—the wars in the Spanish "kingdoms" that had mutated into wars of independence with Bolívar's invasion of Venezuela in early 1817—than the "eastern question," the rebellion of the Greeks against the Ottoman Empire. Onís put forward a persuasive argument for support by pointing to the activities of former Bonapartists disillusioned with the patriot cause who founded a military camp in Texas in 1818 and yearned to serve the Spanish Crown by acting as a barrier to land-hungry Americans. So, too, did the Spanish monarch when he employed the provocative language that "[t]he cause of America is not only the cause of a false and impossible liberty; it is the cause of Napoleon's domination. . . . The American revolution is the European revolution; all that remains is for the Bonaparte family to take a personal part in it."[32]

Certainly, U.S. leaders understood these geopolitical realities. Bolívar's victories, the Riego revolt in Spain against a new counterinsurgency, and, most critically, the British decision to use its naval power to deny any French aid to

Spain for the recovery of its former colonies, among other factors, indeed offered powerful arguments for recognizing that their role in the process of Latin American independence had been limited. But from a *hemispheric* perspective, contemporary U.S. leaders thought about the "western question" differently. The problem posed by the Latin American wars of independence, especially in the Bolivarian theater of northern South America, lay not only in how Bolívar waged war but, more importantly, in what the success of these struggles portended for the unity and political future of the United States. Bolívar as commander of an army of mixed-race troops threatening Spanish Cuba or Puerto Rico was as much of a threat as a Bolívar who crafted a strong defensive Spanish American alliance. The nation's security, it was agreed, depended on weak neighbors.

In the final assessment, then, U.S. political leaders in 1825 measured the success of their own revolution less by any presumed identification with the wars of independence in Latin America than by their ability to articulate a hemispheric policy that resonated with the rapidly shifting sentiments of public opinion and the urgency of articulating a truly national statement. That was a fundamental purpose of Monroe's December 1823 statement. Others interpreted the president's message metaphorically, as a profession that the New World had a purpose and destiny distinctive from the Old World and that the United States had a relationship to America that was different from what it experienced with Europe. The role of "hemispheric policeman" was not yet a self-prescribed obligation but, as Bolívar sensed and later generations of Latin Americans attested, it was certainly implied in what Monroe stated.

Put differently, the revolutionary era can be seen as an era of frustrated hemispheric integration and unity or, conversely, as the beginning of a presumably instinctive U.S. cultural and political hegemony over its neighbors, years when an arrogant United States began to take on the mantle of the benevolent "model republic" even as its sense of racial superiority grew stronger and its expansionist agenda threatened not only North America but an entire continent. These seemingly irreconcilable and incompatible legacies had their origins in Enlightenment thought and revolutionary experience — a liberal Catholic/Spanish tradition reborn in Spanish America and responsive to the nascent inter-American cultural values nurtured by the American Philosophical Society and the naturalists, on the one hand, and, on the other, a United States that would be as menacing to hemispheric liberty as any European power. Inherently contradictory, these are the two images of the United States that have prevailed among the nations of the Americas from the revolutionary era unto the present. The first would sustain the "Western hemisphere idea," and the second, the belief that the United States is not the protector of the Americas but its persecutor.[33]

Both interpretations have survived, but it is the second, much harsher and less forgiving, judgment about the U.S. hemispheric presence that Latin American and a goodly number of Canadian, European, and even U.S. historians believe is warranted. But there is a misperception among scholars about why this second view took hold and who was most responsible for sustaining it. The putative creators of the continentalist agenda are two political leaders from the ranks of the elite, Thomas Jefferson and John Quincy Adams — Jefferson for his articulation of the "empire of liberty" in the western country, and Adams because of his posture toward the Latin American revolutions and his undeniable central role in the making of the Monroe Doctrine. They were not the most consequential players in this undertaking. More important, I believe, were the roles played by George Washington and Andrew Jackson. It was Washington, not Jefferson, who initially conceived the role the western country would play, indeed, must play, in the nation's future, and he sensed it from the moment he first set foot in the Ohio country on the eve of the French and Indian War. Certainly, Adams feared British rebuke if he moved too aggressively against the Spanish for their dalliance in ceding Florida, just as he expressed fears about the prospect of a Bolivarian liberating army of mixed-race insurgents invading Spanish Cuba. Although it worked to his advantage, Adams was just as apprehensive about the excesses Jackson took in his invasion of Florida and rumors that "Old Hickory" was plotting to incite a slave revolt on the island and use it as pretext for an invasion![34]

And it was Jackson who expressed more fervently than either Jefferson and Adams just how strongly ordinary Americans felt about security in the borderlands, the importance of Texas as well as the Floridas, and who articulated — crudely but unambiguously — the quintessential belief of ordinary Americans of his generation that it was justifiable to help the Latin American cause, but the United States should do little in the way of entering into any formal commitments with their governments. (His enthusiasm for the Monroe

Doctrine and his hostility toward the Panama Congress amply illustrated that difference.) The eponymous symbol of the democracy taking shape in the country after 1815, Jackson reflected in his policies and rhetoric a sentiment that belied what critics of the U.S. role in the hemisphere in these and later years are often reluctant to admit — the most fervent expansionist impulses that we identify with continentalism and "manifest destiny" sprang less from those at the top but from ordinary people who held strong views about slavery, were inspired by the evangelical fervor of the day, and for whom the proverbial "social question" often turned on racial or ethnic considerations.

The "scream of the American eagle" was democratic, nationalistic, and religious. Jackson understood the latent power of these beliefs better than any of his contemporaries. He would draw on them to craft a powerful political movement that would dominate the political culture for two generations and create a militant American democracy that threatened its hemispheric neighbors and ultimately convulsed in a civil war that proved to be a hemispheric test case for the survival of union and the revolutionary legacy of human rights.[35]

2   Manifest Destiny

Thomas Jefferson often used grand and inspirational phrases — "America is a hemisphere unto itself" — but one of his most memorable expressions was an "empire of liberty," the belief that the young United States could avoid or at least delay the problems of overpopulation and class conflict that some believed would inevitably threaten its newly won freedoms. As the president who had masterminded the Louisiana Purchase of 1803, he had enabled the country to double that empire. A half century later, following a decade of diplomatic wrangling with Great Britain over the Oregon country and what some contemporaries believed was an unjust war with Mexico, the United States fulfilled what a New York journalist called its "manifest destiny."

The idea of manifest destiny conveyed as much a practical and strategic agenda as a providential one — to add territories that would eventually become states, to preserve the fragile federal system crafted in the Constitution, and, more than anything, to satisfy the seemingly relentless land hunger of old-stock Americans and the waves of mostly Irish and German immigrants entering the country. To other hemispheric governments, particularly Mexico and Great Britain, manifest destiny served principally as the means of extending U.S. territory and power at the expense of its neighbors and the vulnerable Indian peoples who lay in the country's path. After all, the origins of the American Revolution lay not only in the demand for autonomy or equality within the British Empire but also with fundamental differences about developing the trans-Appalachian frontier acquired in 1763. Later, Washington had prophesied that the survival of the republic depended on retention of the western country. Continental mission, Americans were persuaded, would ensure that the West would be "the last home of the freeborn American."[1]

Such expansive visions of their future prompted Americans of the era to dismiss the monarchical and republican projects of the other Americas and their peoples as politically, culturally, and even spiritually inferior. The American Revolution had been the exceptional revolution, they were persuaded. British North America appeared irrevocably divided between English and French cul-

tures. They believed Spanish Americans were largely the victims of two debilitating legacies — three hundred years of Spanish misrule and the daunting task
of incorporating the vast mixed-race peoples of the continent into a republican
society, a judgment made by Simón Bolívar in his famous 1819 address before
the legislators gathered at the Congress of Angostura and in less severe phrases
by Alexis de Tocqueville in his classic account, *Democracy in America*. The
Spanish record in the subjugation of indigenous peoples may have been bloodier, but by comparison the British record of imperial management was sloppier
and less effective. At bottom, the sectarian diversity and haphazard colonial
experience of British America as contrasted with the religious conformity and
complex society of Spanish America help to explain why the transition to independence seemed far more difficult in the latter.[2]

To U.S. leaders of the era, there was nothing comparable in Spanish America
to the unifying and mobilizing spirit most Americans identified with manifest
destiny. Yet its consequences would be the collapse of the nation and a civil
war that in its ambiguities and savagery more closely resembled the kind of
war Bolívar had fought and would alter, sometimes in subtle ways, the image
and place of the United States in the Western Hemisphere.

Old Hickory in the Americas

In 1830 such a prospect seemed not only unlikely but far-fetched. Jackson was
now president, and he subscribed to none of Adams's or Clay's notions about
"good neighborliness." Unlike them, he believed the best way to preserve the
union lay through expansion into the West. Few U.S. leaders of this era voiced
the platitudes of manifest destiny more confidently than Jackson. Jefferson's
dream of an "empire of liberty" inspired later generations, but Jackson in both
word and deed set the pattern by which the U.S. government, with laws, treaties, and force, acquired 1.85 billion acres of Indian lands in North America in
the century after the American Revolution. Jackson believed that the removal
of the major Indian tribes from their proximity to white settlements in the
Deep South would not only secure the southwestern frontier but ensure the
peace and prosperity of white settlers. At the same time, he was persuaded that
with the protection of the federal government, the transplanted Indians would

"cast off their savage habits and become an interesting, civilized, and Christian community."[3]

The policy of Indian removal ultimately, and probably inevitably, led to the infamous "Trail of Tears" and devastating loss of life among the nation's southeastern Indians. Jackson believed he was safeguarding the Indian and was shaken by details of this gruesome episode, yet he did not regret the decision to remove the Indians to western lands. His attitude revealed not only the democratic impulses of the era identified with Jackson and, undeniably, the racial character of manifest destiny. For Jackson, a more compelling reason for such action was the security of the western frontier.

Expanding American commercial interests, not forging hemispheric bonds, was central to his Latin American policy. Inept and shortsighted policies undermined what remained of the goodwill generated by the recognition of the new independent governments of mainland Latin America. To Central America, which had fashioned a weak federation in 1824, Old Hickory dispatched commercial agents and canal promoters, none of whom showed much interest in the fragile cause of isthmian unity. Nor was he disposed to invoke Monroe's now vaguely remembered "doctrine." When the Central Americans requested his support in their protest against the British presence in Belize by reminding him of its prohibitions against European expansionism in the New World, they were politely but firmly rebuked. Jackson did recall the meddling William Henry Harrison from his post in Colombia but soon showed his irritation over less than satisfactory commercial relations with Bogotá by cultivating the rebellious Venezuelans, whose defiance had shattered the union forged by Bolívar. Colombia, wrote the American minister, was a "bigoted Catholic country controuled [sic] by the Priests . . . [but] Venezuela on the other hand is rapidly developing her resources and marching forward with the spirit of the age."[4]

Elsewhere in South America, the U.S. presence followed a different pattern, notably with monarchical Brazil. On the eve of that nation's declaration of independence in 1822, the Portuguese court incorporated the Banda Oriental (the future Uruguay) in order to gain access to the Rio de la Plata. In retaliation, the Argentines tried to displace them, inciting a regional conflict. In 1825 a rebel group in the Banda declared war, which in turn precipitated hostilities between Argentina and Brazil. Vainly, the Argentines attempted to persuade the U.S. government to come to its aid on the grounds that British favoritism toward Brazil violated the Monroe Doctrine. The Adams administration permitted Argentine ships to use U.S. ports, which precipitated a vigorous Brazilian protest. By the time Jackson became president, the British had arranged a truce between the warring parties and effectively brokered the birth of independent Uruguay.

Relations with the Brazilians improved. With Buenos Aires, however, they rapidly deteriorated. In the preceding decade American shippers had descended on Buenos Aires, bearing flour, liquor, butter, salt, furniture, and lumber for a country that projected to the world the dual image of cosmopolitan elites in the capital and unlettered barbarians out in the provinces. In both city and country the Americans were distant competitors to the British, yet some Argentines admired the northern republic On the eve of Jackson's election; an Argentine editor wrote: "Of all the nations with which we have diplomatic relations, none has rendered a more unwavering interest in the cause of liberty and independence in the hemisphere than the United States."[5]

Then Juan "Bloody" Rosas, governor of Buenos Aires Province and visible enemy of the Buenos Aires cosmopolites, took power and within a short time a once sympathetic U.S. resident was writing about a country fallen to "countless hordes of savages . . . at the head of which may be found an un-discriminating thirst of blood and rapine."[6] Rosas might have continued indiscriminately persecuting his enemies in the spirit of national consolidation and precipitated little more than American verbal indignation, but he was determined to rectify a recent Argentine grievance in the Falkland Islands (the Malvinas, as Argentines called them).

When Argentina broke from the Spanish Empire, it claimed the rights of state succession over the islands and dispatched a governor to close them off to commercial shipping from other nations. When the governor seized an American vessel for violating the ban, Jackson (in 1832) ordered a punitive retaliation. An American warship, the *Lexington*, arrived off Puerto Soledad, hoisted a French flag, and dispatched a raiding party ashore to retaliate for the earlier seizures of U.S. whalers and sealers. Afterward, the *Lexington* sailed gloriously for Montevideo with six petty Argentine officials in shackles. To Jackson the raid was a necessary policing of an "uncivilized" society by the forces of a "civilized" nation, but Rosas, who often conflicted with British and

French pretensions to "civilize" Argentine behavior, was not easily cowed. Neither was Jackson. When the Argentine government demanded an apology for the indignity, the new U.S. minister wrote, "We have attempted to soothe, and conciliate these wayward fools long enough. *They must be taught a lesson*."[7]

Within two years diplomatic relations had deteriorated into exchanges of acrimonious official notes. The noticeable bitterness even inspired the British to reassert (with obvious American encouragement) their claims of sovereignty over the Falklands. When the British returned, the Argentine government suspended diplomatic relations with the United States and appealed to other hemispheric governments for a collective protest. Jackson weighed the issue and decided that the reoccupation of the islands did not violate Monroe's prohibition of future European territorial expansion in the New World. He could have done little to prevent British actions anyway, of course, but the reluctance to protest alienated another hemispheric republic. Argentina vainly sought U.S. assistance in its claims to the Malvinas twice more in the nineteenth century (1839 and 1884), and, memorably, in the seizure of the islands by the Argentine military government in 1982.[8]

When Americans of the 1830s looked toward Canada, however, they instinctively sensed the possibility of a continental bond created by geographical proximity, a porous boundary, and (except for the French in Lower Canada) ethnic and linguistic similarities. In the 1830s several social movements that swept across Jacksonian America — temperance, revivalism, and anti-slavery, among others — reverberated across the border. Political discontents in both Anglo Upper Canada (modern Ontario) and French Lower Canada (Québec) increasingly found the more open and democratic politics in the United States an alternative to the hierarchical political and social structure of British North America. With good reason, then, Canadian leaders believed that a militant Jacksonian America posed a threat. They were not unmindful of the urgency of the American challenge, but they determined to meet it rather than acquiesce. The British tradition continued to exert a powerful appeal among Canadians.

In the 1830s loyal Canadians turned back two rebellions, each with a U.S. connection. The leader of the Upper Canadian rebellion was William Lyon Mackenzie (nicknamed "The Firebrand"), who praised Jacksonian democracy and the political liberties he avowed were unjustly denied Canadians. His counterpart in French Lower Canada was Louis-Joseph Papineau (Speaker of the Assembly), who railed against the ruling English oligarchy. Of the two, Papineau proved more naive about the U.S. connection. Mackenzie could not easily reconcile his admiration of U.S. political institutions and his anti-slavery convictions, but he did not waver. Papineau spoke approvingly of U.S. annexation of Lower Canada, believing that it was the only sure means of preserving French law, language, and institutions. "Hurra for Papineau and Freedom," an Albany (New York) editorialist trumpeted, which heartened the rebels. But de Tocqueville understood better what annexation meant: "If the [French] Canadians united with the United States," he noted, "their population will soon be absorbed."[9]

Both movements drew on support from American sympathizers in New York and believed they would get a friendly hearing from the Jackson administration. What they had not anticipated was the determination of Canadian leaders to put a stop to their movements and the growing wariness of U.S. officials about their cause. Defeated in Canada, both Mackenzie and Papineau fled across the border into New York. From there, Mackenzie created a provisional government and began a series of cross-border attacks. Incensed, Canadian officials retaliated. In December 1837 they raided a rebel post in Niagara, New York, and in the attack burned a U.S. vessel (the *Caroline*). One American was killed. The incident set off a firestorm of protest, but over the next few years the diplomats, not the firebrands, settled matters. In 1842 Secretary of State Daniel Webster, an Anglophile with some influential British social connections, and Lord Ashburton, the British minister to the United States, settled the latent claims over the *Caroline* affair, resolved a vexing boundary dispute between Maine and New Brunswick, and marked the boundary between Lake Superior and the Lake of the Woods.

The Balance of Power in North America

With Mexico, diplomatic wrangling brought not only acrimony and suspicion but eventually war, a war in which Mexico would lose half its national domain to the United States.

Mexico, wrote David Pletcher in the *Diplomacy of Annexation*, was the "sick

man of North America" in the 1830s and 1840s.[10] Mexican conservatives of
the era would have agreed with this judgment, but not for the same reasons.
In their minds, its troubles were brought on largely by the liberal assaults on
the church and the traditional social order and, most damning, a pernicious
republican political order. In 1821 Mexico had acquired its independence by
an appropriately named "Pact of Equality" between American and European
Spaniards crafted by Agustín de Iturbide, who became emperor of a vast territory stretching from Panama to the present-day Oregon-California border. In
securing Mexico's independence, Iturbide viewed his role as that of a peace-
maker who ended the devastation of a decade-long insurgency and a leader
who welcomed all Mexicans (except those of African ancestry) as citizens.
The empire survived for a year. Iturbide was driven from power, tried to retake his throne, and lost his life. His was an admirable project, writes Timothy
Henderson, but it collapsed "for the same reason the insurgency failed: . . . the
potent legacy of three centuries of Spanish colonialism."[11]

Its first constitution and federal system of government appeared to emulate
the republican model of the United States, but in the estimation of early U.S.
ministers its fundamental character differed sharply from that of its rambunctious neighbor. Little wonder, then, that Washington's ministers who trooped
into the ancient citadel of the Aztecs with political advice (as did Joel Roberts
Poinsett, who became involved in the bitter factional quarrels of Mexico in the
1820s) or generous offers to settle territorial squabbles (as did Colonel Anthony
Butler, Jackson's gauche emissary) alienated a generation of Mexicans. Even
the Mexican men of reason (and the early republic produced its share of en-
lightened political liberals) recognized that accommodation with the United
States meant national dishonor.

Mexican leaders had other reasons to fear U.S. pressures. In 1819 Adams
and Onís had marked the truncated frontier from the Sabine to the Pacific in
the Transcontinental Treaty in which, presumably, the Americans had relinquished all claim to Texas. But even before Mexican independence two years
later, the Spanish viceroy in Mexico City (emulating the tactics of Spanish governors in New Orleans) had granted permission to Anglo families to settle
west of the Sabine. Believing that isolated settlements of Americans, given
large land grants and permission to retain their slaves, would create a barrier
to the hordes of land-hungry farmers trying to get in, Mexico continued the

policy. Mexican optimists argued that these settlers would eventually convert to Catholicism and become Mexican citizens. Years before, Poinsett had predicted what would happen. Texas immigrants, he wrote, were settling on the most fertile soil in the province. Given time and their obstreperous nature, they would become ungovernable. His successor, Anthony Butler, carried an almost identical message from Jackson to Mexican officials with an offer to purchase the province, from the Sabine to the "Grand Prairie."

In 1830 the Mexican government reversed its policy, but immigration across the virtually unguarded frontier increased. Among the newcomers were Kentuckians and Tennesseans, one of whom — Sam Houston — was a confidant (and, it was later charged, an agent) of Jackson. These recent arrivals were less accustomed to dealing with a faraway and sometimes capricious Mexican government than such veterans as Stephen F. Austin, who still believed the Mexican federalist system would tolerate the idiosyncrasies of these American transplants, the "Texicans." Jackson had tried to intimidate and even bribe the Mexican government into selling Texas (all the way to the "Grand Prairie") and California from Monterey Bay north to the Oregon border and had failed. His personally chosen emissary had been duped, then rebuffed. But the transplanted Americans who had migrated into Texas spoiled for a fight. Their defiance was different from their *tejano* allies. As Austin wrote, resistance to the will of faraway Mexican leaders was the only recourse of people who sensed that accommodation would make them "alien subjects of a people to whom they deliberately believed themselves morally, intellectually, and politically superior."[12]

In 1835 all hopes for accommodation by persons of goodwill, Mexican and Texan, perished with the decision of Santa Anna to assert central authority over the defiant North by crushing what was technically a federalist rebellion of "Texicans" and *tejanos* against the center. In the beginning the war went badly for the rebels, but news of the battle of the Alamo and the "massacre" of a Texan battalion that had surrendered at Goliad inspired a generation of Americans to rally to the cause. When Jackson heard of the Goliad affair he went into an uncontrollable rage. As word of it spread from New Orleans to Mississippi and Alabama towns, Texan agents hastily set up booths to lure willing and vengeful recruits to the cause. By the time most of them got to the fighting, the decisive battle of San Jacinto had been fought, and Sam Houston had extracted his famous surrender from Santa Anna. An artist later recaptured the scene in a mural depicting a cringing Mexican pledging to respect Texas independence.

The Texas rebellion was yet another symbol of the havoc that ordinary Americans were capable of creating for two governments. But Santa Anna's surrender was the opening act in a drama for domination of the Gulf Coast, from the Texas-Louisiana border round the Mexican shore, a political battle in which the expansion of statehood and slavery and the European balance of power in North America led to a larger conflict with Mexico. On one side were the small but vocal antislavery spokesmen (among them Congressman John Quincy Adams, a convert to the anti-expansionist cause) who railed against Texas annexation as a conspiracy to expand the slavocracy. Their mortal enemies were championed by John C. Calhoun, no fiery expansionist but a southern spokesman who recognized that an independent Texas might very well become, under the blandishments of British abolitionism, an independent free Texas republic and thus a magnet for runaways.

A hemispheric issue was at stake. Early in the decade the British Parliament's monumental debate over slavery in its West Indian empire had ended with a victory for the emancipationists. The U.S. government had watched this bitterly argued matter with more than detached interest. British abolitionist propaganda increased in Puerto Rico and Cuba, and both the British and French governments displayed an inordinate concern toward the Texas republic. Its initial overtures for statehood had floundered with Jackson's reluctance to stir up another debate over slavery. In France, the Western Hemispheric strategy took form with heavy pressure on Mexico. Using as pretext the mistreatment of French bakers in the capital, the French laid siege to Veracruz, occupying San Juan de Ulúa, the historic fortress. In the engagement the irrepressible opportunist Santa Anna lost his leg, but his daring in the battle won him (and his leg) momentary glory in Mexican history. Shortly, the French pulled back. Their attention turned northward, to the Texas republic.

There was nothing sinister about French intentions in Texas. The architect of French policy was François Guizot, Louis Philippe's foreign minister, who spoke eloquently of implanting a European balance of power in North America. The Texas republic, dependent on French military advisers against the continuing threat from Mexico, would become the bastion of a revived

French Empire. A coterie of Texans had actually promoted stronger ties with Europe. Their early appeals for statehood rejected, the first generation of independent Texans had journeyed abroad looking for friends and commercial partners. They signed trade treaties with Britain and France. For a few years the French were active, offering the Texans an ambitious plan to colonize French immigrants on 3 million acres in west Texas, in defiance of the Mexican government. Guizot talked enthusiastically about constructing a line of forts from the Red River to the Rio Grande.

When the Texas Assembly rejected the scheme, Guizot lost heart. But British agents now took up the challenge of transforming Texas into a protectorate. Since the American rejection of Canning's proposal for a joint declaration on Latin America, British policy had consistently sought to impede American influence everywhere, especially in Spanish Cuba and Mexico. By the 1830s Mexico was a British economic client. An independent Texas, wedged between a threatening United States and a proud but politically volatile Mexico, threatened the stability of the western Gulf. Britain had far more compelling reasons than France to act. Canada, virtually defenseless against American penetration, had just weathered a rebellion abetted by conspiring New Yorkers. A more vigorous British presence in Texas would distract the U.S. government and prompt it to crack down on violators of the neutrality laws in upstate New York. Others saw in the Texas republic yet another opportunity. If British diplomats could persuade a generation of wastrel Mexican leaders that political wisdom dictated the survival of an independent Texas, money levied for armies to retake it might more profitably be directed to satisfying Mexico's British creditors.

In the early 1840s U.S. diplomats began making incautious statements about a British plot to "Africanize" Texas — to ply the Texans with loans and promises if they would abolish slavery in favor of a free labor system. More outspoken British proselytizers called for a crusade to eliminate slavery not only in Texas but in Cuba and Brazil. These were incendiary words to a generation of southern politicians obsessed at being surrounded by free territory. American fears bordered on paranoia. Duff Green, confidant of Calhoun and slavery's "roving ambassador," as Adams derisively called him, spent 1840 in London attending parliamentary debates about the economic consequences of abolition in the British West Indies. British sugar planters now had to compete, to their economic detriment, with sugar economies in Cuba and Brazil based on slave labor. Green discerned a conspiracy. Refusing to admit that its free labor economy was unable to compete with the slave labor sugar isles, the British had decided to wreck the more efficient slave economies of the Western Hemisphere. Their targets were Cuba and Texas. Green's assessment of British determination but not intention was reinforced in the observation of a British diplomat the following year. "By effecting the final abolition of Slavery in Texas," he wrote, "we at once extinguish that horrid traffic in a Country which, without our interference, might become one of the most extensive Slave Markets in America."[13]

Anticipating the worst, the U.S. government in this decade accepted as provocation to its national interests British ambitions in Mexico and Texas. And by a tortuous logic a succession of political leaders, mostly southerners, tried to persuade their northern colleagues that a slave Texas in the Union would expand the nation's internal marketplace. No one spoke more vigorously than Calhoun. In 1844, upon becoming secretary of state after the sudden death of Abel Upshur, he dispatched Upshur's hastily written treaty of annexation to the Senate with a ringing defense of slavery and its benefits. The Whig opposition, voting conscience over cotton, resoundingly turned it down. This apparent defeat of U.S. expansion inspired Aberdeen. To a peripatetic Texas agent in London he proposed a "Diplomatick Act," an Anglo-French guarantee of Texas independence and pressure on the Mexicans to recognize the republic. The only stipulation was that Texas must not become a state. When news of the offer reached Washington, there was renewed alarm about British intentions. The proposal set Texans to quarreling among themselves. In Mexico the news brought renewed demands for vindicating national honor by launching a *reconquista*.

The truth of the matter was that Texas was lost to Mexico but not assured of statehood. In the elections, the Democratic candidate, James K. Polk, emulating Jackson's old fire about dealing with the Spanish dons of Florida, spoke vigorously about resolving the great territorial issues that endangered American security in the hemisphere — California, Oregon, and Texas. The rhetoric about the Oregon Territory, jointly occupied since 1818 by British and Americans, was more belligerent, but Polk was less disposed to compromise with the Mexicans. Jackson had wanted to purchase Texas and California and had been rebuffed. Polk resolved to succeed where his mentor had failed. His narrow victory in the fall was sufficient inspiration for the outgoing Congress. In February 1845, a few weeks before the inauguration, Congress passed the joint resolution that formally proposed annexation of Texas.

Polk was already busily plying the Texans with lofty words about their future as a state and warning them about the perils if they rejected the American offer. In the end the resolution passed handily. Sloganeers spoke of the "re-occupation of Texas" (territory, Jackson had often argued, that was rightfully American but given away by his archenemy Adams). Polk had transformed manifest destiny into a national security issue. European intriguing in the long-standing disputes between Mexico and the United States imperiled not only American interests but the future of republican government in North America. As Secretary of State James Buchanan instructed John Slidell, sent to Mexico to purchase California and New Mexico and obtain Mexican acquiescence in Texas's annexation, the United States would not "tolerate any interference on the part of European sovereigns with controversies in America, [nor] permit them to apply the worn-out dogma of the balance of power to the free States of the Continent. . . . Liberty here must be allowed to work out its natural results; and these will, ere long, astonish the world."[14]

With these words a U.S. secretary of state validated the use of force in the cause of republican liberty. In retrospect, contention that the example of republican government in the United States would inevitably lead neighboring peoples voluntarily to join the noble American experiment — a view advanced by the journalist John L. O'Sullivan, who coined the phrase *manifest destiny* — appears naive. Neither Mexico nor any Latin American state would voluntarily submit to American expansion, however good or noble its intentions. Manifest destiny was more the credo of the belligerent than that of the pacifist, a necessary imperative to preserve the union. Sadly, as a Whig congressman from Illinois who later became president and a young officer who would become his ablest general feared, it had the power to destroy the union as well.

Theirs were muted voices, however. Former president Andrew Jackson viewed the Texas issue in strategic and personal terms. The British were treacherous, he informed an old political ally in 1844: lodged in Texas, they would mobilize Indians and slaves and ultimately their own troops to control the lower Mississippi and the Gulf of Mexico. As president, he had rejected Texas annexation on the grounds that it would exacerbate the debate over slavery's expansion. In 1844 its incorporation into the union was imperative, for Texas was "the important key to our future safety — take and lock the door against all danger of foreign influence."[15]

The Mexican War

Polk's principal interest lay in California, not Texas. Since the beginning of the decade the penny press had written expansively about Pacific Coast issues — the Oregon dispute, until then a diplomatic matter that had quickly become a volatile political issue in 1843, and California, whose ports beckoned eastern commercial interests. In Polk's presidential campaign, however, California did not figure heavily. Only later did he revive the California issue with a warning about British intrigue in the Mexican province. Polk may have been speculating that the Californios, who had begun organizing against Mexican rule, were readying to emulate the Texans. As things turned out, when the Mexicans abruptly rejected Slidell's offer to sell California and New Mexico, the president returned to the border squabble raised by Texas's claim to the Rio Grande as its southern boundary. An incident between Zachary Taylor's dragoons and Mexican troops on the Rio Grande provided a convenient excuse to label Mexico the aggressor, and when war commenced, Polk had a strike force on the California boundary ready to intervene and forestall any California republic.[16]

The war began with armies penetrating New Mexico, California (which was also attacked from the sea), and northern Mexico, where General Taylor encountered unexpectedly fierce Mexican resistance. In the beginning, U.S. military interests concentrated on the Southwest, presumably validating Polk's arguments that the war was "defensive" — asserting American claims over territories in dispute — rather than aggressive, as several outspoken New Englanders were saying. But in February 1847 Polk adopted the strategy of the Spanish conquerors of Mexico — a landing at Veracruz and a plunge into the interior of populous Mexico. His reasons were complicated. Taylor was getting more press coverage than the commander in chief and was running for president from horseback in Mexico. And Polk had been duped by Santa Anna, then exiled in Havana, who had persuaded the president's agent that he would end the war if the U.S. government would subsidize his return to Mexico. Instead, the Mexican leader formed an alliance with the hated Liberals and resumed the presidency, renewing the fight. Polk vowed to reduce Mexico and its government to submission. When General Winfield Scott's invading army finally took Mexico City in September, the war was for all realistic purposes over, although sporadic fighting continued until early 1848.

If one discounts the invasion of Upper Canada in the War of 1812, the Mexican War was the nation's first foreign war, a crusade that rounded out the continental domain and validated the era's romantic expressions of political and cultural superiority. For its opponents the war introduced a noticeably racist element into U.S. diplomacy and, more disturbing, reinforced their fears that the United States had jeopardized its republican character by acquiring so much new territory. Such self-doubts about the American mission did not linger, though the rising political figure Abraham Lincoln expressed a fairly common Republican sentiment in the following decade when he described the war as the abuse of a neighboring republic. With the passage of several more generations most Americans forgot they had added roughly a third of the national domain at the expense of almost 50 percent of Mexican territory. By the end of World War I, when nationalist reaffirmation reached its zenith, Justin Smith wrote confidently in his two-volume treatise that the Mexican War represented a great crusade. A quarter-century later, during World War II, Samuel Flagg Bemis was blunter when he defended the American victory by rhetorically asking if any American retained such guilt over the immorality of the war that he would restore the Mexican cession to Mexico.[17]

Most contemporaries believed that the victory destroyed forever any possibility that the European powers might create a balance of power in North America. On the eve of the conflict the British had proposed a solution to the crisis. Had Mexico accepted London's mediation, Texas's independence would have been guaranteed, and the Mexicans would have found solace for the loss of their northeastern province by preventing the acquisitive Americans from annexing it. Two years later, following a series of stunning victories on the Rio Grande, in California, and, finally, in Winfield Scott's triumphant march from Veracruz into the capital of the Aztecs, Americans found another reason to celebrate.

In faraway Europe, monarchy had suffered a grievous blow in the revolutions of 1848. News of the calamitous events arrived in the United States only a few weeks after a band of gloating Democrats and disconsolate Whigs joined to approve a peace treaty negotiated on the Mexican plateau between a disowned U.S. emissary and a peace delegation with no precise authority to deal with him. Republicanism was victorious on two continents, trumpeted the expansionist penny press editors, who had written laudatory columns about the crusade against arrogant Mexico. Some illogically attributed the success of revolutions in the Old World to vindication of republicanism in the New World. As the *New York Herald* boasted, the United States in victory had won a coveted place in "the history of civilization and the human race."[18]

By such reasoning, depriving a neighbor of half its national territory was a justifiable price to pay for the survival of republican government and the defeat of European political intrigue in North America. A story largely forgotten in modern accounts of the war was the intrastate conflict in the Mexican north between Mexicans and indigenous peoples that was ongoing from the early 1830s. By the time the U.S. Army invaded the area, Mexicans of the region were exhausted and debilitated by the continuing strife. The conquering Americans exulted in the belief that theirs was a war of redemption.[19]

One indisputable outcome of the war lay in the victory of what Europeans described as a ragtag army of volunteers over an army they had always presumed was more capable. The war had advanced something more than U.S. determination to "spread the blessings of republican liberty" to the sparsely settled northern regions of Mexico. It had brought a conquering army into the heart of populous Mexico, where illiterate, rambunctious Missourians and Texans and Kentuckians marched arrogantly among once-proud savants who had written contemptuously about the coonskin republic next door. With Scott's plunge into the Mexican highlands, the movement for the acquisition of all of Mexico gained renewed vigor, its adherents arguing that territory acquired by conquest should not be readily given up. But just as quickly the movement dissolved when others pointed out that absorbing populated regions of Mexico would also mean taking on that country's factious politics and alien culture.

A month after the war ended, an offer went out from isolated Yucatecos, offering the province to Britain, Spain, or the United States. The penny press took up the cause of Yucatán annexation. Even the poet Walt Whitman joined the crusade. Yucatán soon entered another bloody phase of its lamentable history, with pro- and anti-annexationist elements battling for control and, more alarmingly, resuming the caste war between Indian and white that plagued the peninsula from the 1830s to the 1880s. Annexationist Yucatecos even raised the specter of European violation of the Monroe Doctrine to promote their cause. Once before, citing British interference in California, Polk had invoked the doctrine. Now he raised the issue again, warning the Europeans against creating a protectorate in the Yucatán. At the same time he rejected the notion of U.S. annexation.

Monroe doctrine

Mexico lost half its national domain to the United States, but the nation's defeat, paradoxically, accomplished a long-standing political goal for Mexico in Latin American international politics. The rapidity of American conquest aroused much of Latin America to the expansionist menace from the north. Yankeephobia, until the 1840s largely unknown (except, of course, in Mexico), suddenly became an ingredient of the Latin American variation of Pan-Americanism. Its impact came too late to unite the other republics on Mexico's behalf and virtually destroyed Mexican ambitions to fashion an anti-American confederation until revolutionary Mexico undermined Woodrow Wilson's plan for a Pan-American defensive alliance in World War I.

Insensitive to the browbeating of a neighboring country and unmindful of the war's political consequences for their own country, Americans experienced in this conflict an unparalleled cultural nationalism. The Mexican War and the surge of U.S. interest in the Caribbean and Central America that followed the war validated two disturbing elements in the relations between the United States and the other Americas. The first was the widespread acceptance of the belief of American exceptionalism expressed as territorial aggrandizement at the expense of another hemispheric republic. For ages philosophers had debated whether creation of an empire would cause a republic to lose its political virtues. On occasion the issue had befuddled the revolutionary band of brothers, who were sufficiently familiar with the fall of Rome to speculate about a similar fate befalling the young United States. But the conquerors of Mexico underwent little philosophical torment about this problem. Even John L. O'Sullivan came round to Polk's forceful expression of manifest destiny. Indeed, the victors over Mexico convinced themselves that republican liberty might perish if the United States did *not* wage war against its putative tyranny. Republican institutions were sustainable not only by the dissemination of the idea but also by the acquisition (forcibly if necessary) of ever greater amounts of territory on which to build those institutions. In other words, republicanism, like prosperity, had a territorial imperative.[20]

The second and equally disturbing legacy of the Mexican War lay just beneath the egalitarian surface of U.S. justification for charting a belligerent course against Mexico — ethnocentrism.[21] More bellicose exponents of manifest destiny exhibited few qualms about waging war to spread the domain not only of republican institutions but of the "Anglo-Saxon race." By the 1830s the more benign view of the first generation of independent Americans about the ability of other cultures to absorb republican values had given way to a narrower view that such accomplishments were largely confined to white Americans. Sam Houston, a founding father of Texas and twice its president, often spoke of the republic as a monument to Anglo-Saxon superiority. And Thomas Hart Benton, the Missouri senator and eloquent spokesman for westward expansion, expressed his consternation that England, the citadel of Anglo-Saxon political institutions, would impede the march of that "race" in North America.

Caribbean and Central American Projects

Even before the victory over Mexico, Latin American governments had become apprehensive about U.S. intentions in the hemisphere. Their delegates convened at Lima in 1847 (and at Santiago de Chile in 1856) to reaffirm Pan-American solidarity and a parallel commitment to national sovereignty. The first was a warning to Europe, the second, a reaction to the annexationist impulses they feared in the republic to the north.[22]

In the decade following the triumph over Mexico, manifest destiny turned southward into the Caribbean and Central America. As Mexican officials had ultimately acknowledged in their experience in Texas and California, the vanguard of U.S. penetration in the Caribbean and in Central America was made up not only of U.S. officials but also private Americans, each prompted by diverse motives and interests. In earlier years, the overriding American concern was security, slave rebellion, or "Africanization." By the early 1850s, commercial and political opportunism were added to the agenda.

For the first but not the last time, the annexation of Cuba and the activities of Cuban rebels became powerful and divisive issues in U.S. politics. In 1825 John Quincy Adams had prophesied the island's fall, like a ripe apple, into an outstretched American hand. At the height of the war with Mexico, journalist John L. O'Sullivan, who had the president's confidence, recommended offering Spain $100 million for the island. The Spanish rebuffed the idea with a proud reaffirmation of Spain's destiny in Cuba. In the U.S. government the rejection confirmed long-held notions about Spanish recalcitrance. Among southerners concerned about the limits of the cotton kingdom and slavery in the West, the prospect of Cuba's liberation and then rapid acquisition as natural slave territory kindled expansionist ambitions. Cuban planters, property owners, intellectuals, business leaders, and exiles — most of them white, wealthy, and fluent in English — readily adapted to U.S. culture and its friendly political milieu. They founded the *Consejo de Gobierno Cubano* in New York City; its leader, a Creole planter, married Sullivan's sister. But most of their kindred spirits in the United States lived in the South. Indeed, the aspirations and fears of southern slaveholders and Cuban elites often converged. Both opposed independence on the understandable beliefs that it would exacerbate social disorder and racial strife. Both favored annexation but only as a long-term goal. In the short run, both preferred a continuation of Spanish rule.[23]

Alert to U.S. instincts about Spanish rule, Cuba's putative liberators raised the flag of rebellion on American soil. They found a leader in a disenchanted Spanish soldier, General Narciso López, who had served in Venezuela and had joined the retreating Spanish army on the "ever faithful isle," the slogan Spaniards often applied to Cuba during the wars of independence. López found his benefactors among southern opportunists. Beginning in the summer of 1849 he launched three expeditions against Spanish Cuba. The first never left American waters, but in summer of 1850 the second embarked from the Florida Keys and struck Cárdenas, east of Havana. After a short battle López and his invaders retreated to their ships and the sanctuary of friendly Savannah. There a federal attorney charged him with violation of the neutrality laws, but he was promptly acquitted by a sympathetic jury. He headed for New Orleans to organize his third invasion. This time López had fifty Americans, among them a few sons of plantation owners, in his army. The expedition landed at Bahía Honda, an isolated cove west of Havana. A Spanish officer, alerted to their arrival, dispatched a force to intercept it, and they were all captured. Unwilling to risk arousing American wrath, the Spanish promptly tried the Americans and shipped them to Spain for a year of hard labor in the mines. The Cubans were executed. Their leader was publicly garroted in Havana Square.[24]

In the sobering aftermath the Spanish dispatched their second offer for a tripartite guarantee of Spanish Cuba (the first was in 1825) to Paris, London, and Washington. The British and French were uninterested, and the American response was even more vigorously worded than Adams's 1823 pronouncement on Cuba. The island, wrote Secretary of State Edward Everett, was a geographical extension of North America. A New Englander, Everett was no defender of southern slavery and certainly no advocate of the nation's acquisition of more slave territory. But his successor, William L. Marcy, though no slavocrat, was nonetheless responsive to powerful Democratic pressures from the south to settle the "Cuban question." In the aftermath of López's death, the South reverberated with warnings that Spain was on the verge of abolishing slavery on the island. This would mean the "Africanization" of Cuba and the presence of a free labor economy a hundred miles from the slave South.[25]

The fear inspired one of the more bizarre episodes in the influence of slavery in the United States on the nation's evolving hemispheric relations. Marcy dispatched to Madrid a passionately pro-slavery Louisianan, Pierre Soulé, bearing an offer of $125 million for the island. When the Spanish rudely declined, the infuriated Soulé retreated to the small French border town of Aix-la-Chapelle for a strategy session with two fellow diplomats, James Buchanan, minister to Great Britain, and John Y. Mason, his counterpart in France. There they drew up a secret document (the Ostend Manifesto), which advocated American seizure of Cuba if the Spanish refused to sell. On the trip back to the United States the document was purloined from the diplomatic pouch and found its way into the abolitionist press and, ultimately, validated northern suspicions of a southern conspiracy to extend the empire of slavery southward. But in the South the dream of tropical empire did not perish.[26]

After the Cuban fiasco, southern attention shifted to the isthmus, where energetic U.S. diplomats and equally vigorous American entrepreneurs had already established a Yankee foothold in what had been a British preserve. The

British presence dated from 1824, when the five Central American states had banded themselves into a federation (the United Provinces of Central America) and promptly saddled the new federal government with an onerous loan from the London firm of Barclay, Herring, Richardson, and Company. In the following decade, as American jealousy of the British foothold mounted, the federation came asunder, mostly from provincial animosities. But the Central Americans blamed the intruding British, who had allegedly encouraged separatist factions in Guatemala and Costa Rica. Nicaragua and Honduras particularly resented the British encroachment into the Mosquitia, the vast eastern lowland the Spanish had neglected throughout the colonial period. When U.S. efforts to secure trans-isthmian concessions began in earnest on the eve of the Mexican War, these four states looked to the United States for help.

To the southeast lay a less vulnerable nation, New Granada (Colombia), where the Americans encountered yet another European rival, France. In the years after Bolívar's death the Colombians endured one Panamanian separatist movement after another. In 1839 they fought a bitter civil conflict over the issue of Panamanian autonomy. Rumors circulated about a British-supported invasion by the Venezuelan-born strongman of Ecuador, General Juan José Flores. And a short time later two French engineers arrived to survey for a canal or railroad. Just as the Nicaraguans and Hondurans sensed an opportunity to sign treaties with the Americans to offset British influence, the Colombians welcomed the opportunity to gain an American protector against their European antagonists. In 1846 they negotiated with the American minister, Benjamin Bidlack, a treaty that opened the Isthmus of Panama to free transit and gave Americans the opportunity to construct a trans-isthmian passageway across Panama. In return the U.S. government guaranteed its neutrality.[27]

In the 1850s Americans bound for the California gold fields favored the Panama transit, thus enhancing the opportunities for local entrepreneurs — muleteers, boatmen, and prostitutes among others — and enabling people of color to challenge the domination of isthmian social elites. Their heyday lasted only for a few years, as newcomers from the United States took over much of the local traffic with steamers and the Panama Railroad. Clashes between white and colored — the most serious was the 1856 watermelon slice imbroglio between street vendors and U.S. sailors, which precipitated a brief U.S. military occupation — culminated in strengthening the U.S. economic enclave and enabling local elites to suppress the rising influence of people of color.[28]

In Washington there was less timidity over the British presence in the Mosquitia, virtually ignored by the Nicaraguans until 1844 when the British government announced a protectorate over the region and began dealing with a succession of intermediaries known as the Mosquito kings. If the British presence was essentially defensive, the actions of the British consul in Central America, Frederick Chatfield, were unarguably provocative. On the first day of 1848, as the United States readied for a victorious settlement with Mexico, Chatfield unleashed a ragtag Anglo-Mosquito army against defenseless San Juan. Triumphant, the invaders renamed the town Greytown and immediately announced a new tariff schedule. When the infuriated Nicaraguans retook it ten days later, Chatfield sent two warships and 250 men to drive them out. Under protest, the Nicaraguans abandoned the town and by implication acquiesced to the British protectorate.

Greytown's humiliation roused the entire Caribbean coast of the isthmus with rumors of another invasion. In Panama the American consul warned of an attack on Bocas del Toro and reported that Colombian militiamen were preparing for a British landing. Back in Washington the news of Greytown's fall prompted an official denial to British claims in the Mosquitia. The opportunistic Polk dispatched a diplomat, Elijah Hise, to negotiate with the wounded Nicaraguan government. An infuriated Democratic editor fumed about the Pax Britannica in the isthmus: "It seems no longer agitated, whether [Great Britain] shall continue to protect the squalid nationality of some few hundred illegitimate savages, born of indiscriminate concubinage, and leprous from a commixture of every unique blood, to whom she alternately administers crowns, Christianity, and Jamaica rum. . . . What becomes of Washington's, Jefferson's, Monroe's, and Polk's defiance to Europe?"[29]

Hise was indefatigable, a necessary trait, it was often said, for dealing with Central Americans, and he was determined to outmaneuver Chatfield. The Nicaraguans were happy to comply and overwhelmed him with concessions giving the United States (or U.S. entrepreneurs) total rights in constructing a canal using the San Juan and the interior lakes. When the treaty reached Washington, the Whigs (less bellicose about isthmian questions) were ensconced in the presidency, and Hise's treaty was promptly shelved. Hise's successor, Ephraim George Squier, proved no less ambitious in promoting American interests in Central America and no less contentious in confronting Her Majesty's consul. He also found time to begin the first of a dozen treatises on Central America dealing with everything from the isthmus's flora and fauna to its politics and economics. John Lloyd Stephens, one of the star-crossed U.S. emissaries of previous years, had informed his countrymen about the Mayas. Squier told them about everything else in Central America. Shortly after arriving in Nicaragua, he signed another treaty, omitting any clause guaranteeing its sovereignty. Then he moved on to Honduras and negotiated a convention with the manipulable Hondurans providing for the cession of Tigre Island in the Gulf of Fonseca, at the western terminus of the proposed trans-isthmian route. He dispatched the treaties with a self-congratulatory appendage about outwitting that "man of small caliber" Frederick Chatfield. The "man of small caliber" promptly called on a British man-of-war to seize Tigre Island.[30]

Secretary of State John Clayton, the recipient of this Anglophobic missive, was alert to the larger role the United States was playing in Central America; he was also apprehensive about a confrontation with the British. And his often maligned approach to isthmian questions reflected the belief that any trans-isthmian passage must be international—a belief that perished a generation later with President Rutherford B. Hayes's declaration that any trans-isthmian canal was merely a detached portion of the U.S. coast. Clayton encouraged the French to sign a treaty with New Granada similar to Bidlack's pact and invited the British to join the United States in exercising a protective dominion over trans-isthmian routes from the Tehuantepec in Mexico to Panama.

Recognizing that their own interests in Central America might very well be served by accepting his offer, the British sent a special negotiator, Sir Henry Bulwer, to Washington. In April 1850 Bulwer and Clayton signed what was to be the most far-reaching international agreement concerning Central America until the twentieth century. The two countries pledged equality of treatment and a guarantee of neutrality for any trans-isthmian passage. They promised not to exercise dominion of any kind over the Central American states. This treaty gave the Americans confidence that the British would withdraw from the Mosquitia, the Bay Islands, and even British Honduras. They soon discovered that the British pledge covered only future acquisitions; interests already established, London made clear, would be retained. The Clayton-Bulwer settlement was symbolic of Central Americans' frustrations in trying to benefit by maneuvering one power against another, only to discover that the diplomatic combatants could withdraw to their own domain and arrive at mutually beneficial arrangements.[31]

And there was now another foreign presence in the isthmus — concessionaires, soldiers of fortune, southern dreamers of tropical empire — presumably more amenable than the U.S. or British governments to Central American whims. For a generation the Central Americans had welcomed the foreigners in the belief, as Francisco Morazán had proudly declared, that the Englishman or Frenchman or Belgian or *norteamericano* who settled in the isthmus would be transformed into a *centroamericano*. When the controversy over foreign interlopers reached its zenith in the mid-1850s, Nicaragua was in the eye of the storm. As the Central American federation weakened, the Nicaraguan Liberals, who had supported isthmian unity, looked first to the British and then the Americans to abet their cause. Their mortal political enemies, the Conservatives, viewed the foreign intrusion as a menace to the social culture. But the Liberals championed a more "progressive" view. They assiduously promoted the country as a more attractive route than Panama for migrants to the gold fields in California. The most ambitious of these promoters was Cornelius Vanderbilt, who gathered partners to form the Atlantic and Pacific Ship Canal Company to survey a canal route. Recognizing that the gold seekers were impatient to head west, Vanderbilt also created the Accessory Transit Company, which by steamer, riverboat, and stagecoach ferried gentlemen and their "missy ladies" up the San Juan River, across the interior lakes, and on to the Pacific shore. In the early 1850s, however, Vanderbilt's company began to lose out to a rival group in Panama. The commodore got out of the Nicaraguan venture just in time to acquire a profitable interest in its Panamanian rival.

Vanderbilt's abrupt departure offered an opportunity to another generation of Americans with grander ambitions. Their leader was a brilliant, handsome Tennessean who had become a doctor and a lawyer — William Walker. In 1853 he led an expedition of filibusters into Baja California and Sonora, Mexico. Failing, Walker and his men returned to California. There Walker received word about the opportunities in Nicaragua from Byron Cole, another filibuster already in Nicaragua. The Nicaraguan Liberal army was confronted with a Conservative opposition, reinforced with Guatemalan aid. In their desperation the Liberals had offered Cole and other Americans in Nicaragua bountiful land grants in exchange for their services. The message was a godsend to the languishing Walker. He was a man of lofty ambitions with the mercenary's sense of opportunity, if only he had the will to act. In June 1855, accompanied by the fifty-seven "immortals," the "grey-eyed man of destiny" set foot on Central American soil.

By early fall he had risen to commanding general of Liberal forces and had taken the old Conservative citadel of Granada. Terrified Conservatives hastily agreed to a coalition government with one of their own, Patricio Rivas, as president but with Walker as military chieftain. Ensconced as commander, Walker disbanded the Conservative army and, in keeping with an isthmian political tradition, exiled his enemies. Within a year the U.S. minister was trumpeting the accomplishments of the regime. Commodore Vanderbilt's commercial rivals began subsidizing Walker, as they had supplemented the treasuries of his Nicaraguan predecessor. Mexican War veterans arrived with expectations of receiving generous land grants. Before long, Walker had a force of twenty-five hundred. From the isthmus came ominous rumors of a new slave state and, possibly, an attack on Spanish Cuba.[32]

Central Americans, it is often said, can never unite unless they confront a common foe. In Walker they had one. The initial protests came from Conservatives in Guatemala and the Costa Ricans, who saw themselves as the protectors of isthmian civilization and the "race" against the Protestant hordes from the north. Happily, the British funded the anti-Walker coalition, as did Vanderbilt, who was indignant that his commercial rivals were using Nicaragua to undercut his Panama route. On 1 March 1856 four Central American states formally declared war on Nicaragua.

Besieged on all sides, his troops decimated by a cholera epidemic, Walker took to the offensive. Tossing out the Conservative puppet, he proclaimed himself president of Nicaragua, declared English the official language of the country, and announced the restoration of slavery. Throughout the American South the cry went out for reinforcements. In November 1856, when the Costa Ricans sent an invading force into Nicaragua, Walker retaliated by burning Granada. He left as monument to the destruction a crude sign, "Aquí fué Granada" ("Here was Granada"). But his Central American enemies showed they could persist as well. They received aid from Peru, and a timely British blockade of Nicaragua's ports cut Walker's supply lines. In spring 1857 the Costa Rican leader sent word that any American requesting passage home would be granted safe-conduct.

Walker's men began deserting by the hundreds, leaving him with a skeletal force and almost certain defeat. But once more he was spared. President James Buchanan dispatched a U.S. warship to rescue the now famous Walker and return him home. Back in New Orleans, Walker recruited another invasion force. This time he managed to reach Greytown before the U.S. Navy intercepted him and returned him to stand trial for neutrality violations. The filibuster's charm still worked its persuasiveness on juries, and he was shortly freed. Migrating to New York, he began appearing at the Metropolitan, sitting grandly in his box and occasionally acknowledging the admiring glances from the audience below with a gesture. Ever the publicist, he found time to publish a book about his exploits.[33]

For a year or so the dream of a southern tropical empire revived. Had Walker remained in the United States, he might have found a ready outlet for his considerable martial talent in the Confederacy. But in 1860 he headed back to New Orleans and there put together his third invasion force. This time he had an "invitation" from yet another disaffected element in Central America — the English-speaking residents of the Bay Islands angry with Britain's sudden decision to restore the islands to Honduras. After a glorious welcome in the islands, he believed, there would follow a swift invasion of the Honduran mainland, then a revived isthmian union with Walker as its master.

The expedition arrived off Roatán in June 1860, discovered that the British garrison had not yet departed, and prudently sailed for Trujillo, the old port on the north Honduran coast. It quickly fell before Walker's superior force. But the captain of a patrolling British warship, alert to the nuances of Central American politics, recognized his opportunity. He sent a squad of marines ashore to arrest Walker, pledging safe passage for him and his men. When Walker surrendered, the British turned him over to local Honduran officials. They quickly tried, sentenced, and executed the grey-eyed man of destiny. A Nicaraguan he had betrayed had already written his Central American epitaph: "God will condemn his arrogance and protect our cause."[34]

The Wars of North America

A year after Walker's death, the hemispheric country whose distinctive social and political features Alexis de Tocqueville had detailed in his classic study, *Democracy in America*, collapsed in a fratricidal civil war, one of a series of national conflicts in the Americas in the 1850s and 1860s. In these two decades, Argentina, Chile, Venezuela, Colombia, Central America, Paraguay, Mexico, and Brazil experienced internal warring that pitted liberal against conservative or countryside against city or federalist against centralist. In each case, leaders averred, not only were the political and economic future at stake, but also the very identity of the nation. In the Paraguayan case, the casualties suffered in a war with Argentina, Uruguay, and Brazil not only devastated the country but left a debilitating scar on the national psyche as well. For most hemispheric countries, the impact of the U.S. civil war was indirect and symbolic. The victory of the Union offered proof that unity within a federal system of government could be attained. For North America, however, the war in the United States left far more lasting, albeit differing, legacies.

For Canadians, the American Civil War prompted yet another debate over the uncertain character of the relationship with the mother country and the continuing menace of the republic to the south. In the American Revolution, French Quebecois had solemnly concluded that joining the American cause was simply not worth the price. But in the aftermath of the Mexican War, as the British Parliament dismantled many of the tariff preferences for Canadians, irate Montreal merchants called for annexation to the United States. The enthusiasm on both sides quickly dissipated with reminders that no true Canadian wished to join a country that condoned slavery. From the 1820s black communities cropped up in Upper Canada (Ontario), and by 1861 approximately 35,000 blacks, largely émigrés from U.S. slavery, lived there. Nonetheless, in 1854, the two entities negotiated a reciprocity treaty. Talk of a continental North America revived.

But the outbreak of hostilities between North and South had a subtle effect on the long-standing debate over Canadian Confederation. Most Canadians were ambivalent about the issues of the war. In the beginning of the war, certainly, the prevailing view held that economic factors, not slavery, had largely dictated the southern option for independence. The situation worsened with the British proclamation of neutrality and deteriorated further with Secretary of State William Seward's call for a diversionary confrontation with Great Britain, France, and Spain to protest their coercive pressures against the Mexican government of Benito Juárez (who had declared a moratorium on Mexico's debt payments), and the stoppage of a British ship (the *Trent*) to seize two Confederate envoys. The British cabinet seriously considered a military retaliation over the incident, but as he did in other matters, Lincoln intervened to calm his volatile secretary of state. The only direct threat from Canada was the October 1864 Confederate raid on St Albans, Vermont.

At war's end, the pent-up northern resentments over these incidents prompted calls for retaliation and the seizure of Canadian territory. One casualty of the public militancy was the 1854 reciprocity treaty. A more ominous threat came from the Irish Republican Brotherhood (the Fenians), many of them Union veterans only too eager to carry out raids on Canadian settlements. Again, the threat diminished, largely over the unwillingness of authorities in Washington to encourage such movements with military support, as it had been willing to do in Texas and California, and the equally important resolution of Canadian leaders, notably John Macdonald, to reaffirm the need for a dominion to unite the disparate and fractured provinces. Indirectly, the Civil War and the persistence of Continentalist sentiments among Americans served as a catalyst for the crafting of stronger bonds among Canadians. In the British North America Act of 1867, the two Canadas (Ontario and Quebec) joined with New Brunswick and Nova Scotia in forming the dominion of Canada. By 1871, largely in reaction to a perceived U.S. threat, Manitoba and British Columbia became members.

Some Canadian editorialists gloated that Canada had achieved independence, but the truth of the matter was that Confederation complicated rather than resolved the character of the tripartite relationship between Canada, Britain, and the United States. Canada still did not control its external affairs, and it could not amend its constitution without Parliament's approval. These considerations, however, proved of less immediate importance than a third issue: if Canadians had not united in 1867, the year Seward negotiated the purchase of Alaska from imperial Russia, several Canadian historians have speculated that the United States would have absorbed the provinces one by one, and Canada might have ceased to exist. As one of them astutely noted, the U.S. threat "performed the function of saving [Canada] from drift and indecision."[35]

Mexico followed a different, more violent path to national unity. After its defeat in the war with the United States, the nation turned inward. Those who had supported the peace settlement with the Americans fell into disfavor, and in 1853 Santa Anna returned triumphantly to power. It was his last performance on the Mexican political stage, but, fittingly, he profited. The U.S. government, which had paid only $18 million for the entire Mexican cession, provided Santa Anna with $10 million for the Mesilla Valley in southern Arizona. Two years later, his administration hopelessly indebted by the grafters and sycophants who surrounded him, Santa Anna tried to sell even more of the national domain to the Yankees. This time all Mexico declared against him, and he was driven from the City of the Aztecs.

Mexico lapsed into twelve years of civil strife and foreign intervention, even as the United States fell into discord and civil war. Their parallel internal struggles produced, at least momentarily in their troubled relationship, a sense of common struggle for nationhood. And in these struggles in both countries two remarkable leaders emerged — Abraham Lincoln and Benito Juárez — each of whom appeared unsuited for the role of building a nation.

Juárez was a Zapotec Indian from Oaxaca with a Liberal determination to drive the cleric and the soldier from their positions of privilege in Mexican society. Lincoln emerged as a regional opponent to slavery's expansion. Their rise to power was curiously parallel — Juárez's in the breakdown of the old hierarchical order before the concerted attacks of the Liberals in the mid-1850s, Lincoln's by the growing fears in the North about a national government dominated by southern sympathizers and apologists. Late in the decade, when Juárez and his political allies pushed through laws divesting the church of its lands and the military of its "privileges," Lincoln and other Republicans were roundly criticizing the undisguised opportunism of President James Buchanan's administration in taking advantage of Mexico's plight. In 1858 the defenders of the church and the military formed an alliance with the monarchists railing against the Liberal heathen and raised the flag of rebellion. Desperate for funds to prosecute the sedition, Mexico turned to Washington, offering transit concessions across the isthmus of Tehuantepec and the northern third of the republic (with the authority to protect the routes with U.S. troops) for $10 million. The political outcry from Republicans, uniformly suspicious of Buchanan's motives in dealing with Mexico, prompted him to withhold the treaty from Senate consideration.

In the midst of these troubles, Juárez became president, only to have his enemies drive him from the capital. He took refuge in Veracruz. From there he waged both guerrilla and political war, sending his illiterate soldiers to ambush Conservative patrols and promulgating confiscatory decrees against his clerical enemies. In January 1861 he returned to the capital, dressed in the somber black of the Liberals and riding in a simple coach. Two months later, in similarly portentous circumstances, Lincoln took the presidential oath. Two hemispheric republics plunged into civil war — one before the retaliation of its European creditors, the second before the divisive forces the sudden conquest of territory had unleashed. In the challenge to republican government, the image of the United States in both Mexico and the rest of the hemisphere changed again.

Both governments were now imperiled, but it was the Mexican government that succumbed to European intervention. In 1861 Great Britain, France, and Spain joined in an expedition to punish Mexico for Juárez's declaration of a moratorium on the national debt. When Mexico's creditors extended an invitation to the United States to join their pact, Seward indignantly refused, but he used the offer to extract a pledge from the British disavowing any expansionist intention in Mexico. Seward did not mention the Monroe Doctrine. The British promise meant that the weak alliance with Spain and France would be of short duration. When the allies finally landed their forces at Veracruz, the Mexicans took advantage of their obvious divisions to entice the British into a separate agreement. Shortly, the Spanish, disillusioned with the notion of a *reconquista*, departed and satisfied their imperial ambitions with the reoccupation of the Dominican Republic, where they immediately confronted another guerrilla insurgency.

Only the large French army remained on Mexican soil. By spring 1862 it had pushed into the mountainous interior as far as Puebla. On 5 May (the *Cinco de Mayo*, a holiday now celebrated as far north as Chicago), Juárez's troops defeated them. But the French regrouped, defeated the Mexicans, and marched on the capital. In the following year they returned with a conquering army to install Maximilian, the Austrian archduke whom the Mexican Conservatives had discovered in their long European quest for a Hapsburg to sit on a restored Mexican throne. Their benefactor, Napoleon III, had often dreamed of this venture. Two decades before, in prison, he had written a tiny but ambitious volume, *The Canal of Nicaragua*. A coup d'état and accession to power brought to his court the importuning Mexican clerics, who argued for a Hapsburg to restore order and God in the heathen republic of the Liberals.

Viewing Mexico's defeat from afar, Seward pursued a narrow course between condemnation, which meant invoking the Monroe Doctrine, and acquiescence in the French venture, which no dedicated proponent of republicanism could tolerate. His notes to the French government on the Mexican intervention are masterpieces of diplomatic wording. France had a right to punish Mexico for its financial misdeeds, he wrote, but the Mexican people preferred republican to monarchical government. Meanwhile, the U.S. minister to Juárez, isolated in the remote North during these years, conveyed the repeated assurances of Seward that the cause of Juárez and the cause of Lincoln were the same. When the Confederacy dispatched its own emissary bearing promises, the stoic Zapotec was disbelieving. His patience was ultimately rewarded.

Seward's protests did little to alleviate Juárez's immediate problem or the suffering of ordinary Mexicans. But his criticism of the French venture (and the skills of the Mexican minister in Washington, Matías Romero, in rousing congressional opposition to the intervention) invigorated the *juarista* cause. As the American conflict entered its final year, a powerful sentiment took hold in the Lincoln administration to confront the French over the issue. Napoleon III, alert to the Prussian threat and the disturbing reports from his own ministers about rapidly diminishing public support for the intervention, had apparently already decided to withdraw French troops from Mexico. Maximilian had become a liability, the Confederacy was doomed, and Juárez's reputation was rising even among Europeans.

Seward sent the French a timetable for withdrawing their troops, which Napoleon meekly accepted. Already, the victorious Union had dispatched an army perilously close to the Mexican border, but its presence proved more symbolic than decisive in Maximilian's fall. The real victors were the *juaristas* and Juárez himself, who throughout the conflict had maintained vital links with a United States he distrusted and, at bottom, feared. While Seward pressured the French, Juárez moved against the cities of central Mexico, hoping to lure Maximilian into defending them. By then most of his protective French army had departed. Taken prisoner after a hundred-day siege at Querétaro, the last Mexican emperor stood trial, was found guilty, and was sentenced to death. From Europe and even the United States came pleas for clemency, but the Zapotec who had waged guerrilla war was implacable. Maximilian's execution would serve as a reminder to others who conspired to restore monarchy in Mexico. Seward had condemned the restoration of European monarchy in the Americas; Juárez and his *mestizo* guerillas had defeated it. The Mexican leader had achieved victory with U.S. assistance. In his most desperate days, he had moved his government to El Paso. With Lincoln's acquiescence, he had bought arms and hired mercenaries to continue the fight. For the second time since the winning of independence in 1821, Mexico rejected monarchy.

The Legacy

Yet it was the Civil War in the United States — the apocalyptic finality of the American Revolution — and not the arguably more significant Mexican struggle that inspired hemispheric admiration. And some Latin Americans began to realize that the United States might be richer in its cultural and political tradition and less menacing than the expansionist republic they had earlier feared. Here, again, the key issues of the American struggle — slavery, emancipation, states' rights, and military rule — were to Latin Americans of less importance than the symbol of Lincoln, whom they saw as a unifier standing against all enemies. Although he lacked the warrior spirit of Theodore Roosevelt, the magnetic appeal of John Kennedy, or the moral decency of Jimmy Carter, never again would any U.S. president convey the traditional Hispanic traits of the good leader so closely as Lincoln did for Latin Americans. The explanation lay not so much in his ultimate command of the crusade against slavery, but in his symbolic role as the "just leader" who innately senses the "will of the people" and leads them. Lincoln stood as the champion of central authority against disruptive chieftains and recognized the spiritual issues at stake in the war for the Union. The unconstitutional exercise of power attributed to him meant little to Latin Americans. What mattered was the moral and even spiritual legitimacy of his cause. Such judgments were likelier to emanate from Chileans or Argentines than from Mexicans or Canadians, but they were reminders of the ambivalence of U.S. attitudes toward the other nations and peoples of the Americas and, conversely, their ambivalence toward the United States and its people.

In retrospect, the century between the end of the French and Indian War and the civil war constituted the formative era in the shaping of U.S. policy toward the other Americas. In this era, both the U.S. government and the American people revealed contradictory faces to their hemispheric neighbors, particularly toward Mexico and Canada. One was aggressive and expansionist; a second exhibited progressive and democratic beliefs in a presumptive "civilizing mission" of the nation and in what successive generations of U.S. leaders called "good neighborhood." The first was about power; the second, about purpose.

Sorting these multiple views into neat and simple categories, however, can be problematic and indeed misleading. Some were fueled by religion (a predominantly Protestant reformation of Catholic societies); others, by a strong sense of providential mission that offered both promise and threat (oppressed peoples deserved liberation, but because they were of "mixed-race" and "backward," they required tutelage and pacification and, like the freed slave or Indian, could be discriminated against). There are other considerations — an underlying fear that the chaos and uncertainties that came in the wake of the wars of independence threatened not only the security of the state but its future; the acknowledgment that progress might come at the expense of human rights; and, among others, the persistent cultural prejudice (shared by some literati and intellectual giants) that contact with Latin Americans, especially those Mexicans in the territories acquired in the Mexican War, degraded and corrupted American society and culture.[36]

For many Latin Americans and a lesser number of Canadians, racial and expansionist imperatives, the slave power, and commercial opportunism — not the example of democratic society and republican governance — more accurately represented the reality of the United States in the Americas in the era of manifest destiny. What such a view presumes, however, is a uniformity of opinion and purpose between the central government, the states, and the people about the security, prosperity, and unity of the republic during years of rapid territorial expansion, growth of slavery and the slave power, and, most impressively, revolutions in communication and technology, social movements, and the myriad democratic political cultures that both inspired and perplexed Alexis de Tocqueville as he journeyed about the country in the 1830s. When he turned his attention to the newly independent governments of Latin America, de Tocqueville was persuaded that the United States had achieved a unity and peace that contrasted sharply with the warring and jealousy that had destroyed Bolívar's plans for Spanish American unity and what most U.S. leaders believed were anti-democratic and military-dominated governments.

The truth of the matter was that U.S. policy in the hemisphere, particularly in North America, was driven as much by fear and uncertainty as by purpose. Even at the height of public exaltation over U.S. victories in the Mexican War, there was a somber realization that the federal government was not the advance agent in continental expansion but a follower of the people — mountain men, filibusters, opportunists, land speculators, slaveholders, abolitionists, and ordinary citizens and immigrants on the move. True, it had encouraged these movements, but increasingly national leaders were confronted with a problem similar to that faced by the British in 1763 in trying to stem the flow of colonials into the trans-Appalachian country. The creation of new states, as Jefferson once averred, offered a way for the United States to avoid the poverty associated with concentration of population on the land as well as to provide security against the threat of the Holy Alliance and a resurgence of British and French power in North America. Just as fervently, Bolívar affirmed the confederation of former Spanish American colonies would serve to safeguard the newly independent republics from a similar fate. By the 1850s, the ability of the federal government to contain the powerful human and economic forces unleashed by the democratic impulses of the age and the ambitions of the slaveholding states by the traditional means of political compromise had weakened.

The collapse of the Union into Civil War, the abolition of slavery, and the creation of the leviathan state offered a sobering reminder that the United States was not immune to the divisive forces and flaws its leaders had attributed to the newly independent Latin American states or, for that matter, the Canadas before the Confederation of 1867. In the century after the 1763 Peace of Paris ending the French and Indian War, the United States had achieved independence and preserved the fragile Union that Lincoln commemorated in the Gettysburg Address. But the victory proved less a triumph for the kind of republic imagined by the founders than a recognition that the United States was but one of several hemispheric countries that had rid itself of slavery and divisive federalist wars yet arrogantly believed that unlike its hemispheric neighbors, it had proved itself ready to join the European concert of nations.

By its economic and technological achievements, such a judgment was warranted. But in that first century of independence commemorated in 1876, the record of the United States in dealing with the debilitating legacy of slavery and racism, incorporating its indigenous peoples and immigrants into national life, or in coming to grips with mounting labor strife remained problematical. By the measure that some Americans applied to Latin American republics in the 1830s and 1840s, the United States was no longer the "model republic" but one of the "failed states" of the hemisphere in the 1850s. A generation of political leaders who now believed that the victory of the union had largely resolved the fundamental political and social questions confronting the republic soon discovered that the nation they imagined had not yet been achieved. Nonetheless, some of them were eager to embark on an imperial path.

PART 2
Empire

3   The Imperial Design

In 1876 Americans celebrated not only their independence but, equally important, the survival of the republic after four years of fratricidal war with powerful implications for European powers and especially other hemispheric nations. For those French republicans who had suffered under the monarchical rule of Napoleon III, the Union victory had validated the cause of republican liberty, a triumph that French liberals would honor with ambitious plans for the Statue of Liberty as a gift from the French people to their republican comrades across the Atlantic. But Lincoln's call for "a just and lasting peace among ourselves and all nations" had also touched a generation of Latin American liberals — among them the Argentines Domingo Sarmiento and Juan Alberdi and the Chilean thinker Francisco Bilbao. Alberdi praised England and the United States as the protectors of freedom in the nineteenth century. Where some vilified the acquisitive Yankees, Sarmiento responded: "Let us not detain the United States in its march. . . . Let us emulate the United States. Let us be America, as the sea is the ocean. Let us be the United States." In scornful prose, Bilbao castigated the Spanish political and cultural imprint for its debilitating legacy, but the liberal tradition implanted by the British in North America had bequeathed "the United States, the foremost of nations, both ancient and modern."[1]

Such anti-Spanish sentiments echoed those that Bolívar had voiced fifty years earlier, and that a generation of U.S. leaders would reiterate on the eve of war with Spain in 1898, but the sobering truth of the U.S. Civil War was that it had settled only two issues: the illegitimacy of state secession and chattel slavery. Beyond that, the internal political and social troubles afflicting the nation at 1876 seemed almost as formidable as those on the eve of the war fifteen years before. The difference — and it was an important difference — lay in the reminder of six hundred thousand casualties, a revival of southern resistance to Reconstruction, and a growing northern indifference to the plight of the southern Negro.

Despite these obstacles, the promoters of the centennial doggedly persisted in their call for a fair that would not only bring about "perfect reconcilia-tion" between North and South but also reaffirm the promise of America to a still skeptical world. With small share donations, they purchased a site in Philadelphia's Fairmont Park and solicited exhibits from most of the states and thirty-nine countries. In 1875, workers began the erection of two hundred buildings, among them a twenty-acre Main Hall purported to be the largest enclosure in the world. On 10 May 1876, President Ulysses S. Grant opened the Exhibition by starting the 680-ton steam engine powering the manufactur-ing marvels in Machinery Hall. Eight million visitors — among them, Emperor Dom Pedro II of Brazil — strolled through the halls of what pundits described as evidence of the national reconciliation and material promise. Along with Western Europe, some enthusiasts trumpeted, the United States had entered the second Industrial Revolution.

Not surprisingly, some commentators voiced skepticism. A few foreign cor-respondents were quick to contrast the pretentiousness of the Exhibition with the visible poverty, urban decay, and spreading labor unrest in eastern cities. A few days after the exuberant July 4th fireworks, there was more unsettling news — the defeat of General George Armstrong Custer's Seventh Cavalry at the Little Big Horn in Montana, an omen of the Indian wars of the next fifteen years; and a mob attack on African American celebrants in South Carolina. Doubts about national reconciliation deepened as the contentious presiden-tial campaign got underway in the fall, and disgruntled Democrats threatened armed uprising if their candidate, the New Yorker Samuel Tilden, won the popular vote but was denied the presidency. More and more, it became clear that the surest means to retaining a Republican presidency lay in abandon-ing the freed slave to the political whims and domination of a vengeful and resentful South. A parallel belief held that the country's unity and its economic future depended on a government dedicated to serving the interests of a rising generation of capitalist tycoons; and its political future at home and prestige abroad lay in its ability to pacify those who threatened internal order (Indians, laborers, radicals) and its willingness to carry out a more ambitious role in the world, particularly in the Western Hemisphere.

A generation later, in yet another celebration — the 1893 World's Columbian Exposition or Chicago World's Fair — designers honored not only technology, especially electricity, and manufacturing but also classical architecture and the arts. At Chicago, historian Frederick Jackson Turner delivered his iconic essay on the end of the frontier in U.S. history, a mythical view of national development that would nonetheless persist among successive generations of westerners and historians and students of U.S. expansion as a fundamental guide to understanding how and why the country developed at home and even abroad. Occupying center stage at the Chicago Fair was the Court of Honor, or "White City," a reminder, as social scientists presumably verified, that progress depended on the "whitening" of society.

By then, sometimes haltingly, other times aggressively, the nation had already embarked on what Walter Nugent has described as "Empire II," the acquisition of largely extra-continental territories, beginning with Alaska in 1867, Hawai'i in the wartime summer of 1898, and Puerto Rico and the Philippines before another year had passed. In the new century came the creation of a Caribbean and Central American protectorate system that persisted until the early 1930s and was then altered in form but not so noticeably in purpose by the Franklin D. Roosevelt administration. By comparison with those who had crafted the continental empire traced in part 1 — what Jefferson called the "empire of liberty" — the architects of Empire II also pursued territorial acquisitions, but the central motivation was not such divisive matters as the expansion of slavery or removal of indigenous peoples but other, still controversial considerations — from racism and the sometimes brutal and inhumane treatment of demonized subject people to spreading the "American dream," the search for markets, and even expansion as a valedictory for the "ideal" of manliness.[2]

Greater North America

The Cuban-Spanish-American War of 1898 and the crushing of the Philippine insurrection, it is generally agreed, marked the direction the nation would take in shaping its insular empire. But there are several critical military undertakings and decisions in the last third of the nineteenth century that shaped American thinking in the making of the second empire. One element lay in what Theodore Roosevelt — the exemplar of a U.S. president with strong and almost spiritual convictions about empire — called the winning of the West or what more accurately might be labeled as the conquest of the West. The historian Frederick Jackson Turner believed it occurred with the closing of the frontier, but that proved imprecise. Others pointed to the Army's pursuit of Geronimo, the Apache leader who for years eluded capture. Still others identified it as the hideous massacre of largely helpless Indians at a place called Wounded Knee. For some contemporaries, the Indian wars from the late 1860s to the 1890s exemplified an unjust crusade against a hapless people no longer a threat. For others, these wars, both in their bloodletting and accompanying militant rhetoric, demonstrated what white Americans perceived as a democratic, civilizing mission. Those without any mercy called for a purge of the savage forces threatening the nation or a war of extermination. When the U.S. Army officer initially leading the Geronimo chase expressed some compassion and understanding for the ill done the western Indian, he was removed from his post. His successor, Nelson Miles, felt no such compunction. (Miles was named commanding general of the army and later led the U.S. invasion of Puerto Rico during the Spanish-American war.) The modern description is ethnic cleansing. William F. "Buffalo Bill" Cody essentially captured its meaning in his handout at his show at the 1893 Chicago World's Fair: "The bullet is the pioneer of civilization, for it has gone hand in hand with the axe that cleared the forest, and with the family Bible and school book."[3]

That imperative expressed the essence of what many Americans of the late nineteenth century believed to be a divine mandate for those committed to make war on "savage" Indians or repress an equally threatening menace, organized labor. Ironically, most Americans of the era rarely reflected on the fact that the Canadian experience in western development, which roughly paralleled that of its southern neighbor, resulted in far fewer casualties. From 1865 to the mid-1890s, the U.S. Army fought a thousand military engagements with western Indians; their Canadian counterparts, seven. In search of an explanation for this unsettling disparity, Canadians are quick to point out that in the United States the people got to the West before the law, but in Canada the reverse was the case. In truth, Canadians placed far greater emphasis on controlling the behavior of white immigrants.[4]

Canadians drew on their history, as we drew on ours. More accurately, both depended on their respective memories for guidance and for inspiration. As

Secretary of State William H. Seward envisaged it, the imperial design of the late nineteenth century exhibited some of the features of the age of manifest destiny — for example, a continuing belief in national mission and exceptionalism — but it engaged more fully other, equally pressing and urgent, mandates. Arguably, as David Pletcher has shown, the fractious character of national politics, particularly between free traders and protectionists, and the inordinate attention political leaders had to give to domestic issues, among other matters, have obscured any identifiable pattern of a coherent extracontinental or imperial design. But the elements were there. The difficulty lies in measuring how the disparate hemispheric issues, challenges, and opportunities that confronted the U.S. government in the three decades before the war with Spain would coalesce to revive a public militancy as strong as that exhibited in the Mexican War. Presumably, as U.S. business became better organized and eager to expand foreign markets, particularly in the Caribbean and Central America as well as the western Pacific, its leaders favored a more aggressive foreign economic policy.

The reality was that business leaders and congressmen were often fearful that these policies might do more harm than good. And in an era when U.S. politics was becoming ever more polarized over the issue of race and parallel debates over immigration and labor, a policy of diverting attention to hemispheric challenges in order to ease societal tensions and forge a stronger national unity made sense, particularly if promoted with invocations of taking up the "white man's burden" or "civilizing the savages." In truth, there were equally compelling arguments that expansion into lands peopled largely by persons of color would prove debilitating and ill served those making the case for empire.[5]

Seward did not live to witness how these implicit dilemmas and contradictions of empire would often befuddle and confuse leaders of the 1890s, when all the romantic notions about the meaning of the American experience were being tested in a nation convulsed with political and social challenges at home and abroad. For him, the expansionism that mattered lay not so much in conquest by war but in acquisition through peaceful means, such as the Alaska purchase, which *was* a stupendous stroke of achievement, however long it took to really make the investment pay off. Or it took form in the more vigorous pursuit of commerce or hastily conceived plans not to people new domains but to control their economies and politics. Frankly, that was naive, as the British and French and particularly the Spanish had already found out. Expansion meant pacification, no matter how noble your purpose. But at the onset of the building of Empire II, expansion through peaceful means rather than by force, seemed not only possible but achievable. After all, the republic had endured four years of mindless slaughter and loss of life during the Civil War, and it had survived. Surely it possessed, if not a hemispheric mission, a rightful claim to serve as example for those hemispheric countries striving to achieve unity and purpose.[6]

Those still pressing for incorporation of Canada (or at least a portion of the country) now discovered that they had kindred spirits among a generation of several influential Canadians (among them, the prominent Liberal Goldwin Smith) who felt betrayed by John Macdonald's accommodation to the imperial agenda in the Treaty of Washington. Smith and his followers sought not independence but a union with the United States similar to that of Scotland with England. Smith was dreaming the impossible dream: there was no commonwealth or United Kingdom "model" in the U.S. experience. The Constitution provided for neither. Nor could there be autonomy. Macdonald knew that. Independence in the metaphorical if not the absolute sense in Canada lay not in revolution *against* empire, as had occurred in the American Revolution, but evolution *within* empire. For Canadians, that was the self-evident truth.

And in Latin America, some of those liberals frustrated over the persistent civil conflicts and tardiness of economic progress turned an admiring gaze northward to the United States, which had achieved unity and then began to demonstrate what riches a modern capitalist system was capable of generating. Often they exaggerated and distorted, at times more so than their U.S. counterparts. Not surprisingly, those Americans who ventured into Latin American and Caribbean business and trade in the three decades after the Civil War heartened to these sentiments. From the early nineteenth century until the Mexican War, the agents of continental expansion had been the U.S. Army, the states, and the people, at least indirectly; in Latin America and the Caribbean, the U.S. Navy and the foreign entrepreneur or merchant. They adjusted to the political reality or did not long survive. Those who fared well — such as

W. R. Grace in Peru, who built a commercial empire on the west coast of South America — learned how to operate by the political or, more precisely, social priorities of the host country. A succession of Germans and Americans pushed railroad projects in Costa Rica, for example, but the wily *ticos* of the central plateau resisted until Henry Meiggs (who had laid track in Chile and the Peruvian Andes) and Minor Keith (one of the founders of United Fruit) convinced them that Costa Rica's economic future lay in a rail line to the Caribbean coast. In time, of course, the entrepreneurs founded companies whose resources and clout dwarfed those of local governments. When their interests conflicted, the governments sometimes bowed and occasionally resisted. In the latter instances, Latin America became an early supporter of the Calvo doctrine, by which a foreign company agreed to settle disputes in national courts. By the twentieth century, certainly, the multinationals had begun to appeal to their own governments for support, either by diplomatic pressure or, if necessary, by more forceful means.[7]

Mexico after Maximilian offers a good example of economic transformation and its social cost. It became the raw materials supplier for an invigorated North American industrial economy. In both Mexico and the United States political leaders sought a new economic order. Mexico again turned inward but after its victory over European monarchy strived to blend its Hispanic authoritarian past with the economic promise offered by industrial Europe and America. In Europe the modern industrial order expanded its global frontiers by extending its formal empire. The United States sought markets, bases, and influence. Mexico, like most of Latin America, adjusted because the requirements of modernization seemed to dictate doing so. It promoted industrial development by importing foreign capital, technicians, and entrepreneurs. It permitted an aggressive landed class to diminish the historic social role of the hacienda (where the master provided for his charges) by transforming the landed estates into plantations that produced for export, devouring small farms and those who survived on them. Its government extended to foreigners the privilege of mining for the subsoil riches of the country and the opportunity to construct rail lines to unite the domain of domestic producer with the outside world. In the process, it has been argued, an economic system was imposed from without, on the backs of downtrodden people whose only value was their labor. An informal empire took form. Its creators were Mexican and

American, and its beneficiaries were Mexican and American. But its victims were *los de abajo*, those on the bottom.[8]

In Mexico, the visible impact of the Industrial Revolution was impressive. This country, which Americans and Europeans had long regarded as a political and economic backwater, now had a leader, Porfirio Díaz, who brought order to the countryside and positivist credos to the state and in the process gained a grudging respect from U.S. leaders. Mexico joined the gold-standard fraternity, discouraged bullfighting and the festivities of its Indian past, and acquired a respectable image among its former detractors in Europe and America. The ideal was a modern Mexico, unified by a dynamic middle class attuned to the promise of an imported economic philosophy based on material, not ideological, credos. In the half century between the Civil War and the 1910 revolution, Mexico became both an economic and cultural laboratory for British, German, and, especially, American entrepreneurs, promoters, and even missionaries. The last espoused a version of the American dream unfamiliar to many Mexicans: social mobility, Protestant teachings, free market capitalism, democracy, and the consumer values of a generation.

The U.S. economic foundation began during the Juárez years and picked up dramatically after Díaz began to consolidate his power in the mid-1880s. American capital moved into mining and railroads. By century's end, two U.S. companies, American Smelting and Refining and Anaconda, dominated the industry, especially in the northern states. (By 1910, U.S. investors owned more than 80 percent of mining capital in Mexico.) At the same time, a U.S. consortium gained control over Mexican railroads, and U.S. manufacturing and industry sent finished goods — chemicals, steel, copper wiring, machine tools, motors, electric machinery, among other products. Lacking a significant home market, Mexicans concentrated on light industry. The impact of these changes on both city and countryside was dramatic: the large cities, notably Mexico City and Monterrey, acquired many of the attributes of modern metropolises. Railroads brought the countryside into contact with the city. But with economic modernity came expropriation of land and an internal migration. Three hundred thousand Mexicans from the populous center migrated north to work in the mines, foundries, ranches, and factories where for the first time since the Mexican War they confronted not the Yankee soldier but the American landowner, inventor, railway worker, and technician.[9]

Caribbean Ambitions

Those American leaders who charted the "new empire" did not consider their quest a traditional imperial undertaking. They were more concerned with the pursuit of markets, in the challenge posed by British economic supremacy in Latin America, and, as were earlier generations, with American security in the larger Caribbean. There was no single architect of this unified strategy, although Seward, whose career as secretary of state virtually spanned the decade of the 1860s, certainly grasped the relationship between the U.S. Navy's determination to acquire West Indian naval bases and the American farmers' clamoring for markets. In 1866 Seward commenced a vigorous campaign in the Caribbean. He signed a treaty with Denmark for the acquisition of the Danish West Indies and a canal pact with Nicaragua and initiated efforts to secure a site for a naval base in the Dominican Republic. Though none of these was approved in the nineteenth century (all but the last were achieved in the twentieth), Seward's general prediction about eventual U.S. dominance in the Caribbean was a portent of the course of American policy.[10]

His successors proved no less enthusiastic about commercial expansionism, even though they were divided on the political implications of a quest for "informal" empire. In 1870 the U.S. Senate politely asked the Ulysses S. Grant administration about the state of hemispheric trade and received from Secretary of State Hamilton Fish a reaffirmation of the Monroe Doctrine. Fish threw down the gauntlet by declaring that American economic interests in Latin America would inevitably relieve the continent from its dependence on British trade. In the ensuing years secretaries of state pursued commercial treaties in both the independent and colonized Caribbean, urging both to accept the revered U.S. principle of reciprocity.

Despite the urging of naval strategists such as Alfred T. Mahan and Stephen Luce and private commercial promoters for a more vigorous U.S. role in Latin America, most Americans remained apprehensive about the political implications of such ventures. The United States might achieve informal empire, they acknowledged, as had Great Britain, but it should not create formal empire, which meant the burdens of colonies and outposts to defend, an unwanted obligation the British were already reluctantly undertaking. Mahan argued that the nation did not have to emulate European colonialism to enjoy the benefits of empire — markets could be achieved without the burden of governing subject peoples. But if the nation did not modernize its navy, protect the sea lanes for its commerce, and acquire political influence in strategic places, it was doomed to enter the new century in an inferior relationship to its European rivals.

Three crises of the 1870s and 1880s illustrate the changing character of the country's approach to Latin America. The first came with Grant's disastrous campaign to annex the Dominican Republic. Even before the Civil War the United States had been drawn to Hispaniola. In 1850, alert to European interests in the squabbles between Haiti and the Dominican Republic (which had won its independence in 1844 after twenty years of Haitian domination), Congress had initiated a special inquiry into the island's problems. An American emissary, William L. Cazneau, had negotiated with a larcenous Dominican executive a treaty ceding Samaná Bay for a naval base site, but French and British protests killed the plan. In 1861 Spanish troops returned at the invitation of General Pedro Santana, who wanted protection from an aggressive Haitian government. The Spaniards spent four years fighting a sporadic counterguerrilla war and abandoned the republic in frustration. U.S. fascination with a Dominican naval base quickly revived, and Seward sent his son Frederick to offer the new Dominican leader $2 million for a lease.

The younger Seward never consummated a deal that for the navy would have been better than Alaska. In Grant's first year as president, a band of American promoters (Cazneau among them) descended on Santo Domingo. The new Dominican leader was Buenaventura Báez, who apparently believed Cazneau was prepared to deal for the sale of the entire country. Cazneau returned to Washington and plied Grant with grandiose schemes not only for obtaining a much needed base for the U.S. Navy but also for settling remote portions of the Dominican Republic with hardy Anglo pioneers. In presenting the treaty Grant argued that annexation would raise the lowly Dominicans to a more civilized level. But Senator Charles Sumner effectively demolished Grant's argument with the persuasive logic that the Dominican Republic represented an alien culture that could not be molded into a tropical Anglo-Saxon outpost. However limited its cultural achievements, the Massachusetts solon declared, the Dominican Republic belonged to the Dominican people, who had no desire to join the United States. Annexation, he solemnly declared, would serve only to provoke resistance and would "impair the predominance of the colored race in the West Indies."[11]

Grant touted Dominican annexation as both a commercial and a moral enterprise. To Europeans, such exhortations smacked of American moralization of expansionist policies, which the European governments themselves were doing in Asia and Africa. Both were pretentious, but American pronouncements appeared to indicate that the United States really *believed* it sought a higher purpose in the world and that its empire, informal or formal, would be different. Thus in 1868, when Cuban rebels raised the flag of revolt, they aroused the country's moral conscience against "heathen Spain." Congress was swept away by pro-Cuban sentiment. But the reality of the weakness of the Cuban cause and Fish's determination to prevent a confrontation with Spain blocked the congressional firebrands' demands for action. In the first year of what became a ten-year struggle, Fish tried to negotiate Cuban independence, promising the Spanish a handsome financial settlement if they would quit the island. When they indignantly refused, another generation of American adventurers, gunrunners, and opportunists plied the waters between the Florida coast and the island.

Fish still refused to budge, though in late 1873 the capture of a U.S. gunrunning vessel and the shooting of fifty-three of the crew threatened his policy of restraint. Spain apologized and paid an indemnity, and official anger over the incident dissipated. In the aftermath Fish noted perceptively that Spanish rule over the island was doomed. He championed the island's liberation (and, by implication, Puerto Rico's) but never fully accepted the notion that the island could achieve independence without American sustenance or protection. Nor could he accommodate the view of an inner circle of Cuban rebels that the real war for independence went beyond the cry for political self-rule but encompassed the dismantling of the sugar economy, source of the island's wealth but also of its social inequities.[12]

Until the 1890s the United States confined its expansionism in Latin America to commerce and, occasionally, to displays of its naval power. When the French under Ferdinand de Lesseps began excavating a canal across the Isthmus of Panama (the area in which the United States had pledged in 1846 to safeguard the neutrality of the passageway) President Rutherford B. Hayes solemnly declared that *any* trans-isthmian canal was merely an extension of the U.S. coastline. American politicians, invoking the Monroe Doctrine, routinely denounced the 1850 Clayton-Bulwer Treaty, its spirit of Anglo-American cooperation, and the hallowed idea of an international, neutral canal. Even the Colombians, long resentful of European maneuvering in the western Caribbean, appeared taken aback by American rashness. In 1885, when one of the periodic Panamanian revolts against Colombian rule could not be quelled and in the opinion of the manager of the Panama Railroad threatened the neutrality of the isthmus, the U.S. government invoked its treaty right to intervene. In the largest U.S. military expedition to foreign soil since the Mexican War, the U.S. Navy landed several companies of marines and bluejackets (armed seamen) and crushed the revolt. Lacking specific authority, local commanders pressured the Colombians for information about possible bases in Panama or offshore islands in the event the navy wished to occupy them in time of civil unrest.

The leader of the revolution, Pedro Prestán, was publicly executed in Colón. For years afterward, observers remembered the authoritative presence of U.S. naval power. Indeed, the 1885 landings in Panama represented something more ominous in the exercise of U.S. power in the region — a "dress rehearsal" for the 1903 Panama intervention.[13]

Pan-Americanism, Yanqui-style

Four years before the impressive demonstration of American firepower on the Panamanian isthmus, the United States had displayed its own version of Pan-Americanism in South America. Fittingly, it came from one of the more bombastic of late nineteenth-century American leaders, James Gillespie Blaine, twice secretary of state and presidential aspirant. As secretary of state in the James A. Garfield administration, he enthusiastically supported U.S. interests in Peruvian nitrates. Chilean engineers were already developing the nitrate industry in Antofagasta and Tarapacá (provinces of Bolivia and Peru, respectively). Anticipating trouble, the Peruvians and Bolivians had signed a secret pact to defend their interests. In 1879 the War of the Pacific broke out. The Chileans were victorious, routing the Bolivians and dispatching an invading army to Callao. Blaine took office just as the conquering Chileans were on the verge of a stupendous triumph. With a diplomatic naïveté that convinced the Chileans he was cleverly trying to promote U.S. economic interests in Peru, Blaine tried to mediate the conflict. As U.S. ministers in Santiago and Lima embarrassed Washington by identifying with the cause of the respective warring governments, Blaine dispatched a special emissary to the region, bearing invitations to his grand design, a Pan-American conference in the United States. Among other matters, Blaine told the Chileans, the Latin American nations would perhaps wish to discuss the recurring interstate wars of South America.

His pledge not to use the proceedings for an official inquiry into the war did not placate Chile, which announced that its government would not participate. After President Garfield's untimely death in September, Blaine lingered for several months and then left office. His successor questioned his meddling in the War of the Pacific and shelved the Pan-American venture. The Chileans had their own conception of a South American balance of power, and they expected the international powers to accept it, but they recognized their limitations in dealing with Europe and the United States. They prosecuted the war against the Peruvians and in 1884 imposed what the American government considered a punitive peace settlement. Peru lost Tarapacá; Bolivia, its Pacific littoral, Antofagasta. The Peruvian provinces of Tacna and Arica, which figured prominently in Chilean calculations, fell under Santiago's domain for a decade, their future ultimately to be decided by President Herbert Hoover in 1929.[14]

Blaine did have a higher motive. Questioned by a suspicious Congress and rebuffed by the Chileans, he nonetheless established the view that the United States had a special obligation to mediate intra-hemispheric conflicts. If its intrusion deterred European powers, so much the better. In Central America, he plunged into a long-standing territorial dispute between Mexico and Guatemala, encouraging the hapless Guatemalans to look to Washington for diplomatic protection. When the meddling Blaine formally proposed arbitration, neither Mexico nor Guatemala accepted. The United States had not yet assumed the protective role it would later play, but American intentions foreshadowed gunboat diplomacy.

Blaine returned to the State Department in 1889, in time to preside over the first modern Pan-American conference. He had lost none of his earlier commitment to a hemispheric economic war against British capital. He reinforced this commitment with another popular sentiment, "America for the Americans," expressed in an ambitious but impractical proposal for a hemispheric customs union that would enhance the political image of the United States throughout the hemisphere. Contemporaneous literature, especially the hortatory (and racist) social scientific tracts, portrayed a heathenish, popish, but redeemable continent. The fundamental question was whether Latin America would be redeemed by goodwill, emulation of the United States, or forceful persuasion. When the Latin American delegates finally arrived, they were already bored with Blaine's notion of a customs union and took umbrage at his notion that American companies with legal problems in a Latin American country should have diplomatic recourse to Washington before submitting their cases to national courts.[15]

To Blaine, economic solidarity would protect against European intrusion and, perhaps, be a forerunner of hemispheric political cooperation. All save the Dominican Republic attended this conference, but the visiting Latin American delegates saw in Blaine's slogan "America for the Americans" merely the substitution of the United States for European economic intrusion into their affairs. They inspected the American industrial empire, dutifully impressed with the awesome machinery that symbolized man's technological triumph but perhaps fearful of the social disruption an industrial democracy portended. They approved the establishment of an International Bureau, forerunner of the Pan-American Union.[16]

In the end, however, the delegates, led by the Argentine and Chilean representatives, emasculated most of Blaine's more ambitious plans for molding continental economic linkages. Inspired by their demurral to a Yankee economic model, the Cuban essayist, poet, and revolutionary José Martí (who covered the proceedings for a Buenos Aires newspaper), sensed they were kindred spirits only too willing to champion what would ultimately become the cause of Cuba Libre. After all, the Argentine delegate, Manuel Quintana, joyously proclaimed that America (by which he meant Latin America) was a single entity. A few years later, Martí expressed similar sentiments in his famous essay "Our America." In truth, save for the smaller countries of Central America and the Caribbean, most leaders of the larger mainland countries of the continent proved as suspicious of the activities of Cuban revolutionaries and the idea of independence for the island as a generation of U.S. leaders. The United States was no cultural model for them, certainly. Neither was the revolutionary cause of Cuba Libre.[17]

The Splendid Little War

For the United States the 1890s brought political crisis wrought by economic dislocation and a political struggle often described as the "battle of the standards," the tumultuous 1896 presidential campaign of William McKinley versus William Jennings Bryan. The decade ended in war and in a fervent debate over imperialism and the prosperity that some associated with it. Latin America, especially the Caribbean, took on greater strategic importance for the United States. Its place in American calculations proved a welcome distraction from the political and social conflict that racked the country. The navy rapidly modernized, and ideologues talked of "looking outward." Disputes transformed into confrontations, problems into policies, and incidents into strategies. It may be wrong to argue, as some have, that the United States sought a fight in these years, but it did not strive to avoid one.

Early in the decade, for example, the country came perilously close to hostilities with remote Chile. Animosities still lingered from our meddling in the War of the Pacific and, later, from the official American sympathy with the Chilean president, Jorge Balmaceda, in the bitter civil war between Balmaceda and the Chilean Congress in 1891. Balmaceda, a forerunner of the modern Latin American economic nationalist, had Blaine's support. Europeans (mostly British) with heavy investments in Chile feared Balmaceda would nationalize the nitrate deposits, so they championed the congressional faction. After the Congress won, Balmaceda took refuge in the Argentine embassy until the last day of his term, and then shot himself. A party of American sailors, on leave in Valparaiso from the U.S.S. *Baltimore*, was mobbed by a band of Chileans, and two Americans died. In Washington, news of the incident led the Harrison administration to demand an apology from Chile, threatening retaliation if refused. After several tense months of negotiation (interspersed with press warnings of Chilean warships steaming up to attack the defenseless California coast), the Chileans capitulated. A decade before, confident Chileans bettered the United States in a diplomatic confrontation. This time, however, the combined problems of a civil war and hostility from its neighbors gave Washington the edge. "Santiago had blundered into a confrontation it could not win."[18]

American power intruded in other incidents and confrontations in the hemisphere. In September 1893, a mutiny by the Brazilian navy, begun by monarchists intent on toppling the new republic, threatened international shipping in Brazilian ports and thus prompted a forceful American naval demonstration on behalf of the government. Four years before, the Brazilian military had forced the ailing monarch Pedro II to abdicate. The rebels created a republic. In the beginning, the U.S. response was enthusiastic about the triumph of republican governance over monarchy and the end of slavery on the South American continent. The origins of the naval mutiny lay over deep-seated resentments about the privileges and the power accorded to the army in the new order. What had begun as a demonstration of naval protest turned into a seven-month siege of Rio de Janeiro harbor.

Throughout the crisis, U.S. leaders grew increasingly concerned that the revolt was a British plot to restore the monarchy and effectively curtail U.S. commercial interests in Brazil. In the harbor, the situation grew worse. In late January 1894, U.S. and rebel ships exchanged fire as a U.S. warship escorted an American merchant vessel to the dock. The incident probably helped to stave off further tension, as local residents had grown weary of the blockade. Throughout, the U.S. government professed that its sole purpose lay in protecting legitimate U.S trade and the prevention of European intervention.[19]

In the following year, Venezuela's dispute with Great Britain over the Guiana boundary brought the American government to Venezuela's defense. Secretary of State Richard Olney, responding to anti-British sentiments in the country, used the incident to inform Britain that the United States was "practically sovereign" in the Western Hemisphere and that its "fiat was law." A more blunt view, expressed by a generation of jingoistic Republicans including Theodore Roosevelt and Henry Cabot Lodge, held that Europeans could expect American interference in their disputes with Latin America.

For Venezuela and the Caribbean these statements heralded a more assertive policy with profound implications. After the Venezuelan imbroglio, the United States regarded any European gesture of force in negotiating with a Caribbean state — a not uncommon way for the nineteenth-century powers to handle their problems with smaller countries — as its own strategic concern. Europeans trying to fathom American intrusion into the Caribbean naturally assumed the United States was intent on joining the imperial family. Anti-imperialist rhetoric remained strong in the United States. Its obverse side was not identification with the Caribbean republics but reaffirmation of earlier beliefs that their political future required American guidance. The United States welcomed their break with Europe; it did not welcome them as sister republics.

The century ended with a "splendid little war" against Spain that ended one empire in Cuba and Puerto Rico and imposed another that had been taking shape for three decades. To the Cuban rebels whose forerunners had fought that empire for seventy-five years, their American liberators established another in its place.

The explanation for how and why that happened would require a separate volume, but we must begin with what President William McKinley referred to as "ties of singular intimacy" between the United States and Cuba — a nineteenth-century tradition of white Cuban adaptation to and acceptance of American cultural norms and a parallel nurturing of a Cuban struggle for independence. Those belonging to the first longed for autonomy within the Spanish empire with assurances of their privileged status; if Spain could not provide that, they preferred acquisition (and, presumably, eventual statehood) by the United States to an independent Cuba dominated by a black and colored majority. Those of the latter group believed fervently in independence, the end of slavery and the accompanying racial divisions it engendered, and the creation of a modern Cuba that would take its place in what Martí imagined would be a modern West Indian civilization. That required the end of slavery (which indeed came almost a decade after the end of the Ten Years' War), armed struggle, a more diverse economy, and what Martí called the reformation of Cuban society.

The links of both groups with the United States grew stronger after the Ten Years' War, when a migration of a hundred thousand Cubans (10 percent of the island's population), departed for Europe and, especially, the United States. Cigar factories closed in Cuba, new ones opened in Florida. (By 1900, the cigar industry in Tampa was valued at a staggering $17 million dollars. Other Cubans settled in Boston, Philadelphia, New York, Wilmington, and Baltimore. Creole planters, businessmen, and merchants, many as fluent in English as Spanish, journeyed back and forth between the island and the major metropolitan areas of the Atlantic seaboard. They acquired U.S. citizenship. Their children attended U.S. schools. Returning migrants brought with them not only U.S. manufactured items — clothing, furniture, bicycles, railroad materials, elevators — but also a preference for North American cultural traditions (including baseball) and an increasing disdain for everything Spanish. Those representing the Cuban working-class migrant (including Martí, who wrote for several Latin American newspapers and for a time supported himself by teaching Spanish) often experienced discrimination, especially if they were Afro-Cuban or dared risk involvement in the labor union quarrels of the era.[20]

More than any nineteenth-century Cuban opponent of Spanish rule, Martí changed both the purpose and the strategy of the struggle. In 1892 he founded the Cuban Revolutionary Party, and over the next few years he inspired Cuban exiles and immigrants with his columns in the revolutionary newspaper, *La Patria*. Drawing on the support of Cuban workers in New York and Tampa, he recruited volunteers and raised moneys for renewing the war. More important, he emphasized that the purpose of the struggle was the creation of a new Cuba — independent, democratic, and committed to ending the debilitating legacy of slavery and racial discrimination. As much as U.S. leaders feared the chaos resulting from the collapse of Spanish rule on the island, they were equally apprehensive about the triumph of a movement they could not manipulate or control.

When the Cuban rebellion erupted again in 1895, it quickly captured the imagination of the hemisphere. In their struggle against Spanish rule, the rebels assumed mythically heroic proportions as valiant warriors for freedom hurling themselves against an archaic political and economic system that, Americans believed, had brutalized the island for four centuries. From the beginning Washington put the Spanish government on notice that its tolerance for another prolonged struggle in Cuba was limited. Even the phlegmatic Grover Cleveland, who stood forthrightly against bellicose congressmen threatening to declare war to settle the Cuban "mess," expressed his moral disapprobation of Spanish rule and military measures in the Cuban conflict.

But the situation on the island proved far more devastating than Cleveland or, indeed, most Americans were able to comprehend. With the tragic death of Martí early in the war (he had returned to the island early in 1895 and was killed in a skirmish), the rebel commander Máximo Gómez declared a moratorium on sugar production. Those estates in violation would be burned, their factories destroyed. Workers who dared assist planters would be executed. Persuaded that the Spanish could not hold out, Cuban planters, merchants, and business leaders appealed to Cleveland to intervene. His secretary of state, Richard Olney, warned of racial war if the rebels won. In the end, the bewildered Cleveland ran out of solutions. He was only too relieved to turn over the Cuban mess to the victor in the bitter 1896 presidential election, William McKinley.

For more than a year after taking office McKinley anxiously watched the human toll that the revolution and Spanish counterrevolution took on the island. As Americans cheered on the journalists and filibusters who ventured south to cover the war or to offer their services, the president realized that the combatants were waging more than a grisly conflict that sickened those Americans who read daily accounts of its human toll. If the war went on — and McKinley had the unsettling reminder of the Ten Years' War of 1868–78 — the Spanish would either inflict an unacceptable punishment on the civilian population, especially in the east, or, just as ominous, the rebels would lay waste to the rich sugar plantations in the west. Thus the president urgently pressed for a diplomatic solution in fall 1897 after the Spanish had cut a trench midway across the island and herded civilians into special camps in the west and after a rebel army under Antonio Maceo had begun devastating raids on the sugar plantations. When the harassed Spanish government finally succumbed to American pressures for Cuban autonomy, a proposal the rebels condemned, McKinley blamed not the Cubans but the Spanish.

The Spanish offered reforms and autonomy, but there were too few takers. The rebels wanted independence; the loyalists, a vigorous prosecution of the war; the property holders, U.S. intervention; and the U.S. government, the determining role in Cuba's future. In mid-February 1898, when the U.S.S. *Maine*, dispatched to Havana harbor to safeguard American lives in the beleaguered city, was blown up, the event galvanized the widespread anti-Spanish sentiment in the country. Within the U.S. government, the explosion (which the public generally attributed to Spanish saboteurs) reinforced the view that only the United States could bring a "humane" settlement to Cuba. The following month, as the Spanish anticipated American intervention and desperately sought European allies, McKinley delivered a peace proposal to Madrid that called for U.S. mediation of the conflict. For the Spanish, his ultimatum meant either humiliation or war. Spain reluctantly chose the latter.

American entry into this war was no miscalculation, no aberration brought on by frustrations generated in the bitter political divisions in the country. The United States went to war against "heathen Spain" in 1898 because the public wanted it, because American business had at last concluded that the loss of Spanish-American trade would be offset by the prospects of expanding American economic interests in the fallen Spanish Empire, because the U.S. military (especially the navy) appeared prepared to fight it, and because the president of the United States had an uncanny ability to shield his international strategic calculations with appealing homilies. Beyond these immediate reasons, the United States had long coveted Cuba for strategic and economic reasons, had a self-ordained role in shaping the island's future, and believed the Cuban rebels were so irrational in their destructive campaigns that they could not be entrusted with power and thus required tutelage. "Against the landscape created by the receding tide of Spanish sovereignty," Louis Pérez Jr. has written, "Washington confronted in Cuba the anathema of all U.S. policy makers since Jefferson — the specter of Cuban independence."[21]

Europeans looking at the coming of this war assumed that the United States was provoking Spain into a war that would advance its ambitions in the Caribbean and the western Pacific. Although the United States pledged not to annex Cuba — a move demanded by congressmen wary of assuming the enormous Cuban debt — the intervention in Cuba (and Puerto Rico) opened up American political and military influence in the Caribbean on a scale that ultimately surpassed the European role in the region. Less apparent to both Americans and Europeans — even those who expressed moral doubts about intruding into this conflict — was the impact of U.S. intervention on Cuba's economic future and, ultimately, its social and political future. The coming of American troops guaranteed one revolution but destroyed another. Americans had come to accept Cuban independence and saw themselves as the island's liberator, but they had no intention of accepting its economic or social restructuring. In the past Cuban rebellion had failed, Americans told themselves, because it had not been sustained by moral resolve and determination to fight until independence was achieved.

The exhausted Cuban rebels who survived the Ten Years' War learned a different lesson: real independence could be achieved only by demolishing the island's rigid social structure, which meant destroying the sugar economy. This sentiment was not universal among the bands of revolutionaries who fled to Europe and the United States after 1878, but it was dogma to the inner core of rebels who renewed the struggle in 1895. It explains why their drive into the relatively prosperous western provinces, where the most successful sugar estates were located, left in its wake burned fields and razed mills. A goodly portion of this property represented the $50 million that Americans had invested in the Cuban sugar industry. But it also symbolized a social and economic system the rebels were determined to expunge from Cuba's future, whatever the cost.

The intervention was no misadventure or miscalculation, nor a signal that the United States intended to create an empire in the Caribbean and the western Pacific resembling those the Europeans had crafted in Africa. Europeans may have had few illusions about American purposes, but any Latin American sympathy for Spain and its cultural legacy in the hemisphere diminished by the U.S. pledge on the eve of its entry into the war not to annex Cuba. Certainly, McKinley had been disingenuous when he professed that the United States entered Cuba to end the war, not to seek domination of the island. A prominent rebel leader, Calixto García, initially angered by the refusal of Washington to make any agreement with the Cuban provisional government, had concluded that the United States was indeed committed to the freedom and independence of the island. What García failed to understand was the shallowness of that commitment.

The territorial benefit of victory over Spain — military occupation of Cuba and annexation of the Philippines and Puerto Rico — did, however, provoke a debate over empire within the United States. Anti-imperial sentiment could be identified among all social and economic classes and in both political parties. But the debate was about what should be done in the aftermath of the war and not about the justification for intervening in Cuba. Throughout ran warnings and rebuttals about the fitness of those Spanish colonial charges the

United States had liberated for self-government and the dangers of bringing alien cultures under U.S. rule. Equally unsettling to some was the tarnishing of America's cultural image in the experience of this war. In the hullabaloo before the war, the press portrayed the Cuban rebels as bronze variations of Anglo-Saxon warriors fighting a traditional struggle for freedom.

When the Americans finally got to Cuba in June 1898, they encountered an essentially guerrilla force with unsettlingly dark-skinned common soldiers and officers. Before long U.S. officers were casually ridiculing the fighting spirit of their putative allies and praising the bravery of the Spanish enemy, a noticeably different assessment from the earlier favorable expressions about Cuban warriors from American soldiers of fortune and volunteers to the rebel cause. American blacks ("smoked Yankees") served in this campaign, earning, many of them said, more respect from the Spanish than from their own officers, who made derogatory references to the Cuban "mambises," the black shock troops of rebel contingents. Increasingly, white Americans on the island sympathized more with those social groups who were fearful of Afro-Cuban rule. "If we are to save Cuba," noted a reporter for a New York paper, "we must hold it. If we leave it to the Cubans, we give it over to a reign of terror."[22]

After the war, when the occupying U.S. military decided to disarm the rebel army, it did so for political and racial reasons. American troops came as conquerors, and they ruled as conquerors. The political consequences proved as devastating for the Cuban rebels, it soon appeared, as for the defeated Spaniards. The U.S. military denied the Cubans a seat at the peace table, created a postwar military government as the inherent right of the conqueror, and assumed the obligation to police a ravaged country. The independent Cuba that emerged from this experience was stunted from its birth with self-doubts about its national identity. Equally as troubling was the decision to take Puerto Rico, which had won its autonomy in 1897, as reparation. In less than a year the island passed from being a Spanish colony with considerable freedom and economic sufficiency to an outpost of the United States, conquered territory over which the U.S. flag but not the Constitution prevailed. In both islands the political culture suffered such debilitation that a major legacy of the experience was to be the Caribbean defiance that still troubles modern Americans, who believe they liberated both from Spanish oppression and prepared both for a brighter future.

Annexation of Puerto Rico was just compensation for the cost of waging that conflict; annexation of the Philippines, as McKinley told a group of inquisitive clergymen, was motivated essentially by a commitment to Christianize the Filipinos. Rarely did Americans question their leaders' motives in undertaking empire; they asked only where it should be undertaken or how it should be pursued. The peace treaty debate, which focused almost exclusively on Philippine annexation, was the last stand of the old-line anti-expansionists and their once persuasive arguments that extending American rule over other cultures would ultimately debase the character of the "old republic." For successive generations, historians assessing the fundamental issues of the debate over the U.S. penetration of the Caribbean in the late nineteenth century and the presumed "plunge" into empire at the turn of the twentieth century have concluded that the imperialist architects, employing racial ideology and a sense of benevolent assimilation, readily accepted the notion of the "white man's burden." In reality, they were deeply troubled by the thought of dispatching white Americans into insular "hot zones" inhabited by people of color.[23]

The U.S. Caribbean empire was different but not for the reasons Americans believed. In 1900 the Supreme Court, in a series of cases, declared that the Constitution did not follow the flag to Puerto Rico. The only colony in the region until 1914, when the United States purchased the Virgin Islands, remained largely neglected until the United States entered World War I. Promised its independence on the eve of war, Cuba waited four years to attain it, and then, to get the Americans to leave, its leaders had to accept a constitution laden with obligations to the United States. Americans who flocked there considered Cuba as much a colony within American domain as Puerto Rico. As had those Americans who had earlier ventured into Mexico and Central America, they viewed themselves not as conquerors but as exemplars of America, especially its faith in economic opportunity and its conviction that property and its protection constituted the foundation of a modern society. In Cuba and in the banana enclaves of the Central American coast, where opportunity beckoned a generation of Americans, their impact on local economies ultimately became so large that it extended to the entire country, its politics, and even its culture.

In 1900 a thoughtful Puerto Rican emissary to the United States, Eugenio María de Hostos, solemnly informed President McKinley that by intervening in Puerto Rico the United States had an obligation either to grant the island its freedom or to annex it as a state to ensure the equality of Puerto Rican culture within U.S. domain. To do neither, he warned, would unleash powerful nationalistic outcries that would inevitably center on the disparity between U.S. actions and professions. De Hostos was more prophetic than he realized.

From the early 1880s, the onset of successive waves of immigration from southern and eastern Europe complicated traditional ideas of governance and citizenship, ideas of entitlement to the promises of American life, and, most fundamentally, ideas about color and identity. The stresses caused by this racial and cultural "pummeling" would indirectly impact on the country's more aggressive hemispheric policies in the 1890s and its experience in the Pax Americana in the first three decades of the twentieth century. Great Britain and to a lesser degree France had sufficient historical experience and a sense of cultural identity to carry out their imperial mission. For the United States, however, the consequences proved far different. Despite appeals from such prominent military figures as Leonard Wood, the United States developed no colonial army to police its new domains and no colonial service to manage them. Rather, it would improvise, using a "creative pragmatism" in its Pax Americana. One feature was the implanting in the Treaty of Paris (which officially ended the war with Spain) a clause upholding the right to acquire new territories but with no parallel commitment to admit them as states. The phrase "unincorporated territory" along with "protectorate" soon became part of the vocabulary of U.S. empire.[24]

The Imperial President

The nation lacked a colonial army or a colonial service, but in Theodore Roosevelt it found someone who spoke about imperial mission although in a distinctive American idiom. In 1900, when the McKinley administration negotiated a new treaty with the British, pledging the neutrality of a future canal, Roosevelt, then governor of New York, denounced the pact for failing to permit the United States to defend the waterway. The treaty was altered to meet his specifications. After assuming the presidency following the assassination of McKinley in September 1901, Roosevelt was either indirectly or even directly implicated in some of the most consequential decisions in U.S.

military intervention and political involvement in the circum-Caribbean. He withdrew U.S. troops from Cuba in 1902 only when the disgruntled Cubans accepted the Platt Amendment, thus converting the island into a protectorate that persisted for another thirty years. Acutely sensing the public concern over British and especially German pressures against debt-ridden Venezuela, he intruded in the controversy in late 1902 and early 1903 in a manner that some viewed as unnecessarily reckless. At the same time, his irritation over what he considered Colombian dalliance and deception in the negotiation of a canal treaty prompted him to sponsor the Panamanian Revolution of November 1903. Indeed, his controversial role in what was called the "Panama Affair" dogged him for another decade. In late 1904, following his impressive victory in the presidential election, he boasted that the United States would exercise a policeman's role over indebted and disorderly Caribbean states to prevent their harassment by European creditors, and declared in 1905 a customs receivership in the Dominican Republic.

Roosevelt demonstrated he could also challenge the British in Canada as well. When British diplomats conceded U.S. control over the Panama Canal route in 1901, they effectively lost any leverage over the still unsettled boundary between Alaska and Canada.

The issue became more acute with the discovery of gold in the largely unsettled Yukon Territory in 1897, which precipitated a rush of successive waves of fifty thousand American migrants into the region. Both the U.S. and Canadian governments took extreme positions on the precise location of the boundary, although old Russian maps appeared to confirm the U.S. claim. McKinley proved amenable to negotiate the difference, but not Roosevelt, who made it clear that he would not arbitrate. In the end, a six-member commission settled the matter, with the Chief Justice of England siding with the two undeniably prejudiced Americans. For years, Canadians remained convinced that the motherland had "sold out" their rightful ownership of the coastal strip between British Columbia and Alaska. In reality, Roosevelt made it clear that if the commission had decided otherwise, he was prepared to defend the U.S. claim with troops. The embittered Canadian prime minister, Wilfred Laurier, vowed that Canada would achieve in the twentieth century a society morally and materially superior to that of its southern neighbor.[25]

These actions, Roosevelt argued, were necessary and unobjectionable, representing not aggressive behavior but forceful restraint, a policy of "velvet on iron." He correctly surmised that Great Britain would tolerate (indeed, welcome) a more dominating American political and military presence in the Caribbean. And he sensed that the American public would look on the heightened German presence in the region with misgivings. He mixed bellicose rhetoric with determined action. The intent was to achieve precisely enough involvement in Latin America to ward off European interference yet avoid becoming bogged down in turbulent internal problems that continually beset the smaller republics. The *public* Roosevelt insisted on American domination of the canal, demanded protectorate status for Cuba, warned against the German peril in the Venezuelan debts crisis, and talked of a policing role among turbulent little republics whose leaders often got in the "revolutionary frame of mind" and had to be chastised. The *private* Roosevelt confided to his transatlantic pen pal, the anti-imperialist George Otto Trevelyan, that his dispatch of troops into what some writers called "the American Mediterranean" was not an American version of European imperial behavior.[26]

In brief, then, Roosevelt personified the quintessential American-style imperialist — attuned to public opinion, at times calculating and on other occasions reckless. He expressed little regret over the savagery of the U.S. suppression of the Philippine insurrection, although he lamented more than once that the acquisition of the islands might prove to be a strategic risk, as indeed history proved to be the case. In his language and even in his behavior he could exhibit characteristics, as the British ambassador reputedly observed, of someone with the emotional maturity of a twelve-year-old. He was also a nineteenth-century New York aristocrat whose entire persona had been shaped by his twin experiences of life in the Dakotas and in the often violent arena of industrial America. He understood, as had Washington and Lincoln, the obligations of leadership and the reality that in a nation as diverse and still unformed as the United States the leader must take a position, must chart the way, and must articulate a definition of national purpose. The world, like the Dakota Badlands, could be unforgiving and uncertain in its course. So could the thousands of laborers who massed under the banner of workers' rights. In Roosevelt's day, socialism represented more than an intellectual discourse. He understood this reality. His strength lay in the widely unacknowledged and, to Europeans, disturbing reality that Roosevelt's America exhibited all the industrial might and military pretensions of a European power but frankly lacked the maturity and national self-assuredness possessed by the French and the British or even the Germans. Roosevelt often spoke about the difference between a "Buchanan" and a "Lincoln," and implicitly he believed the kinds of crises the United States faced in the 1890s and in the first decade of the twentieth century replicated those of the Civil War and post–Civil War generation.

In the Venezuelan crisis, for example, he waited until the public furor over the Anglo-German blockade before criticizing the Germans for their actions; then he maneuvered the American fleet in the West Indies in such a way as to demonstrate American resolve without unduly provoking the European intruders. In the Dominican case, which had larger implications for Europeans because of the republic's heavy indebtedness, he probed into the country's internal affairs only to the extent necessary to get the customs receivership. When the Senate questioned his intentions, he confirmed the arrangement as an executive agreement and waited two years for the Senate to acquiesce in a formal treaty. He was unforgivably insensitive toward the Colombians when they debated the canal treaty that Secretary of State John Hay had proffered and doubtless provoked them to reject it by his callous remarks. He did not plot the Panamanian revolt of November, though he certainly provided reassurances to the plotters. He did have legal authority to safeguard the passageway under the 1846 treaty with Colombia. Contemporaries who condemned his peremptory action forgot how many times American troops had landed to enforce it. The difference in 1903 was that the treaty was invoked *against* Colombia, to whom the pledge of maintaining the neutrality of the isthmus had been granted, which not a few lawyers considered a baffling interpretation. He got a better deal with Panama (which was to nurture a bitterness until 1979 because their negotiator in Washington, Philippe Bunau Varilla, had mortgaged the republic's sovereignty to give the Americans virtually a free hand in the Canal Zone). Roosevelt naturally accepted the concessions, but he was reluctant to fashion an American colony in the Canal Zone.[27]

More significant than Roosevelt's imperial posturing was his explicit rejection of hemispheric unity in the face of European pressures. In 1902, on the eve of the Anglo-German blockade of Venezuela, the Argentine foreign minister Luis M. Drago boldly proposed that Latin America's heavy debt should not be cause for European intervention in hemispheric affairs. Though schooled in international law, Drago took his case into the court of American politics. Praising the United States for its opposition to European territorial aggrandizement — in effect, lauding the Monroe Doctrine — Drago argued that Europe's gunboat diplomacy on behalf of its creditors threatened hemispheric integrity. Financial pressures, he believed, led inevitably to intervention. A united hemispheric protest under the rubric of a multilateral doctrine was necessary.

Never, perhaps, had a Latin American managed to articulate a more persuasive argument for collective action only to reinforce a unilateral policy. What Drago had not perceived was the acceptance within the U.S. government and the public generally of an imperial posture in the Western Hemisphere. Rejecting the charge that the United States was imitating the European powers, Secretary of State Hay articulated, and Roosevelt forcefully demonstrated, the modern American role in Latin America. The external menace, Hay informed Drago, lay not so much in the political threat (save, perhaps, for the visible though exaggerated German meddling in the Caribbean) but in the more aggressive economic penetration of European capitalism sustained by the imperial state. As a heavy investor in Cuba and Mexico, the United States (though still a debtor nation) sympathized with European creditors trying to collect from Latin American mendicants. Given its strategic interests in Latin America, especially in the Caribbean, the U.S. government could not permit European powers to collect their Latin American debts by forceful means. Neither did it wish to relinquish the Monroe Doctrine to the Pan-American system.

Within a few years, Roosevelt had rallied public sentiment against European interference in the Caribbean and then declared that the United States must police the region to ward off future European meddling. Drago watched disconsolately as the debts question dragged on in the Permanent Court of Arbitration in The Hague, where the blockading powers against indebted Venezuela won first priority for payment of claims and must have been perplexed at Roosevelt's contention that "intervention to prevent intervention" was justifiable. There was a Pan-American system, which dealt with apolitical questions such as commercial accords or mundane matters. A U.S. system for the hemisphere, however, dealt with political questions, particularly those relating to American security interests. Drago had unintentionally transformed an economic question into a political issue, and neither Roosevelt nor his successors seriously considered submitting it for hemispheric approbation. Drago posed a Pan-American corollary to the Monroe Doctrine; Roosevelt responded with the Roosevelt corollary. As Adams had recognized in 1823, Roosevelt instinctively sensed the domestic political appeal of a unilateral rather than a collective response to the European challenge. In declaring that the United States must carry out the role of policeman in the hemisphere, Roosevelt assumed obligations that his successors and the U.S. military rapidly wearied of carrying out.[28]

Successive generations of Americans often mused about the Roosevelt era as the inauguration of a half-century in which the United States would increasingly assume the hemispheric mandate that the British presumed to exercise in other regions of the globe. That was pretentious, if arguable. Virtually every issue and crisis Roosevelt faced in the hemisphere represented something inherited from the "long" nineteenth century, notably in Cuba and Panama. In truth, there was no precise U.S. imperial design for the Americas, nor even for the more vulnerable circum-Caribbean. In the Cuban revolt against Spain, in Venezuela's defiance of the European powers, in the Dominican Civil War, and in Panamanian rebellion against the central authority of Bogotá, what the United States did was to intrude into conflicts and situations it only dimly understood, and it did so without the historical training and institutional expertise of a traditional European power. As Roosevelt himself sensed, the unsettling reality of the Pax Americana was the task of pacifier, not America in Britain's place but in Spain's place. In Cuba, in Puerto Rico, and in other places in the circum-Caribbean, it would hold local governments accountable for protecting property or holding elections in the name of stability and democracy. To those ends the United States would use not only its political and its military power but even exert a cultural and moral imperative. That role would entail obligations and commitments that would prove more a problem than a solution. The experience of continental empire proved to be poor preparation for that of insular ruler of peoples of color. Over more than two centuries, the United States has not learned the fundamental lesson that it is easier to create a republic from an empire than it is for a republic to carry out the role of an imperial ruler.

4   Pax Americana

In the three decades after the war with Spain, the United States expanded its interests in Latin America by every political, economic, and military measure. It had displaced the Spanish Empire in Puerto Rico and Cuba. In the western Caribbean, it had already begun to chart a more direct role for American power on the isthmus. In South America the United States had assumed a protective role over Venezuela in the 1895 boundary dispute between that country and Great Britain. With the encouragement of the Brazilian foreign minister, the Baron of Río Branco, Washington fashioned what a later generation would call an unwritten alliance. Rejecting Argentine arguments for a hemispheric collective statement on such diverse matters as the forcible collection of international debts and the obligations of aliens to settle their disputes in the courts of the country in which they did business, the United States followed a unilateral course in the region. It asserted its military power in the Caribbean, intervening in the internal affairs of smaller states and creating a string of protectorates from Hispaniola to Panama. Its justification rested on understandable strategic arguments, questionable economic policies, and, in retrospect, political and cultural pretensions bordering on the arrogant.[1]

As the British had already discovered, informal empire with its large benefits and modest overhead ultimately gave way to formal empire with its obligations and increasing imperial surcharges. By the end of the century, a disconsolate inner group of British imperialists had come to the somber conclusion that the British Empire on which the sun never set had gotten too costly, but it had to be defended from without and, increasingly, from within. The United States had no colonial service, no colonial army, and no colonial economic bureaucracy, nor did U.S. officials feel a need to create them. Taking on the imperial burden for the noblest of intentions, however, did not lessen the obligation of defending it. As German interest in the Caribbean and in Mexico heightened after the turn of the century, so did U.S. opposition to it. As American companies intruded in the tropics, especially in Cuba and Central America, U.S. political leaders articulated a Caribbean strategy in political and economic terms.

When the charges of empire became unruly or defiant, they were "chastised" with stern warnings or, if they persisted in the "revolutionary frame of mind," with a "spanking" by U.S. military forces. If their outburst proved threatening to long-term American interests, they suffered occupation, which meant stern-minded military proconsuls in charge of their affairs. In Theodore Roosevelt's day, Americans enthusiastically took on the imperial mission. By Franklin Roosevelt's day, they had grown weary of it.[2]

New World Policeman

To describe the Pax Americana as a U.S. version of the Pax Britannica, as some historians have done, is to gloss over two distinctions between the U.S. role in the Western Hemisphere in the first third of the twentieth century and that played by Great Britain during the "long" nineteenth century.

First, and perhaps most important, one of the fundamental credos of the American Revolution — a belief that persisted through the nineteenth century — was that of self-determination. Throughout its history, the United States has violated that principle in the name of security or its own self-interest, but the nation's reluctance to create a colonial bureaucracy, a colonial army, or a tradition of colonial service has signified deep-seated doubts about its willingness to carry out the kind of imperial mandate the British assumed. Second, the United States, unlike Britain or even Rome, acquired an insular empire and took on its controversial policing role *before* it had matured to nationhood. Put differently, the United States did not become a nation in the modern sense of that word during the Revolution or even as a consequence of the Civil War, despite the symbolism of a union forged in blood and iron, as was Bismarck's Germany. Rather, it achieved its nationhood in the first two decades of the twentieth century, contemporaneously with Canada, Mexico, Brazil, Venezuela, and Argentina. These were years in which the United States wrestled with the sometimes violent and divisive political and social convulsions identified with labor unrest and immigration, exercised an expanded presence in world affairs, and exhibited an economic growth that rivaled the major European nations. In the Caribbean, the model of U.S. empire was not so much the string of protectorates from Cuba to Central America but the

Panama Canal, built with American money, French brains, and West Indian sweat. The trans-isthmian waterway, considered a disastrous and failed enterprise in the mid-1890s, became at completion two decades later what the "new Rome" symbolized. The social cost, however, was high, as the daily injuries and deaths of the sixty thousand West Indian laborers attested.[3]

Despite what the British publicist W. R. Stead called the "Americanization of the world," there were sobering voices who warned that the United States had not achieved a peaceful transition to industrialization. Indeed, such was the conviction of the acknowledged "First Canadian," the Quebecois Wilfred Laurier (prime minister, 1896–1911), who staked his political reputation on a controversial reciprocity treaty with the United States. At the same time, a growing number of predominantly Anglo Canadians came to regard Americans and Canadians as people with a common British ancestry. Laurier (who had cooperated with U.S. officials during the war with Spain) believed that stronger economic ties with Canada's southern neighbor would make for a more peaceful border, ease the growing social tensions within the nation, and convince London that it should pay more attention to Canadian concerns. But the strategy backfired: Robert Borden, Laurier's opponent, argued that the treaty merely accelerated the Americanization of Canada, and the Laurier government collapsed before this challenge.[4]

Canada experienced the throes of immigration but carried no imperial burden to accompany it. Political leaders in the United States, notably Theodore Roosevelt and Woodrow Wilson, called for unity in taking on this endeavor and increasingly urged the newcomer to assimilate by the process of "Americanization." Inevitably, the cultural clash between the older America and the newcomers — peoples disparagingly called "hyphenates" — reverberated throughout national politics and indirectly but noticeably influenced U.S. foreign policy. For some, such as the radical Randolph Bourne, the hostility of the old-stock America toward the later and the parallel efforts to create a uniform "American" culture was a denial of the reality of a unique transnational America. For others, among them the far more influential Herbert Croly (co-founder of the liberal *New Republic*), the "promise of American life" — the title of his 1909 book — depended on the creation of a peaceful American international system in which the United States upheld a commitment to "good government and order in the Americas."[5]

Croly's hemispheric design appeared just as the Roosevelt presidency was ending, when the critique over his handling of the canal project began to escalate and as some congressmen expressed misgivings about how he had used the Venezuelan debt crisis as excuse for intervening in the Dominican civil war and imposing a customs receivership. His critics charged that the Roosevelt Corollary to the Monroe Doctrine — the exercising of a policing role in the circum-Caribbean — was not only risky but riddled with pitfalls and bound to create obligations that the country could ill afford. True, there had been a German threat to U.S. power in the Caribbean, but by the time Roosevelt announced the Corollary, the German high command had already begun to shift to a European continental strategy. (Some military historians point out that U.S. naval intelligence had no way of verifying this shift. Indeed, after the onset of World War I, German designs in the hemisphere escalated, particularly in revolutionary Mexico.)

Others pointed to the Drago doctrine as an alternative to the Roosevelt Corollary, but Drago's recipe for hemispheric cooperation proved too vague to satisfy Roosevelt. Despite his disdain for other hemispheric governments as either too weak or too unreliable to carry out the task of a policing role, Roosevelt was not without reason for his penchant for unilateral action. The Argentines themselves had little use for Drago's position, and Secretary of State Elihu Root, who was far more circumspect than his boss, placated the Brazilians and the Chileans at the third Pan-American conference in Rio de Janeiro in 1906 and spoke grandly of strengthening the commercial ties of the Americas and the U.S. commitment to the rule of law even as he deftly emasculated what Drago had proposed. The big countries of South America proved more interested in developing a stronger relationship with the United States than in advancing Martí's vision of "Our America."[6]

The problem was not the larger countries but the smaller ones, the protectorates that required pacification. Cuba offered an apt illustration of the point, a reminder of how the U.S. presence could act as both conciliator and appeaser to some and as provocation to others. For some Cubans, the Platt Amendment of 1902, which permitted U.S. intervention to safeguard foreign lives and property, offered the only sure guarantee of independence. Other Cubans derided the measure as yet another denigration of the dream of Cuba Libre. The first group found their political icon in Tomás Estrada Palma, the island's first president, who had spent many years in the United States and readily acquiesced in the Americanization of the island's culture and what his critics called the daily humiliation of Cubans before the American lion. Estrada believed the United States would shield him, regardless of the fraud and violence accompanying his government. His Liberal opponents read the Platt Amendment and concluded precisely the opposite: the U.S. government was obligated to intervene to establish a government respectful of lives and property.[7]

At first the Liberals tried to gain power by the traditional route. When this failed, they called for U.S. intervention. Throughout 1905 and early 1906 there was sporadic violence throughout the island, not as devastating as that afflicting Spanish Cuba in its final years but enough to alarm Roosevelt. Under siege, Estrada called for a landing of U.S. troops, stating he could not guarantee foreign lives or property. Roosevelt privately fumed about the anarchy and misrule but tried to placate both sides by sending his rotund secretary of war, William Howard Taft, on a peace-making mission to Havana. It was a mission doomed to failure.

The second Cuban occupation, which commenced in fall 1906, was a test case of U.S. rule in the Caribbean: an army of occupation that disarmed the rebels, creation of U.S.-run civilian departments in which Liberals took part, the drafting of an electoral code, an ambitious but costly economic development plan, and, most important, accommodation of the Liberal politicos at every turn. When the occupation ended, the new president, the Liberal José Miguel Gómez, waved goodbye to the U.S. military governor and launched one of the most corrupt administrations in Cuban history. The Liberals used their power to stifle the resurgent Independent Party of Color, which called for vindication of the rights of Afro-Cubans in the new society. A year after the U.S. soldiers departed, Gómez outlawed the party on the specious grounds that its leaders planned a race war. When they sought to restore the party's legality in 1912, the Cuban army crushed the movement, killing most of them. The campaign proved to be the bloodiest retaliation against people of color in the Caribbean since the British suppression of the Morant Bay uprising in Jamaica in 1865.[8]

With Cuba the United States had the Platt Amendment of 1902, which had created the "special relationship" Cubans came to hate, so Roosevelt was able to say that he had no choice but to intervene to "safeguard" the island's independence. But just as quickly he was plunged into another familial quarrel in Central America. In 1907, with Mexican support, Roosevelt and Root gave their approval to a series of treaties aimed at bringing peace among the warring Central American states. They agreed not to recognize governments that came to power by bullets instead of ballots and to respect the neutrality of Honduras, the warring ground of Central American armies. A Central American court was launched with American blessing. But within two years American hostility to a nationalistic Nicaraguan leader, José Santos Zelaya (who hounded foreign entrepreneurs, exiled his political enemies, and meddled incessantly in his neighbor's politics), made the U.S. government a violator of its own principles. Alienated Nicaraguan conservatives found adherents and financial support from the United Fruit Company (UFCo), which along with lumbering and mining companies dominated the economy of eastern Nicaragua. When the revolution broke out, Roosevelt had already left office. He had not hesitated to "chastise" unruly governments that ran afoul of American strictures with selective, limited use of troops. His successor, William Howard Taft, convinced of the need for financial reorganization of small economies with the support of Wall Street's investment houses, undertook to safeguard American political interests with dollars, not bullets. "Dollar diplomacy" became the motto for maintaining Central American security.

The plan was apparently working in the Dominican Republic. But Central America is not an island, and from the beginning its five states resisted "Wall Street" and its foreign economic manipulations. They could not hold back the penetration of "Market Street" — American companies whose go-getter entrepreneurs were less interested in monetary reforms or honest customs collectors than in paying what was necessary for their political champion to gain power so they would not have to pay any duties on goods they imported for their businesses. The prototype of "Market Street" was Sam "the Banana Man" Zemurray, who in 1911 financed a revolution plotted in a New Orleans bordello that eventually gave him a stake in a Honduran banana empire. In all except Nicaragua, dollar diplomacy was a failure, though the private American economic presence, reinforced by stern diplomatic pressures and the occasional appearance of U.S. warships, reminded the republics of Washington's policing role.

In Nicaragua dollar diplomacy succeeded only when the United States forced Zelaya to flee and then dispatched a major military expedition into the country to protect his pro-American successor with bullets. Two thousand U.S. troops — sent by a government whose leaders believed they confronted in Nicaragua a Latin American variation of the Boxer Rebellion with its attendant disorder — swept through Nicaragua's populous west. To this day Nicaraguans date the immersion of their country into the American empire from this era, and when the last marines finally departed a generation later the memory of the American intervention remained fixed in their collective psyches.[9]

Dollar diplomacy was much more than a narrow economic program whereby foreign governments considered unstable by U.S. investors and officials had to accept financial advisers in order to get desperately needed private loans. In time, the entire process became intertwined with contemporary beliefs that the United States could both stabilize and uplift "backward" peoples without the attendant costs of formal colonization. In this more expansive view of a policy, nineteenth-century liberal ideas about progress — ideas infused with strong racialist notions — could be reinforced with the precepts of the professional-managerial revolution and the Progressives' commitment to the development of the "whole person." Even the American Federation of Labor, an early critic of U.S. imperialism, became a participant in this undertaking, notably in Puerto Rico, Mexico, and Canada.[10]

Pan-American Visions and Latin American Realities

Among the ironies of the Latin American policy of the United States is the record of Woodrow Wilson, who condemned the interventionism of his predecessor and chastised the economic imperialists yet became the greatest interventionist of his age. The difference, explained his defenders to a largely unreceptive Latin American audience, lay in the purpose of his hemispheric policies, not in the sometimes forceful way he applied them. For Wilson and his contemporaries, imbued with a sense of American mission, Latin Americans still reserve a special antipathy. Roosevelt may have treated them contemptuously, but at least he possessed the good sense to believe there was little to be gained in trying to remold their political culture. Wilson accepted their reformation as a challenge. Three-quarters of a century later, the United States has yet to shake off the cultural paternalism he grafted onto the Pan-American tissue.

Wilson, a historian, knew little of Latin America or its history, but he viewed himself as both adviser and judge to hemispheric political leaders. After all, he had experienced firsthand the ravaged American South and its efforts to overcome war's devastation and the onslaught of outsiders trying to extract its wealth and mold its politics to their will. The problem lay in his inability to rectify errors in the American treatment of smaller hemispheric countries and preserve the strategic commitment wrought by sixteen years of Republican foreign policy. McKinley had accepted the colonial burden, Roosevelt had refined it with limited interventions in the Caribbean, and Taft had belatedly acknowledged that brute force, not dollars, was sometimes necessary to maintain American interests. Reviewing this legacy of unparalleled American intrusion into neighboring republics, Wilson was pointedly critical of the stifling of "legitimate aspirations" of captive peoples, yet he could not bring himself to admit that they might willingly choose a distinctly un-American path to the present. He sought a united hemisphere but was never able to shape a policy that fused his rhetoric with Latin American realities. Although Wilson was reluctant to admit it, he subscribed to Herbert Croly's judgment that a viable hemispheric international system depended on the "forcible pacification of one or more . . . centers of disorder" in Latin America and the Caribbean.[11]

Wilson condemned European economic imperialism in Latin America but with the precision of a social scientist crafted an American-directed hemispheric economic strategy. As a political thinker, he championed Latin America's striving for political liberty and "decent government," but as president he unleashed his verbal wrath upon revolutionary leaders who defied his prescriptions. Despite his professions of a new era in U.S.–Latin American relations, Wilson was, at bottom, as deeply committed as Roosevelt to the maintenance of U.S. strategic interests in the hemisphere. Unlike Roosevelt, he genuinely believed a more amicable and certainly more acceptable Latin American policy could be fashioned. He accepted much of the inherited anti-imperialist dogma about the evils of export capitalism and specifically condemned dollar diplomacy. But on taking office he quickly discovered that any desire to chart a new course in hemispheric affairs assumed a secondary role to dealing with immediate problems, as in Mexico, or safeguarding vital military stakes such as the Panama Canal. To his credit, he showed a reluctance to advance the cause of private economic interests in Latin America, as had Taft, yet to the dismay of Latin Americans he undertook even bolder involvement in their internal affairs. Roosevelt had elected to chastise Latin Americans if they got in the "revolutionary frame of mind." Wilson chose to instruct them "to elect good men."[12]

Everywhere in the Caribbean Wilson inflicted punishment in the service of laudatory causes — in Haiti, where a high-minded naval officer landed troops in summer 1915 (after a mob had murdered the president, and political rivals had plunged the country into a rebellion); in the neighboring Dominican Republic, where Wilson imposed his plan for running the country and, when the Dominican leaders defied him, sent in troops to run them out and install a military government; and in Mexico, which sank into revolution in 1911. Like many Americans, Wilson cheered the ousting of the Mexican dictator Porfirio Díaz and believed his successor, Francisco Madero, who had plotted his rebellion in the United States, was a kindred political spirit. Three weeks before Wilson's inauguration, Madero was toppled in a military coup and then taken out and shot. Wilson never recognized the man who replaced him, Victoriano Huerta and, because other revolutionary aspirants raised the revolutionary banner against Huerta, naively believed he could "direct" Mexico's revolutionary course.

Wilson sent emissaries into every Mexican revolutionary camp and stationed the Atlantic Fleet off Mexico's Gulf shore. He twice dispatched U.S. troops onto Mexican soil — to Veracruz in April 1914 in an occupation that lasted seven months and into northern Mexico in 1916 in a futile chase after Pancho Villa. The justification for the first lay in Wilson's determination to bring down a government whose leader had ordered the murder of his freely elected predecessor, and for the second, as retaliation for Villa's raid against Columbus, New Mexico. In Veracruz the U.S. military erected an honest government in an unarguably corrupt city, a record that earned for the United States not the lasting gratitude but the enduring enmity of Mexico, Mexicans, and, indeed, most Latin Americans. From mid-1915 until mid-1916, a year of racial strife along the border, there were thirty raids into Texas. In the Villa chase, the punitive expedition led by John Pershing not only failed to capture

Villa and his band but found itself confronting regular Mexican troops in two engagements. Ironically, in the revolutionary decade (1910–20), the human and economic ties between the two countries escalated: 1.5 million people, many of them refugees, migrated from Mexico into the U.S. Southwest. American merchants along the border continued to do a brisk business trading with and financing Sonoran rebels. Trade with Mexico expanded through the decade.[13]

Elsewhere, in the smaller and more vulnerable countries, the American grip tightened. In the aftermath of the Nicaraguan intervention of 1912, which Wilson had roundly criticized, secretary of state William Jennings Bryan concluded a canal pact with a compliant Nicaraguan diplomat and with it expanded U.S. economic and political influence in Nicaragua. He tried to impose on Nicaragua a variation of the Platt Amendment but failed when incensed Republicans (among them former secretary of state Elihu Root) stopped him. The Wilson administration used the recurring internal discord in Haiti and the Dominican Republic as an excuse to install de facto military governments that persisted for nineteen years in Haiti and eight years in the Dominican Republic. In the same era the Canal Zone was Americanized to a degree the president who had "taken" it would have disapproved, and Cuba, which had emerged in 1909 from its second military occupation by U.S. troops, was thoroughly subordinated to American economic and political domination. Even Costa Rica, which had already demonstrated its distinction among Central American states for political stability, incurred Wilson's wrath in 1917 when the Tinoco brothers seized power. The president, employing the stipulation against recognition of revolutionary governments in the 1907 isthmian treaties, refused to recognize the new government.

Yet, paradoxically, he advanced a Pan-American pact to bind the hemispheric republics in a defensive alliance that, on paper, was stronger than Bolívar's of ninety years before. In 1913 Wilson had pledged in an oft-quoted speech at Mobile, Alabama, that the United States sought no new territorial aggrandizement in the Western Hemisphere. Latin Americans were heartened by his profession of a new era in American policy. Yet they were quickly disheartened by Wilson's interpretation of what a reformed Latin American policy meant. Condemning European economic imperialism in the hemisphere, he sought to advance the economic reach of the United States. Castigating the gunboat diplomacy of his predecessor, he followed with interventionist policies of his own. As often happened, the profession of its "civilizing mission" by America (which called for Latin American cooperation) and the strategic interests of the United States (which required hemispheric domination) were not easily reconciled. As Herbert Croly had noted in his stimulating book *The Promise of American Life* (which dealt mostly with the domestic polity), the United States must carry out its "great work" in the hemisphere as well. Ideally, hemispheric governments would cooperate in the endeavor to shut out European imperialism. In reality, none save the United States was strong enough to contain the external threat.[14]

Thus the "civilizing mission" of America that Wilson proclaimed joined with the "protective imperialism" of the United States that Roosevelt had earlier applied. Viewed in that way, Wilson's interventionist policies appeared reasonable and logical. But Wilson might have had to do less intervening had he preached less about the mission. Latin Americans judged him mostly on what he did for the United States and its interests, not what he said he wanted to do on behalf of America and its mission. As Americans are fond of saying — and as Latin Americans know — actions speak louder than words.

The Pan-American proposal went out to the Latin American governments just as the Veracruz affair was winding down. A number of nations had tried to mediate between the Americans and Mexicans, with limited success; now the Yankees were refurbishing the Bolivarian design and presenting it to them for approval. Six governments, representing mostly small countries under close American scrutiny, heartily approved. But the larger countries, even nominally sympathetic Brazil, expressed strong reservations. And Mexico, now ruled by the determined (and defiant) Venustiano Carranza, who chafed under American incursions into his country, rallied Latin America against Wilson's pact. In both Haiti and the Dominican Republic, where Wilson had proposed undeniably beneficial political advice, the diplomats ultimately turned over matters to the U.S. military, which reluctantly but forcefully carried out his strictures. Inevitably, he turned his concerns to the European war, and in the process the international community he had strived for took on a transatlantic, not a hemispheric, shape.

"To make the world safe for democracy" evoked a higher purpose to U.S. entry in World War I, but Latin Americans had good reason to distrust the U.S. credos. More than a decade before, at Rio de Janeiro, Elihu Root had tried to persuade doubtful Latin American delegates that Theodore Roosevelt's bullying actually represented the policy of restraint. Since then, the United States had reoccupied Cuba, launched a major invasion into recalcitrant Nicaragua, established blatantly military governments in Haiti and the Dominican Republic, and twice invaded Mexico. In every case, U.S. officials pointed out, the situation had warranted our course of action, but the collective impact of these incursions alienated a generation of Latin American intellectuals and disabused their political leaders from looking northward for the model political culture.

Even more befuddling were Washington's policies toward its tropical wards, which vacillated between benign neglect and intensive efforts to reorder what Americans considered backward places. Puerto Rico, largely forgotten since its annexation, achieved a measure of status in 1917 with the Jones Act, which made its inhabitants U.S. citizens but did not accord the island the rights of a state in the Union. Then the island lapsed into colonial desuetude until the mid-1930s, when the Franklin D. Roosevelt administration dramatically publicized another salvage operation. At the southern extremity of empire lay the Panama Canal Zone, technically only a leasehold from Panama. Within two decades after the opening of the canal in 1914 the Canal Zone had become an enclave of propertyless white American supervisors and their West Indian labor force. In Central America lay captive Nicaragua and Honduras — the first a U.S. protectorate and the second an independent country with a political and economic system largely beholden to American fruit companies.

In Haiti and the Dominican Republic, the civilians bequeathed to the U.S. military two more protectorates, ruled by officers committed to implanting the American sense of community in cultures they considered generally unsuited for it. In both countries the military regimes encountered civilian hostility and guerrilla resistance. Several prominent Dominican leaders went into exile, and the U.S. Navy installed a military government. (A few Dominican exiles surfaced at the 1919 Paris Peace talks to make a muted protest about the denial of Wilsonian professions of self-determination.) In Haiti, the U.S. occupiers found a compliant Haitian (Sudre Dartiguenave) to carry out their will and forcibly imposed a new constitution on the republic. The severity of rule in both countries prompted a major investigation by a joint committee of Congress after the war.[15]

Not unexpectedly, then, Latin Americans were somewhat skeptical about American rhetoric when the United States entered World War I in April 1917. Yet except for Argentina and Mexico, where Wilson's meddling had given German agents an opportunity to conduct a secret war intended to provoke a Mexican attack on the United States, Latin American countries were not hostile to American aims. They had rejected Wilson's Pan-American pact and continued to condemn American imperialism, but they did not embrace the German cause. For the smaller republics of the Caribbean, strategic realities made traditional neutrality an impossibility. As American investment and influence diminished with the Mexican Revolution, it advanced in the Caribbean. As Europeans retreated, the long-sought South American market in oil, cables, and finance capitalism expanded. When the war ended, the process accelerated, and with it came American cultural pretensions.

The weak Caribbean republics had already bowed to the American presence, but the mainland South American countries were more insulated and resisting. Argentina looked upon the "civilizing mission" of American trade, investments, and missionary diplomacy as a threat to its own considerable prospect for leading the Pan-American movement. Only the Brazilians, who already spoke of their "special relationship" with the United States, perceived little threat in Wilson's vigorous diplomacy. They had recognized economic realities when their European credit markets collapsed; from 1914 on they had had to look to the larger banking houses of New York. At the urging of J. P. Morgan the largest of these lending institutions had formed a South American Group, agreeing to pool their resources in extending loans.[16]

Direct investments and greater commercial links followed as American lenders were no longer dependent on the Latin American branches of European banks to act as intermediaries. In the summer of 1915, when the administration lifted the ban on loans to belligerents, some of these funds found their way back to Europe, but the general conditions laid the foundation for a veritable American financial assault on Latin America after Versailles. With U.S. entry into the war came the inevitable proliferation of bureaucracies and their coteries of agents, investigators, and experts dispatched to missions in Latin America. They kept watch on German spies and tried to prevent vital products from reaching the European enemy. There was a minor brouhaha over Mexican sisal from Yucatán when enterprising Mexican factors demanded what American officials considered an exorbitant price. Herbert Hoover, czar of the Food Administration, responded with threats to use corn, a staple in the Mexican diet, as a weapon. In the conduct of policy the State Department often found its goals confounded by such intrusions. The Shipping Board and the War Trade Board were especially meddlesome.

The most crucial issue, of course, was Latin America's position on the war. Within the State Department there was apprehension that the animosity against the military governments in Haiti and the Dominican Republic would seriously damage U.S. wartime diplomacy in South America. Washington arrogantly expected the smaller countries to do their duty and declare war. Costa Rica, Nicaragua, Panama, Honduras, Guatemala, Cuba, and Haiti willingly complied. Among South American governments, Brazil declared war following the sinking of the steamer *Macao*. In words as defiant as any Wilson had used, Brazilian president Wenceslau Brás avowed that the "dignity of the nation" must be confirmed.[17] Argentina and Mexico were determinedly neutral; Chile, Colombia, Paraguay, Venezuela, and El Salvador joined them. The remainder — Bolivia, Ecuador, Peru, Uruguay, and the Dominican Republic — broke diplomatic relations with Germany and her allies. (The U.S. military government in the Dominican Republic refrained from declaring war in order to relieve Washington of obligations for economic assistance.) In declaring its neutrality, the Uruguayan government announced what eventually became a principle of inter-American public law: though itself a neutral in the conflict, Uruguay regarded other hemispheric countries that declared war as nonbelligerents.

John Barrett, the former diplomat who had become director of the Pan-American Union, zealously argued that South Americans were not pro-German. When several governments criticized him for impertinently speaking for them, he compounded his gaucherie by suggesting that official envoys be dispatched into Latin America to solicit support for the war effort. In the end he lost his job as director of the Pan-American Union and slipped into obscurity. Washington followed this embarrassment with yet another. George Creel, head of the Committee on War Information, launched a propaganda drive to persuade Latin Americans that the United States was fighting for ideals, not territory, in Europe. The Mexicans were unconvinced, but the Argentines, usually condemnatory of U.S. policy, lauded American entry into the war as inspiration for a new Pan-Americanism. But the Argentine president, Hipólito Irigoyen, was not sufficiently moved to break diplomatic relations with the Central Powers.[18]

Latin America's greatest burden remained the dislocation of its economies brought on by the loss of European markets. The hemisphere was largely unprepared for the economic impact World War I had on the republics. In 1915, at the First Pan-American Financial Conference, the delegates had discussed problems in trade, transportation, and finance and made minor adjustments, but they could not realistically anticipate that more severe measures might be required. Guatemala, which had sold its high-quality coffee to Germany, was compelled to dump the crop of 1917–18 at low prices in San Francisco. Other commodities, such as iron and steel, now came from the United States, which imposed limits on exports of vital wartime materials or, when available for the hemispheric market, charged exorbitant prices for them. Most Latin American countries found themselves far down the priority list for goods now obtainable only from the United States.

As Americans replaced European lenders and suppliers, Washington expected hemispheric governments to cooperate in everything from confiscating German property to blacklisting native firms doing business with German companies. With these measures the Wilson administration interfered in such mundane transactions as the import of coal in Argentina and the sale of Chilean nitrates. In its determination to wrest control of Latin American trade from British domination, the United States occasionally took reprisals against British companies. Toward the end of the war the Departments of War and Navy objected to Britain's sale of war supplies to South American governments and opposed a British coaling station in Peru. The answer to European military influence in Latin America, the admirals said, was the prompt dispatch of U.S. military missions.

Relations with Canada, which had figured prominently in the prewar calculations about dollar diplomacy, reemerged after the war as part of the political reconfiguration of U.S. relations with Britain and Washington's more ambitious role in the hemisphere. Canadians harbored deep resentments about the tardiness of the U.S. commitment in the war, arguing that Canadians had died while Americans had profited. In the postwar era they became even more dependent on their powerful southern neighbor. In part, their predicament was of their own making and the decision of the British government to give members of the commonwealth a greater amount of latitude in their own affairs. The 1921–22 Washington naval conference, which allocated to the British, U.S., and Japanese navies a dominance in their respective territorial waters, effectively made Canadians more autonomous — a choice favored by the Liberal prime minister William Lyon McKenzie King (1922–30) — but more vulnerable to U.S. economic and even cultural influence. As cynical Canadians reminded their countrymen, U.S. money came north as Canadians went south. The sense of vulnerability deepened with the onset of the Depression, when financially strapped U.S. communities deported foreign-born residents who became public charges, including Canadians and even some Mexican Americans born in the United States. The 1931 Statute of Westminister validated Canadian autonomy within the British commonwealth of nations, which meant that Canada was no longer a pawn in the British-U.S. equation, but the new status did little to retard the growing U.S. economic presence in the country or alter the infuriating ambivalence in the relationship between the two neighbors. In a decade when an Anglo-American war over Canada was a fantasy, both Canadian and U.S. military planners had a war plan. In the estimation of the U.S. Army's Strategic Plan Red scenario, the conquest of Canada would lead to the making of new "states and territories of the Union [and] the Dominion government will be abolished."[19]

The Twenties

World War I enabled the United States to supplant Europe in the economic balance of power in Latin America. Europe's decline as hemispheric economic power had begun before the war and escalated rapidly in the aftermath, and it represented not a simple Marxian evolution of the dollar following the flag (or the flag in supportive pursuit of the dollar) but, more precisely, the parallel endeavors of private and public economic interests.

During the war, when it was apparent that the patterns of U.S. commerce and investment in Latin America were shifting, Congress became more supportive of private economic interests in the region. The Edge and Webb-Pomerene acts permitted American banks to establish branch offices in foreign cities and freed export houses that combined efforts to gain access to foreign markets from prosecution under the antitrust law. There was immediate concern that at war's end European competitors would challenge the United States in controlling Latin American petroleum reserves and cables (then of considerable strategic value) and regain domination of the Latin American credit market. The threat of this economic challenge turned out to be greatly exaggerated, and within a few years the State Department declared that it would no longer render judgments on private loans to Latin American governments. American petroleum, cable, and international investment concerns had already grown weary of the political restraints imposed from Washington.

There were exceptions to this apparent divorce between public and private actors on the hemispheric economic stage. In Mexico, where revolutionary nationalism, expressed in the 1917 constitutional declaration that the nation's subsoil wealth belonged to the people, collided with long-standing foreign mining and petroleum leases, the U.S. State Department doggedly supported the American companies.[20] And in the Caribbean, where the United States was dismantling the military occupations of the previous decade, it insisted on retaining certain financial prerogatives. As part of the price for ridding themselves of U.S. proconsuls, the Dominicans obligated themselves to pay off the bonds issued by the occupation government. In Cuba, the U.S. ambassador often imparted his financial guidance to usually compliant Cuban leaders.

Contemporary critics, particularly the vocal socialist analysts of export capital in the 1920s, saw little substantive difference between dollar diplomacy, which symbolized the official promotion (and use) of private investment, and the diplomacy of the dollar, which stood for a less conspiratorial relationship between Washington and Wall Street. The latter brought supportive technical advice to Latin American governments improperly schooled in public finance. Under the stern guidance of Secretary of Commerce Herbert Hoover and the chief of the Bureau of Foreign Trade, Julius Klein, Washington insinuated an unexpected moral tone in this effort. Klein perhaps best expressed this blending of American cultural and economic credos. Latin American countries, he wrote, "deserve the most effective collaboration from their Northern Anglo-Saxon neighbors, not simply in capital, but in technically trained personnel and in schooling for their own native experts. . . . Indeed, the whole of our westward march across the continent, our struggles with precisely similar frontier difficulties, and our prolonged experiences with the same problems in transportation, mining, forestry, and agriculture, should certainly provide abundant sources of helpful experiences in solving these problems."[21]

On a hemispheric scale, then, Hoover sought the same cooperation with the private sector that he pursued on the domestic front — the associationist state with Washington acting as friendly mediator between private American investors and Latin American governments. The smaller Caribbean states, in the face of the lingering threat of Yankee intervention, had no choice but to yield. But South Americans, suspicious of American motives, never accommodated the persuasive rhetoric emanating from Washington. They accepted foreign banking, mining, and petroleum ventures as means of promoting national development and employment. Halfheartedly they listened to Hoover's strictures warning against loans for the purchase of armaments or some other impolitic diversion of funds.

Hoover and Klein were the last of a line of American economic advisers to Latin America in the tradition inaugurated by Elihu Root at the Rio conference in 1906, continued under John Barrett's direction at the 1911 commercial conference, and pursued more aggressively after World War I. The intent was the promotion of *functional* as opposed to *authoritative* government, a belief grounded in the political wisdom that the duty of government lay in the sustenance of sound economic philosophy carried out mostly by private enterprise. That Latin America's economic and political values were rooted in the centralist philosophies of authoritarian Spanish and Portuguese monarchs — rather than in Adam Smith or John Locke — was of little consequence to Hoover.

In the 1920s Latin American intellectuals largely rejected the business ethic that prevailed in the United States. The movement had begun a generation earlier in the writings of José Enrique Rodó, the Uruguayan writer, who had condemned American materialism. The United States had brought its power, and its wealth, and its technology southward, but despite its professions of godliness, he argued, it had abandoned God in its quest. Abruptly Latin American thinkers who had once written admiringly of the northern industrial democracy began to look more closely at their own cultures as models for the future. Rodó spoke of a Latin race that repudiated the unholy combination of Protestantism and materialism. In *Ariel*, published in the aftermath of the American triumph over hapless Spain, Rodó employed Shakespearean images to show that American materialism led to mediocrity. Latin America, by extolling idealism, must reach for spiritual heights. The literary outburst continued with Rubén Darío, the Nicaraguan poet, perhaps the greatest poet in the Spanish language, who spent a dissolute life in Paris but inveighed against Yankees trudging across his native land.

Such an achievement, it seemed, was impossible as long as Latin Americans retained their jealousies of American wealth and power. Rodó's response, echoed by Manuel Ugarte in *The Destiny of a Continent*, held that the United States possessed no culture worthy of admiration. The collapse of Europe in the carnage of the war removed the Old World as a symbol. In the void Latin Americans must construct their own version of civilization. In Argentina the cause took the form of glorification of the nation's turbulent *gaucho* past; in Brazil, praise for the country's natural resources and climate; in Haiti (still in the grip of American power), the resurgence of negritude, the nation's African roots; and in Peru, the country's Incan past. Everywhere the late nineteenth-century positivist credo, which Latin Americans had once embraced from the European and American model, stood in disrepute.[22]

For some Latin American thinkers, the Mexican Revolution represented the collective protest of an oppressed people against American-style order and progress. That was the view from outside the nation. In other ways, however, the triumphant revolutionaries — certainly the northerners who had taken over with Álvaro Obregón in 1920 — retained the Porfirian state and most of its trappings. Labor remained dependent; the peasants, without land. Powerful economic barons still controlled manufacturing and sought government protection. After receiving U.S. diplomatic recognition in 1923, the government began to encourage a different form of revolutionary nationalism. Bureaucrats drove the priests from the schools and dispatched their own educational zealots into the countryside. José Vasconcelos, the educational czar, wrote of the cosmic race. The muralist José Clemente Orozco glorified Mexico's Indian past. Culture and nationalism were fused into a new dynamic, "spiritual nationalism," which transcended the narrow political variety. A generation of Americans looking for a cultural alternative to the crass materialism of their own country found inspiration in things Mexican.[23]

Out of it the first generation of post-revolutionary leaders fashioned a new political order. They did not create a democratic or an egalitarian Mexico, but they drew on the xenophobic heritage of its people to raise the cultural banner against the outside world and its credos. Throughout the decade of the 1920s Mexico resisted U.S. diplomatic pressures to accommodate American petroleum and mining companies, its strategy of charting the course of Mexican finance, and American efforts to mediate the bitter church-state conflict. The nationalism born in the Mexican Revolution and its violence no longer tolerated passivity before American power. There were confrontations and threats of U.S. retaliation and rumors of war against "Bolshevik" Mexico, but the country did not lower the flag of defiance.[24]

Just as the image of a democratic United States had deteriorated with the exercise of the police power and the big stick, so, too, had the stature of the enterprising Yankee in the Latin American marketplace. In Mexico the revolution wrought an anti-Americanism that persisted, making not only American business but even tourism a riskier matter. Farther on, the banana companies of Central America, once familial operations, had by the 1920s evolved into powerful challenges to the state. United Fruit, incorporated in 1899 by three Americans, was the dominant economic force in Guatemala and Honduras and had extensive holdings in the tropical lowlands of eastern Costa Rica. In Honduras, the only reliable sources of government revenue were the Cuyamel, Standard, and United Fruit companies. In Venezuela and Bolivia, American oil companies loomed ever larger on the economic horizon. The presence of American multinationals — the term was not widely used then but accurately reflects the scope of their operations — confirmed leftist suspicions that Latin America was rapidly slipping under U.S. economic domination. But the more ominous challenge of these powerful companies, which in the smaller republics had become the largest employer of "native" labor, lay in their imprint on national culture.[25]

Guatemala's relations with United Fruit illustrated the apprehension its leaders sensed about the penetration of an American economic giant into a stratified society of master and man. At the turn of the century, the country had fallen under the sway of Manuel Estrada Cabrera, who virtually enslaved its Indian masses in a modern labor system. When United Fruit began to shift its operations away from the Nicaraguan Caribbean coast, it looked to Honduras and its rich northern coastland and fertile sites in northeastern Guatemala. Unlike compliant Honduran executives, who generally gave the banana tycoons anything they wanted, Estrada was determined to be their partners. He resisted efforts from Washington to transform the country into a financial protectorate but struck deals with Minor Keith, one of United Fruit's founding fathers, to establish banana enclaves in the sparsely populated Guatemalan east. Keith was then permitted to build a rail line into the interior that ultimately expanded into the United Railways of Central America. Estrada made sure that the banana laborers — many of them descendants of black West Indians who had settled on the neglected Caribbean coast after the mid-nineteenth century — remained in the protective enclaves around Livingston, Puerto Barrios, and the Montagua River Valley. In such manner the Guatemalan shielded his people from whatever economic and political dynamic such operations generated.

Years before, when he was carving his banana empire in Limón Province in Costa Rica, Keith had struck a similar arrangement with the Costa Rican elite in the highlands. He built hospitals and schools for his black laborers and connected the capital to the Caribbean with a railroad. United Fruit governed in the lowlands, but it kept its black subjects from migrating into the highland interior. As did their American counterparts elsewhere in Latin America, the banana companies accommodated the elite. But the manner in which they operated — their organizational structure with its dependence on a managerial elite, along with the profits they generated — offered a tempting prospect of material reward and a social stature that depended on what one did for a living. Latin America's critical intelligentsia may have written off the American intruders as crass émigrés from a materialist culture, but the day laborers under their sway discovered that a few jingling coins in the pocket made one feel less like a peasant.[26]

Yankee Imperialism at Bay

A foreign policy predicated on strategic necessity, economic expansion, and political tutelage can inspire gratitude but only among those subjects who benefit from its presence. Among them it leaves unforgettable impressions of what a great power can do. Unintentionally but inevitably, the intruding country — whether it comes to do ill or, in the case of the United States, to do good — will inspire an opposition. The opposition may take the form of a cultural defiance, in which the people simply pretend to adapt or change their ways long enough to benefit from the largesse of an intruding benefactor. Toward the end of what most Americans considered a benign intrusion into Latin America, their Caribbean charges were no closer to democracy than they had been in the beginning. American browbeating, interventions, and an occasional occupation government had momentarily gotten them out of the "revolutionary frame of mind." When the American grip began to relax in the mid-1920s, the opposition to American rule, which had diminished but never disappeared, resurfaced in more violent form.

Shortly after the war ended, the architects of Wilsonian penetration of Latin America found themselves under assault. In 1919 the military narrowly averted a scandal over alleged atrocities committed during the campaign against *caco* "bandits" in Haiti. A year later, during the heated presidential campaign, the American imperial structure came in for harsh assessment from the most unimaginative of political candidates — Warren Gamaliel Harding, who declared that as president he would not instruct West Indians in the art of democracy with bayonets. In responding, Democratic vice presidential candidate Franklin D. Roosevelt publicly boasted that he had written Haiti's constitution, which the country had been virtually compelled to adopt by the presence of U.S. Marines. It was an impolitic assertion, indicative of the callousness of Wilsonian rule. What occurred in Haiti and in the Dominican Republic was a breakdown of a regime that enunciated twin policies of racial paternalism and economic development. Ordinary Haitians and Dominicans saw those who resisted the occupations as freedom fighters. In Haiti, more so than in the Dominican Republic, some marines began to lose confidence and, to use a popular expression, went "native." As the resistance heightened, daily violence became more routine, the demands of the two regimes for forced labor grew, and the suppression became more severe. An imperial nation whose political traditions are infused with the rhetoric of liberty and self-determination cannot succeed in imposing its will and mandate on another, however "backward" and weak.[27]

The nation's blunders in the Caribbean did not determine the outcome of the election, but Harding's triumph indicated a public weariness with the Caribbean burden his predecessor had undertaken. For Latin Americans the

apparent lessening of American will presented both an opportunity and a dilemma. It meant, among other things, that the United States was admitting it
held no lasting formula for Latin America's problems. At the same time, as had
been made clear in Article 21 of the League of Nations covenant, the United
States had no intention of retreating from the tradition of regional domination, expressed concisely in the Monroe Doctrine. Apprehensive about foreign
intervention, nine Latin American states (Brazil, Bolivia, Cuba, Guatemala,
Haiti, Honduras, Nicaragua, Panama, and Peru) became charter members of
the League in 1919, and several others joined in the 1920s. One of the more
enthusiastic proponents of hemispheric unity, the Uruguayan foreign minister Baltasar Brum, boldly advanced the idea of a Pan-American League
of Nations.

After an intensive congressional investigation in 1921–22, Washington declared it was withdrawing its troops from the Dominican Republic and reor-
ganizing the Haitian occupation. In this atmosphere of retrenchment from the
Caribbean empire, the fifth Pan-American conference met at Santiago, Chile,
in 1923. Latin American delegates were eager to tout the League of Nations
and denounce the lingering American empire in the tropics. The U.S. delegation, instructed not to discuss the League in the wake of the Senate's adamant rejection, listened gloomily as Latin American spokesmen extolled the
Bolivarian dream of hemispheric unity and assailed Washington's domination
of the Pan-American Union. They championed the efforts to codify inter-
American law — which had gotten underway at the 1902 meeting in Mexico
City and had revived with the creation of a Commission of Jurists at Rio de
Janeiro in 1906 — and insisted on discussing "political" questions. In the end
the Americans declared that the United States preferred a Pan-American system distinct from the League and that the Monroe Doctrine, which Wilson
had advanced momentarily as hemispheric policy, had reverted to a unilateral
policy of the United States.

The willingness of the Americans to listen to Latin American complaints
probably countered the rhetorical assault of the Argentines, who desperately sought a hemispheric declaration on naval armaments to check Brazil's
rapid expansion in shipbuilding. Of greater significance was Latin America's
participation in both the Pan-American system and the League of Nations,
thus demonstrating, apparently, that it was possible to belong to the Western

Hemisphere and to the world. A recurring theme in Latin America's protestation was U.S. intervention in hemispheric affairs and the manifest need for the Pan-American system to avow the principle of nonintervention and reaffirm the rights of states. Until the end of World War I, when the European threat to hemispheric security had subsided, the American response held that the Pan-American system had neither produced an effective hemispheric structure nor codified a hemispheric law that all the states supported. Latin American delegates — especially the Argentines — continued to speak of the rights of states; their American counterparts, to speak of the "rights and duties" of those states. Unless the Pan-American system required the second, declared a succession of U.S. secretaries of state, hemispheric governments could not reasonably expect to enjoy the full benefits of the first.

Behind the formal sessions another drama unfolded. As so often for the United States in its hemispheric endeavors, the irritant was Mexico. Denied American recognition because of disputes over Mexico's 1917 Constitution, which boded ill for U.S. companies still operating in the country, the Mexican government had refused to send a delegation. But every day a number of Latin American participants trooped over to the residence of the Mexican ambassador to Chile to discuss Mexico's position on this or that matter. More embarrassing was the sight of a mute Henry Fletcher, chief of the American representation, under express instructions *not* to respond to the effusive praise of Woodrow Wilson delivered by the president of Paraguay.[28]

Later that year, Secretary of State Charles Evans Hughes, in a centenary address on the Monroe Doctrine, reaffirmed that the United States was retreating from empire and recognized the juridical equality of Latin American states but would not join them in a regional security pact. At the same time the United States boldly reasserted its primacy in Central America in a series of treaties aimed at containing isthmian discord by the expedient of recognizing neither revolutionary governments nor anybody related to a revolutionary who gained power by the electoral process. The restriction was even more severe than that laid down by Theodore Roosevelt in 1907. In its determination to chastise Nicaragua for its meddlesomeness, the U.S. government had ignored that treaty and invaded the country in 1910.

In late 1926 Nicaraguan disturbances brought yet another intervention. The United States had no Platt Amendment with Nicaragua, as it did with Cuba,

but since 1912 Nicaragua had been a virtual protectorate with a marine lega-
tion guard symbolizing the reach of American power. In the mid-1920s the
State Department quietly withdrew them. A few weeks later the country was
plunged into a political crisis. The new president had tried to placate the opposition party with jobs; his efforts only served to irritate his own political family.
The leader of the disgruntled was Emiliano Chamorro, called affectionately
the General, who had helped the Americans crush the revolt of 1912. Through
intrigue and intimidation he drove the president from office and maneuvered
himself into the executive chair. His putative friends in Washington either had
to accept him or find some alternative. They chose the latter.

Technically, Chamorro had violated the 1923 treaties, which the United
States was bound to uphold. But Chamorro's seizure of power had precipitated
a revolt in the name of the ousted vice-president, Juan Sacasa, who had assembled a dozen revolutionary groups vowing to place him in the presidency.
Whatever its displeasure with Chamorro, Washington was not prepared to
tolerate Nicaraguans settling their own affairs in a revolution that threatened
its interests. In late 1926 the U.S. minister pushed Chamorro out. In his exit
the General was able to prevent Sacasa from taking power. The Nicaraguan
National Assembly, with the blessing of the U.S. government, selected Adolfo
Díaz as president. Shortly afterward, U.S. troops began landing on Nicaragua's
eastern coast, ostensibly to safeguard the considerable foreign business there
but in reality to influence the outcome of Nicaraguan politics. A larger intervention occurred on the west coast, and in spring 1927 the president's special
emissary, Henry Stimson, arrived, urging mediation and pledging fair elections. All except one of the rebel leaders struck a deal. The holdout, Augusto
César Sandino, raised an army of men, women, and children and declared, in
words of defiance heard as far away as China, that Nicaraguans possessed the
right of self-determination.[29]

Policy in Central America made no provision for such a claim, nor could
Americans understand how Sandino could mold a revolutionary army on such
a slogan. But in time Sandino had volunteers from all but one Latin American
republic. To Americans, he was an improbable leader: he would not stand and
fight, he ran into the mountains, and (when the marines pursued him) he ran
off to Honduras or Mexico. Yet somehow he managed to acquire a following

and a vaunted hemispheric fame. Dutiful to its pledge, the United States supervised an indisputably honest election in 1928. When Sandino denounced the American presence as imperialism, President Calvin Coolidge dispatched five thousand marines to roam the Nicaraguan north in a vain search for a man their commander derisively called a "mule thief." The Sandino chase was denounced throughout the hemisphere, in the U.S. Senate, and in the press. Senator William E. Borah of Idaho, alluding to Coolidge's statement about "our special interests" in Nicaragua, decried the intervention as an "oil and mahogany policy." In truth, the American commitment posed a more troublesome issue than safeguarding foreign property in Nicaragua. There were indisputable security interests in Nicaragua; the issue lay in the means of maintaining them.

Roosevelt's notion of intruding into unruly societies in limited interventions, exercising a police power, had yielded to the Wilsonian view of intervening more intensely to "teach them to elect good men" and inculcate a respect for political order. That policy was now failing. It suffered not from the failure of U.S. military strength but from the lack of will to sustain it against even a poorly equipped foe. The civilians had given the task of community building in the Caribbean to the soldiers more than a decade before. But they could not govern until they had intervened, and where they had dispatched troops — in Veracruz, in Hispaniola, and now in Nicaragua — they could not easily escape the burden of the colonizer. Even at its height, the British Empire had strained under the continual burden of policing its outposts. Americans had always believed the United States could avoid this dilemma by largely rejecting colonialism and exercising its influence through informal but effective political measures. What Americans did not understand was that for Latin Americans the distinction Americans made between their purpose and those of Europe's formal empires was not that important. What mattered was U.S. actions and, more important, the American presence on their soil.

The jungle war in Nicaragua convinced a generation of civilians in the State Department that they must retake command of Latin American policy. Nicaragua provided the opportunity. At the height of the intervention, the sixth Pan-American conference convened in Havana. Coolidge himself led the U.S. delegation, arriving in a U.S. warship. He was greeted at the dock by

Cuban president Gerardo Machado, the cattle thief turned businessman who had clamped down on dissent and promised the nervous Americans an uneventful meeting.

Urged on by Mexico and Argentina, the Latin Americans were determined to debate Nicaragua. Coolidge delivered a predictably uninspiring address and looked to former secretary of state Hughes to hold back the verbal tide. Expecting platitudes about political order and the security of the Panama Canal, the delegates heard instead mild assessments of the U.S. position. When the final plenary session took up the issue of intervention, the rhetoric escalated. Anti-American diatribes rang throughout the hall. Hughes responded with a defense of the Monroe Doctrine as a protective shield for Latin Americans. States have an obligation to protect their citizens in countries that cannot safeguard their lives and property. This was not intervention but "interposition."

It was a euphemism, perhaps, but Hughes's choice of words momentarily salvaged American prestige. The Argentines had tried to get an absolute ban on intervention but failed and stalked out. Hughes electrified the audience, won praise for confronting the issue, and returned to the United States realizing that some other basis for protecting American interests must be found. In 1930 the solicitor general of the State Department, J. Reuben Clark, declared the Roosevelt Corollary an unsound and impolitic legal basis for intervention. Roosevelt had transformed the Monroe Doctrine, he said, from a policy of United States versus Europe to United States versus Latin America. There was an immediate outcry about retreating from responsibilities, and the "repudiation" of Roosevelt's Corollary was abruptly repudiated.[30]

But there was no turning back to the large-scale interventions of the past. The following year Stimson, now secretary of state, announced that American property owners in Nicaragua must look to Managua, not Washington, to safeguard their interests. As for U.S. strategic interests in the region, international law provided the nation with sufficient foundation to safeguard its interests, by intervention if necessary. Washington wanted a "special relationship" with Latin America; it would not relinquish its historic unilateral interests in the Caribbean without a firm commitment that the smaller countries of the region would safeguard them.

It found such an assurance in a generation of Caribbean strongmen, leaders it did not really want, did not particularly like, and ultimately disowned. It accepted them, frankly, because their interventions in U.S.-crafted governments had achieved military security for the United States in a region vital to its interests and opportunity for private American capital and companies. It accepted them, finally, because the cost of a policing role in the Caribbean had gone beyond U.S. willingness to pay for the service with troops. In fragile and unstable small countries the United States confronted backward yet changeable economies and political systems but resilient cultures with their own priorities, their own ways of doing things, and their own unappreciated strengths.[31]

The American performance at Havana confirmed Latin American intellectuals' generally contemptuous assessment of U.S. cultural unworthiness and innate aggressive instincts. The Mexican Isidro Fabela had expressed a widely held sentiment two years before: "Every dollar that crosses our frontier not only has stamped on its obverse the North American eagle but carries also in its hard soul the flag of the stars and stripes, which is today the most imperialistic in the world."[32] From the Mexican border towns to Patagonia, the continent's philosophers railed against a crass United States inflicting its Protestant materialism on a hapless but proud culture.

Some, like the Argentine philosopher José Ingenieros, called for the "moral union" of Hispanic peoples against the menace of Wall Street. Others, inspired by a Chilean proposal, urged a Latin American league to supplant the spiritless Pan-American Union of Yankee domination, a cause advanced before the League of Nations in 1930 and in 1971 when Salvador Allende proposed an Organization of American States without the United States. There was a limited but publicized Hispanic countercultural invasion in the defiant work of the Mexican muralists Diego Rivera and José Clemente Orozco, who parodied American capitalism in their artistry on public buildings from California to New York. Less subtle in his assault was the Peruvian populist Víctor Raúl Haya de la Torre, who had visited New York in the mid-1920s and sailed away thinking how Wall Street had overtaken the Statue of Liberty as America's conscience. He returned to Peru and began preaching another creed. The real Latin America, said Haya, must rediscover its Indian past and reject the domination of U.S. business. He formed the American Revolutionary Popular Alliance (its Spanish acronym is APRA), which preached hemispheric unity, internationalization of the Panama Canal, neutrality, and socialism appropriate to Indo-America.

The Good Neighbor

Such condemnations had become an issue in American politics and within the U.S. government. In 1928 Franklin D. Roosevelt, who had played a minor role in shaping the Wilsonian empire in the Caribbean, confessed that the United States had few supporters among the Latin American states. His discovery was not limited to Democratic aspirants. The Coolidge administration had already confronted an obstinate generation of revolutionary leaders in Mexico. The president's college friend Dwight Morrow had descended on Mexico City professing to "like" Mexicans, which had prompted the Mexican president, Plutarco Elías Calles, to ease somewhat the government's pressures on American oil companies in Mexico. But when Morrow tried to get the Mexicans to accommodate U.S. suggestions in their financial planning (a not uncommon practice of U.S. diplomats in the 1920s) he encountered Mexican resistance. Under pressure from American Catholics, he tried to mediate between church and state in the bitter Cristero revolt, when priests displaced by government teachers rallied peasants in central Mexico against them. The government retaliated with harsh anticlerical laws. Morrow placated them, and the churches reopened, but the revolutionary decrees remained on the books.[33]

The massive show of military strength in Nicaragua had amply demonstrated American domination in the hemisphere. Yet, unexpectedly, the frustration of the Sandino chase, the inability to chastise the Mexicans, the withdrawal from the Dominican Republic, and American defensiveness at the Havana Pan-American conference had collectively exposed the inherent disability of U.S. policy in the Caribbean after the triumph over Spain. Even Herbert Hoover, who as secretary of commerce had orchestrated a Latin American policy of commercial and financial enlightenment through the Bureau of Foreign Trade and Commerce, sensed the limitation of American influence. Shortly after trouncing Al Smith in the 1928 presidential election, he embarked on a goodwill tour of Latin America, disavowing any intention to play "big brother" in the hemisphere.

The decline of public enthusiasm — especially congressional support — for the Nicaraguan intervention and the onset of the Depression were practically simultaneous. The cost of intervention made its political acceptance even less palatable. Condemned at home, the capitalists found few sympathizers for dispatching the marines to safeguard their investments in the tropics. In 1931 the House Committee on Appropriations listened gloomily as the quartermaster general explained that marine operations in Haiti, the Dominican Republic, and Nicaragua from 1915 had consumed $9 million of public money. The anti-interventionists, predictably, considered this a heavy charge for the cause of expanding democracy in the tropics and of "teaching them to elect good men." From those who had identified the country's strategic interests in the Caribbean as a justifiable motive for interventionist policies, there was a reluctant admission that some means other than the use of military force had to be found to carry out U.S. policy.

As the Depression sank in, even true believers in the country's democratic mission began to question the practicality of interventionist policies. In 1930 six civilian governments in Latin America, among them Argentina and Peru, fell under military rule. In South America the demise of professedly democratic governments brought scarcely a murmur of American disapproval. But even among nominally compliant Central American republics, American tolerance of antidemocratic elements proved surprising. In Guatemala and El Salvador revolutionaries shot their way into power, in defiance of the 1923 treaties that forbade recognition of coup d'état governments, persisted, and eventually won U.S. recognition. In subservient Panama, where a public outburst had killed a revision of the hated 1903 canal treaty, a middle-class reform movement tossed out the president in a bloodless coup and escaped American interference — despite cries of threats to canal security.

In Nicaragua the numbers of U.S. troops began to decline sharply after 1929, and a dispirited U.S. military shifted its policing and the U.S. government its political burden to Anastasio Somoza García and the National Guard. In 1930 a political crisis (and a hurricane) provided Rafael Leonidas Trujillo with the opportunity to inaugurate a thirty-one-year tyranny in the Dominican Republic. To Cuba, Roosevelt dispatched a special emissary, Sumner Welles, whose task was to persuade Gerardo Machado to step down as president. Already, however, a generation of Cuban professionals and youthful idealists, who had been fighting Machado for several years, had raised the flag of rebellion. Machado resigned, and following several hectic weeks, a reformist junta under Ramón Grau San Martín took power.

For five months, the revolution of 1933 held sway — altering Cuba's political, economic, and social culture — as a nervous Roosevelt watched. Roosevelt named Welles ambassador, gave him extraordinary latitude to operate in the confusing Cuban political scene, and surrounded the island with the menacing firepower of the U.S. Navy. In the meantime his secretary of state was in Montevideo pledging the administration to a policy of nonintervention, limited only by the obligations of treaties and the rights of nations under international law. The Pentarchy of Grau instilled a momentary revolutionary triumph among a generation of young Cubans who had plotted against the Machado dictatorship and suffered the indignities of the Platt Amendment. But in the end, it fell — the victim, many Cubans still believe, of American nonrecognition and the plotting of Welles and Fulgencio Batista. All three dictators — Somoza, Trujillo, and Batista — received Washington's approbation. Inevitably, when their rule degenerated into sordid familial tyrannies, the Good Neighbor policy espoused by Roosevelt and his generation would be lambasted as evidence of American sustenance of Caribbean dictatorship.[34]

But this was not a choice easily made. The changing priorities of U.S. policy toward the hemisphere are often overlooked. Until the 1920s, American security interests had taken precedence, followed by promotion of U.S. trade and investments, which had escalated after World War I. The Nicaraguan intervention severely damaged U.S. political standing in the hemisphere, which Hoover and especially Roosevelt sought to correct by more than symbolic gestures. Just as potentially harmful was the collapsing American economic stake in Latin America, which followed closely in the wake of Latin America's virtually united condemnation of U.S. policy at Havana. From 1929 until the eve of Roosevelt's inauguration, American exports to Latin America declined in value by more than 75 percent, while its imports from the republics declined by 68 percent. Bond creditors heard equally grim news. In the 1920s American brokers had merrily sold American investors bonds on Latin American governments and municipalities. In the global repudiation of debt after the collapse of the American economy, Latin America was in the forefront.

Embarking on a program of economic nationalism at home, Roosevelt and especially Secretary of State Cordell Hull recognized that restoring hemispheric trade was crucial. For Hull, an unreconstructed Wilsonian, the means to accomplish this lay in a vigorous reciprocal trade program. If the United States lowered its tariffs, imported more from Latin America, and signed regional and bilateral commercial agreements that opened up the hemisphere to American products, he believed, trade barriers elsewhere, especially in the more desirable industrial markets of Europe, would tumble. Latin America provided the opening because its economies had been historically more responsive to pressures from the industrial economies of Europe and the United States. Pan-American economic cooperation thus became a State Department slogan from the beginning of the Roosevelt administration. When the Reciprocal Trade Agreements Act became law in 1934, the president could expand American exports to Latin America and jeopardize neither domestic industry, which faced no competition from the south, nor domestic commodities because the covered imports were materials such as rubber, bananas, bauxite, and platinum, which Americans did not produce.

The Good Neighbor credo was "nonintervention, noninterference, and reciprocity." Roosevelt pledged not to send marines to chastise Latin Americans, and not to browbeat their governments with heavy-handed policies, but he asked them to reciprocate by accommodating his international economic program. In practical terms, this meant that he expected the smaller republics in the Caribbean to acquiesce in Washington's economic priorities, but he was willing to make concessions that cost very little. The Panamanians, for example, negotiated the end of the humiliating protectorate and won a few economic concessions. More indicative of the ulterior purpose of the Good Neighbor was not Roosevelt's willingness to relinquish the Platt Amendment, which had made Cuba a protectorate in 1902, but the steadfast opposition to a revolution that threatened American sway over the island's economy. In Cuba, always a special case in its calculations, the United States tossed aside the general principle of an economic open door, thoroughly subordinated the Cuban economy to its own, and kept it largely closed to any except American products.[35]

The success of the Good Neighbor policy — indeed, even its origins — cannot be precisely measured. In trade advantage, the United States relinquished little, particularly in the vulnerable circum-Caribbean. The record in South

America proved to be modest, however much the U.S. leaders counted on a revival of hemispheric trade as a means of restoring economic well-being. By the general assessments in economic development and the goals of dollar diplomacy, the record was mixed. Undeniably, the "money doctors" had succeeded in introducing a degree of professionalism and managerial expertise to several Latin American governments. Yet in those places where U.S. advisers should have accomplished much more, the record proved embarrassing. The de facto colony of Puerto Rico in 1935 was a "basket case" of economic backwardness and the mission of cultural transformation an abject failure. With good reason a New Deal governor called the island a "stricken land." And in one of the tragic episodes of Depression-era history, local communities and states expatriated almost two million Mexicans (many of them U.S. citizens) from the country. In the economic and even the political sphere, the Pax Americana was no success, if not precisely a failure as a military venture.

In 1900, fresh from the U.S. military victory over a weak and dispirited Spain, the nation's leaders had embarked on an imperial venture with a sense of mission and purpose even as they resisted pressures to create the institutions and military to sustain that mission. The Pax Americana was not a republican model of the Pax Britannica. Even as he touted the image of "policeman" in the Caribbean and boasted about the nation's might and purpose, Theodore Roosevelt fretted about the country's vulnerability (especially in the western Pacific) or the machinations of Dominicans or Cubans or Panamanians trying to manipulate him into greater involvement in their domestic affairs. More than that, he doubted the willingness of the American people to sustain an imperial mandate, however ready they appeared to be in taking on the role of hemispheric policeman. Woodrow Wilson believed he could alter the purpose of that mandate through instruction and example, not reliance on military power. That effort withered under the combined pressures of World War I and resistance — directly through guerrilla war, indirectly by other means — to the U.S. intrusion. A decade later, the collapse of the stock market and the liberal capitalist model that successive generations of U.S. leaders had touted further weakened American resolve throughout the hemisphere.

Yet, in sometimes subtle ways, the bonds between North and South had strengthened. Examples varied from the fascination of Americans for Argentine boxing to the qualified acceptance of the idea of a distinctive American international law to fascination with a romantic and exotic Mexico, not as revolutionary challenge but alternative to the U.S. model of mass industrialization. Some, such as the historian Herbert E. Bolton, offered a historical perspective on a "greater America." Others, notably the writer Waldo Frank, promoted a view of a North-South fusing of countercultures that sharply contrasted with older values of the capitalist society. In unappreciated ways, Fredrick Pike has astutely noted, the American loss of confidence in "uplifting" and assimilating the Indian may have contributed to its weakened resolve in carrying out a similar task in the hemisphere and seeking greater accommodation with its Latin American neighbors.[36]

In the political and economic turbulence of the 1930s, the place and reputation of the United States in the hemisphere remained an uncertainty. In 1936 — the year he won a resounding re-election victory — Franklin Roosevelt knew he could not reprise the role of hemispheric leader with the same bluster and resolve his distant cousin Theodore had demonstrated. But there was no doubting the growing threat to U.S. security and interests.

PART 3
The Global Crisis

5   A Hemisphere at War

In March 1933, when Franklin Roosevelt took the oath of office as the nation's thirty-second president, domestic, not hemispheric, issues dominated both his and the country's concerns. Within the first hundred days of his administration, he plunged into a fundamental reshaping of the role of the federal government in the economy. Yet, despite the understandable priorities of Depression politics, hemispheric issues increasingly distracted him. In the strategically important Caribbean and Central America, he continued the work of his Republican predecessor in dismantling the formal protectorate system, although his administration would do so in a manner that to some critics looked like a continuation of previous policies but in a different form. The arrogant character of imperial America remained, only now the United States had surrogates to keep law and order. With Mexico, formerly an alienated, revolutionary neighbor and hemispheric irritant to U.S. ambitions, the readjustment proved more problematic. In part, this stemmed from the determination of a nationalist president, Lázaro Cárdenas — the most radical of Mexico's leaders — to reaffirm the revolutionary promise by siding with labor in a bitter dispute with foreign oil concerns and peasants disgruntled over the failure of the government's agrarian policies. The decision put Mexico on a collision course with powerful U.S. interests, including religious leaders who condemned the government's anticlerical mission. Both looked to the Roosevelt administration for support.

In retrospect, it became apparent that what Cárdenas was doing replicated in essence what Roosevelt was doing — saving the capitalist system and asserting control over increasingly militant labor unions, although he was doing it in a manner more relevant to Mexico's one-party tradition. In 1938, when the Mexican crisis broke, Roosevelt had already confronted a challenge from a Panamanian government determined to renegotiate the despised 1903 canal treaty. But Panama proved to be a special case for the Roosevelt administration because of the canal and its critical role in the nation's economic and strategic planning. The canal was not only an economic lifeline; it also enabled the United States to get by without a two-ocean navy. But in 1935 the War Department further complicated matters with a sobering report that the U.S. Army could no longer defend this vital waterway with its land forces in the Canal Zone but would require air defense installations in the republic. The once-heralded limitations treaty signed by the great naval powers after World War I, which had presumably given the United States the ability to defend its security interests in the northern zone of the hemisphere, now seemed outmoded with the capability of an enemy to launch attacks against the canal from carrier-based aircraft.[1]

The Chaco War

Strategic matters complicated the ongoing negotiations over the canal, but these presumably could be dealt with through bilateral negotiations. The conflict between Bolivia and Paraguay over the Gran Chaco proved far more complicated and exasperating for the administration. It was one of three South American border wars that prompted U.S. diplomatic involvement in the 1930s, but it was by far the most serious. Not only was the Chaco a long way away, but in Southern Cone politics, Argentina, not the United States, was the power player in the 1930s.

The origins of this war lay in rival claims of two ambitious nations to a territory the size of Wyoming reaching from near the eastern Bolivian city of Santa Cruz to a point south of Asunción, the capital of Paraguay. Until the early twentieth century, the Bolivians largely ignored the Chaco, but soon afterward the government began to erect forts in areas claimed by the Paraguayans. The settlement of the Tacna-Arica dispute between Chile and Peru further complicated matters by ending Bolivia's hopes for a Pacific Ocean outlet, and the nation's leaders began to look more and more at the Chaco and a route into the La Plata River and the southern Atlantic. When fighting erupted between the two governments, the League of Nations intervened, a decision that irritated the United States and prompted Washington to organize its own multilateral negotiations. That effort in turn collapsed, largely because of Argentine opposition and the reality that the U.S. government possessed little more beyond moral persuasion to prevent a full-scale war.[2]

Argentina, not the United States, appeared to be the mediator of peace in the Southern Cone. In 1932, the year before the seventh inter-American meeting convened at Havana, a dispirited Brazil and Chile conceded to the Argentines the opportunity to decide whether there would be peace or war between Bolivia and Paraguay over the Gran Chaco. But not even the Argentines could prevent the outbreak of a war. The impoverished Bolivians, fired by an impulse to break out of their isolation by obtaining access to the Atlantic, unleashed their attack on underpopulated Paraguay in June 1932. Paraguay could not resist unless it had Argentine support; its status as an economic appendage of Argentina virtually assured that Buenos Aires had the power to determine whether the nationalistic Paraguayans would be victorious or suffer a humiliating defeat.

With diplomatic legerdemain the Argentine foreign minister, Carlos Saavedra Lamas, skillfully exploited this crisis, which rapidly escalated into a gruesome war, to achieve Argentine mastery over Southern Cone international politics. A few months after U.S. secretary of state Cordell Hull launched his trade program, the Argentines signed a commercial pact with the British, which provided Buenos Aires with an economic status roughly akin to a dominion in the empire. Saavedra Lamas publicized an antiwar treaty linked to the League of Nations. Then Argentina insinuated itself into command of a commission to mediate the Chaco dispute by obtaining a hastily arranged membership in the League of Nations, which meekly deferred to Buenos Aires' direction in the settlement. When the compliant Hull arrived in Montevideo, ready to yield on Latin American demands for an absolute prohibition on intervention, the Argentine press unleashed a virulent anti-American propaganda campaign. Saavedra Lamas was ingratiating: the United States and Argentina, the Argentine told his American counterpart, will "become the two wings of the dove, you the economic, and we the political."[3]

In reality the Argentines were carving out their own economic arrangements that defied Hull's reciprocity program, and Saavedra Lamas's cynical exploitation of Latin American and the League of Nations' despair over the Chaco soon made clear that there would be no peace between Paraguay and Bolivia unless the Argentines wanted it. The Brazilians complained of Argentine manipulation of the conflict; the Chileans, frustrated over their inability to support the ravaged Bolivians, blamed Buenos Aires for the failure of peaceful negotiations by the League. When the Chileans tried to negotiate a commercial treaty with Peru in the spirit of Hull's reciprocity program, the Argentines (who furnished 50 percent of Peru's wheat imports and stood to lose by the arrangement) vigorously complained. The U.S. government could not afford to offend Buenos Aires. The Bolivians finally grew so exhausted with their war that they were compelled to turn to Argentina, clearly the only country in the hemisphere that could determine peace in the Southern Cone.

Peace did not come in the Chaco until January 1936.[4] Although the Bolivian Indian conscripts fought well when the Paraguayans had pushed eastward and threatened the oil fields, in the July 1935 truce Paraguay gained 90 percent of the disputed territory. The combined death toll was heavy: a hundred thousand lives, the hemisphere's deadliest conflict since the U.S. Civil War. Throughout, the Americans had yielded to Argentina as the political arbiter in the Southern Cone and had gotten little in return. With Hull his most enthusiastic supporter for the honor, Saavedra Lamas was accorded the Nobel Peace Prize. In the meantime the Argentine economy, fueled by a 150 percent increase of its exports to the United States (which was unable to break the 12.5 percent duty on American products entering Argentina) prospered while that of its South American neighbors stagnated. The docile Peruvians had to accept Argentine wheat on the same terms as Chilean or pay a hefty surcharge for selling its petroleum to Buenos Aires. From Washington came praise for the Argentine success in bringing peace to the Southern Cone and recognition of its economic accomplishments in the face of adversity. As the encomiums poured forth, the Argentines ordered seven warships from Great Britain. Saavedra Lamas was named president of the League Assembly and at the direction of Adolf Hitler received the Star of the German Red Cross for his labors in settling the Gran Chaco War.

Despite the Argentine diplomatic triumph over the United States and its defiance of Hull's trade program, Washington persisted in wooing Latin America to the Good Neighbor policy. Roosevelt himself led the diplomatic challenge at the Conference for the Maintenance of Peace, which convened in Buenos Aires in late 1936. The president sailed for the meeting aboard a U.S. warship — not as conqueror but as the true good neighbor who had purged U.S. policy in the hemisphere of its odious tradition of interventionism and dollar diplomacy. He was saluted everywhere. Stopping in Rio de Janeiro he was greeted by schoolchildren waving the American flag and singing the U.S. national anthem. Getúlio Vargas, who in the following year announced the "New State" in Brazil (which to democrats bore an unsettling similarity to European fascism), declared a national holiday to honor Roosevelt. The Brazilian leader further pleased Washington by naming the pro-American Oswaldo Aranha as ambassador to the United States.[5]

Not to be outdone, the Argentines promptly followed with their own national holiday to commemorate their distinguished visitor. Roosevelt and Hull reaffirmed the commitment of the United States to absolute nonintervention, and the Latin American delegates cheered the "Pan-Americanization" of the Monroe Doctrine. Then they promptly followed the Argentines in demurring on any strong commitment to bind the hemispheric republics in an alliance against German penetration. Spruille Braden, U.S. ambassador to Argentina, was so irritated with the intransigent Saavedra Lamas that he personally appealed to the Argentine president, General Augustín B. Justo. But Saavedra Lamas had the satisfaction of final defiance. He not only torpedoed Hull's laborious efforts at the conference but also submitted to the secretary of state a parting indignity by declining to say good-bye when the American delegation left for Washington. From that moment, Hull remained convinced the Argentines would obstruct U.S. efforts to obtain a hemispheric security agreement.[6]

Defining the Hemispheric Threat

In this and other experiences with Latin America in the coming years the U.S. government learned a painful reality about what can happen to a dominating power that with considerable publicity alters its interventionist habits in the affairs of its more vulnerable neighbors. Anticipating a menace to U.S. security in what they believed was Latin America's vulnerability to European fascism, U.S. diplomats ventured into these conferences calling for hemispheric unity to confront what they deemed a threat. But Latin American leaders intellectually disposed to the notion of the "organic" or "corporate" state — in which the government served not as "broker" but as unifier (and dominator) of the nation's diverse social, political, and economic sectors — the German and Italian examples were inspirational. But until the fall of France and the Low Countries in summer 1940 (which signaled a German opportunity to acquire the West Indian dependencies of the defeated countries) U.S. protestations about the "fascist menace" fell largely on Latin American governments more concerned about maintaining their economic links with Europe. The United States had necessarily chosen economic nationalism in 1933, Latin American leaders contended, and so, too, must they.[7]

Germany, Italy, and Japan no doubt posed a threat, but to most of Latin America the more visible peril was American meddling or hypocritical preachments of economic liberalism in an era when their European connections offered more immediate economic rewards. U.S. diplomats extolled the "democracies" of the hemisphere, but the political fear they harbored was a string of republics stretching from Mexico to Argentina, with governments that they believed too closely resembled (in content if not in form) the authoritarian regimes of Italy and Germany.

Authoritarian governments in Latin America were, of course, not entirely repugnant to U.S. leaders, especially if they offered a realistic alternative to the uncertainties of the revolutionary nationalism that had exploded in Cuba in 1933. The danger lay in the obstacles to Washington's efforts to solidify the republics in a common defensive network posed by regimes wary of American intentions and presumably responsive to aggressive German economic and political overtures. By the time the eighth Pan-American conference met at Lima in 1938, Germany had mounted an impressive trade program in the hemisphere that had brought about political dividends. The Third Reich had not only recovered to the levels of Germany's pre–World War I trade with Latin America but had become a more important supplier than Britain. German firms, relative newcomers, were less resented in those countries where the British had long been accustomed to dealing with their Latin American customers in a domineering fashion. Even in Central America, for years under the political shadow of American power, German economic penetration (especially in Guatemala and Costa Rica) had achieved impressive levels.

The United States associated the surge of German commerce (and of the Japanese in Ecuador and Peru) with a more vigorous German cultural and political pressure. German settlers who lived in Chile's southern frontier had their own schools that were, the government presumed, vulnerable to German propaganda. Across the Andes, the British reach still prevailed, but throughout the Southern Cone the Germans had made great headway. The German colony in Buenos Aires numbered 250,000, and although it was not united in its support of German ambitions in Argentina, it was viewed by the Auslandsorganisation (the network of German nationals in foreign countries) as a useful political and cultural tool for German interests. Argentines were alert to the danger of foreign ideologies, whether of the Right or Left: the government outlawed the Communist Party. When Nazi agents began circulating among the German community urging the teaching of Nazi propaganda and the Nazi salute in the schools, resentful Argentines called for an investigation. In 1939 they heard frightful (and untrue) stories about a German conspiracy to seize Patagonia. Under public pressure the government outlawed the Nazi Party, but another German organization rose in its place. Argentina's strong economic ties with Germany dictated a policy of accommodation, not confrontation. When hostilities commenced in Europe in September 1939, Argentine president Robert Ortiz voiced tentative support for the Allies, but many in the nation's foreign policy bureaucracy perceived such sentiments as an indirect approval of U.S. designs for domination of the inter-American system.[8]

In the Brazilian south the German population reached almost a million, of whom a tenth were alleged to be Nazis — ready, it was presumed, to advance the German cause in South America's largest nation. Vargas, who had seized power in 1930 to protest against a stolen election, perceived enemies on both the Left and the Right. After a failed communist revolution in November 1935, Vargas instituted a state of siege and gradually eroded the power of the National Congress. By 1937 he was ready to do away with the legislature altogether. Proclaiming the New State (Estado Novo), a Brazilian variation of fascism, he dispatched "interventors" into the Brazilian states and banned political parties. In Washington there circulated fearful rumors of a German fifth column in Brazil, sustained by the Integralistas, a movement organized in 1932 by a novelist and political ideologue, Plinio Salgado. Quite unexpectedly, the Integralistas attempted a coup in May 1938, surrounding the national palace. Vargas managed to hold them off until troops arrived. The Integralistas spoke of "Brazil for the Brazilians," as did Vargas, who more than Salgado expressed his displeasure over German efforts to divide the loyalties of Germans living in the Estado Novo and undertook repressive measures against political and cultural organizations with foreign connections. He closed German schools and commanded his soldiers, armed with German-made weapons and trained in the German tradition by German-speaking officers, to speak Portuguese. Thousands of Germans departed for the fatherland, but Vargas did not sever the German supply line of Krupp arms.[9]

How did Roosevelt perceive the ominous warnings from the south about the Nazi menace? There was no dearth of sensational literature, from both American and Latin American writers, about the German intrusions. The writer Carleton Beals (who had been the bane of American interventionists in Nicaragua in 1927), with predictable but credible hyperbole, warned in *The Coming Struggle for Latin America* that the continent was awash in fascism. Only a U.S. government sufficiently committed to social justice for Latin America's downtrodden could hold back the German tide. Within the State Department, Beals was largely written off as an alarmist, but not just a few of the department's hemispheric observers, including Adolf Berle, were issuing similar warnings to Roosevelt. Ironically, as the U.S. government grimly assessed the Nazi penetration in the hemisphere, the German foreign office had come to similarly morose judgments about the American challenge to German ambitions in Latin America. The Nazi ambassador to Argentina was called to Berlin, was informed that the German image in Latin America had suffered from its high visibility, and returned to Buenos Aires with a stern message for the Auslandsorganisation minions.[10]

More disquieting for Roosevelt were stories emanating from Latin American capitals about German sympathy among the *nacistas* of Chile, who, in an especially bitter political campaign in 1938, attempted to overthrow the conservative government of Arturo Alessandri. When the Integralist putsch failed in Brazil, it was widely believed, the German agents shifted their attention to Chile. The rebels took control of two government buildings and called for help from Chileans fearful that Alessandri would choose his successor. Alessandri's troops brutally crushed the uprising, and the vengeful president ordered sixty-two of the rebels executed. His reaction probably guaranteed the victory of the Popular Front candidate a short time later.[11]

This and other dreary tales about the precarious state of Latin American democracy, coupled with credible warnings about German political opportunism, inspired reassessments about the place of the hemisphere in American strategy. What elevated Latin America to a position of high priority among policymakers was the certainty with which Americans professed their determination to avoid involvement in another European war—even during the tense days of the Sudeten crisis—but their obvious willingness to shore up American security in the Western Hemisphere. In *The Ramparts We Watch*, Major George Fielding Eliot wrote confidently that Britain, France, and the Soviet Union could deter Germany in central Europe, but fascism, soon to be installed with Francisco Franco's triumph in Spain, would spread to Portugal, then across the Atlantic, and ultimately corrode the political cultures of Latin America. That notion was farfetched, admittedly, but it carried sufficient credibility to inspire the analysts in the War Department to amplify their requests for defense sites in Panama with scenarios about fifth columnists and saboteurs and the vulnerability of the canal to attack from aircraft carriers at sea. Indeed, the U.S. Senate's growing concern about the military threat in the isthmus explained its three-year delay in approving the 1936 canal treaty.[12]

The Mexican oil expropriation crisis, which had begun earlier in the year with the decision of the Lázaro Cárdenas government to nationalize foreign oil properties (mostly British and American), now assumed strategic importance. In the beginning, Cordell Hull, reinforced by an outraged British government, had put heavy pressure on the Mexican government to make a settlement agreeable to the companies. Confronting the harsh rhetoric from the north, Cárdenas resisted. When the Americans and British refused to buy or transport Mexican oil, he struck a deal with the Germans (who privately regarded him as a socialist and an enemy of the Reich but nonetheless sensed an opportunity to undermine American interests) to exchange oil for aircraft. From Mexico City, Josephus Daniels, Roosevelt's boss in the Wilson administration and now his ambassador, toned down the abusive instructions coming from Hull—and thereby risked being recalled. Secretary of the Treasury Henry Morgenthau Jr. apparently persuaded the president that strategic interests in Mexico were being jeopardized.

By the time the foreign ministers met at Lima later in the year, Hull had acquiesced in Cárdenas's decision not to meet the companies' demands. Cárdenas, too, softened his criticism of his northern neighbor. Although at the Lima conference Mexico reaffirmed its commitment to nonintervention, the continuing antigovernment violence in the countryside and the rise of the conservative National Action Party meant that Mexico could ill afford to risk alienating the United States or pursue a similar course to that chosen by Carranza in World War I. Roosevelt sensed Cárdenas's dilemma and responded by supporting the 1940 government candidate (Manuel Ávila Camacho) in one of Mexico's most corrupt presidential elections.[13]

Roosevelt dared not challenge the isolationists and their determination to keep the United States out of European conflict, but he accurately sensed the insecurity the country felt about its position in the Western Hemisphere. The Munich crisis did not dispel isolationist sentiment, but fear of German penetration in Latin America provided a credible rationale for undertaking more ambitious defensive policies with the other American republics. The grander design, which Adolf Berle called the "north-south axis," anticipated not only economic but political commitments — the first designed to knit the hemisphere in commercial and investment ties and the second, equally vital, to sustain vulnerable governments from the powerful influences of pro-Axis movements. There must be no Axis undermining of Latin America, Berle said, by a fascist Trojan horse. On the eve of the Lima conference, scheduled to meet in December 1938 in a country with strong ties to Benito Mussolini's Italy and newly signed commercial pacts with Germany, the Division of the American Republics in the State Department grimly anticipated more troubles from pro-German elements everywhere in Latin America.

Roosevelt's detractors, predictably, and even some of his defenders have portrayed these frenzied political efforts in the inter-American system in the years before World War II as yet another example of duplicity in his approach to the global crisis. Clearly, Roosevelt exploited the apprehension about German intrigue in the hemisphere, and certainly Hull realized that a policy of globalism stood no chance against the entrenched strength of isolationism unless the United States followed the hemispheric defensive strategy Roosevelt's military advisers now advocated. As in the first two decades of the twentieth century, when German imperial ambitions in the Western Hemisphere, particularly in the Caribbean and Mexico, appeared more a menace to American interests than subsequent analyses revealed, so did Washington's interpretations of Hitler's intentions perhaps exaggerate Germany's capabilities to undermine Latin American governments. But the cumulative impact of irrefutable statistics of German and Italian economic and military ties with Latin American governments coupled with the undeniable philosophical appeal of corporatism (the euphemistic name for the political and economic structure that fascism and Nazism symbolized) made for a disturbing assessment of the Latin American condition in the aftermath of the Munich crisis and the prospect of a Falangist victory in Spain. Hitler was a continentalist, but he was determined to restore German influence in the world. The conquest of South America, he told a confidant, would not require German troops but could be attained on the strength of German settlers, the better social classes, and fifth columnists.[14]

The thought may have been fanciful, but analyses of Berlin's limitations in Latin America could not dispel the data about German influence, which the old Wilsonian secretary of state perceived as conspiracy. Arriving in Lima, he became alarmed when he heard that German agents and Italian propagandists had already implanted stories of the threat to Latin America's "Latin and Mediterranean conscience" by this emissary from the north. There was a palpable cultural slant to the proceedings. On the opening day of the conference, José María Cantino, the Argentine foreign minister, paid faint praise to hemispheric unity, then proudly reaffirmed, "If to the mother country [Spain, Portugal, or England] we owe the basis of our literature, then to French culture we owe the basic formation of our intellectual life, and to Italy and Germany all the vital aspects of our evolution." Then he departed, delegating responsibility to an underling and leaving Hull again infuriated at the craftiness of Argentine diplomacy and the American entourage fearful of being isolated in a hemisphere the United States was striving to unite.[15]

Sumner Welles, left behind because he tended to dominate in negotiations with Latin Americans, had argued that if the United States must accept a less satisfactory hemispheric pact to get Argentina's participation, it should do so. Often in disagreement over tactics in hemispheric policy, Hull and Welles believed unanimity was upper-most in American strategy at Lima. The U.S. delegation, noticeably annoyed with Buenos Aires' refusal to break the European connection, confronted in the Mexican and Colombian governments a seemingly unshakable determination to defy the fascist menace with a unifying pact more provocative than Washington thought was necessary. In the end, Hull got less than he wanted, but the U.S. delegation went home with the satisfaction that the Declaration of Lima, which extolled "continental solidarity" and promised "consultation" in the event of a threat to it, had been approved by all the republics. Samuel Guy Inman, who had brought to the inter-American cultural program and the Good Neighbor policy the missionary's zeal, proudly declared that the Monroe Doctrine had now been Pan-Americanized into a "fighting platform for American democracy."[16]

In truth, the "platform," like the dream of hemispheric unity, was more a spiritual than a tangible military foundation — but at least it was a beginning in the American determination to confront the European threat by following a Latin route.

The outbreak of World War II in Europe in September 1939 enabled the United States to accomplish in Latin America what intervention and a vigorous expansion of the American export economy had failed to achieve — the incorporation of the hemisphere into its global strategy. In mid-1939, on the eve of Hitler's attack on Poland, the Roosevelt administration had not broken the transatlantic cultural and economic bonds between South America and European fascism. In the inter-American political arena, U.S. diplomats had wavered under Argentine determination to prevent a stronger declaration at Lima, and Hull's spirited promotion of American exports had not shaken South America's faith in its own credos of economic nationalism.

Even the larger South American republics, traditionally resentful of U.S. pretensions, perceived the need to oblige Washington, principally for economic reasons. At Panama, where the foreign ministers convened only a few weeks after the outbreak of hostilities in Europe, the U.S. delegation reaffirmed U.S. intentions to aid the republics in overcoming the debilitating economic impact of ruptures in hemispheric trade with Europe. They adopted Roosevelt's notion of a hemispheric "safety belt," an imaginary (and indefensible) line three hundred miles outside the United States and Latin America, and forbade the European belligerents from waging war inside the "neutral" hemispheric waters. Most considered the safety belt unenforceable and even laughable but recognized that economic exigencies warranted their acquiescence. They renewed their efforts for an inter-American development bank, which the State Department pledged to take up with the Inter-American Financial and Advisory Committee. The committee dispensed questionnaires and by May 1940, despite some reservations about their ability to help fund the bank, eight of the republics had signed the charter. When the administration went to Congress for funding, however, it encountered strong opposition from conservatives, who saw the bank as a competitor to private banks.

American economic strategists were now arguing that the outbreak of war in Europe dictated a shift away from Hull's free trade philosophy and toward a hemispheric economic policy that reinforced American security. The Export-Import Bank, not the reciprocal trade program idealized a few years before, charted the nation's course in a world economy in which the Wilsonian ideal of free trade, a policy of dubious success in a world economy devastated by the Depression, now was imperiled by war. In the two years of hemispheric neutrality, the U.S. government had placed far greater emphasis on stockpiling strategic materials, withholding vital supplies from export, and attaching political stipulations to its loan and investment policies for Latin America. From 1938 to 1940, Latin America not only lost much of its trade with continental Europe but found itself locked out of the British imperial economy. Latin Americans bought from Americans at less competitive prices; they sold to Americans at lower prices. In these two years, the United States increased its imports of Latin American products by 37 percent and its exports to the hemisphere by 45 percent. When U.S. representatives proposed an inter-American trading corporation to act as purchaser of Latin American products for resale in Europe, the larger countries of South America, led by the defiant Argentines, resisted the plan as yet another effort to subordinate the Latin American economies to the United States.[17]

The European belligerents promptly violated the Panama safety belt in a dramatic and potentially dangerous naval battle between three British warships and the German pocket battleship *Graf Spee* off Uruguay in late 1939. The commander of the German ship took refuge in Montevideo, Uruguay, but was ordered out of the port by the Uruguayan government. Rather than do battle with the pursuing British ships, he scuttled his ship in international waters. Argentina took his crew in internment. Throughout the Americas the incident demonstrated the vulnerability of the Southern Cone and the inability of the U.S. Navy to safeguard hemispheric waters.

The following June, when the fall of France precipitated yet another hemispheric crisis, Roosevelt had already resolved to press the issue of hemispheric security, but the American public and the U.S. military were more concerned with the Caribbean, where the northern republics of Latin America had become alarmed over German submarine patrols and the disquieting prospect that France and the Netherlands, now under German domination, would cede their Caribbean possessions to the Fuehrer. Among the U.S. military the need to acquire bases in Panama, which a nationalistic government under Arnulfo Arias was resisting, became necessary to safeguard the canal, and in the War Department arguments for defense facilities in Venezuela, the Dominican Republic, Colombia, and Brazil were strengthened. Frank Knox, a Republican critic of the president, who joined the cabinet as secretary of the navy in these troublesome days, had earlier advocated seizure of the European possessions in the West Indies to prevent their falling under German control and for safeguarding the Panama Canal. The Army-Navy Joint Board confirmed the recommendation in its Rainbow 4 Plan.[18]

In July 1940 the foreign ministers convened again at Havana. The discussions were more somber, the resolution to protect the vulnerable European possessions from German control more determined. Still, as in earlier Pan-American meetings, the Latin Americans were seemingly more concerned with traditional national interests than with hemispheric unity. In the United States fretful observers called for seizure of Europe's hemispheric possessions. The British, responding to a Dutch appeal, landed marines in Aruba and Curaçao to shield Dutch oil facilities that suffered attacks from German squads. Already the U.S. Congress, echoing an 1811 resolution that had prohibited the transfer of Spanish Florida to another European power, resolved not to recognize the transfer of any European colony in the West Indies to Germany and empowered Roosevelt to enforce it. When the German foreign office denigrated the resolution, the State Department responded with an even broader commitment to a Pan-Americanized Monroe Doctrine. Again, the Latin Americans exacted their price for acquiescing in American strategic priorities. Guatemala, Venezuela, and, especially, Argentina (which had claims on British Honduras, British Guiana, and the Falklands, respectively) wanted special consideration for their support. Eventually they gave in when Hull pledged to meet their peculiar economic needs with Export-Import Bank loans. Under pressure the Argentines had capitulated but not without grumbling about renewed U.S. penetration of the Caribbean. Even so, the pro-Nazi government in Vichy, France, so alarmed the U.S. military with its yielding to German pressures that Secretary of the Navy Knox recommended seizure of the French West Indies, which the Act of Havana, if broadly interpreted, permitted. As things worked out, French officials in the West Indies, recognizing the vulnerability of the islands, declared their neutrality and thus avoided American occupation.[19]

These moves, however, did not necessarily mean that the Roosevelt administration had committed itself to the notion of a fortified hemisphere isolated from the European conflict. In fact, Canada's declaration of war against Germany had prompted reminders of Roosevelt's statement during the fall 1938 Munich crisis that the United States could not be indifferent to any threat to Canada from a European power. By the 1931 Statute of Westminster, each British dominion had the constitutional right of neutrality, but Canadian prime minister William Lyon Mackenzie King had skillfully mobilized a pro-war vote seven days after London's declaration. The delay permitted Canada to obtain much-needed military supplies from its southern neighbor before U.S. neutrality laws took effect.

The fall of France effectively ended U.S. neutrality. In August 1940 Roosevelt negotiated a deal with Churchill that gave the British fifty destroyers in return for long-term leases to British installations from Trinidad in the West Indies to Newfoundland, which the Canadians desperately wanted to incorporate as a tenth province. In the same month Roosevelt and Mackenzie King declared a de facto alliance in Ogdensburg, New York, only a short distance from Canadian soil and in the presence of six U.S. Army divisions. At the time, most Canadian defense forces were in Britain and thus Canada was vulnerable to a German invasion, but Mackenzie King and his military staff resolutely refused to bring them home. To deal with his predicament, Roosevelt proposed a Permanent Joint Board of Defense to shield the northern half of the hemisphere. Prime Minister Winston Churchill and Roosevelt had fashioned a historic personal bond, but Roosevelt had not bothered to inform his British ally of the details of the pact until the deed was done. When Churchill learned what Mackenzie King had agreed to, he was taken aback, but the Canadian had taken the only action available to enable his country to defend the empire. It was a lesson about their security in the Western Hemisphere the British could not stomach, but they had to digest it.[20]

World War II

The Japanese attack on Pearl Harbor did not elicit a commitment to a hemispheric defensive alliance. Washington entered the war largely with the same hemispheric allies that had signed on to its World War I crusade to make the world safe for democracy. On the same day (8 December 1941) that Roosevelt spoke of a "day of infamy," Guatemala, Costa Rica, Honduras, El Salvador, Haiti, the Dominican Republic, and Panama declared war on Japan and, a few days later, joined by Cuba and Nicaragua, on Germany and Italy. But on the South American mainland there was hesitation: Colombia and Venezuela broke diplomatic relations, and the other republics, reluctant to offend the Axis powers without the reassuring presence of U.S. or British naval protection, maintained a discreet neutrality. When the foreign ministers gathered at Rio de Janeiro in January, Welles pressed the case for severance of diplomatic relations as the only effective means for harassed governments to deal with German subversives. The Colombians, Mexicans, and Venezuelans supported the American proposal, but, as before, the Argentines were predictably hesitant, and the Chileans demurred on the credible grounds of their vulnerability to Japanese naval supremacy in the Pacific and the inability of the Americans to safeguard their long coastline. In the end, despite Hull's wishes for harsher pressures on the recalcitrant Argentines, Welles retreated, accepting a resolution that recommended rather than demanded a severance of relations. But the diplomatic battle triumphed in other ways; before the conference ended Brazil, Paraguay, Ecuador, Uruguay, Bolivia, and Peru severed relations with the three Axis countries.

The Good Neighbor at war strived to forge a unified hemisphere out of countries with seemingly disparate cultures and political traditions. Philanthropic endeavors of the 1920s were transmuted into formal programs in the Division of Cultural Affairs of the Department of State, whose ideologues (some of them harsh critics of gunboat diplomacy in the old days) now spoke of understanding and the bonds of democracies at war. In the Office of the Coordinator of Inter-American Affairs, a budget that escalated from $3.5 to $38 million in two years enabled its energetic chief, Nelson Rockefeller, to launch a highly publicized propaganda campaign of "America for the Americas" to combat Nazi subversives, extend U.S. technical assistance, discourage revolutions, and expand American exports. The true believers — like Inman, the former missionary, and the disciples of the historian Herbert Bolton, who had spoken so eloquently of the "epic of Greater America" and a unified Western Hemisphere — sensed no insurmountable obstacles in the path of cultural unity. Others, such as Samuel Flagg Bemis, who published his *Latin American Policy of the United States* in 1943, and the Yale political scientist Nicholas Spykman, who startled the hemispheric unionists with his *America's Strategy in World Politics*, were politely disdainful of the prospects for a defensive alliance built on cultural sympathy rather than the realities of international politics.

American rhetoric, expressed in radio transmissions, advertisements in pro-American newspapers, slick publications such as *On Guard*, movies and cartoons geared to a Latin American audience, and the description of the Monroe Doctrine as a statement of collective hemispheric defense, among other things, conveyed one message to Latin Americans. But U.S. actions, it was alleged by formerly critical observers such as the Peruvian Haya de la Torre, gave quite another view of American intentions. To counter German military influence in the hemisphere, particularly in South America, Washington increased the number of its military missions from a paltry five in 1938 to one in each of the republics two years later. In 1940 the War Department expended $500 million on the program. Junior Latin American officers were trained "in the American way" in the United States, and the Latin American militaries began receiving war materiel at cost before Lend-Lease became law. The goal was not only to discourage Latin American military ties to Europe but to validate American purpose in the defense of democracy and the belief that a modernized Latin American military could more ably confront the inner menace of Nazi agitators and fifth columnists. The legacy, though unintended by the U.S. government, was to reinforce the strength of the Latin American military as a political instrument.[21]

Dictators lined up with the United States in defending democracy in a totalitarian world, and in their own countries they permitted U.S. agents to fashion counterespionage networks and cracked down on Germans, some of whom were guilty of nothing except being German. Throughout the Caribbean — an important theater of war because of German submarine attacks on Allied shipping — Mexico, and Central America, entire economies were drawn into the wartime economy of the United States. American health and sanitation officials and engineers descended on the republics to combat disease, lay sewage lines, and construct roads — probably the most significant accomplishment of U.S. proconsuls in the tropics earlier in the century. The war effort required agricultural and industrial labor, and throughout the circum-Caribbean and in Mexico and even in South America hundreds of thousands supplied it. Monocultural economies lost their European markets for sugar, coffee, and bananas; Americans bought those items. When their productive energies went into vital products and they could not grow enough food for their population, the United States provided it. When their country people began drifting in from the outback to the cities looking for work and were unable to find it, U.S. emissaries promoted public works programs to employ them and urged the extension of the vote to instill the American conception of "democracy." In Brazil, America's most important wartime ally, the United States helped build Volta Redonda, the steel mill symbolizing the Brazilian industrial future, just as in Mexico it provided economic sustenance for the future Mexican steel industry at Monclava.

As part of its wartime goal of stemming German influence in the Americas, the United States followed an aggressive policy against German expatriates on the sometimes questionable grounds that most were spies, saboteurs, or Axis sympathizers. The State Department pressured Latin American governments to deport targeted Germans back to Germany or on to the United States. Some were interned; others were exchanged for U.S. citizens held by the German government. Still others were farmed out in work programs, some of them in defense plants. Those who managed to avoid deportation or internment from their Latin American homes suffered deprivation of civil rights or lost their properties.[22]

The smaller countries rushed to acknowledge their commitment to the American hemisphere by declaring war, but the larger countries — Mexico and all South America — hesitated. Willing to break diplomatic relations, they were reluctant to plunge into the global struggle with a U.S. government unable — or unwilling — to accommodate their priorities. Mexico hesitated until the sinking of a Mexican vessel off Florida unleashed an outburst of anti-German sentiment and gave the Avila Camacho government an excuse. With the declaration of war Mexican authorities "intervened" in German (and later, Italian and Japanese) businesses, cracked down on German social clubs, and used the outpouring of antifascist sentiment to smash the Sinarquistas in central Mexico. Even the Mexican Left, symbolically represented by former president Lázaro Cárdenas and the chieftain of Mexican labor, Vicente Lombardo Toledano, joined in the government's program to unite Mexico with the Allied cause. Mexico supplied vital raw materials, dispatched an air unit to the Philippines, and demanded (and ultimately received) sufficient economic and technical assistance to facilitate the Mexican economic miracle of the postwar era. Under a 1942 *bracero* agreement, Mexican agricultural laborers worked on U.S. farms, on the railroads, and in industrial plans. A quarter of a million Mexicans served in the U.S. military; almost 15,000, in a war theater. Economic bonds were strengthened. As the Mexican foreign minister attested, the nation's northern frontier became "a line that unites rather than divides us."[23]

But the social price was high: Mexican productivity was geared to the American economy, and the prices for consumer goods and foodstuffs escalated by 400 percent from 1939 until the last year of the war. By then the urban population confronted serious shortages of even basic foodstuffs, and a black market expanded in such items as coffee, fruit, and vegetables. Wages rose, but prices outstripped them. All told, Mexico's participation in the war accelerated the nation's industrial growth, tripled national income, and laid the foundation for a modern economy and nation no Mexican visionary of the Porfiriato could have imagined. But the achievement of these goals came at a price: the denial of the revolutionary promise of emancipation from the U.S. economic grip.[24]

Mexican leaders had made their choice, for better or for worse. So, too, did the Brazilians. Vargas, the "proto-fascist," as a few American cynics called the Brazilian leader, broke diplomatic relations with the Axis but stopped short of declaring war. Brazil, Vargas told confidants, would "stand or fall" with Washington. He began cracking down on German aliens, disbanded the remaining German social and political clubs, and closed German schools.

Though Brazilians grumbled about obnoxious U.S. servicemen and the tightening economic grip of Washington, Vargas cleverly exploited Hull's scarcely disguised hostility to the Argentines and demanded greater amounts of military aid. And despite Washington's hesitation in accepting Brazilian troops for the European campaign (lest the other South American countries demand equal treatment, thus necessitating an even larger dispersal of vital war equipment), the Brazilian generals, declaring that they did not intend to be "spectators," pressed for a direct role in the crusade against fascism and dispatched troops for the Italian campaign. Brazil as a participant, Vargas realized, augured well for its future international status.[25]

The war fundamentally altered U.S.-Canadian relations, yet in sometimes subtle ways the experience deepened Canadian resentments about the American presence. Mackenzie King had angered Canadian nationalists by signing the Ogdensburg agreement, but to these critics he rightfully responded that he had no realistic alternative for protecting the nation. After Pearl Harbor, however, he was relegated to a secondary and even tertiary role in Joint Allied planning. Reluctantly, he agreed to put Canadian forces under U.S. command if North America came under attack. On the other hand, the two governments did cooperate in the development of nuclear weapons and in petroleum development, for in both the United States depended heavily on Canadian resources. Canadian officials also acquiesced to U.S. pressure to construct the 1,500-mile Alcan Highway linking Alaska to the lower forty-eight states. At war's end, Canada paid for the road and other U.S. installations. By most economic measures, admittedly, Canada benefited. In early 1944 the two missions created in 1927 were elevated to embassy status. Not surprisingly, some U.S. observers sarcastically identified Canada as the "49th economic state," but such comments belied fundamental differences. If the United States became more so a "melting pot" during the war, Canada remained a distinctive mosaic. Where the U.S. cultural presence seemed overbearing, as in the behavior of U.S. military personnel, Canadians (like the British and the West Indians, too) expressed their displeasure.[26]

Under American prodding the other South American republics — except Argentina — fell into line. Midway in the war it had become obvious to most of them that breaking diplomatic relations with the Axis countries was insufficient if they were to play a role in the collective alliance of antifascist belligerents fashioned in 1942 and in shaping the peace. Venezuela concluded a peaceful adjustment with the oil companies that differed significantly from the Mexican example and declared war, contributing its vital petroleum to the Allied cause. Colombia had less oil to contribute, but since 1939 (when the government had rid its airlines of German, Italian, and Austrian nationals), it had, like Venezuela, identified with the United States. After Pearl Harbor, the U.S. military had access to strategic sites in the country. When the Germans sank several Colombian vessels in late 1943, the government declared a state of belligerency and formally adhered to the United Nations. U.S. officials expressed skepticism about the sympathies of populist president Isaías Medina Angarita for the Allied cause, but after the Pearl Harbor attack he permitted the stationing of U.S. military personnel in the country.[27]

In Bolivia, Enrique Peñaranda, who ruled largely at the behest of traditional oligarchical interests, committed the country to war after a succession of agreements with Standard Oil (whose properties had been nationalized by a socialist military regime in 1937) and the Export-Import Bank. He was promptly tossed out in a "national socialist" coup headed by a discontented military officer, Gualberto Villaroel. Initially supported by the Revolutionary Nationalist Movement (MNR), a political faction considered as pro-fascist, Villaroel readily turned against the group in order to obtain U.S. recognition. Unlike many of his twentieth-century predecessors, he ran the Bolivian government without the approval of the tin barons, committed political heresy with fitful efforts to incorporate the abused indigenous population into national life, and tolerated the creation of a mine workers' union. His innovative politics proved to be his undoing, however. Outraged tin moguls fashioned a symbiotic opposition of right-wing and Stalinist parties in order to harass him. Saddled with a dispirited military unable to protect him, in July 1946 he was dragged from his office by rioters and hanged from a La Paz lamp post.[28]

In Washington (and elsewhere) it was generally assumed that the rightist coup in Bolivia was the work of the Argentines, who persisted in ignoring the declarations of the Rio conference, maintained their ties with Berlin, and casually tolerated a visible German presence in Buenos Aires. In neighboring Paraguay, General Higínio Morínigo, ruled in a scarcely disguised authoritarian state that was economically (and, it was alleged, politically) beholden to Argentina. Good Neighbor diplomats descended on Asunción with pledges of economic and military aid in the expectation that Morínigo could be weaned from his proto-fascist convictions. When the Brazilians joined in the overtures, the suspicious Argentines, ever alert to the dynamics of Southern Cone international politics, responded with their own commitments to the suddenly courted Paraguayans. Yet throughout the region the carrot-and-stick policies of Washington isolated the Argentines.[29]

In 1943 the wrath of Sumner Welles fell on Chile, whose government was accused of ignoring the resolutions of the Rio conference about cutting economic ties with the Axis and cracking down on German-owned businesses and Nazi propagandists. To the Chileans, the Germans were not goose-stepping Huns but the hardworking (and largely anti-Hitler) German farmers who had settled in the south. Under pressure to fall in line, the Chileans broke diplomatic relations with no strong intention to go further, but in late 1944 came the unsettling announcement (provoked, it was said, by Soviet insistence) from Washington that only belligerents could take part in the forthcoming United Nations conference. In early 1945 the "associated states" of Ecuador, Peru, Venezuela, Uruguay, Paraguay, and Chile, unwilling to risk U.S. disfavor, declared war.[30]

Argentina now stood alone. After the Rio conference it had defied Washington by maintaining its ties to Germany. Brazil proved far more accommodating to Washington's requests, and its military stockings were filled by the grateful Americans, who declared that a corresponding generosity for Buenos Aires would come only if Argentina severed its ties with the Axis. Pressed by a military that perceived him as vacillating, Argentine president Ramón Castillo promptly turned to Berlin. But it was not enough to satisfy the hardliners in uniform. In mid-1943 a military coup spearheaded by a rightist coalition, the Group of United Officers, drove Castillo from office. Its seizure of power commenced a three-year confrontation with the Americans that ultimately culminated in the political triumph of its leader, Juan Domingo Perón, in 1946. Castillo's war minister, General Pedro Ramírez, assuming executive power, dispatched a naval reserve officer to Germany to procure armaments. The emissary was arrested en route by the British and under questioning confessed he was a German spy. With this information and details of Argentine involvement in the Bolivian coup, Hull, ever determined to bring the Argentines to heel, increased the pressure on Buenos Aires. In January 1944 the embarrassed Argentines suddenly announced a break with Germany and Japan. The next month, Ramírez turned over the presidential seal to his vice-president, General Edelmiro Farrell.

Hull was not yet convinced of Argentine compliance. For a year Washington withheld diplomatic recognition on the grounds that Argentina's commitment to hemispheric unity against the Axis was shallow, prompting the Argentines to look again to the Germans for military supplies. By this time the Germans had little to provide. Hull remained unrelenting in his stalking of the recalcitrant Argentines, prompting increasingly vocal criticism (from the Latin Americanists within the department and from Welles, whom Hull had driven from power) and warnings that his policy of isolating Buenos Aires was harmful to hemispheric unity. But the secretary, reinforced by Berle, clung tenaciously to his charges of Argentine perfidy. When Buenos Aires appealed for understanding to the other Latin American governments, Hull publicly denounced Argentina for "openly and notoriously . . . giving affirmative assistance to the declared enemies of the United Nations."[31]

The Argentine plea did not go unheeded among other Latin American governments. Again, as in earlier inter-American confrontations, the Mexicans stepped into a bitter diplomatic battle between Washington and Buenos Aires. At the Inter-American Conference on Problems of War and Peace, which convened at Chapultepec Heights in Mexico City a month before Roosevelt died, the gestures of good neighborliness culminated in Argentina's declaration of war against the Axis. Argentina gained admission to the United Nations, American Lend-Lease supplies entered the country, and the Farrell-Perón coalition made concessions to hemispheric unity by blacklisting German firms. Most of the Latin American governments understood the Argentine position: they saw it as a reflection of political and economic reality. But the Americans remained unforgiving.[32]

A few months after Chapultepec, Spruille Braden, who had clashed with the Argentines before, publicly declared on his arrival in Buenos Aires as U.S. ambassador that his mission was to promote democracy in a putatively undemocratic state. He threw down the gauntlet to Perón, who had already announced for the presidency, by demanding surrender of the German assets in the country. Braden returned to Washington as assistant secretary of state, but he persisted in his verbal attacks, referring to Argentina as an "ex-enemy."

Perón retaliated with his own barrage in the Argentine press. It was a battle he won in 1946, after Braden had issued the tactless *Blue Book* detailing Argentine perfidy during the war. Perón's response was an ingenious appeal to Argentine nationalism: "Whom do you choose — Perón or Braden?"[33]

By then American priorities in Latin America had already begun to shift to Washington's global calculations. Roosevelt, who had spoken often of the Good Neighbor and "giving them a share," had altered the American image in the hemisphere, but the Good Neighbor policy indisputably expanded U.S. military influence in Latin America as the only realistic and politically acceptable way of defeating isolationism and bolstering American defense efforts. This meant, inevitably, that Latin Americans confronted political and economic realities seemingly beyond their control. As in the past, American security interests required stable governments; global economic patterns, disrupted by the war, meant dependence on the external market.

The Good Neighbor policy had sought to bridge the gap between North and South in the Americas and had succeeded in ameliorating their historically troubled diplomatic relations, forging economic bonds that had not existed before the war, and fashioning a cosmetic cultural understanding. The wartime alliance offered opportunity but required Latin America's accommodation to Washington's priorities. The United States provided loans and grants, bought strategic and surplus commodities, and tried to improve Latin American transportation, agriculture, and industry. Through financial agreements and technical assistance, Washington had shielded Latin America from some of the harsher impacts of the war. The balance sheet was uneven. The postwar Mexican economic miracle depended heavily on its wartime economic relationship with the United States; Mexican economic dependence has its origins in the same place. Brazil, Haiti, Bolivia, and Ecuador gained less from the American development projects than promised. Argentina fared better in the war, and its defiance of the United States is often cited as justifiable as a way to avoid economic dependence, yet in the postwar years the Argentine economic record was not as impressive as Brazil's or Mexico's.[34]

The Good Neighbor policy did not perish with Roosevelt, but the experience of war altered the nation's hemispheric priorities. As a geopolitical thinker, Spykman had insisted the part of the world that mattered politically, economically, and even culturally to the United States turned on an east-west, not a north-south, axis. Latin America, in this scheme, now seemed less vulnerable to a threat from abroad. Spykman was arguably correct about American global interests and Latin America's place in U.S. strategic thinking, but he and many other Americans profoundly underestimated the revolutionary potential latent in Latin America's political and social structure.

Lamentably, something else was lost in the triumph of democratic capitalism — the momentary vision of American intellectuals such as Waldo Frank of an inter-American harmony based on mutual respect of differing cultural identities. Hundreds of West Indian Canal Zone laborers, promised U.S. citizenship, had volunteered for military service. Thousands of Latin Americans had appeared at U.S. embassies to join America's struggle against the Axis. In the wartime alliance Americans found in the Latin American (largely Hispanic) sense of cultural preference — of friendship over work, of quality over productivity, of spiritual rather than material well-being — more admirable symbols. There was an innocence in this view, Fredrick Pike has observed, but the Americas, north and south, had profited, spiritually if not economically. In retrospect, such cultural bonds would have better served American interests in Latin America than Washington's future prescriptions for hemispheric unity.[35]

The Legacy of War

The United States emerged from World War II as the most visibly dominant economic and political power in the world. To wage the conflict that had brought this stupendous victory it had integrated Latin America into its global strategy. It had dealt with dictators and democrats, sometimes in a manner that displayed a preference for the former over the latter. It had challenged and defeated the German economic and political threat to its sway throughout the Americas, and it had cultivated a new image among Latin Americans. It had sought and largely achieved the integration of the Latin American economies into its international economic strategy. It had sought and largely achieved the dependence of the Latin American militaries on American tutelage of its officers. It had sought and largely achieved the creation of a postwar inter-American system that did not conflict with its global political strategy.

Yet for all these triumphs, the efforts to forge an American hemisphere of common political, economic, and cultural aspirations had already begun to disintegrate. Latin Americans expected a more just economic, social, and political order, but they could not agree on the means or, ultimately, on the social and political price they were willing to pay to achieve it. Awed by American power and material bounty, they retained traditional convictions that they were morally if not materially superior. Their wartime ally both attracted and repelled them. The country they had once condemned as a predator had gone to war against predatory fascism in the service of humanity. With an unexpected generosity it had shared its scientific and medical knowledge to assist ravaged peoples, had linked isolated communities throughout the Americas, and in these and other tasks had conveyed that Yankee enthusiasm for getting things done — all without the inspiration of the profit motive. But often Latin American wartime visitors to the United States, overwhelmed by the factory transformed into an arsenal, were taken aback by American superficiality, conformity, and stultifying lifestyle. And in Latin America, the Yankee too often exhibited the worst characteristics of the intruder who believes the only things that count are those that can be counted. The wartime experience had thus produced cultural shock, which required adjusting to the trappings of the modern society America symbolized. For the United States, the experience of the war had transformed the country from a regional into a world power and in the process altered American thinking about the place of Latin America and Canada in its postwar calculations.

What hemispheric leaders wanted after the war was development, which the United States applauded but would neither adequately sustain nor safeguard against American economic penetration or the uncertainties of a world market. At the Chapultepec conference, called at the urging of the Mexicans to reconcile the Argentine and U.S. governments, the U.S. delegates extolled the United Nations while the Latin Americans spoke about their preferences for a regional system to safeguard the peace and address their economic problems. In what the Americans regarded as a concession, the hemispheric alliance was validated in Articles 51 and 52 of the UN Charter. Of equal concern to the Latin American delegates was their own economic charter. A State Department official had forthrightly expressed the justice of their case: "We asked for and obtained the help of Latin America in the prosecution of the war — Latin America will ask, and we must give, help in the transition from war to peace."[36]

The high expectations Latin Americans had developed during the war meant that the cost of postwar aid was not only high but, more important, beyond the ability of the United States, given its global commitments, to offer. Latin Americans had suffered economic deprivation during the war; they believed American commitments of postwar assistance would not only be honored but channeled according to their developmental preferences. American assistance had been critical: bereft of a world market for their primary products, they had found in the United States a purchaser at a guaranteed price. They had built up huge dollar reserves ($4.4 billion in foreign reserves) and an unsatisfied appetite for American consumer goods. Now, at war's end, they believed the relationship must continue. In the inter-American system lay their best prospect for catching up with the industrial nations of the north and escaping the nineteenth-century economic order that still encumbered the republics. Latin America could do so only with massive credit and assistance. Instead it encountered a postwar United States that raised prices for its commodity exports and devalued the dollars Latin Americans held. From 1945 until 1948, the higher costs of American products consumed $2.7 billion of their reserves. Of more consequence, they confronted a United States that directed its primary attention to the shattered economies of Europe and Asia.

With the broader objectives of the Latin Americans — continued use of resources until victory over the Axis was achieved, a stable and orderly economic transition to a peacetime economy, and a long-range development goal for industry and agriculture — the U.S. government was in agreement. But it demurred on the question of economic nationalism and the Latin American insistence on using the state to promote economic development and shielding national economies from the competitive forces of the more advanced industrial countries. On this matter the usually suppressed cynicism of the Latin American delegates erupted in sarcastic comments about a nation that protected its own industries and agriculture but refused to concede the same advantage to others. The American draft of the economic charter spoke of tearing down barriers to trade and establishing safeguards for private investment — a point of view considerably distant from the Latin Americans' predilection for closely supervising the investment dollar. At the UN organizational conference at San Francisco in May, the Latin Americans renewed their pressures for a regional pact, voicing their own apprehensions about Soviet ambitions in Latin America.

It was a pledge not fulfilled until two years later at Rio de Janeiro, when the U.S. government had crafted the containment doctrine and made Latin America's economic development secondary to American security in the Western Hemisphere. In the meantime Washington directed its hemispheric energies to harassing the defiant Argentines by trying to prevent the election of Juan Perón. To this end Spruille Braden induced the Uruguayan foreign minister, Eduardo Rodríguez Larreta, to issue an appeal for collective intervention to ensure democracy and respect for human rights in the Americas. With no particular enthusiasm for Perón's cause, the other Latin American republics politely rejected the idea as a violation of strict nonintervention.

Perón triumphed and launched his own brand of economic nationalism that he called "Justicialismo," which Braden incorrectly labeled a form of fascism. In the mind-set of Washington in 1946, Justicialismo laid the groundwork for communism in the Southern Cone. A few — Rockefeller, who reflected Wall Street's sentiments when he pointed out that Perón's domination of highly political Argentine labor offered a buttress against communist intrusion; Arthur Vandenberg, the Michigan Republican who had taken a special interest in Latin America's incorporation into the United Nations; and George Messersmith, who replaced Braden in Buenos Aires — saw in Perón's politics an effort to shape a modern Argentine economy and political culture in a country where the traditional landowning classes and the military had lost their credibility. At a time when the hemisphere remained vulnerable to American pressures and could be subordinated to U.S. strategic priorities, there was lessening tolerance in Washington for the policymaker with a "regionalist perspective."

Rockefeller was eased out in 1945. Two years later, with Vandenberg calling for the long-delayed Rio meeting (which Braden had opposed), Braden himself fell from grace, largely at the Michigan senator's insistence and, frankly, because he found it difficult to shift from an antifascist to an anticommunist focus. For his unwilling retirement Braden exacted as price the fall of Messersmith, who had been decorated by Perón for his efforts to promote American-Argentine cordiality. Ironically, throughout the war ordinary Argentines remained fascinated with American culture, particularly film and Hollywood stars, even as the political relationship between the two governments worsened. To some U.S. leaders, such a bipolar attitude was both inexplicable and illogical, but it made sense to many Argentines, who demonstrated that it was indeed possible to admire much about American culture without approving of the policies of its government.[37]

In an atmosphere of uncertainty, confusion, and sometimes bitter departmental conflicts, U.S. postwar hemispheric policy evolved. Latin American aid was assigned a secondary status to that apportioned to Europe, a not unexpected decision, but Roosevelt's words about "giving them a share" and the wartime enthusiasm for hemispheric economic development rapidly dissipated. The Brazilians, for example, expecting much larger amounts of U.S. aid after the war, were given less and politely informed that the United States had other commitments for its public funds. Latin American countries that depended on raw material exports for their economic well-being wanted industrial equipment and technology from the United States but needed a higher price for their exports to pay for them. American manufacturers passed on rising costs to their Latin American purchasers; with the support of their government they kept down the prices they paid for Latin American imports.

If there were genuine fears of internal communist subversion or involvement by Perón, as in Chile in the last years of the Popular Front, Washington provided a minimum of financial assistance and its political support to a beleaguered government. In Chile the stake was deemed high enough to invest: a government with a working arrangement with the communists, but confronted by a labor strike in American-owned copper mines and in the coal mines, had to acquiesce to American demands to crack down on the miners to survive. Ambassador Claude Bowers identified the crucial issue: "The strike is Communist and revolutionary and [as a] result will have inevitable effect throughout South America. . . . In view of the world contest between Communism and democracy it seems incredible that we should be indifferent to the major battle Communism is waging in Chile. . . . Unless we can and [will] do [more] we may prepare ourselves for a grave Communist triumph in our backyard . . . which will spread to other American nations."[38]

In the increasingly simplified context in which Washington gauged Latin America's place in its global perspective, the hemispheric delegates met at Rio de Janeiro in March 1947. A makeshift truce had been arranged with Perón, who had already voiced concerns about the Soviet peril in the world, had requested arms to confront it, and had begun receiving them. A surface cordiality reappeared when discussions focused on the safeguarding of the Western Hemisphere. The United States obtained the first of several Cold War alliances that followed in the next half dozen years. The Inter-American Treaty of Reciprocal Assistance (the Rio treaty) restated the principle that an attack against one hemispheric nation obligated the others to come to its defense in a succession of responses culminating, if necessary, in war. Senator Vandenberg, who had served as delegate, returned with a glowing description of the defensive alliance as "sunlight in a dark world," a subtle reference to Soviet expansionism. The Senate approved the pact in an overwhelming vote. A year later, at the ninth inter-American conference in Bogotá, the State Department dispatched with its representatives a guide entitled "U.S. Policy Regarding Anti-Communist Measures Which Could Be Planned and Carried Out within the Inter-American System" but suggested that they should avoid anticommunist agreements with the other republics and concentrate on anticommunist resolutions.

In both conferences, the United States generally got what it wanted; the Latin Americans did not. Washington fashioned the Rio treaty and the Organization of American States (OAS) charter, the first a hemispheric defensive alliance and the second a hemispheric institutional structure, to conform to its own priorities and — as the United States had done in its prewar commitments to Latin America — to provide a military and political example for its global anticommunist network. At Bogotá there was an ominous prelude. A popular Liberal, Jorge Eliécer Gaitán, who had run as an independent in 1946 and appeared to be the favorite for the 1950 election, was assassinated on the street. A wave of riots and destruction known as the *bogotazo* followed, with the government blaming the communists for much of the damage. Secretary of State George Marshall arrived in Bogotá with a warning about international communism, and the delegates responded with a resolution declaring that "international communism or any totalitarian doctrine is incompatible with the concept of American freedom."[39]

As a mark of its consistency with the global implications of Latin American policy, the Department of State, initially lukewarm to the rearming of Latin

America's militaries (on the credible thinking that they consumed too much of depleted public treasuries), reversed its position and moved to revive the moribund Inter-American Defense Board, reinforcing its recommendation with the comment that Latin Americans had their own priorities for their militaries, and if the United States provided the arms it would increase its influence among them.

In retrospective and occasionally scathing evaluations of the course the United States chose in Latin America after the war, it has been often argued that Latin America deserved more than it got from its wartime ally. Further, if Latin America had received the developmental assistance its beleaguered economies required, if the United States had given its support to the proposed inter-American development bank, if (as the ambassador to Brazil William Pawley suggested) the United States had sustained a "Marshall Plan" for Latin America, then communism would not have been the threat Marshall and the hard-liners in the State Department warned about. Almost casually, President Harry S. Truman at Rio de Janeiro and Marshall at Bogotá spoke of European priorities and the expectation that private sources offered the Latin American mendicants their only realistic alternative. Such a choice was a developmental model that did not meet the hemisphere's needs because it conformed to American and not Latin American priorities. In denying Latin Americans the aid they solicited, Truman spoke of the differing problems confronted by Europe and Latin America. The task in Europe was reconstruction, which could be achieved by public aid. "The problems of countries in this Hemisphere are different in nature and cannot be relieved by the same means and the same approaches."[40]

His comment anticipated, doubtless unintentionally, the severity of solutions to Latin America's problems that has persisted ever since. The United States had industrialized and in the process had raised the standard of living for its peoples. But the government had created some of the basic political, economic, and social institutions necessary for that task in the transformative years from the Wilson era to Pearl Harbor. World War II had enabled it to accelerate that goal without a fundamental social transformation. What Latin America required, some economists believed, was not reconstruction but restructuring of its economy and politics. More conservative observers believed such an undertaking would require a restructuring of the social order.

The truth of the matter, it can be argued, proved to be more complicated, for the implications of the *bogotazo* of 1948 proved to be more critical for the hemispheric future than the alliance crafted at Chapultepec a few weeks before Roosevelt died and Harry Truman became president. In those three momentous years, the United States demonstrated, through word and deed, that its foreign policy priorities lay in Europe and even in the western Pacific and not in its wartime alliance of hemispheric nations. This was understandable, given the international political dynamics of the age and the U.S. Congress's willingness to support the kinds of foreign economic policy initiatives called for by the Truman administration, but it boded ill for the future. Truman himself viewed the *bogotazo* riots as the work of international communism. As Secretary of State Marshall observed, "It is the same definite pattern as occurrences which provoked strikes in France and Italy [in the postwar years]. . . . In actions we take here regarding the present situation, we must keep clearly in mind the fact that this is a world affair — not merely Colombian or Latin American."[41]

In the process, the hope of a generation of countercultural artists, writers, intellectuals, and even political leaders in the 1920s and 1930s that the United States would assume a more benign view of its role in the hemisphere dissipated under the pressures and agendas of postwar triumphalism. In the United States, the cultural mandate of the Good Neighbor policy became the victim of a relentless anticommunist crusade. It could not be easily replaced with a foreign policy that could sustain the kind of social agenda for postwar governments that some in the hemisphere now advocated. Accordingly, U.S. intellectuals had to forsake their ties with Marxism or risk alienation from mainstream public opinion. In increasing numbers, their presumed ideological allies in Latin America and the Caribbean absorbed more fully Marxist-Leninist rhetoric. As each group shifted in different ideological directions, the capitalist credos of individualism and growth gained strength in the United States and withered south of the Rio Grande. In this atmosphere of suspicion and recrimination, the Cold War in the Americas took shape.[42]

In retrospect, it is difficult to conclude which approach proved the more realistic or more naive. The dynamics of the Cold War reverberated differently almost everywhere in the Americas — different in the cities from in the countryside and different in the larger countries from in the smaller ones. Viewed within the context of more immediate and arguably far more consequential threat to U.S. interests in Europe and Asia, it is perhaps understandable why U.S. leaders did not accord Latin American pleas for greater aid a higher priority in the postwar years. After all, the policies and agencies we identify with these early Cold War years — the Truman doctrine, the Marshall Plan, the National Security Council, and the Central Intelligence Agency, among others — acquired their initial importance in discussions about threats in Europe and Asia and secondarily in Latin America. The solution, it was generally agreed, involved meeting the communist challenge on every front but with a variety of means, from a more vigorous economic assistance program to military measures, including destabilizing governments and counterguerrilla measures. In their euphoria of wartime victory and the growing determination to meet a presumably implacable communist challenge, U.S. leaders and a goodly portion of the American public failed to appreciate the fragility of the wartime alliance or the depth of anti-Americanism in the hemisphere in the postwar years. The bitterness ran deepest, ironically, not in faraway Argentina or Chile but closer to home, in Cuba, Mexico, and, surprisingly, Canada.

Cuban and Mexican resentment could be explained in part by the long history of U.S. pressure and interventions and, indirectly at least, all three by lingering animosities over Americanization.

Indeed, the unparalleled wartime collaboration between Canada and the United States belied the reality of two peoples who were "strangers beneath the skin." Undeniably, Americans and Canadians harbored equally intense and even racist sentiments toward Japanese minorities during the war, but Canadians made no effort to use "loyal" Japanese as combatants, and Canada did not permit internees to return to the Pacific coast until 1949. On a more mundane level, the Canadian government also restricted the entry of U.S. comic books. At bottom, however, lay Canadian indignation over U.S. self-satisfaction over its role in the war and corresponding U.S. blindness or indifference to the Canadian contribution. More than that, most Americans could not fully appreciate that the Canadian sense of independence and nationhood ran just as deep as their own. After all, in the postwar "free world," Canada was the third most powerful country and justifiably wanted to be a major player, not merely a bystander.[43]

6 The Cold War

In some important respects, 1948 was a successful year for U.S. goals in the Americas. In the previous year at Rio de Janeiro, the U.S. delegation had persuaded the other republics to support a far-reaching inter-American defense pact. In spite of the violent backdrop of the *bogotazo*, which cost a thousand lives, the participating governments in the ninth Inter-American Conference created the Organization of American States, a continental political and economic structure that far surpassed what Secretary of State James G. Blaine had in mind for the 1889 meeting. The OAS structure included three critical subagencies — the Economic and Social Council, the Council of Jurists, and a cultural council. In the American Treaty of Pacific Settlement, or Pact of Bogotá, the signatories agreed to settle their disputes by peaceful means. In the American Declaration of Rights and Duties of States they pledged a human rights agenda far more inclusive than the U.S. Bill of Rights. More pointedly, and in a direct reference to the perceived communist threat, the conference declared that "by its antidemocratic character and its interventionist tendencies the political activity of international communism or any totalitarian doctrine is incompatible with the concept of American freedom."[1]

These were admirable sentiments, but the political and social climate bespoke a different reality. In 1948 Latin America suffered six coups, none of which offered reassurance of the survival of democracy in the hemisphere. Nor, ironically, did a resurgence of dictatorships, uniformly anticommunist, indicate that Latin America was more fully integrated into the U.S. global anticommunist design. Troubled by such critics as the Argentine economist Raúl Prebisch of the UN Economic Commission for Latin America (ECLA) — who held that Latin American poverty originated in the industrial prosperity of North America and Europe, which drained the continent of its raw materials — and the broadening appeal of statism, symbolized by Perón's Argentina, the U.S. government altered its tactics in dealing with hemispheric governments.[2]

Hemispheric Optimists and Realists

The architect of the new style in Latin American policy was Edwin Miller, an aggressive but *simpático* careerist who became Secretary of State Dean Acheson's point man on the hemisphere in 1949 as assistant secretary of state. He barnstormed the Latin American capitals, preaching the anticommunist message but with greater understanding of Latin America's resentment over the U.S. tendency to "impose" its own "political system" on the hemisphere. The recent instability that plagued several countries was distressing but a reality the United States had to accept. Economic development was necessary for the flowering of democracy in the hemisphere. To implant democracy by intervention, as the American record in the Caribbean had amply demonstrated, would not bring Latin America closer to "maturity."[3]

A dictatorship or revolutionary government, though repugnant, would be offered recognition but would not have U.S. blessing. When Anastasio Somoza installed himself in the Nicaraguan presidency by unconstitutional means in 1947, Washington complained but ultimately recognized his government. A similar logic prevailed elsewhere with other dictators. They were naturally appreciated as being solidly anticommunist, but their political credentials did not automatically guarantee U.S. approbation. Acceptance of their legitimacy was a means of exercising influence in the hemisphere while simultaneously striving to wean them from their dictatorial ways through economic assistance and inter-American cordiality. But George F. Kennan, the principal architect of the postwar policy of containment, intruded with his precise strategic calculations about Latin America's place in the global agenda. Given the political disparities between the United States and the hemispheric republics, he doubted the efficacy of the inter-American system as a means for achieving American goals. Latin America produced governments we liked and governments we didn't like: the crucial issue was not hemispheric political or cultural compatibility but whether or not we had "satisfactory relations" with them.[4]

Perhaps Kennan was right about the expedient way to achieve a secure hemisphere. But Miller thought more as hemispheric not global strategist, so he pressed ahead, citing Latin America's lukewarm response to American pressures to identify with the UN commitment in Korea. He encountered again the globalists, whose arguments about the communist threat were reinforced by the Korean War, and who fashioned a dozen military pacts with Latin American governments. Ironically, Miller's advocacy of increased economic aid to the hemisphere, his polite tolerance of dictators, and his insistence that Latin America be integrated into U.S. Cold War policy facilitated Kennan's approach.

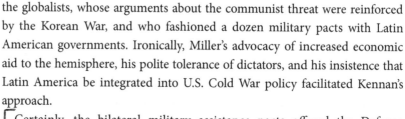

Certainly, the bilateral military assistance pacts offered the Defense Department an immediate reassurance that something was being done to contain communism in the hemisphere. From 1952 to 1955, the United States signed defense pacts with twelve Latin American and Caribbean governments — Cuba, Colombia, the Dominican Republic, Haiti, Honduras, Guatemala, Ecuador, Nicaragua, Brazil, Peru, Chile, and Uruguay. Some of the old-timers in the Department of State who had tried to adhere to the undeniably admirable tenets of the Good Neighbor policy — notably nonintervention, noninterference, and collective solidarity — lamented that the country seemed to be returning to the old days of gunboat diplomacy.[5]

If such a policy translated into coziness with dictators — even decorating a few of them with U.S. medals — or inured the United States against social or political change, it was an unpleasant and, in retrospect, a distasteful choice. At the time it seemed to be the only realistic choice. When military security is the goal of policy, success in results is more highly valued than the political or moral character of the ally. More disturbing, perhaps, was the unmistakable reluctance of the Latin Americans to identify American priorities in the Cold War as their priorities. They took American aid, received U.S. military hardware, and voted with the Americans in the United Nations on Cold War issues, but their accommodation revealed less a genuine commitment than a realization that they had little alternative unless they were willing to pay the price of defying Washington. Clearly, the United States had drawn a line in the postwar world, and it expected its hemispheric allies during World War II to go along with its priorities. The distinguished Mexican historian Daniel Cosío Villegas perceived the stakes when he wrote, "Is it possible . . . that the United States will find it necessary to create a retrograde, reactionary world made of antiliberal and antidemocratic forces?"[6]

With the outbreak of the Korean War in June 1950, such a choice seemed likelier. Ironically, the United States had been able to push through a critical UN Security Council vote calling for a forceful response to North Korea's invasion of the South because of the support of two nonpermanent members (Cuba and Ecuador). In the aftermath, several hemispheric governments responded favorably to the U.S. appeal for a hemispheric anticommunist and by implication anti-Soviet stance. As the conflict wore on, however, such sentiments withered under the acknowledgment that the United States had little intention of pursuing the issue beyond a country-by-country approach.

Accordingly, the scenario assumed a different pattern from place to place. In 1949 Perón declared that in the event of a war between the United States and the USSR, Argentina would be on the American side, and he spoke grandly about sending Argentine troops to Korea. When the fighting started, Perón just as quickly changed his mind and went so far as to suggest that the ABC powers (Argentina, Brazil, and Chile) combine into a neutral bloc. His Brazilian counterpart, Getúlio Vargas, spoke favorably about the U.S. role in the war but had to withstand growing domestic criticism for his stance. In Chile, the last of the Popular Front triad — Gabriel González Videla — succumbed to a growing hostility to U.S. copper companies and the improbable return of the old Chilean warrior, Carlos Ibáñez, the General of Hope. Initially a champion of the left, Ibáñez ridiculed the nation's defense pact with the United States and called for legalization of the Communist Party. Once in office, however, he proved unable to stem the downward spiral of the economy. In the end he resorted to tactics he had employed in the 1920s — repression of labor and the left. In turn, Washington demonstrated its approbation by restoring limited financial assistance.[7]

The support of other hemispheric governments — notably Mexico, Canada, and Colombia — did not stem from any strong beliefs in the U.S. prescription for internal political or economic development or world order. Mexico's pro-business president, Miguel Alemán (1946–52), received an enthusiastic welcome in his 1947 visit to the United States, proudly declared that Mexico stood forthrightly for democracy, and acknowledged the expanding economic ties between the two countries. But he just as resolutely refused to sign a military security pact with the United States, and in 1952 Mexico became the only Latin American country refusing to endorse a hemispheric military assistance agreement, the Inter-American Reciprocal Aid Treaty.[8]

Both Canadian prime ministers Mackenzie King and his successor Louis St.

Laurent were outspoken anticommunists. Canada joined the North Atlantic Treaty Organization (NATO) and sent troops to Korea, but along with many Canadians these two leaders harbored doubts about the growing militancy of U.S. foreign policy. The reality, as the Canadian historian Denis Smith acknowledged, proved to be the instinctive Canadian apprehension about Soviet expansion: the "politics of fear." Although its government confronted a civil war, Colombia, too, dispatched a military contingent to the fighting. Its Conservative and pro-Catholic president, Laureano Gómez, voiced political sentiments that pleased U.S. leaders, who now seemed willing to supply Colombia with military assistance despite some reservations that Gómez would employ the weapons to suppress domestic political enemies.[9]

One Civil War, Two Revolutions

In other words, the choices were never easy, as the United States had already found out in its response to the 1948 Costa Rican civil war and would again learn in the Bolivian and Guatemalan revolutions.

The Costa Rican war — the most traumatic in the nation's history — had erupted after the breakdown of one of Latin America's most admirable electoral systems, when disgruntled landowner José Figueres raised the flag of rebellion against a government that had wrought impressive social reforms but had depended on the communists to attain them. During the war, when Figueres had criticized the government for seizing German property, the president sent him into exile. He returned to a triumphant reception in a Costa Rica bitterly divided over the communist issue. The communist leader, Manuel Mora (already something of a legendary figure in Costa Rican life), tried to soften the party's image among an increasingly suspicious population, but the opposition was unrelenting. The campaign extended into the United States, where ominous warnings about a Russian beachhead in the isthmus found their way into the press. Within Costa Rica, the Social Democrats, the government's most formidable opposition, maintained their anticommunist journalistic assaults against a government whose spokesmen were unambiguously pro-American on the international issues of the day.

To Washington such conciliatory gestures were unconvincing; to Figueres, who had conspired to overturn the government since his return from exile, they meant nothing. Figueres had not only a national but also an international network of conspirators and supporters. The Caribbean Legion, dedicated to the overthrow of Caribbean dictators, supported him in exchange for his prior commitments to their cause. Juan José Arévalo, the leftist president of Guatemala since the tumultuous days of 1944, when dictators had fallen in Guatemala and neighboring El Salvador, pledged arms and troops. Figueres needed only an issue to raise his volunteers against a government whose successive leaders from 1940, Rafael Calderón Guardia and Teodoro Picado, had brought social reforms and with them governmental corruption and ideological conflict into national politics.[10]

The contested election of 1948 provided Figueres with the opportunity to launch his rebellion. In a bitterly contested race, a social conservative, Otilio Ulate, had apparently triumphed, but the National Congress, dominated by Calderón's followers, declared the election void because of irregularities. Calderón himself, it was widely assumed, would now be designated as president. Throughout the central valley that dominates Costa Rican social and political life, Don Pepe's prediction four years before that Calderón would never relinquish power unless forced to do so seemed prophetic. Figueres now had his long-awaited opportunity. The battle began on 10 March 1948. Pressed from without by the war of national liberation, the government began to crumble from within. With only a token army, it was compelled to rely on Mora's San José legion of workers to defend it. Every gesture of Picado toward the communists brought down the wrath of the opposition, predictably, but also the vocal displeasure of such hemispheric socialists as Haya de la Torre, who warned of "another Czechoslovakia" in the Americas. In desperation Calderón called on Somoza in Nicaragua to intervene in the struggle against Figueres, who had vowed holy war against him. Costa Rica was spared the larger and even bloodier conflict that might have resulted. Somoza dispatched units across the border and took Villa Quesada but pressed no farther. From his lair Figueres called for negotiations but rejected any settlement that left the Popular Vanguard, the communist militia that held San José, with its arms. He vowed to march on the city if the communists resisted.

His declaration came a week after the *bogotazo* and its frightening portent of urban violence carried out by communists. Costa Rican president (and

Calderón ally) Picado decided that San José should be spared a comparable fate. In an admirable gesture of conciliation he saved Costa Rica from national disintegration. Calderón and Picado took immediate advantage of the terms hammered out between the diplomatic corps and Don Pepe and went into exile in Somoza's Nicaragua to plot their revenge. Within a week Figueres and the National Liberation were parading in the capital. The nation, he declared, had been saved from the communist scourge. This pleased U.S. officials, some of whom had casually referred to Don Pepe as a Nazi only a few years before. In his defiance of the political order, Figueres had assured the restoration of the Costa Rican landed elite in national life. National Liberation had also validated the primacy of the social order, not ideology, in the political culture.

For Costa Ricans, the civil war was a formative event in the nation's history; for the United States, it was a lesson in how the weak can manipulate the strong. Whatever doubts U.S. officials had about Figueres — he became, alternately, a Nazi and then a communist in their estimation — he possessed impressive staying power in the estimation of U.S. officials. Figueres was suspect for his political views, but Picado and Calderón were unacceptable, period. The junta headed by Figueres gave way in 1950 to the Ulate presidency. In 1951, National Liberation became an official party. Three years later, Figueres himself became president. In the ensuing years, the Costa Ricans alarmed Washington by nationalizing the banking system and creating what some called a middle-class socialist society. Figueres championed the Caribbean Legion. In 1954, when Dulles browbeat smaller Caribbean and Central American countries into supporting his "death-wish" sanctions against the leftist government of Guatemala at Caracas, Figueres defiantly boycotted the conference. Not many leaders of small Latin American or Caribbean governments had that much courage, but Figueres did because he was an anticommunist. He knew just how far he could push the Yankee giant, and he survived.[11]

But in Bolivia the feudal aristocracy perished before middle-class revolutionaries of the Nationalist Revolutionary Movement (MNR). During the war MNR officials had occupied important positions in a government that was, in Washington's view, pro-fascist. In the discord that wracked Bolivia in the late 1940s, an era of declining tin prices and agitation among workers, Víctor Paz Estenssoro had effectively purged the volatile Bolivian political arena of his leftist opposition and won labor's support. The Bolivian military, once MNR's ally but now fearful of its political reach, vowed to crush the movement. Unlike the rural dons of Costa Rica, the Bolivian landed aristocracy (believing that a movement of the dedicated without guns posed no real threat) decided to watch the struggle from the sidelines. When MNR organizers called for strikes, the military violently suppressed them, and the party went to the barricades, confronting military units throughout Bolivian cities. In this challenge to the government, MNR lost out, but in the process it had united the tin miners with urban workers. And the ordeal had convinced Paz that the only way to revolution was that path long advocated by Juan Lechín and his following of former Trotskyites — defeat and then disband the military.

In 1951, when the MNR made its last attempt to gain power by the ballot, Paz was in exile. But he ran for president at the head of an MNR ticket, and the party won a stupendous victory. The army again intervened, installing a rump government, and frantically searched for a civilian political base to sustain it. By now the erosion of Bolivian traditional political life had virtually run its course, and in the cities, where a new political culture had taken its place, MNR leaders began passing out weapons not only to the party faithful but to anyone who would help them gain the power wrongfully denied. Two years before, they had hesitated to arm civilians, fearing a destructive civil war. An unexpected dispute with the United States over the low price Washington was offering for Bolivian tin abetted the rebel cause. Bolivian authorities decided to shut down production, a decision that worsened economic conditions and precipitated more unrest. In April 1952 the party called for the final assault. It seized the armories in the capital and distributed the weapons to the populace. Armed miners descended on La Paz. After three days of intense fighting and six hundred dead, the Bolivian army surrendered.

With its defeat came the collapse of the old order and, more ominously, demands for a revolutionary new order from those who had made the triumph possible. The victors had shifted from the Right to the Left in their constituency in only six years. Paz Estenssoro and the MNR now had power, but the country's economy was grossly distorted. Tin, the only marketable export, cost more to produce in Bolivia than anywhere in the world. The country had few manufacturers because it had few consumers of manufactured goods. It had a landed aristocracy who were largely absentee and whose estates could be taken without much protest. Its tin owners, if adequately compensated, were eager to rid themselves of inefficient operations. The revolution had assumed political command of an exhausted society, a wretched economy, and a state with no defense save the masses MNR had armed. They would not wait for the revolution to fulfill its promises.

The revolution that had been inspired from above now found itself pushed from below — by tin miners demanding greater benefits and by Indians, who had historically been denied participation in national life but who now had the vote. A movement that had begun with moderate economic plans undertook a social and economic restructuring of the nation. Although their reforms for the tin industry were unacceptable to the workers, Paz and his MNR chieftains nationalized the holdings of the tin barons, Patino, Hochschild, and Aramayo. More frightening than the urban dislocation was the breakdown of rural society. Throughout the remainder of 1952 and into the next year bands of *campesinos* organized themselves into militias, seizing estates and expelling their occupants. By the end of 1953 the countryside, which had been largely spared in the revolution, was devastated. The old rural social order, banished from the land, collapsed.

Less than two years in power, with a bankrupt economy, an agricultural system that could not feed the nation, and no money for the social programs they had promised, the revolutionaries chose the expedient course. Rather than nationalize the entire economy and alienate their middle-class supporters, they chose to accommodate Washington's strictures about running the country. Alert to the pressures the U.S. government was bringing on the Guatemalan Revolution, they offered compensation to the owners — a move that displeased the more radical tin workers but that virtually assured Washington would render its polite approval because there were few U.S. investors in Bolivian tin. Within a short time U.S. officials announced that the United States was doubling its purchases of Bolivian tin and that Bolivia would begin receiving food exports.

Over the course of the decade Bolivia received $100 million in American aid, more than any Latin American nation. The money flowing from a government dedicated to hemispheric anticommunism provided the Bolivian government with a third of its budget, enabled it to feed its urban population, and made possible the improvement of social services and transportation to its rural people. Indisputably, the price Washington exacted was high: Bolivia had to conform to the economic model the Americans imposed. In 1956, when American aid began trickling off and the MNR confronted yet another economic and political crisis, those who had made the revolution four years before concluded that they had only three choices. They could impose socialism, accept a potentially disastrous inflation, or look again to Washington. They chose the last option, and with the approval of U.S. officials and the International Monetary Fund, Bolivia announced a stabilization program.[12]

The Eisenhower administration and the Bolivian revolutionaries did not reconcile their differences out of common purpose or understanding. Bolivia could not afford the social and political costs unleashed by the revolution MNR had begun but feared to complete. The United States chose to subsidize that revolution for fear of something even more destructive. The critical issue was MNR's dismantling of the Bolivian military. Without a loyal army to sustain the new political order, the revolutionary party in power had to persevere until it could create a military. That course meant, in turn, U.S. subsidies and U.S. influence over a revolution now beholden to Washington. Even the anti-imperialist leader Juan Lechín privately acknowledged that the government had no alternative but to choose U.S. aid. Unlike the Cubans after the revolution that unseated a dictatorship, the Bolivians had no benefactors. When conditions worsened, they could, and did, use the threat of political collapse or send tentative feelers for assistance to Eastern Bloc nations in order to ply more moneys from the U.S. government. But the economic commitments from Washington in the 1950s proved sparse and, except for food shipments, inadequate to what was required for rebuilding a shattered economy. What this predicament portended for the nation's future was anybody's guess, but there was little reason for optimism.[13]

The Guatemalan Intervention

In Central America President Dwight Eisenhower and Secretary of State John Foster Dulles were able to exercise their Cold War policy more forcefully.[14] They were less understanding of the obstacles facing a new generation that had come of age. In 1944, invigorated by a democratic spirit that had swept the isthmus, urban revolutions had driven from power Jorge Ubico in Guatemala and Maximiliano Hernández Martínez in El Salvador. Five years later their Honduran counterpart, the old dictator Tiburcio Carias Andino, succumbed, though the quintessential banana republic suffered no disruption of its social order. Somoza persevered in Nicaragua but not without occasional American disapproval of his meddling in Costa Rican affairs. Somoza and Pepe Figueres were blood enemies. In 1954 the two fought a border skirmish when Figueres's enemies, who had been given sanctuary by Somoza, launched a raid from Nicaraguan soil. Washington did not especially approve of Figueres and his notions of state intrusion into the economy, but neither did it want a destabilized isthmus, so the U.S. Air Force dispatched planes to San José, and the OAS intervened to settle the dispute. Somoza backed off from his personal vendetta, and Figueres emerged from the crisis with Washington's begrudging support. As he often remarked, Figueres knew how far he could push the Americans and get away with it.

His kindred spirits in Guatemala did not. Under a formerly exiled university professor of economics, Juan José Arévalo, they had begun a social transformation in Central America's most rigidly structured social order. The 1944 overthrow of Ubico, orchestrated largely by reformist students and faculty at the University of San Carlos, heralded profound changes for the country. Inspired by the wartime rhetoric of commitment to a more democratic Latin America and their disgust at their nation's debilities, Arévalo's vanguard looked to a national reformation guided by this idealistic generation. Arévalo spoke of "spiritual socialism" as a remedy for a nation subject to the domination of an entrenched oligarchy and the church. The dream was a new Guatemala where Indian peasant and urban laborer — theretofore excluded from the political culture — would take their rightful place.

Arévalo showed purpose but had no dependable political support to sustain his cause. Labor, for example, rapidly increased its economic standing in the new "humane capitalism" but soon fell under the sway of communists, who began operating schools for future organizers. Like the urban militants of Bolivia and Costa Rica, Guatemalan workers had long suffered from exploitation and indifference. They had never counted for much in the political and social order. Promised a better day, they became more militant. When Arévalo left office in 1950, Guatemala was a better place for the dispossessed, but "spiritual socialism" had not triumphed. Arévalo had failed to create a cohesive political culture. He did not disband the military, which chafed under his social reformism and twenty times attempted to overthrow him. He managed to hang on, usually by arming the urban faithful, but he left the military intact. Toward the end, ominously, the extremes, the Right and the Left, moved farther apart. "Spiritual socialism" was neither a reconciling nor a unifying doctrine. But at least Arévalo survived his term.

His successor, Jacobo Arbenz, was not so fortunate. Assessing the fortunes of a revolution only six years in power, Arbenz decided the only realistic course was invigoration of the government's promise to the Guatemalan peasantry. The Bolivian revolutionaries had made their peace with country peasants by giving them land. In Costa Rica the triumphant rural elite had not given peasants land but provided a benevolent paternalism and acquitted itself with a pervasive myth that in Costa Rica there was no peasantry. By any standard of social decency the Guatemalan country dwellers deserved the agrarian reform that Arbenz announced in June 1952, expropriation with compensation of untilled land above a certain acreage. Landless *campesinos* could now gain title to lands they had worked as migrants or use of the land in return for a percentage of their crop. In retrospect, the law was mild, but Arbenz did not possess the political stature of the Mexican or Bolivian revolutionaries who had carried out more drastic reforms. More crucially, the Guatemalan revolutionaries were striking directly at the most powerful foreign entity in Central America, United Fruit.

UFCo, which Central Americans derisively called "the Octopus," was not only a huge landowner but also the proprietor of Guatemala's railroad and public utilities.[15] To many the company was Guatemala's last fiefdom, long accustomed to having its way because it had friends in high places, especially in the Eisenhower administration. Under Arbenz's reforms UFCo lost more than two hundred thousand acres, for which the government promised to pay what company officials considered a woefully inadequate compensation. Back in the United States UFCo publicists undertook a blistering propaganda campaign to portray "Red Guatemala" as a menace not only to international capitalism but to American security. Largely unseen by American observers — and thus too little appreciated by them — were the disparate but collectively ominous social disturbances caused by roving bands of *campesinos*. Wanting more than the government was capable of delivering in its agrarian reforms, they had fallen under the sway of militant rural leaders who inspired them to seize not only UFCo lands but also the holdings of all foreigners. In time, even sympathetic Guatemalan reformers who lived in the countryside grew fearful of these bands. They had struggled for democracy and national reformation. But the rural disturbances had resurrected old fears that reach deep into Guatemala's history: the unanticipated dangers that sometimes followed political and economic reforms, when formerly oppressed peoples, incapable of being satisfied with moderate, "rational" gestures from their rulers, sense in their collective strength the capability to bring down the prevailing social order and construct their own.

Eisenhower and Dulles required no encouragement to target the Guatemalans for punishment. Dulles, who had once served in the law firm of Sullivan and Cromwell, which represented UFCo, had already singled out the Guatemalans for their deviation from American guidance in the United Nations. Both Figueres and Arbenz had irritated Washington, but Arbenz was more vulnerable and, in Dulles's eyes, more culpable. He had not isolated and disarmed the communists but instead tolerated their rising influence over Guatemalan labor and permitted them to organize the *campesinos*. In Dulles's mind the communist presence in Guatemala confirmed Soviet penetration of the hemisphere. Other Central American governments, alert to American predilections in the Cold War, joined in the condemnation.

The conspiracy against Arbenz commenced early in the Eisenhower administration. It had already begun within the Guatemalan oligarchy and its supporters in the military in 1952, when Carlos Castillo Armas and Manuel Ydígoras Fuentes vowed war against Arbenz in a gentleman's agreement in San Salvador. But they required American aid and inspiration. Eisenhower was alert to the dangers in an overt assault against the defiant Arbenz, but he remembered his wartime experience and was especially mindful of what could be accomplished by a military intelligence operation. This explains why the Central Intelligence Agency's (CIA) anti-Arbenz plan, appropriately called Operation PBSuccess, was so appealing to an administration dedicated to the dismantling of a leftist government but sensitive to international and especially hemispheric criticism.

One assault against the Guatemalans was carried out through the inter-American system. At the tenth inter-American conference, which met in Caracas in

1954, Dulles led the diplomatic offensive. He introduced a resolution declaring the "domination or control of the political institutions of an American state by the international Communist Movement" a menace to the inter-American system and requiring appropriate response under the Rio treaty. Guatemala, which had not yet signed the pact, denounced this Declaration of Caracas as a pretext for interfering in its internal affairs. Although offended by Dulles's remarks, the other Latin American republics went along when he declared, "I believe there is not a single American state which would practice intervention against another American state."[16]

This reassurance, coupled with expectations of U.S. economic aid, got Dulles the authorization he needed. With the declaration in his pocket he headed for Washington, and Operation PBSuccess and the Guatemalan counterrevolution commenced their final drive to extinguish what rightist commentators called "the Red Star over Guatemala."

Anticipating that Castillo Armas would invade, Arbenz frantically tried to shore up his faltering government with political and military measures, but he was frustrated at every turn. Denied arms from the United States since 1948, the Guatemalans looked first to Western European sources. When the Americans blocked them, they appealed to Eastern European governments. News of a shipment from Poland on a Swedish freighter prompted a revival of American charges of Soviet involvement. Within the country, Arbenz's security agents rounded up suspected revolutionaries and subjected them to harsh treatment, including, it was widely reported, torture. On the diplomatic front, Guatemala appealed to the UN Security Council, proclaiming to the world that the United States, in complicity with United Fruit, was conspiring against a small republic. On the military front, Arbenz withstood Castillo Armas's first attack, destroying two of his three bombers. On both battlefields the initial triumphs quickly deteriorated in frustration, then defeat. In the United Nations, the Americans brought heavy pressure on the British and French, who made a prudent diplomatic retreat. Eisenhower replaced the planes Castillo Armas had lost, and the invaders, beaten on the ground, subjected Guatemala City to a bombardment more psychologically than physically destructive.

Arbenz might have survived if he had been able to rouse an armed populace to the government's defense, but the erosion of his support had gone too far. CIA agents had already gotten assurances from the Guatemalan military that it would not distribute arms to Arbenz's loyal civilian militias. When the air attacks began, Arbenz possessed sufficient airplanes to defend the capital, but the CIA operatives, in a brilliant ploy, broadcast over a rebel station the announcement of the defection of a government pilot. The story was untrue, but Arbenz believed it and grounded his planes. In the final days of late June, threatened by his generals, he tried to shift executive power to a presumably loyal officer. But the U.S. ambassador, John E. Peurifoy, a putative member of the conspiracy from the beginning, foiled his efforts by insisting on a candidate more amenable to Washington.

Its choice, of course, was Castillo Armas. In a national broadcast, Dulles lauded Guatemala's salvation from international communism, and Castillo declared that UFCo's lands would be restored. He demolished the labor unions and disfranchised a generation of Guatemalans who had been incorporated into the political culture in less than a decade. A grateful Washington provided the liberators of Guatemala with a $6 million loan.

The Guatemalan intervention bequeathed an ambiguous legacy, not only for the Eisenhower administration but for Guatemala as well. The CIA proved capable of adjusting to the changing events on the ground, but the agency's claim that Arbenz capitulated because of the propaganda campaign against him is a distortion of the facts. He lost power because the Guatemalan military, anticipating a U.S. military intervention, turned against him. Worse, his successor proved to be so inept that he survived for only three years before becoming a victim of an assassin's bullet. The entire affair would unleash two powerful and destructive forces — a deepening of the latent anti-Americanism and resentment of U.S. influence in the region and the onset of a civil strife that persisted into the 1990s.[17]

Rebellion or Revolution

In undermining Arbenz the United States offered no effective rebuttal to the Latin Americans who had reluctantly approved the Declaration of Caracas with the expectation that U.S. economic aid would shortly follow. Marshall had pledged his government to a hemispheric economic conference as early as 1948. When it finally convened in 1954 at Quintandinha, Brazil, Prebisch and the ECLA disciples were prepared with a report on the hemisphere's economic realities. Latin Americans only appeared better off, said Prebisch. In reality, the continent was even more dependent on the industrial north, its share of world trade had declined, and the United States could expect more trouble because of rising expectations and decreasing economic performance. If the challenge were not met, a turbulent future was inevitable. The U.S. emissary, George Humphrey, responded that private not public aid offered the mendicant Latin Americans a more prosperous future.

Others (including the president's brother Milton, who summed up the case for a more aggressive economic program in a special report) warned of a calamitous future for Latin America if social and economic issues were not addressed. The United States was not insensitive to these appeals. Ultimately, in its acceptance of the Inter-American Development Bank and the Alliance for Progress, Washington adopted a developmental strategy far more ambitious and even revolutionary than any contemplated in the early 1950s. But there were always limits to what it would or could do for Latin America, just as there were limits to its tolerance for Latin American governments that deviated from American prescriptions for economic development. After Richard Nixon's visit in 1958, when angry crowds in Venezuela and Peru spewed out their disgust over everything from the Eisenhower administration's coziness with crass dictators to the intrusion of American multinationals into traditional societies, the U.S. government supported such programs as the ambitious housing scheme of the Peruvians to meet the relentless demands of the urban squatters who had already begun to fester in squalid rings circling Lima. As the president expressed matters, homeownership deprived the communists of new recruits.[18]

Communism in Cold War Latin America was a perceived rather than a visible threat to American interests. In the revived anti-Americanism of the era, the United States mistook the outbursts against its domination as the work of the communists — with less vehemence but essentially the same logic that Nixon used to explain the riots his appearance provoked. Communist parties throughout Latin America, in fact, went into decline after World War II. By the mid-1950s, as America's global anticommunism assumed an uncompromising stridency, most hemispheric governments had broken diplomatic relations with the Soviet Union (which was still willing to concede to the United

States a sphere of influence throughout the Americas). American liberals who chided the Eisenhower administration for its inattentiveness to hemispheric economic concerns and its casual indifference to Latin America's historical antipathy to American intervention correctly identified these outbursts as potentially troublesome for U.S. policy.[19]

Several countries, notably Brazil, initially accommodated U.S. Cold War priorities in order to obtain desperately needed economic assistance. In both the Truman and Eisenhower administrations the prevailing view held that Brazil could be an acceptable capitalist model for Third World economic development. After World War II, Nelson Rockefeller and the auto magnate Henry Kaiser undertook private economic development programs in Brazilian agriculture and its nascent automobile industry that soon exceeded in scope the funding under the Good Neighbor policy. As the Cold War in the hemisphere deepened, however, the Brazilians became increasingly frustrated with the "Europe-first" priorities of U.S. leaders. To counter this trend, the Brazilian government began to revive old economic ties to Germany to obtain investment funding.[20]

Latin Americans wanted development, but *neither* the American *nor* the Soviet model. To the U.S. response that it could not realistically extend aid without stipulations — neither Congress nor the American public would have sustained a program for which the borrower set the terms — they offered a reaffirmation of traditional priorities. As the brilliant Venezuelan man of letters Mariano Picón-Salas expressed it: "Although we Latin Americans are requiring a technology as effective as that of the North American for the improvement of our material conditions, at the same time we wish to preserve our conception of life and culture which, from many points of view, is opposed to that of the United States. The worst thing that could happen to us would be to transform ourselves into second-class Yankees or to have their culture imposed upon us or to suffer an adulteration of native spiritual values, like that which a badly organized North American education has produced in Puerto Rico."[21]

Puerto Rico was an apt choice as an example of Latin American apprehension of Americanization, although few Americans (of that era and today) understood what Picón-Salas was trying to say.[22] The island was an oddity in the American experience in Latin America. In 1917, when it gained what amounted to territorial status, Washington had dispatched a generation of educational zealots to mold an English-speaking culture. By the time the Depression set in, the program was in shambles. The New Dealers came along with a Puerto Rican development scheme, which promised much and delivered little, although it did alert a generation of Americans to the severity of what Rexford Guy Tugwell, appointed governor in 1941, called the "stricken land." Just as troubling as the island's depressed social and economic condition, however, was the nationalist agitation of a Puerto Rican elite for independence. In 1937 police, angry over the murder of their chief, fired into a crowd of Nationalist Party members in Ponce. During the war anti-Americanism flourished among both the Left and the Right, and in 1945 what to do with (or to) the island remained a conundrum.

Most Puerto Ricans recognized that independence would free them from their felt obligation to conform to American culture but would doom them to economic ruin. For those Puerto Ricans torn between the cultural identity the independence movement promised and the better life the American connection held out, Luis Muñoz Marín, leader of the Popular Democrats, had a deceptively simple and thus reassuring message. Shortly after the war, when President Truman declared that Puerto Rico had three choices (independence, statehood, or dominion), Muñoz responded by rejecting the first two and, in a modification of the third, called for a "commonwealth of the associated people of Puerto Rico." A commonwealth would enable the island to protect its economy and its cultural distinctiveness. The fact that the U.S. Constitution made no provision for such an arrangement escaped those U.S. leaders desperately searching for an alternative to the Puerto Rican conundrum.

Muñoz Marín became Puerto Rico's first elected governor in 1948. Two years later, Congress validated the commonwealth in Public Law 600, which it submitted to a plebiscite in an island wracked with uncertainty over what it meant. The Independence Party boycotted the voting. The Nationalist Party called for insurrection. They attacked police stations and even the governor's residence. Muñoz declared a state of emergency and called out the National Guard, which took over the University of Puerto Rico, where nationalist sentiment ran strong and its sympathizers regularly gathered. Eventually, the guard suppressed the insurrection, but not before two dozen had perished. In one highly publicized incident on 30 October, the guard stormed the home of the fiery old nationalist of the 1930s, Pedro Albizu Campos, who was teargassed into unconsciousness in the assault. The following day two Puerto Rican nationalists tried to assassinate Truman. For years the nationalists kept up their protests, arguing with considerable validity that Muñoz's characterization of Puerto Rico as a "freely associated state" simply masked with deceptive words the reality of a continuing colonial status. Muñoz was less *riqueño*, perhaps, but craftier. He now joined the U.S. delegation in the United Nations in arguing that Puerto Rico no longer belonged on the UN list of non-self-governing territories because Puerto Ricans had voted to accept Public Law 600.

Already, however, the American colony had begun to assume the economic character that became its blessing and, unintentionally, its burden. In its determination to rid the island of wartime government "socialism," Congress in 1945 authorized the Aid to Industry Program, by which private businesses could lease factories at very low rates, and two years later revolutionized the program with the Industrial Incentives Act, which forgave corporate taxes (and local taxes for a decade). Attracted by Puerto Rico's ready supply of low-cost labor, corporate America moved to the island. Almost immediately the *independentistas* condemned the transformation as simply another variety of colonialism—an industrial rather than a plantation colonization, but still a self-perpetuating dependence.[23]

In the 1950s Puerto Rican "colonial whining" (a phrase Tugwell often used) diminished noticeably because of the spectacular growth rates of the U.S. economic policy, called Operation Bootstrap, which in its most frenzied years led to the establishment of a factory every day. In the decade after 1947 the island's gross national product doubled, and on the eve of Castro's revolution in Cuba, which became in the 1960s the competitive economic model, Puerto Ricans enjoyed the highest per capita income in Latin America. Even as the economy lagged behind that of the mainland, the quality of life for Puerto Ricans rose impressively. Little wonder, then, that Puerto Rico became for the United States the economic model for the Alliance for Progress.

Puerto Rico proved to be a test case for U.S. postwar strategy in the Caribbean in other ways as well. During the war, U.S. officials persistently urged the British to step up the movement toward decolonization in the West Indies. In the late 1940s, however, the British grip on the region weakened before nationalist movements, the activities of West Indian migrants to the United States, and the undeniable economic costs of maintaining the empire.

Alert to the need to maintain British support in their Cold War strategy in mainland Latin America, U.S. officials joined the British and West Indian reformers in supporting the transition to greater self-governance. These efforts paid off in the creation of the West Indian federation in 1958, which reinforced the commonwealth tradition and relinquished security issues to the United States. But in 1962, the federation collapsed, the victim of Jamaican and Trinidadian jealousies and the U.S. reluctance to relinquish its military base at Chaguaramas, Trindidad, as a site for the federation's capital.[24]

By then, the Caribbean was in the "eye of the storm." Puerto Ricans and West Indian nationalists were rebellious and defiant, but they were not revolutionaries. The revolution against a U.S.-dominated hemisphere occurred in what most postwar Americans considered the most "Americanized" place in the Americas — Cuba.

The Cuban Revolution

When Fidel Castro triumphantly entered Havana in early January 1959 and ended what most Cubans and many Americans considered an odious dictatorship, progressive elements in the hemisphere cheered his victory. His war against Fulgencio Batista had at last brought down one of the triumvirate of tropical rulers — each identified with the U.S. presence in the Caribbean — whose long and sometimes ghastly rule ended in the following two decades. The second, Rafael Leonidas Trujillo Jr., who had wielded power as Caribbean Caesar in the nearby Dominican Republic, fell in May 1961, the deserving victim of assassins in his own military. The third, Anastasio Somoza DeBayle, whose father had molded a familial dynasty in the waning days of marine-ruled Nicaragua, fled to the United States during the final days of a civil war that consumed fifty thousand Nicaraguan lives. Unwanted in a nation whose president feared he was conspiring to reverse a revolution most Americans and virtually all Nicaraguans believed offered Nicaragua hope for a democratic future, Somoza sought sanctuary in Paraguay. He died a year later when terrorists ambushed his car.

Before these dictators departed from power, the United States had already distanced itself from them. (In Trujillo's case, the CIA abetted the assassins by providing arms.) In its expressions of support and its offers of economic assistance, the U.S. government welcomed their successors with the twin expectations of furthering hemispheric democracy and charting their economic and social courses. By abandoning the strongmen it had helped to install in power and sustained through long years of misrule, it naively believed that good intentions, economic assistance, and its military credibility would enable the United States to "guide" the revolutions that triumphed. But Castro and later the Sandinistas had their own priorities, their own agendas, their own timetables. Only in the Dominican Republic did the American political and economic prescription, reinforced by an overwhelming military presence, hold sway over the new order.[25]

In Venezuela, there were signs that the United States might find a reformist, anticommunist ally. After World War II, Venezuela became something of a laboratory for those who believed that there was indeed an alternative to the "ugly American" personified by the diplomat and the businessman. The "missionary capitalist" exemplar was Nelson Rockefeller, who believed that in Venezuela the United States could carry out not only an economic mission but a social mission as well — the first through the International Basic Economy Corporation (a for-profit entity) and the second via the American International Association, an agency dedicated to social improvement. Rockefeller was convinced that the world economy depended on the economies of the developing world. Venezuela seemed the appropriate place for such an exemplary effort. American culture, notably film, baseball, and particularly a materialist acquisitive instinct were noticeable middle-class Venezuelan traits. And Venezuela's petroleum made the country even more important to U.S. political leaders.

In 1953 Venezuela was in the political grip of a military dictator, Marcos Pérez Jiménez, admired by the anticommunists in the State Department and even decorated by President Eisenhower but vilified by the Venezuelan Left and the nation's reformers (including Rómulo Betancourt of Acción Democrática, which had briefly held power in a coalition government at the end of WWII). Both the Truman and Eisenhower administrations had reason to criticize Pérez's high-handed ways, but neither was going to crack down on a regime that nurtured a powerful petroleum industry and promoted closer economic ties with the United States. Private citizens and groups, such as the Inter-American Association for Democracy and Freedom, kept up the pressure to change things. The chorus of disapproval of the U.S. connection rose dramatically throughout the decade, reaching an explosive height in May 1958, when Vice President Nixon endured taunts and stone throwing in an ill-advised Caracas motorcade that nearly cost him his life. In the tense political atmosphere, Betancourt was viewed by many, especially U.S. leaders looking for an alternative to an odious dictatorship, as the solution. In December 1958 (as the Eisenhower administration was quietly trying to rid itself of the Batista dictatorship in Cuba), Betancourt won the Venezuelan presidency. He would join other Latin American leaders as the "alternative" political solution to a continent seemingly drifting inexorably left.[26]

In the calculations of most Cold War social scientists, Cuba should have been the least likely place for a socialist revolution — a ready place for a liberal assault against dictatorship, certainly, but not the kind of upheaval that Americans and Europeans identified with Soviet satellites of Eastern Europe. Cubans in the postwar era were perhaps the most Americanized of all former U.S. protectorates, more so than the Puerto Ricans. They absorbed American cultural values, from food preferences to architecture, and in response Americans delighted in listening to Cuban music. The economy of the island was virtually an extension of the mainland economy, as U.S. companies dominated Cuban telephone, telegraph, railways, sugar, bananas, tobacco, and petroleum. Cuba, in short, seemed fully integrated into the U.S. economy and thoroughly imitative in its slavish devotion to American cultural preferences.

By the early 1950s, Cubans of all social classes, not just the lower order, had come to resent the U.S. connection, albeit for different reasons. For those who nourished traditional ideas of Cuban identity, the link with the powerful neighbor was humiliating, particularly when Cubans looked at the role of organized crime in their beloved Havana. In 1944 the reformist leader effectively denied power by the United States in 1933 finally achieved victory, but in the ensuing eight years and two presidents (Ramón Grau San Martín and Carlos Prío Socorras), political corruption and graft convinced a generation of middle-class Cubans that something was terribly wrong with the political system. When the former dictator/president Fulgencio Batista launched his military takeover in 1952, most of the pro-American Cuban community and the U.S. government were pleased with the quick restoration of order and normal business. Others, however, viewed these events as yet another example of the denial of Martí's dream of an independent, sovereign republic.[27]

Castro launched his revolution against Batista's government with the disastrous attack on the Moncada barracks in Santiago in July 1953. His rallying cry was the restoration of constitutional government in Cuba, not the removal of American economic and political influence that had shrouded the island from the early years of the century. At his trial, when he delivered the "History Will Absolve Me" speech, he spoke largely for the benefit of Cuba's disgruntled professional and business classes who lived in a country that boasted the fourth highest per capita income in Latin America and had a vigorous intellectual and political community but suffered under a crass dictator widely regarded as an American puppet. And he spoke to another generation of Cubans, increasingly discontented and alienated, who believed him when he castigated a presumably modern Cuba where urban dwellers looked visibly prosperous and fun-loving while a countryside of illiterate cane workers lacked the necessities of life. He reminded Cubans of the ignominy of the foreign presence, largely American, which controlled the nation's utilities and 50 percent of its arable land. The Eisenhower government, at least indirectly, abetted Castro's cause by expressing its displeasure with Batista, even to the point of instituting an arms embargo (March 1958) and in a last-ditch appeal to easing the dictator out with promises of a safe haven exile in Miami. But he was too proud or too pigheaded to accept the offer. A few weeks later, he left the country.

Victorious over the despised Batista, Castro began with pledges to restore Cuban democracy, which heartened those middle-class Cubans who had repudiated Batista. But they quickly realized that Castro owed little to this group for his victory, and because of that they had little influence over him or his plans for restructuring the Cuban economy. Washington had dispatched a presumably sympathetic ambassador to Havana, Philip Bonsal, who issued no protest when Ernesto "Che" Guevara, Castro's economic czar, nationalized Cuba's American-owned telephone system. Castro followed with a dramatic visit to the United States, where he was lionized by a still admiring American public and press. Reluctant to appear as a mendicant to wary Cubans who had watched previous leaders make deals with Washington, Castro declared that he wanted not a loan but a new economic understanding with the United States. He met with Vice President Richard Nixon (President Eisenhower was vacationing in Augusta), who apparently liked Castro but was suspicious of communist influence in the revolution. To allay this and other charges, Castro denounced dictatorship and pledged to his American listeners that his revolution was not communist. As a symbolic gesture of his politics he snubbed the Soviet ambassador during a reception at the Cuban embassy and reminded Americans that his government had not restored the diplomatic relations with the Soviet Union that Batista had broken in 1955. But as he spoke, Cuba's ties with the United States were already unraveling.

Castro severed the American bond because the United States posed the most formidable international opposition to his plan to transform Cuba into a socialist nation — in other words, to "de-Americanize" the island.[28] He was dedicated to the long-held but never-realized dream that Cuba could play a pivotal if rarely decisive role in international politics. But the Cuban Revolution began with a calculated restructuring of the economy. The takeover of Cuba's telephone system was but the first of a series of measures that struck at American property interests in Cuba and, more fundamentally, challenged liberal American beliefs about the social and economic reforms that Cuba merited. In May 1959 the government announced a sweeping agrarian reform law, which applied to American holdings. Ambassador Bonsal upheld Cuba's right to expropriate foreign property if the government compensated the owners. Castro reassured him and then proceeded to move against large American-owned ranches. His rhetoric was alternately strident and conciliatory. Often in the same speech he denounced Washington for trying to control the course of the revolution and then offered soothing words to the same government he had assailed for its history of unjust intervention in Cuban affairs.

During the ensuing months, as seizures continued and irate owners criticized the arbitrariness of revolutionary justice and the executions of thousands deemed enemies of the revolution, statements from both governments indicated that disagreements over Cuba's economic policy might be reconciled through continued negotiations. By the end of the revolution's first year, Bonsal was still cautiously optimistic. Early in 1960, when the two governments seemed headed for a fundamental understanding, Castro proposed sending a delegation to the United States to talk about their differences, but he wanted pledges that Cuba's sugar quota, vital to the country's economic interests, would not be reduced. Washington refused.[29]

Afterward, the revolutionary course again shifted to the left. In February, Soviet First Deputy Anastas Mikoyan descended on Havana and signed a commercial treaty with the Cubans. The Soviets were not yet ready to make larger commitments, and Castro waited until May to restore diplomatic relations with Moscow. Even then it was not clear that the revolution was heading inexorably toward the creation of a communist state. What was apparent was Castro's determination to rid Cuban politics of naysayers and to purge the regime of its critics. He molded urban labor and rural *campesinos* into an alliance. Middle-class Cubans who had not yet abandoned the faith were denounced as enemies of the revolution. In June came the order to foreign refineries to process Soviet crude oil. Under pressure from the Eisenhower administration, they refused, and Castro further infuriated Washington by ordering their seizure. When the companies dispatched key personnel back to the United States, Castro brought in foreign technicians to run the plants. Significant, too, was the calculated decision to limit the involvement of urban groups who had proved critical to his victory.

Eisenhower had already suspended Cuba's sugar quota of nine hundred thousand tons, a severe blow to the island's economy but one that did not deter Castro or mitigate his defiance of Washington. By late summer, as the U.S. presidential campaign between Vice President Nixon and Senator John F. Kennedy was getting under way, the "Cuban question" had already become a political issue in the United States. By now, American public opinion about Castro had diminished from the early enthusiasm of his first months in power to doubts about where the revolution was heading and widely held skepticism about Castro's democratic professions. This shift in opinion roughly paralleled government policy and explains why Cuba became such a volatile subject in the fall and why Kennedy, in a narrow race for the White House, spoke often about Cuba's "loss."[30]

By then the Eisenhower administration had stepped up its timetable for dealing with Castro as it had dealt with Arbenz in Guatemala six years before, but the plan, which had emanated from Nixon's encounter with Castro in spring 1959, was not one the vice president could now use as rebuttal to a vigorous young senator determined to exploit the issue of "communism ninety miles from American territory." Fearful of communist penetration of Arbenz's government, the United States had moved quickly to unseat him. Guatemala was a lesson the intelligence bureaucracy often cited as reports of communist intrusion in the Cuban Revolution grew more frequent. Washington had rid the hemisphere of a leftist government in Guatemala; for even more compelling reasons it now proposed to topple Castro.[31]

Nixon had talked privately about the plan, but its gestation lay in the CIA, which had Operation PBSuccess (the scenario for the Guatemalan intervention) as proof of its expertise in handling such irritants elsewhere in the Caribbean and in Iran. To the generation that had masterminded the Guatemalan affair, the decision to topple Castro was perhaps more problematical and certainly fraught with more difficulties but, to use a favorite bureaucratic word, no less "doable." Castro defied American power and influence in Cuba; his revolution challenged the American prescription for Western Hemispheric development. Arbenz and the Guatemalan revolution had confronted American power, and the United States had rebuffed him. But in the process it had no alternative to Latin American liberals of the mid-1950s who were calling for a "Marshall Plan" for the Western Hemisphere.

The Eisenhower administration had learned one lesson from the Guatemalan affair — a revolutionary government that does not have the support of the military can be readily brought down without using U.S. troops. Castro learned this and more from the events of 1954: if the United States could not accept the Guatemalan Revolution, it most certainly would never accept the more radical Cuban variant. More important to Castro was his conviction that if he raised the stakes of the confrontation between Cuba and the United States to a level at which the United States would *have* to dispatch its soldiers to the island to destroy the revolution, it would not do so. Eisenhower had the benefit of U.S. intelligence operatives in Guatemala who verified the unreliability of the Guatemalan officer corps in the defense of the Arbenz government. Kennedy did not have such a reassurance about Operation Zapata, the outline for the Cuban operation, because Castro quickly eliminated anti-revolutionary officers from the Cuban military, most of them by execution. This, of course, U.S. officials knew, but they came to successive erroneous conclusions about the fighting capability of Cuba's military, the loyalty of a Cuban populace already outspoken in its criticism of the revolution, and what steps Castro would take to remain in power.

Thus was born what has been called the "perfect failure." The plan for unseating Castro had the sanction of the intelligence and military communities and a ready and willing army of former Batistianos, alienated middle-class exiles, and even vengeful former Castroites who had become disillusioned with the revolution and had fled to the United States. In retrospect, the former Castroites had the most persuasive strategy for dealing with Castro. Their spokesman, Manuel Ray, had organized a resistance movement against the *líder máximo* within Cuba, and in fall 1960 still another guerrilla operation had sprung up in the Escambray Mountains. Both sought CIA support but were discounted by agents as too isolated and too weak to cause much damage. Eventually, Castro's forces wiped out the Escambray guerrillas and sent Ray into exile.

In the United States, Ray pleaded for a resumption of the anti-Castro guerrilla campaign, but no one in the CIA was much interested. By then, the general plan called for a conventional landing of Cuban exiles in a remote spot along the southern Cuban shore. The assault troops would be sustained by American supply ships until they established a beachhead; then they would move inland (where disaffected Cubans would join them) and create a "legitimate" government that the United States and ultimately the international community would recognize. Ray criticized the plan as hopeless, arguing that the presence of so many former Batista officers among the exiles doomed the credibility of any invasion among even disaffected Cubans. But the CIA, whose agents moved about Miami with cash and advice, was determined to run things with the same gusto it had managed Operation PBSuccess. Besides, there was no one in the agency who believed Ray when he said that "Castroism without Castro" was the only way to get support from the large numbers of Cubans who chafed under Castro's rule. Even after the training camps were moved into Guatemalan boondocks, far from prying journalists, CIA trainers brooked little criticism from the Cuban charges and sent the complainers back to Miami. Shortly before the invasion, Kennedy insisted that Ray and his group (who called themselves the Revolutionary Movement of the People) be allowed to participate in the invasion, but the CIA effectively undermined the order by taking its leaders to an isolated farm outside Miami and holding them incommunicado.

Their presence among the invading brigade in April 1961 would probably not have altered the outcome of the battle at the Bay of Pigs, but their plan for toppling Castro, although it called for a prolonged struggle and American support, was in retrospect more realistic than that concocted by the CIA. Kennedy had his doubts about the latter but no acceptable substitute. Once Kennedy had acquiesced in the general plan for getting rid of Castro, he inquired as to its feasibility and was dutifully informed that it had a "fair" chance of success, which, he found out later, meant one in four. U.S. military support and, if necessary, the landing of U.S. troops would, of course, have dramatically altered this somber prognostication. But Kennedy was alert to the continuing barrage of invasion rhetoric from Castro's minister to the United Nations and to American credibility in the Third World. He stipulated that no U.S. troops were to take part in the invasion. He was committed to removing the Cuban nemesis but desirous of maintaining the nation's image among Latin Americans historically antagonistic to American intervention. In brief, the U.S. response to the revolution in April 1961, unlike those of 1895–98 or 1931–33 — interventions largely at the behest of Cuba's white elites — proved to be too little and too late. The exodus of disaffected Cubans had already begun: 62,000 in 1960, 67,000 in 1961, and another 66,000 in 1962. Most departed with every expectation that they would be able to return when — not if — the U.S. government removed their nemesis.

The success of the operation depended on American actions that the president was loath to take. Those lacking, it rested on variables within Cuba that Castro was able to control. The invaders left Nicaragua, where they had been relocated after publicity had prompted them to vacate Guatemala, believing that American planes would knock out Castro's puny air force, that American supplies would sustain them on the beach, that dissident Cubans would rally to their cause, and, more than anything, that the U.S. government would not abandon them. In all of these expectations they were mistaken. Castro took command of Cuban defenses, dispatched his planes to the Bay of Pigs to sink one of the supply ships, and ordered the arrest of thousands of Cubans suspected of collaboration with the invaders. In the United Nations the U.S. ambassador, Adlai Stevenson, defended a hopeless cause and stood humiliated. Throughout Latin America Kennedy was condemned for going too far in dealing with the Cubans, a sentiment widely expressed by an American public and press that had become suspicious of Castro and generally supported their government's pressures against him, but in the end they were uneasy with the methods employed to overthrow him.[32]

"Those Who Make Peaceful Revolution Impossible"

The outcry among Latin Americans was not unexpected; the reaction of the American public to Kennedy's acquiescence in the Cuban invasion and then, when it was imperiled, his inability to make sure it succeeded, damaged his political prestige. Neither, however, was a lasting disability. Castro's revolution and his defiance of American power left other legacies. The Bay of Pigs was a crossroads for both Castro and Kennedy. In its aftermath the prospects for reconciliation dwindled.[33]

Even before the Bay of Pigs, Castro had carried his challenge to the United States into Latin America. Shortly after returning from his 1959 American trip, he embarked on yet another venture, to participate in a hastily called meeting in Buenos Aires of the Committee of 21, which had been convened to discuss Latin American economic issues. Already the Cuban Revolution had increased apprehension about revolutionary outbreaks elsewhere. For the first time the United States encountered the "new Cuba" in a hemispheric forum. Castro himself led the Cuban delegation, sporting the now famous fatigues from his days in the mountains and smoking an iconic Cuban cigar. He was accompanied by fierce-looking bodyguards, but his popularity, especially among younger Argentines, seemed universal. Even inside the meeting hall, as he sat listening to dreary intonations from the other speakers, he continually distracted the audience with his nervous shifting of his legs and tugs on his moustache. When he rose to speak, few knew what to expect, but after a halting introduction he began what was for him a mild assessment of Latin America's troubles. Hemispheric governments were unstable, he said, because they ruled over backward economies, and they had to change. Latin Americans were not culturally unsuited for democratic governance, as European and American political observers had often said (and Latin Americans too often believed), but they were condemned to political retardation because they were denied the opportunity to develop their economies. He ended with a challenge to the United States to provide the continent with $30 billion in aid for the next decade.

Roy Rubottom, speaking for the U.S. delegation in a noticeably irritated tone, reminded the audience of U.S. support for the Inter-American Development Bank and rejected Castro's proposal. The delegates voted to table the Cuban request. Castro departed and did not participate in later inter-American meetings. When the foreign ministers convened in Santiago, Chile, in September, the Americans pushed for a collective disapproval of Cuba's relations with the Soviet Union. The Latin American response was a restatement of economic priorities, but in early 1960, when the ministers met again in San José, Costa Rica, Cuba's sponsorship of invasions and subversion in Panama, Haiti, and the Dominican Republic prompted the delegates to censure its government. Raúl Roa, Castro's emissary to the meeting, stormed out in protest. When the Committee of 21 met in Bogotá in September, the Eisenhower administration was prepared to support a Social Progress Trust Fund with $500 million to underwrite housing, education, and health projects in the hemisphere. U.S. delegates spoke less of relying on the private sector to underwrite Latin American development needs. It was obvious to the alert Latin Americans that Castro's revolution was largely responsible for this offer of American largesse.[34]

In the campaign of 1960 Kennedy spoke forcefully about Cuba, but he also seized on ideas originally put forth by Latin American reformers (notably, Brazilian president Juscelino Kubitschek and the leaders of the Economic Commission for Latin America) who called for a bold new development program for the troubled hemisphere. To a generation of Latin Americans accustomed to hearing shopworn phrases about "hemispheric unity" and "common goals" from U.S. political leaders, Kennedy described a hemisphere whose people unjustly suffered authoritarian rule and economic deprivation that the Alliance for Progress would address. The task was gargantuan in its dimensions — housing, jobs, agrarian reform, health, and education for the millions of Latin Americans who had abandoned hope of a better life. It demanded a "peaceful revolution." Without that effort, Latin America confronted violent upheaval.

In some of its proposals, such as the call for a Latin American free trade area and a Central American common market or American financial support to help certain hemispheric nations stabilize the often rapidly fluctuating commodity market, the alliance was not particularly revolutionary. But the thrust of the program was toward social reform and economic development on a scale unprecedented in Latin American history. Agrarian and tax reforms, literacy campaigns, and the extension of health measures to Latin America's poor were not only costly but threatening to the hold of the established social and political order. Kennedy made clear in later statements that such an ambitious program could best be carried out by civilian governments inspired by reformist leaders committed to economic development and social change. Accompanied by his wife, who spoke briefly in Spanish, the president formally inaugurated the Alliance for Progress in a ceremony before the Latin American delegations in March 1961. A month later occurred the fiasco at the Bay of Pigs.

The architects of the program were an impressive group. Though some, such as historian Arthur Schlesinger Jr. and Richard Goodwin, knew little of Latin America, they were eager students and willing to apply their considerable intellectual talents to overcome the hemisphere's vast but to them not insurmountable obstacles. Others, such as Teodoro Moscoso, Adolf Berle (chairman of the Latin American Task Force), Lincoln Gordon, Robert Alexander, Arthur Whitaker, and Arturo Morales Carrión, were knowledgeable about the region and brought a sense of urgency to their mission, as demonstrated by Moscoso's comment, "It is one minute to midnight in Latin America." And Kennedy, unlike his predecessor, did not follow absolutely the dictum of the Mutual Security Act of 1951, which used anticommunist criteria and national interest as the guide for allocating aid to mendicant Third World countries. The stress on economic development and social reforms appealed to a generation of "action intellectuals" who responded to Kennedy's style of cutting through the bureaucratic maze to "make things happen" with a program that offered Latin Americans a realistic choice to the society Castro's revolution was bringing to Cubans.

In August 1961, when the inter-American economic conference convened at a resort outside Montevideo to discuss hemispheric goals, the Alliance for Progress squad flew down to confront America's hemispheric adversaries. "Che" Guevara led the Cuban delegation. Although more ideological than Castro, Guevara nonetheless held out a tentative peace offering to Washington and met formally with the presidents of Argentina and Brazil. But there was little hope of reconciliation, and Guevara renewed the challenge with the af-firmation that the Cuban Revolution would achieve the goals of the alliance. The Americans were already pressing for the expulsion of Cuba's government from the OAS, and the other Latin American governments, though occasionally grumbling about Washington's harassment of Cuba, recognized American priorities and began cutting diplomatic ties with Havana. When the Venezuelans shut their embassy doors in November, Castro retaliated with a convoluted address in the Plaza de la Revolución about his "conversion" to Marxism-Leninism. In early 1962, Washington finally succeeded in expelling the Cuban government from the OAS, though this triumph, critics pointed out, resulted from considerable browbeating and bribery. A huge crowd gathered in Havana's Plaza de la Revolución to hear Castro's defiant response to the expulsion: "The OAS was unmasked for what it is — Yankee Ministry of Colonies and a military bloc against the peoples of Latin America."[35]

Cynical Latin Americans were already calling alliance funding "Fidel's money." Castro's emissary walked out of the conference with the ringing declaration that Cuba could be kicked out of the OAS but not out of the hemisphere. Shortly, Castro began calling for a united Latin America against U.S. imperialism, which elicited the praise of the Chinese Communists, then international champions of guerrilla war, but irritated the Russians, who were busily promoting peaceful coexistence with Latin America. Castro soon convinced them to pay closer attention by cracking down on dissidents within the country and exhorting Cubans to revolutionary solidarity. Cuba was undertaking the building of a socialist society, he declared, and until it was achieved the revolution must be safeguarded.

Nikita Khrushchev, assailed by Beijing for his betrayal of the revolutionary struggle against imperialism, began looking more closely at this still untamed revolutionary who mocked the United States yet now exhibited the revolutionary prudence to realize that socialism must be constructed within a country before the revolution could be exported. Had the Americans done nothing about Castro, Khrushchev would have understood; had Kennedy followed up the Bay of Pigs with an invasion and gotten rid of Castro, Khrushchev would have understood. In either case the Russians would have done little to help the Cubans and would have confined themselves to denunciations of American imperialism in the United Nations. But Kennedy had elected a third course and in the process had been indecisive. In their meeting at Vienna a few months after the Bay of Pigs, Khrushchev had bullied Kennedy, and the young American president had returned home recognizing that he had to redeem his reputation. Over the next year, his brother Bobby, in reality a "Deputy President," oversaw a series of poorly planned, poorly executed efforts to disrupt the Cuban economy and eliminate Castro ("Operation Mongoose"), to provoke a revolution that did not require backup by U.S. forces. When Kennedy finally got confirmation that the Russians had put missiles in Cuba, he felt betrayed, as if dealing with Khrushchev was tantamount to making an informal arrangement with a U.S. urban politico like Richard Daley of Chicago. The president — and, indeed, Khrushchev — learned a hard lesson in the Missile Crisis: the significance of this most dangerous moment in the Cold War was not only military but political and psychological, and resolution of the crisis proved to be essentially a question of character and not game theory.[36]

Thus the Cuban Revolution and the Alliance for Progress, each parading as the inescapable alternative for a distressed hemisphere, became the captives of history and circumstance. Expelled from the hemispheric system, the Cuban government (and Castro personally) embraced the Soviet Union, an alliance of two countries with dissimilar cultures and frankly dissimilar leaders born of Cold War politics and Cuban defiance of all geopolitical logic. When the superpowers squared off in the missile crisis of October 1962, none of the central issues dealt with the alternative Cuban and American proposals for Latin American political and economic change. In the settlement of the crisis, Kennedy and U.S. policy appeared vindicated by his courageous challenge to the Soviets and the support he received from the Latin American nations. Beneath the glow of victory lay a disconcerting reality: the United States had left the thorn implanted in the American side, a reminder of Cuban defiance.[37]

In the long run, the significance of the Cuban Missile Crisis often depended on the "angle" of the observer. For Kennedy, the Cuban threat was yet another challenge from an ambitious and expansionist Soviet Union and Premier Nikita Khrushchev. Castro, Kennedy naively believed, was little more than a surrogate for Soviet ambitions in the Americas, and like his predecessors, he framed the confrontation of October 1962 in the strategic, ideological, and even personal context in which he viewed the Cold War and the global threat of communism. The last proved to be of no small consequence in Kennedy's dealings with Conservative Canadian prime minister John Diefenbaker, a mild-mannered anticommunist who had supported the Bay of Pigs invasion and spoke of Cuba as a Marxist beachhead. But in Kennedy's mind, Diefenbaker lacked resolve, and for that reason the State Department made Diefenbaker privy to their decisions during the Missile Crisis only at the last hour. As two Canadian historians bluntly put the issue, "the United States ignored Canada, its closest ally, during what it believed to be the gravest crisis of the Cold War."[38]

In the initial assessments of the crisis, Kennedy received uncommon praise for his steadfastness throughout what is generally regarded as the most dangerous week in the history of the Cold War. Now that students of the crisis have access to most of the details, their assessment of his resolve and the decisions of all three men are more cautious — and more sobering. The Russians swore not to be caught again lacking the capability to respond to U.S. military might. After Khrushchev's removal from power, the Kremlin embarked on a military spending spree that ultimately bankrupted and then brought down the regime. Overconfident, the United States set itself on a disastrous military course in Southeast Asia that ended, humiliatingly, in the debacle of the fall of Saigon.[39]

Over the years, one thing has become clear: Castro may have felt left out in the critical exchanges between Kennedy and Khrushchev, but he was far from being a passive spectator in this crisis, and from his perspective he saw himself as a victor. Undeniably, his reputation throughout Latin America suffered in the initial months after the crisis, as the OAS resolved to use whatever means necessary — individually or collectively — to remove the missiles. Two years later, U.S. efforts to isolate Cuba in the hemisphere culminated in yet another OAS resolution condemning the Cuban government for violating the Río treaty by its interference in the internal affairs of Venezuela. All except Mexico approved a recommendation for OAS governments to break diplomatic relations with Cuba. (The Mexican government dispatched a team to Washington, D.C., to explain that the nation's revolutionary tradition forbade such an act but that Mexico resolutely opposed communism.)

By then, sadly, Kennedy was dead, assassinated by a pro-Cuban Marxist sympathizer, Lee Harvey Oswald. (Some conspiracy theorists continue to believe that Oswald shot Kennedy because of the latter's visceral hostility toward Castro.) For his presumed humiliation at the hands of the young U.S. president, Khrushchev lost power. But Castro survived and indeed became more daring in his challenge not only to the United States but to Soviet leadership of international communism. So, too, did the revolution long promised to generations of Cubans from 1892 and Martí's founding of the Partido Revolucianario Cubano and twice thwarted by the United States and its Cuban surrogates. When Castro got word about the OAS resolution against his government, he responded defiantly that "the people of Cuba consider themselves to have equal rights to help . . . the revolutionary movements in all countries that engage in such intervention in the internal affairs of our country."[40]

PART 4
The Modern Era

7   Years of Uncertainty

The Cuban Missile Crisis had a sobering impact on Kennedy, on the Russians, and on most everyone except Castro, who reputedly became so infuriated over the deal made between the young U.S. president and his Soviet counterpart that he began courting the Chinese and promoting himself as a Third World leader. Yet Kennedy clung to the belief that the United States could sustain a development policy that would raise the standard of living for a generation of Latin American and Caribbean peoples and thus prevent the kind of violent revolution that came in the aftermath of any sudden reversal of an improved standard of living. Havana had its propaganda machine; Washington possessed the United States Information Agency, which skillfully (and without attribution) used the television news program *Panorama Panamericano* to disseminate information about the Alliance for Progress as a liberal alternative to the socialist promise for a more prosperous and free hemisphere.

At the same time, Kennedy restated his doubts about military takeovers to prevent such threats from the left. Six weeks before the president's assassination in Dallas, Assistant Secretary of State Edwin A. Martin, in a major speech approved by the White House, affirmed that military takeovers constituted an impediment to political stability and democracy. Martin acknowledged that the United States could not deny the reality of a resurgent military in the volatile political culture of several Latin American countries. Kennedy made clear his priorities. "Every resource at our command," he stated shortly before his death, must be employed "to prevent the establishment of another Cuba in the hemisphere."[1]

For Kennedy, the confrontation with Cuba was personal. Indeed, in the goals and hatreds of these two hemispheric adversaries the world witnessed over the next fifteen years what can happen when advocates of conflicting ideologies and polities collide. From the Missile Crisis to the fall of Salvador Allende's socialist government in Chile in September 1973, the peoples of the Americas would experience profound changes in not only the political culture but in more fragile social relationships. Some related directly to the salient issues raised in the volatile exchange between Washington and Havana; others, such as the student protest, the civil rights movement, racial confrontation, decolonization, and immigration, appeared as secondary to the more explosive hemispheric confrontations we identify with the U.S. response to the Cuban Revolution and the controversial episodes of the inter-American experience during these years.

The defiant and rebellious island nation that José Martí had prophesied would be the center of a great West Indian civilization, the protectorate an exasperated Theodore Roosevelt called an "infernal little Cuban republic," and the neighbor Americans described metaphorically as ripe fruit, child, woman, and playground became John F. Kennedy's most formidable hemispheric challenge.[2]

Thus, the Kennedy legacy for the hemisphere remains a conundrum — modernization theory masquerading as ideology, counterinsurgency assuming the role of rural development and pacification, the Peace Corps and the Partners of the Americas indirectly abetting the intelligence work of the CIA — these and related contradictions in the young president's approach to hemispheric affairs proved a continuing problem for later generations of Latin Americans and Americans. At the same time, the emotional impact the young U.S. president had on a generation of Latin Americans, particularly young people, heralded a new day for hemispheric affairs.

The Alliance Balance Sheet

Kennedy's untimely death, it is often said, deprived the Alliance for Progress of its most dedicated advocate. The reality was that the fundamental problems in the alliance had already become visible before his death, and the entire program, to use Chilean president Eduardo Frei's words, began to "lose its way." Its diminishing momentum lay not so much in the example of Castro's revolution as alternative but in obstacles, some anticipated and others unforeseen, in the Latin American condition. One problem lay in the financing. The United States pledged $1 billion for the first year and an impressive $20 billion for the decade, but in the course of affairs the Congress committed half that amount with the expectation that private investors would contribute $10 billion and the Latin American governments, a whopping $80 billion. Out of each hundred dollars spent, only two dollars went to the poor.

Nonetheless, there were impressive accomplishments in agrarian reform, education, health, housing, industrialization, and employment. Seven of twenty-one recipient countries achieved the growth rate of 2.5 percent. But at the end of the 1960s, a U.S. government report gloomily concluded, Latin Americans had actually fallen behind in each of these categories. From 1960 to 1967 a million rural families were resettled, yet ten times that number remained on marginal plots with little hope of a better life. Too often those who had escaped the poverty of the countryside found a similarly depressing environment in the mushrooming slums and squatter settlements that surrounded Latin America's rapidly expanding metropolises. In education the Alliance for Progress sought an enrollment increase of 6 percent annually, an ambitious rate, but the preschool population grew so rapidly that, as in the agrarian resettlement program, programs could not keep pace with demand. Child mortality was reduced but at less than half the goal, and housing fell woefully short of the 15 million units needed. In the 1950s, when Latin America lacked the supportive economic underpinning of the alliance, more newcomers to the job market found employment than in the subsequent decade.[3]

Why had the alliance gone awry? Had Latin American elites, fearful of the disruption of profound changes to the social order and alert to the anticommunist priorities of the United States, placed insurmountable obstacles in its path? Had Washington abandoned its commitment to "peaceful revolutionary change" to achieve peace of mind? Or (as more thoughtful analysts have suggested) when the threat of Castro's revolution receded, did both Latin America *and* the United States decide the social and economic issues of Punta del Este no longer to be so compelling and the cost of achieving them to be so high as to make them unobtainable goals? Few faulted Kennedy for lack of good intentions or commitment. Of the postwar presidents, he was second perhaps only to Jimmy Carter in his zeal for understanding the region's major problems. Certainly, the security issue was uppermost in his mind, but he was also genuinely committed to helping the poor. At bottom, both the method and the means to achieve these twin goals were fraught with problems: essentially too much faith in the prevailing development model (modernization theory) and the belief that "one size fits all." At the same time, he became increasingly willing to use destabilization and covert methods against presumed enemies and more tolerant of military dictatorships. In a sobering assessment in June 1963, President Alberto Lleras of Colombia noted "the danger of a serious corruption of the spirit of the Alliance, its progressive weakening. . . . [T]he disappointment of the people with it . . . was obvious toward the end of 1962, when the enormous rehabilitation enterprise of Latin America began to be talked of as a new form of imperialism [and] . . . a gigantic publicity stunt."[4]

Early in the 1960s the alliance began to lose the democratic political sustenance required to achieve its social and economic goals. First came the dramatic resignation of President Jânio Quadros of Brazil, who believed his abrupt decision would lead to popular demands for his return. Then there was the military ouster of President Arturo Frondizi of neighboring Argentina, who had managed to alienate most of the country's powerful groups, followed in summer 1962 by a military coup in Peru. By the time the antidemocratic cycle ran its course, sixteen civilian governments fell to military seizures in the first eight years of the alliance. The official U.S. reaction, at least initially, was hostile. Washington expressed its displeasure at what it considered a return to the political authoritarianism of an earlier day. Kennedy was pointedly critical of the Peruvian military for its violation of the spirit of Punta del Este. Later that summer, as members of the Trujillo family threatened to disrupt a planned election in the Dominican Republic, the president dispatched warships to Santo Domingo to intimidate them.

In the Peruvian case, Kennedy took the position that the military had acted to prevent Manuel Odría (one of three candidates for the presidency) from winning by fashioning a political alliance with Haya de la Torre's *Aprista* Party, the nemesis of the Peruvian military. Such a move would deny the office to the reformist Fernando Belaunde Terry, favored by both the military and the Kennedy administration. On the surface, at least, the action taken in the Dominican Republic seemed less ambivalent both in purpose and results. Had the president chosen not to deploy those ships off the Dominican capital, the despised Trujillos might have been able to reassert their power.[5]

But there were limits to his antimilitary resolve, and, predictably, Cuba figured heavily in his calculations. In Guatemala, where a military coup forestalled the return to power of Juan José Arévalo (the former president, whose leftist reforms had irritated the United States), Kennedy was discreetly approving. In British Guiana, his concern about the political appeal of Cheddi Jagan, a Marxist, prompted Kennedy to pressure the British to delay granting independence until a more suitable candidate could be identified. In the aftermath of the missile crisis, as Castro's threat lessened, so did Kennedy's hostility to the Peruvian generals who had driven out a civilian leader by ramming a Sherman tank through the gate of the national palace. The British Guianan case proved more complicated. There the contest for power lay between Jagan, a self-professed Marxist, head of the People's Progressive Party, and of South Asian descent, and Forbes Burnham, of African descent and leader of the People's National Congress. The British clearly wanted to get out of Guiana. Neither they nor the U.S. government liked either Jagan or Burnham, but the latter was no socialist and that made the difference. So, Kennedy elected to use the AFL-CIO and the newly created American Institute of Free Labor Development to foment racial discord among the two groups and prevent Jagan from becoming the president of an independent Guyana. The ploy worked, much to the lasting embarrassment of both Washington and London.[6]

The turning point may have been military coups in Ecuador in July and in Honduras in October 1963.[7] The latter, which brought down the Liberal reformer Ramón Villeda Morales, prompted a rethinking of U.S. policy in the White House and, more fundamentally, the place of the Latin American military in hemispheric strategy. Edwin Martin, Kennedy's assistant secretary of state for Latin American affairs, in a public declaration, ruefully noted the grim prospects for reform under a military regime but acknowledged the difficulty of trying to sustain a civilian leader with economic coercion or even military pressure. Martin believed the most realistic course for the United States would have been to identify its Latin American policies with what scholars were calling the "emerging middle sectors," who were presumed to be committed to civilian rule and the development of a professional military.[8]

This admission was, at least, a recognition that Latin America was different, but the prevailing wise men in Washington still held fast to the notion that Latin Americans' political, economic, and social priorities were generally those that Americans ascribed to them. The complaints that had surfaced about the Alliance for Progress — in Congress and among some of the more grumbling recipient governments — had dealt with costs, procedures, and predictable bureaucratic muddling. Few in Washington or Latin America seriously questioned the Rostowian article of faith that development and democracy went hand in hand, that economic diversification and cooperation offered Latin America an opportunity to break the bonds of an agricultural past, or that civilians were preferable to generals in the running of public affairs.

What was lacking in the American prescription for Latin America was a fundamental awareness not only that Latin America was different but also that its politics, its economy, and its social structure fit together differently, worked differently, and expressed different values. If democracy meant the dispersal of power, as Americans believed, then in Latin America, where legislators often represented traditional interests opposed to social and economic reforms, democracy was an obstacle to development. Latin America had to develop its economy, but it needed also to develop a parallel real democracy, which imperiled the ruling social order. Not until 1966 did the U.S. Congress, which had become increasingly disillusioned with the diminishing fortunes of hemispheric democracy, insist that American aid for development projects should be conditioned on participation of local governments and social organizations.[9]

For most Latin American leaders, unaccustomed to sharing decision making with those on the bottom, this was truly a radical notion and precipitated considerable grumbling about American interference, but it revealed that Congress had a vague awareness of the limitations of an aid program that lacked political purpose. Latin America had to identify social and economic goals — in education, agrarian reform, employment, and housing — which it undertook, often with enthusiasm, but it then had to integrate its marginal people into the social order, and do so in a way that did not threaten those accustomed to obedience as well as gratitude from the beneficiaries. Ironically, some of the most telling criticism came from those running the program (among them, the Puerto Rican Teodoro Moscoso) or congressmen who visited Latin American countries and returned to Washington voicing complaints about the snail's pace of projects. In November, the State Department finally relented to the pleas of two Latin American presidents — Kubitschek of Brazil and Alberto Lleras Camargo of Colombia — to create an Inter-American Committee for the Alliance for Progress, with a board dominated by Latin Americans. The move placated some but did not quell the grumbling. In the summing up, hostility among Latin Americans toward the United States in the 1960s varied from place to place. It was often ambivalent, a juggling of positive and negative features, attitudes sometimes referred to as a "love-hate" relationship. The U.S. response to anti-Americanism, often decried as crude or an overreaction, often proved resilient.[10]

The Perils of Pragmatism

At the time of Kennedy's death the alliance was not yet in disarray, but Washington's approach toward Latin America had already become more pragmatic. As the United States increased its financial and diplomatic pressures, the recipients of its largesse became more defiant. The civilian president of Argentina, Arturo Illia (who had succeeded the military regime in 1963), had assumed office vowing to cancel foreign oil contracts, which he believed were illegal. Warned that such a move would jeopardize American aid and prompt Congress to invoke the Hickenlooper Amendment (which mandated termination of foreign aid to any country that did not compensate for seized American property), Illia moved ahead. The Hickenlooper Amendment was not applied, but aid to Argentina fell dramatically, from $135 million in 1963 to $21 million the following year.

President Lyndon B. Johnson, a strikingly different personality from Kennedy, proved no less committed to preventing "another Cuba," but in his dealings with hemispheric problems he displayed none of his predecessor's magnetism. Although Johnson pledged to make the Alliance for Progress a "living memorial" to Kennedy, it soon became apparent that his approach would follow the style of a Democratic politico who had acquired from his mother a strong moral imperative to do good and an unparalleled determination to succeed. With his fellow Texan Thomas Mann as his "point man" on Latin America, Johnson soon took the practical approach to hemispheric issues. He talked about Panama or Mexico or the Dominican Republic or even revolutionary Cuba in the political vernacular he used when dealing with a recalcitrant senator "bucking him" on a piece of legislation. There were those who could be pressured or bought off, but in some cases there were limits to hardball politics. A June 1964 telephone conversation with Mann about what to do with Castro is illustrative. When Johnson casually inquired about "getting rid" of the Cuban leader, Mann set him straight. As long as the Cuban military supported Castro, his removal was unlikely. Besides, Mann astutely noted, if Castro were gone, who would replace him?[11]

Johnson had already confronted trouble in Panama, where a serious dispute over the flying of the U.S. and Panamanian flags in the Canal Zone had deteriorated into a dangerous confrontation in January 1964. The origins of this breakdown in U.S.-Panamanian relations stemmed indirectly from the frustration of a generation of young Panamanians determined to rectify long-standing grievances over the canal and the symbolism of the Canal Zone as de facto, if not de jure, U.S. territory. Initially, President Kennedy responded favorably to Panamanian requests to allow Panama to benefit more from canal operations and to permit Panama to fly its national banner at selected places in the Canal Zone. As Kennedy soon discovered, the Canal Zone had its own constituency in the U.S. Congress, and the combination of congressional pressure and reluctance of U.S. military commanders in the Canal Zone to endorse the president's policy prompted Kennedy to rethink his decision. In the midst of the crisis, the embattled Canal Zone governor elected to order the lowering of both flags in the zone. When Panamanians learned that a promised sea-level canal might not be constructed because of U.S. pledges not to use nuclear devices to excavate the waterway, they were outraged. To Panamanians, the hoisting of the national flag in the Canal Zone had a powerful symbolic value: the need to protest an invasive American enclave that not only physically divided the nation but whose very existence made Panamanians feel like aliens in their own homeland.[12]

The shooting erupted when Balboa High School students defied the governor's order and raised the flag at their school. In response, Panamanian students marched into the Canal Zone and tried to hoist the Panamanian banner. The ensuing scuffle between the two groups quickly escalated into a local battle and then more serious violence that the police could not stop. Only the combined actions of the National Guard (which aided isolated Americans trapped in Panama to reach the safety of the Canal Zone) and U.S. troops brought order. For several months relations between the two governments were suspended. In the end, and with his customary flair for the dramatic, Johnson promised the Panamanians that they would eventually get a new treaty and held out the promise of a new sea-level canal — but they had to wait.[13]

This was the pragmatic approach to Latin America. If Latin Americans wanted more control over their economic future, they would have to pay a political price. The intellectual guru of this policy was Mann, who characterized public aid as ineffectual and favored a businesslike approach to the hemisphere. This idea translated, his critics charged, into inordinate sympathy for American private investment in Latin America. It was perhaps an exaggeration, but with Johnson's blessing, Mann assumed control over State Department and Agency for International Development (AID) operations in Latin America, replacing Martin and Moscoso. He called in U.S. ambassadors to the hemispheric republics and laid down the new priorities — a preference for economic growth over social reforms, protection of U.S. investments, neutrality toward Latin American governments, whether reformist or rightist, and an unambiguously anticommunist temper to U.S. policy.

Six months earlier, Martin had spoken hesitantly about the resurgence of Latin America's military. Mann's inspirational lecture quickly had its impact. A few weeks later, the Brazilian military, attentive to Washington's demonstration of its displeasure with the populist João Goulart, drove him from office in a coup. Ambassador Lincoln Gordon had learned of the projected overthrow several months earlier from disgruntled São Paulo businessmen, and the CIA had funneled money to U.S. private interests in the country to subsidize anti-Goulart marches in the city. The Johnson administration, which obviously applauded Goulart's fall, recognized the new military government in only twelve days. Once in power, the generals unleashed their wrath on Brazilian radicals, stripping political rights from three former presidents, six governors, fifty-five assemblymen, and prominent labor organizers and intellectuals. Gordon contemplated resigning in protest, but he was persuaded that the United States could exercise a moderating influence on the Brazilian military. That may have been an unrealistic and even naive assessment, given his involvement in the affair. Forty years later, the National Security Archive made available declassified documents revealing that President Johnson had not only authorized the use of covert measures on behalf of paramilitary forces in Brazil but also had ordered a U.S. naval task force to the Brazilian coast in support of the coup.[14]

But the ships never made it to Brazilian waters. The Brazilian generals — some of whom had experience in the World War II Italian campaign—did not require U.S. military aid. Purged of its leftist members, the Brazilian Congress chose army chief of staff Humberto Castelo Branco (who had led the takeover) as the new president. In his most pessimistic forecasts, Gordon could not have foreseen the vigorous economic expansion and political repression that lay ahead for Brazil, which became in the decade after the coup a bloody symbol for those who believed that economic growth flourished in the authoritarian state. Washington demonstrated its appreciation by showering its praetorians with $1.5 billion in aid in the first four years after the military seizure of power. In retrospect, some have argued that without U.S. acquiescence, the Brazilian military might not have undertaken the repressive policies that followed the coup nor would they have systematically "denaturalized" Brazilian cultural identity. Brazil's military leaders resolved to act, with or without Washington's approbation. Both Kennedy and Johnson disliked the leftist shift of Quadros and Goulart, but the military feared even more his inability to reconcile the conflicting political forces in the nation. In the end, Goulart could have mobilized a resistance, but he chose to spare the nation a bloody confrontation. The Brazilians were not following a U.S. "playbook" in this crisis. As Lyle McCalister has observed, "Militarism in Latin America is an indigenous phenomenon . . . a response to tensions in societies" and not a direct response to U.S. influence.[15]

In Bolivia, however, the U.S. impact on the course of events was more direct. American dissatisfaction with the presence of Juan Lechín, vice president in the government of Víctor Paz Estenssoro, grew so intense that Paz turned against his former political ally. In the late 1950s, as the United States pressed its financial stabilization plans on Bolivia, Lechín had shielded the Left. When Paz took him on as vice president, Lechín became more conciliatory, visiting Washington to affirm his anticommunist convictions. But even a trip to Nationalist China did not convince the Americans that he had abandoned his radical notions and his support of the Bolivian Workers' Central, which Washington and the International Monetary Fund perceived as an obstacle to their Bolivian financial scheme. Alert to American wishes, Paz turned against Lechín and tried to break the grip of the Bolivian Left on the Nationalist Revolutionary Movement (MNR).

When that failed, he turned to the Bolivian military, which the revolution had virtually demolished in its seizure of power in 1952, arguing that the country now confronted the peril of internal subversion. American military advisers streamed into the country to train the counterinsurgency force that three years later triumphed over Che Guevara's peasant revolution. In a calculated move, Paz cemented his alliance with the military by taking on General René Barrientos as vice president, but the disintegration of the MNR offered opportunity to the revolution's enemies. Two months after the election, the generals, with Barrientos in the fore, took over. They rejuvenated agrarian reform, declared war on urban labor, and enthusiastically supported foreign investment.

What occurred in Bolivia offered a dual lesson for U.S. leaders, the first reassuring but not the second. Ernesto "Che" Guevara had come to Bolivia convinced that its marginalized and oppressed peasantry would be willing recruits to his revolutionary message. But the MNR had done enough to extend the benefits of the 1952 revolution to mollify Bolivia's indigenous people, and the Bolivian military easily defeated his guerrilla force. At the same time, befuddled U.S. agents watched as Bolivian leader René Barrientos cynically used his populist image to undermine the social reforms of earlier years, crack down on dissidents in the labor unions, and enrich himself. Accused of being a CIA lackey, he ultimately was estranged from his U.S. benefactors and sought friends in the Soviet Union. In his obituary in U.S. newspapers, he was hailed as a populist general committed to democracy, yet another distortion of the reality of a man placed in an orphanage at an early age but at his death leaving an estate of $10 million.[16]

And in Argentina, the military, alert to the financial rewards that their Brazilian counterparts had gained, tossed out the middle-class civilian president, Arturo Illia, in June 1966. The generals then installed one of their own in his stead, prorogued the legislative assembly, and banned political parties. Afterward, Washington augmented its aid package to Buenos Aires. The United States had not abandoned its support of democratic civilian governments in the hemisphere, but Mann had clearly rearranged the hemispheric agenda. In a major speech at Notre Dame in June 1964, he had reaffirmed American support for representative democracy and American commitment to press for elections in countries where the military had seized power. Condemnation of the military for its illegal seizure of power served little useful diplomatic purpose. In any case, the issue of communism was a different matter, for it raised vital questions of hemispheric security and national interest.[17]

The Dominican Intervention

The crisis in the Dominican Republic demonstrated just how complicated such an approach could be. After Trujillo was killed, the U.S. government had identified its policy with his most popular critic, Juan Bosch.[18] In the aftermath of Kennedy's dispatch of naval vessels to prevent a return of the Trujillo family to power, Bosch swept to victory. For seven months, this unpredictable, chain-smoking Dominican poet-revolutionary fascinated a people ground under by indisputably the most gruesome tyrant in the history of the Western Hemisphere. But his American benefactors and the Dominican military grew increasingly, and noticeably, irritated. He did not lead, was weak, and, worst of all, was said to allow the communists to organize. Bosch responded that it was better to have them in the open rather than drive them into the mountains to wage guerrilla war, but this was not the democratic toughness Washington wanted. Nor, apparently, what Bosch's generals wanted. In fall 1963 they drove him into exile. Kennedy denounced the coup but reluctantly acknowledged he had to recognize the new regime. Ambassador John Bartlow Martin, who had praised Bosch's pluralism, soon found himself "out of the loop" in State Department communiqués about the Dominican situation. For the time being, the outward demonstration of indifference to the coup appeared to work.[19]

The generals ran the government for a few months and then installed a triumvirate, headed by Donald Reid Cabral, a civilian. Satisfied that the Dominican military had the Left under control, Washington turned its attention elsewhere in the Caribbean. Reid called for austerity and stability, twin credos that pleased the Johnson administration. They were not especially welcomed by Dominican business and professional elements, who grumbled about his tight-money measures and doubtless welcomed the demonstrations, strikes, and comical plotting that disrupted his tenure. Dominican social conservatives found their hero in Joaquín Balaguer, who had served Trujillo but did so, they believed, under duress, an understandable and to them forgivable predicament. More serious was the challenge of a band of junior officers in the Dominican military who called for the restoration of constitutional government and looked to Bosch as their leader.[20]

Their revolt, which began in late April 1965 with the takeover of a radio station and the arrest of a general dispatched to placate Bosch's partisans, appeared initially to offer no serious challenge to Reid. He sent reinforcements to Ozama fortress, and national police readily dispersed crowds that had gathered in the capital's central district. But Reid did not move against the dissident colonels within the military. They renewed their demand for Bosch's return. When Reid refused, they seized the fire station and began taking positions in the city. Unable to rely on his own military for protection, he put in frantic calls to Washington and the U.S. embassy in Santo Domingo.

Washington's principal concerns were the safety of Americans in the capital and, as the situation deteriorated, the communist influence among the pro-Bosch elements. U.S. officials presumed that real power lay with the Dominican generals holed up at San Isidro Air Base outside Santo Domingo, who would, they believed, prevent Bosch's return, even if it meant another military takeover. They had not taken accurate measure of the hesitancy of the generals to maintain Reid, and they underestimated the resolve of the junior officers, who moved decisively by organizing Bosch's civilian partisans. Their leader, Colonel Francisco Caamaño Deño, personally arrested Reid and proclaimed Bosch's imminent return on Dominican radio.[21]

For the Dominican generals and for Washington, of course, the issue was not constitutional government but the prospect of Bosch returning to power, which they believed would throw the country into civil war. If that happened, the communists would surely take advantage of the chaotic situation to install themselves. Their numbers (as journalists covering these events soon revealed) were grossly exaggerated, as was their influence among the junior officers, who championed Bosch's restoration. Yet in the early calamitous days of the revolt, while Bosch supporters roamed the streets, sending foreigners scurrying into the Hotel Embajador, the grim reports coming into the Operations Center at the State Department made for unsettling reading. The rebels wanted no confrontation with the United States. They vowed to protect American lives and property. When the generals at San Isidro began mobilizing against them, they appealed to Washington to mediate. Ambassador W. Tapley Bennett Jr. arrived back in Santo Domingo just as the anti-Bosch military faction unleashed a ferocious attack on rebel positions. The Embajador and the embassy came under sniper fire, presumably from the rebels. With rifles cracking in the background, Bennett made the frantic call to Washington that precipitated Johnson's decision to intervene. On 28 April five hundred marines from the

USS *Boxer* went ashore in Santo Domingo. In a national television address that evening Johnson declared that they had landed to safeguard American lives and to prevent "another Cuba" in the Western Hemisphere.[22]

Within a week reinforcements arrived, taking up position at San Isidro Air Base. Their presence, Johnson argued, was justified by the stream of disturbing reports about communist infiltration in the revolution. Initially, their putative role was to maintain a tenuous neutrality among the armed political factions. In reality, as several prominent Latin American governments charged, their purpose was to provide hemispheric validation of what they called the Johnson Doctrine: unilateral American intervention to prevent a communist takeover. When the American command decided to send the larger San Isidro force into the capital to join with the initial contingent of marines, thus bringing the Americans into conflict with the rebels, all pretense of neutrality evaporated. Johnson was not indifferent to hemispheric criticism, but the outcry provoked his legendary vulgarity. As a hastily assembled Dominican crisis team arrived from Washington, the U.S. government pushed through a resolution in the OAS (which Johnson had said "could not pour piss out of a boot if the instructions were written on the heel") authorizing an inter-American peace force of 9,100 U.S. and 2,000 Latin American (mostly Brazilian) troops to provide for an orderly transition. They remained for almost a year, guaranteeing that Joaquín Balaguer, not Juan Bosch, would guide what the U.S. government styled a controlled democratic experiment.[23]

The Dominican intervention did not erase the American commitment to Latin American development, nor did Latin American criticism shut off the flow of aid, public and private, from the United States. What the dispatch of American and Latin American troops into Santo Domingo symbolized was the chasm between U.S. priorities and Latin America's needs and the American disillusion with the Alliance for Progress. At the heart of the debate is not only Johnson's action in this crisis but the character of the man himself. As did Kennedy, he believed in restraining communist expansion until, according to the prevailing wisdom, it collapsed for failing to satisfy the needs of the individual. Johnson believed that containment of communism meant more than military alliances or hardware but also required a direct response of government to people, especially those in the Third World. At the same time, he felt compelled to control the divisive forces within the nation, not only his critics on the left but even more so the powerful anticommunist right. To rely on the OAS to settle the Dominican Civil War, he feared, was to risk further outcries from this power sector about his anticommunist credentials and in the process would endanger his goal of achieving the Great Society. He tried to satisfy both liberals and conservatives and in the end satisfied neither.[24]

Political Divides

Although the analogy did not quite fit, that was for some critics the problem of the Alliance for Progress in the shifting political climate of Latin America. In this critical decade, the laudatory social reforms of the alliance — in education, health, agrarian reform, literacy, and the like — weakened before the demands of private investment and Latin America's increasingly burdensome obligations to use aid to repay debts or to absorb American exports. But they also weakened before unanticipated Latin American priorities. By every economic measure Latin America appeared better off in 1968 than in 1960, but those who benefited were largely those who had been better off in 1960. American planners had believed that commitment to development and democracy would nourish the Latin American middle class, which would in turn sustain the social and economic programs that would serve as a bulwark against communism. They could not easily foresee that the middle-class beneficiaries of their largesse had a more fearful view of social philanthropy and a more somber appraisal of democracy.

Undeniably, the United States shifted its efforts from social programs to the private sector as the linchpin of economic development. It did so, in part, for security reasons. Thus agricultural development gave way to agricultural pacification. But there was a more fundamental reason. As the decade wore on, the United States was confronted with a dilemma. The model the Alliance for Progress had chosen for its program of economic development was Puerto Rico, hailed as the alternative to the Cuban Revolution. Latin Americans did not deny the impressive statistics of the Puerto Rican economy, but they were unwilling to accept its development scheme as one to emulate. Puerto Rico's development architects had taken advantage of the rural labor force on the island and extended incentives to manufacturers and industrialists to relocate there. That was unobjectionable — even to Latin America's elites. But they were hesitant to accept the impact that Operation Bootstrap had on lower-class Puerto Ricans who moved into San Juan or New York. Though the dream eventually vanished before the reality of urban squalor, their expectations had been raised, and more important, the poor of San Juan refused to accept something their parents and grandparents in the countryside had traditionally accommodated — the Hispanic's view of the social order and one's place in it.

Kennedy committed the United States and its economic strength to the Alliance for Progress in the name of America and its political values; he confirmed Latin America's place in U.S. Cold War strategy. Latin Americans adored him for the first, and they forgave him for the second. His successor continued that aid and reaffirmed with troops Washington's strategic priorities in the hemisphere. Latin Americans disliked him whether he did them good or ill, but neither Kennedy nor Johnson was singularly responsible for the failure of the alliance and the end of the democratic dream in the authoritarian nightmare. Development and democracy coexisted in American developmental theory but not in Latin American reality. In 1960 Latin American dictatorship was in decline and civilian democracies in the ascendancy. In the course of the decade, Latin American militarism and authoritarian governments were reborn, sometimes with U.S. acquiescence and even encouragement and, it must be remembered, with the acquiescence and encouragement of a Latin American middle class that valued its well-being more than it valued the incorporation of Latin America's marginal populations in the social order.

In such circumstances, the lower classes lost out — not only in income but also in any meaningful social advancement. In a curious and entirely unexpected way, however, they found an opportunity to move up the social ladder — in the military. Americans decried the growing militarization of Latin America in the 1960s as a threat to political democracy but overlooked the impetus that a military career gave to social democracy and, indeed, to the notion that the military can run the state and manage the economy more efficiently than civilians. The American trainers at the School of the Americas in the Canal Zone thought they were tutoring a generation of Latin Americans in the art of counterinsurgency, but they were also conveying to impressionable students (as the U.S. Army had done to the Brazilians in the Italian campaign in World War II) the belief that the soldier can run things if he has to. This was an unintentional but unmistakable legacy of the counterinsurgency program.

At the beginning of the 1960s, Latin Americans, it was confidently believed, confronted two choices for their future — the Cuban revolutionary model, which had not yet assumed its Soviet economic or political character, or the agenda offered in the Charter of Punta del Este and the promise of peaceful revolution. Ten years later, Latin America had two unpalatable symbols of what had been wrought: Cuba and Brazil. For those who had yearned for social justice and a better life in a democratic society, neither offered much reassurance of Latin America's political future. Cuba undeniably had achieved much in the decade. In education, public health, and the integration of rural and urban sectors, the revolution went farther than any Latin American country in attaining the objectives of the Alliance for Progress, but as Castro himself confessed, it had not achieved its developmental goals. It was a failure only partially explained by the U.S.-led economic embargo against Cuba and the island's isolation in the Western Hemisphere.

For democratic Latin Americans, the Cuban model offered little solace. But, then, neither did Brazil, for accompanying its impressive economic growth was a ruthless suppression of liberties carried out with such gruesome effectiveness that it sickened even social conservatives. Brazil at the close of the decade was the domain of generals and technocrats propped up by a coalition of financiers, industrialists, large landowners, and a new middle class. The dissenters (students, labor organizers, intellectuals, the remnants of Goulart's populist forces, and Catholic priests) were isolated, harassed, imprisoned, tortured, and sometimes killed. When the military had seized power in 1964, few believed the regime could persist, but the generals held power for two decades.

Yet there were less noticed variations on these political and economic models. The Peruvian military, which had ousted a civilian government in 1968, offered a curious fusion of social reform and repression. The generals enthusiastically promoted land reform, nationalized a highly visible foreign company (International Petroleum), throttled the press, and imposed their will on the judiciary. With a logic that befuddled American liberals and conservatives, General Juan Velasco Alvarado (one of the Peruvian generals who had led the military takeover) explained the zigzag course the junta had chosen: "When one is pursued by a herd of maddened bulls one has three options. One is to kneel, close the eyes, and pray. The second is to fight the bulls, which is as good as the first option. The third is to lead the stampeding herd into terrain that is more advantageous to the pursued. The masses in Latin America are starting to stampede. We the military are the only ones who are capable of leading them — and us — into safe ground."[25]

The 1968 Peruvian Revolution deeply shook the political culture. Not only did the military government end the International Petroleum Company's (IPC's) activities in the country, but the entire affair dramatically altered the nation's relationship with the United States. The focus of public attention now shifted away from U.S.-Peruvian links to the revolution itself and its imprint on Peruvian culture and society. The foreign presence remained, of course, but Peru's new leaders now determined they must exorcise the prevailing assumptions of dependency on foreign investment and advice from the United States.[26]

More palatable was the route taken by Chile, Venezuela, and Colombia, where those in power had resolved to permit their political opponents to campaign more or less freely while promoting economic development and the broadening of the social order. In Colombia, this conciliatory approach (in which Liberals and Conservatives had agreed to alternate in the presidency) had been critical in mitigating the volatile legacies of the civil war. In Venezuela, the Democratic Action Party, whose leader, Rómulo Betancourt, had served as Kennedy's prototypical Latin American democrat, had dominated politics through the decade and had carried out reforms that for the time being had placated the Left. In Chile, the Christian Democratic party of Eduardo Frei, identified as "the last best hope" by his U.S. admirers, had won power in 1964.

But in each of these there were problems. In Frei's case, the principal intent of the United States was to prevent the election of the socialist candidate Salvador Allende. Frei was a reformist with a nationalist bent. He tried to capitalize on Chilean resentments over a U.S. Army research project to study insurgencies in underdeveloped countries (Operation Camelot), commenced diplomatic relations with Eastern Bloc countries, and pursued a more conciliatory agenda with Cuba. In Colombia, enthusiasm for the Alliance for Progress quickly subsided after Kennedy's death, but President Alberto Lleras Camargo was more to the point when he noted that the rhetoric had proved more radical than the willingness to bring about necessary changes, especially in the volatile areas of agrarian reform and taxation. By the end of the decade Congress no longer had much confidence in the Colombian model. A similar disaffection occurred with Venezuela. Washington admired President Rómulo Betancourt (1958–64) for his commitment to democracy, and because his domestic enemies came from the left they showered him with money. They tolerated his anti-dictatorial agenda. But when his successor, Raúl Leoni, criticized the Dominican intervention, Johnson was outraged, and by the end of the decade one of the continent's most Americanized countries appeared to be moving toward an independent course.[27]

With the sustaining influence of the Alliance for Progress, it was said, their example might have spread elsewhere in Latin America, but in 1969 the United States had virtually abandoned the alliance. Almost simultaneously, Latin America, disturbed by America's altering priorities, lost its enthusiasm for the OAS. In the Dominican crisis the United States had exploited its dominance of the inter-American system to exact compliance with its interventionist policies. When Johnson left office in 1969, Vietnam was obviously the fulcrum of America's global policy, but for Latin Americans, the turning point in hemispheric solidarity had come four years earlier, when a determined American president had reaffirmed, in what they bitterly called the Johnson Doctrine, Washington's old habits and priorities in dealing with its neighbors. In the humiliation the OAS had remained largely silent. In three conferences of the organization from 1965 to 1967, the distrust of the United States, largely brought on by U.S. intervention in the Dominican Republic, hampered long-standing goals of trying to remold the hemisphere's political structure into a more effective force in the settlement of disputes between member states without invoking the Rio treaty. There were exceptions to this unsettling trend, among them Washington's tacit support for the 1967 Treaty for the Prohibition of Nuclear Weapons in Latin America and the Caribbean (the Treaty of Tlatelolco). The determination to prevent another Cuba in the Caribbean may have succeeded, but hemispheric unity suffered for it.[28]

The Rockefeller Mission

When Richard Nixon became president in January 1969, Vietnam, not Latin America, was his concern. The dreary reports about the failures of the Alliance for Progress had confirmed in his mind the direction U.S. policy should take. The United States must maintain its dominating political image and safeguard the interests of the American multinationals with a large stake in Latin America, he argued, yet it must do so without the costs a heavy-handed approach often entailed. This meant supporting "our friends" (the resurgent Latin American militaries) and opposing "our enemies." Latin America had exhausted its efforts to bring about peaceful revolution and in the process had merely inspired the Left to exact ever greater demands on fragile political systems. The generals had reluctantly seized power to preserve the social order. This was a simplistic analysis of the situation, but in considering Latin America, the president and most Americans preferred to think in black-and-white terms. Responding to proposals for greater Latin American access to the American market, which had been raised at the Viña del Mar conference in Chile, Nixon confidently asserted that the Latin Americans wanted not aid but trade, not costly social programs such as the Alliance for Progress but the opportunity for more dynamic free enterprise economies. Such was his developmental strategy for the continent.

Yet in August 1969 Nixon got a report on the condition of the Americas that was disquieting. In the spring he had dispatched his old adversary and former coordinator of inter-American affairs Nelson Rockefeller on a mission southward. Rockefeller had returned bearing grim tidings about the quality of life in the hemisphere. In phrases as compelling and occasionally as eloquent as Kennedy's, Rockefeller spoke of common goals, common bonds, and the need to create a "community of self-reliant, independent nations linked in a mutually beneficial regional system, and seeking to improve the efficiency of their societies and the quality of life of their peoples." This was heady stuff in light of the disappointments of the 1960s, but Rockefeller had not finished. Latin America's dismal condition, he wrote in a remarkably candid passage, was largely a result of American policy. U.S. aid and commercial policies had been carried out in a way that denied the "aspirations and interests of its neighbors," and Washington had often cavalierly displayed a "paternalistic attitude" toward

Latin American governments, interfering in their domestic affairs in an "unseemly" manner as if "it knew what was best for them." The United States had spoken of a "new partnership"; now was the time to practice it.[29]

Latin American reformers were initially heartened by such an unusual American self-flagellation but were just as quickly disillusioned when they read Rockefeller's recommendations for increased American support for the Latin American militaries and American multinationals.[30] Latin Americans were understandably suspicious of foreign companies because they did not understand the benefits they supposedly wrought in the development of democratic societies. Their sufferance of military government was a small but understandable price to pay if their countries were to be shielded from the menaces of guerrilla war and communism. Without order they could not hope to confront the compelling social issues of the day.

Devoid of any central social or political purpose in its hemispheric policy, Rockefeller opined, the United States had fallen back on the older (and to Americans more understandable) strategic and economic strictures in dealing with the hemisphere. With these it could not defuse the popular appeal of the still vigorous Latin American Left. In a politically unattainable but challenging recommendation, Rockefeller proposed the creation of a secretariat of Western Hemispheric affairs to direct all U.S. government activities in Latin America and a hemispheric security council (with its central office outside the United States) to train Latin American military and police in counterrevolutionary warfare. These offices never became a reality, although the U.S. military and even city governments took up the training of Latin American officers and police. Rockefeller's urgency in advocating such measures, coupled with his support for American multinationals, validated in Nixon's mind the approach the United States must take in dealing with Latin America. Some found the report badly flawed by its exaggeration of the threat from the Left — historically more frightening to Americans than Latin Americans — yet Rockefeller had offered the American people a sobering reminder about Latin America's deceptively placid condition.[31]

Nixon spoke loftily about a "new partnership" with Latin America, one in which Latin American recipients of American aid, for example, would not have to "buy American" and could anticipate U.S. support on such diverse matters as debt servicing, technology transfer, and tariff preferences. He coupled these pledges with warnings about Latin American miscreant governments that placed unwarranted barriers against American investment and reminded their leaders of the Overseas Private Investment Corporation, which insured against takeovers of American multinationals. Latin American governments that hoped for a marked change in American economic and commercial policy toward the hemisphere were sorely disappointed. Support for development funding to the Inter-American Development and World Bank fell short of Latin American expectations, as did the reduction of tariff barriers. In 1971, when Nixon declared a 10 percent surcharge on imports — aimed primarily at the Japanese — the Latin American imbalance in U.S. trade patterns was further skewed in Washington's favor.[32]

Very shortly, the "new partnership" looked to Latin Americans much like the old relationship of the 1950s. This was not altogether the result of Nixon's failure to adjust to new realities and expectations. Latin America had changed. The Alliance for Progress, arguably, had not achieved the expectations of 1960, but the Latin America Nixon confronted as president was far different from the hemisphere that had so rudely greeted him on his visit of 1958. In Peru, for instance, he had to deal with a military government whose leaders had strong popular instincts and sprinkled pronouncements with socialist rhetoric. Their populism was, apparently, contagious. In Venezuela, the incoming president, Rafael Caldera, allowed the communists to participate in national politics and initiated a dialogue with Castro. The Argentine military, presumably secure since it had tossed out a civilian government in 1966, ran afoul of the working and middle classes with its economic program and narrowly avoided being overturned. And in Bolivia, where Washington's tightening grip had created, it was assumed, a regime subservient to American wishes, yet another general stormed into power and began nationalizing the holdings of Gulf Oil. When he departed after a year, his successor promptly infuriated Washington by nationalizing even more foreign property.

Latin America had yet to take charge of its future (to employ a phrase of the 1980s), but clearly South America in the 1970s began to refashion its international economic ties. The Russians and the Chinese joined the Germans and Japanese in commercial ventures. This was a challenge Nixon could not ignore. He reinforced government support to American multinationals, cut back on public aid to the defiant regimes, and lauded the "economic miracle" wrought by the Brazilians. In Peru and Bolivia the U.S. government consciously encouraged rightist military officers. In Bolivia, the military responded by tossing out its reformist colleagues and setting up a pro-American government. Washington acknowledged that deed by reinstituting aid. The changeover was relatively inexpensive and easy.

The Chilean Tragedy

But in Chile the confrontation with revolutionary change produced a bloody climax. In 1970, in a bitterly divisive election that produced no clear winner, the Chilean National Assembly had chosen a socialist, Salvador Allende, as president. For more than a decade Allende had capitalized on the alienation of urban workers in a country noted for its middle-class democracy and social tradition. In the 1964 election, Allende asked for and got help from the Cubans and the Soviets. In the end he proved no match for Eduardo Frei, who was not only getting American dollars but who also had the CIA and the American Federation of Labor, using its aggressive Latin American organization, the American Institute for Free Labor Development (AIFLD), working clandestinely on his behalf. In other hemispheric countries where organized labor had become too "political" (that is, too leftist in its orientation), AIFLD performed yeoman service in the anticommunist cause of Washington. Other U.S. agencies targeted Chilean women, traditionally conservative, with stories that Allende and the socialists would undermine the nation's family values.[33]

Frei proclaimed a "Revolution in Liberty" and energetically set out to incorporate Christian Democracy's curious mix of traditional and reformist social philosophies into a political culture that was rapidly becoming polarized. In the spirit of the Alliance for Progress, Frei called for agrarian reform and encountered a phalanx of conservative assemblymen. Responding to long-held Chilean resentments against foreign control of the vital copper mining industry, he proposed a gradual nationalization, "Chileanization," which pleased the leftists, but permitted the foreign owners to continue running the companies, which infuriated them. When after three years the economy began to falter with the decline of copper prices and tax revenues, the social programs lost their urgency. Under pressure from the International Monetary Fund and the World Bank, Frei began austerity measures. Bolivia had earlier yielded to American economic prescriptions; so, now, did Chile.

Still, the Chilean economic collapse did not necessarily pre-ordain an Allende victory. In 1970, as in 1964, the U.S. government determined to keep him out of power. The National Security Council, inspired by Henry Kissinger's assessment of the situation ("I don't see why we must sit with our arms folded when a country is slipping toward communism because of the irresponsibility of its own people"), allocated $500 thousand to be distributed among Allende's opponents.[34] Before the campaign was over, the U.S. government had spent $1 million, and Anaconda Copper and International Telephone and Telegraph (ITT) another $600 thousand, toward Allende's defeat. Even after he had gotten a plurality of the votes, which virtually assured his selection by the Chilean National Assembly, efforts to deny him power did not end. ITT, which had been operating in Chile since the 1920s and had amassed $160 million in assets, was so fretful over a socialist in power that it contrived (apparently with Nixon's blessing) a scheme whereby the Christian Democrats in the assembly would vote for Jorge Alessandri, the former president. He, in turn, pledged to resign, which would mean a new election and another chance to deny Allende the power he had long sought. The plan fell through when the Christian Democrats refused to go along, but ITT immediately followed with phase 2, a plot to cause such economic dislocation that the military would step in, as it had in Bolivia. The CIA, still in the hunt, threw its support to an anti-Allende officer who intended to kidnap General René Schneider, a supporter of Allende's constitutional claim to office. Even Kissinger found the latter too risky, but the Chilean officers went ahead. In the kidnapping attempt Schneider was killed.

In American eyes Allende's triumph was not only a threat to U.S. interests in Chile but also a symbolic challenge to its political stature elsewhere in the continent. He was a Marxist, elected to power in a democratic and capitalist society. Chile would be socialized, Allende pledged, but by peaceful means. This meant nationalization of the copper mines and banks and major industry and agrarian reform, as Chileans had anticipated, but it also signaled an independent foreign policy, the end of dependency, and a restructuring of the social order. The last was the most unsettling to middle-class Chileans because it meant, initially, a redistribution of national wealth to Allende's army of marginals and, ultimately, the formation of a new political culture in which the working class would occupy center stage.

Allende's Chile projected a democratic, socialist image before the world.[35] The government raised taxes, froze prices, and increased wages, which had the effect of augmenting the share of national wealth by wage earners from 50 to 60 percent. In the capital, unemployment dropped. Rising demand for food and manufactures brought increased productivity in agriculture and industry. When the first local elections were held, in April 1971, the socialist-communist coalition, Popular Unity, won 50 percent of the vote, an impressive showing in Chile's multiparty politics. Allende was hailed as the "second Fidel," and his program as the protector of the Chilean poor. But in early 1972, as Allende continued with his program of national reconstruction, his political support began to wane, particularly among Chile's middle classes. The economy, which had enjoyed a brief revival, now began to show the stress of his policies. Production had increased, but demand outpaced it, so the government had to satisfy consumers' wishes with increased imports. In the international economy, the price of Chilean copper fell to the level of 1967, and Chile's standing among international lending agencies plummeted with it. Within the country the reformist political consensus that had seemed possible in the beginning now collapsed as middle-class housewives undertook protest marches over rising prices and the falling value of the Chilean *escudo*. Had Allende maintained his links with the Christian Democrats, who had yielded power to him in 1970, he might have been able to weather the economic crisis. Instead, sensing that their political future lay with the old order, not the new, the Christian Democrats decided to abandon the Left.[36]

With their departure went whatever middle-class political support Allende had enjoyed. His response was to declare a state of emergency. He banned public meetings, permitted the police to arrest persons without a warrant, and authorized the military to censor the press. In Bolivia or Peru such use of state authority to maintain order would have met with sullen acquiescence, but Chile had a historic tradition of political tolerance, and Allende's toughness inspired the discontented to launch a new wave of protests. In winter 1972 storekeepers, angry over high taxes, closed their doors. A few months later, the truck drivers struck, citing shortages of spare parts and government-imposed hauling rates. Professional groups and shop owners followed them into the streets in a series of massive demonstrations that shook the government but did not bring down Allende. In the ensuing elections, Popular Unity fared better than in 1970 — a sign that Allende was compensating for his declining fortunes among middle-class Chileans by expanding his political base among the urban poor. In the next critical election, in March 1973, the poor turned out in force to renew their commitment. The victory, Allende believed, meant the Chilean people approved the socialist path he had charted for them.

For the Chilean military, however, the electoral reaffirmation of Allende's program meant that the ballot box offered little promise of turning him out. The generals had a forty-year tradition of staying out of politics, but they held solidly anti-Marxist political values and had been suspicious of Allende from the beginning. In the aftermath of the March elections, they watched approvingly as the truck drivers went out on strike for a second time and, perhaps unexpectedly, found themselves courted by the Christian Democrats, who pressed Allende to appoint more military men to his cabinet. Throughout Latin America, the Christian Democratic Party trumpeted civilian domination of the military and condemned military domination of the state. Fearful that Allende would arm urban workers, the assembly authorized the military to search for weapons in factories and buildings where leftist organizers gathered. His followers took to the streets in protest, and the politicized urban workers seized factories.

The plotters waited until a prominent general in Allende's cabinet resigned before launching the counterrevolution on 10 September 1973. Allende died the following day, either by his own hand or by another's. The victors established a military government with General Augusto Pinochet as president, and the Christian Democrats and the rightist National Party approved it. In the early days of the coup, soldiers herded thousands into makeshift prisons and executed hundreds of leftists. Then, in a systematic and forceful manner, they began dismantling Chilean socialism and with it the political culture Allende had wrought. They returned the nationalized factories to private ownership, clamped down on the unions, and disbanded the Marxist parties. They broke diplomatic relations with Cuba. They declared the restoration of a capitalist economy and an orderly society. But they did not restore Chilean democracy, nor did they relinquish power.[37]

The collapse of Chilean democracy in 1973 was largely but not solely a domestic tragedy. Allende had become a symbol — the triumph of socialism by constitutional means — that infuriated the Nixon administration and prompted the U.S. government to redefine its anticommunist global strategies. A Marxist government had achieved power in a country with a strong European tradition in its politics. Viewed from this perspective, Allende's Chile was less a harbinger of Marxist takeovers in neighboring Latin American countries than a prototype for the Western European communists to emulate. If they won power by the ballot box, as had Allende, C. L. Sulzberger speculated, the Italian or French communists would be able to split the NATO alliance and destroy the European common market.[38]

In the early months of the Allende government, before Washington's policies had become clear, a consortium of multinational companies, spearheaded by ITT, pressured the administration to block any loans to the Allende government. When Allende nationalized the Chilean copper industry in July 1971, the Agency for International Development cut off the financial spigot. Shortly afterward, the Inter-American Development Bank, which was in the business of making development loans, took Chile off its list of recipients. The World Bank, then under the direction of former secretary of defense Robert McNamara, followed the trend in late summer. The Export-Import Bank, which had extended $600 million in credits to Chile since World War II, abruptly announced that it would not certify new credits until the Allende government made pledges that no more foreign property would be nationalized. With the new ITT president, Harold Geneen, enthusiastically supporting a hard-line policy, the Nixon administration in early 1972 declared that future nationalization without proper compensation would result in further curtailment of credit. Later in the year, after random negotiations of the issues of nationalization and credit, Allende got an extension on Chile's debt repayment schedule, but once Washington learned of the military discontent and plotting in early 1973, its position hardened.

Was the Nixon administration directly responsible for Allende's fall? No. Did it bear a responsibility in Allende's overthrow? Undeniably, yes. For more than a decade, the United States had abetted, sustained, financed, and encouraged Allende's opponents. It provided reassurance to the Chilean military. It imposed economic obstacles to Allende's government among international lending agencies. It did not undermine Allende from within, but it encouraged and funded those who did. Allende himself ultimately bore responsibility for the failure of his socialist revolution in trying to reform a society by restructuring it. Even without American disapproval, he courted discontent and, probably, civil conflict, but with American hostility he confronted inevitable disaster. For the United States there was too much at risk — in the symbolic affront of a democratically elected socialist and in Chilean defiance of American direction. President Gerald Ford admitted that the CIA spent $8 million in Chile to facilitate Allende's downfall. What the United States got for its money was stability; what Chile got was the preservation of the social order, at the price of democracy. In the final analysis, to identify U.S. tacit approval of the military takeover as the principal reason for Allende's fall is to diminish the role of the Chilean military in bringing down civilian governments. It had not knuckled under to Washington's pressures to prevent Allende's inauguration in 1970. As William F. Sater astutely points out, "it is more likely that three years of chaos and the fear of rebellion, not Richard Nixon, inspired Chile's armed forces to depose Allende in 1973."[39]

The North-South Dialogue

So palpably offensive was the Chilean military's eradication of the Left that within a few years even Kissinger expressed disapproval over the collapse of Chilean democracy and the abuse of human rights by the Pinochet government. By then, of course, new descriptive slogans and causes were reverberating through the inter-American system — the New Dialogue and its companion expression, the North-South Dialogue, which inspired the Linowitz report; and SELA, the Spanish acronym for the Economic System of Latin America. The latter represented the spirited defiance of a Latin America prepared, as yet another slogan confirmed, to "take charge of its future."[40]

SELA included Cuba but excluded the United States. Its principal architects, Carlos Pérez of Venezuela and Luis Echeverría of Mexico, wanted to chart a new course for Latin America in the international economic system. Echeverría's shift to the left represented a symbolic effort to restrain foreign, largely American, economic penetration and appeal to leftist sentiments by advancing Mexico's claim as a Third World leader. Venezuela's defiance of

Washington was more complex in its origins. That nation had been something of a showcase of the Alliance for Progress in the early 1960s, but Nixon's indifference to trade issues and congressional measures during the 1974 Arab oil embargo (Venezuela was a founding member of the Organization of Petroleum Exporting Countries in 1960) worsened matters. Venezuela had opposed the embargo and even continued to ship oil to the United States, but Congress, indifferent to the fact that it was an *Arab* oil embargo, retaliated by withdrawing the General System of Preferences from the Trade Act of 1974. Despite Pérez's protestations of the unfairness of the retaliation, Venezuela stood condemned. Over the next year, relations between the two countries continued to deteriorate. As Pérez touted a populist defiance and called for fairness to developing nations in trade practices, President Gerald Ford, in an address before the United Nations, condemned the wealthy petroleum nations for squeezing the consumer with high prices. By mid-1975, however, tensions subsided. Kissinger began to call for a "dialogue" between north and south. Venezuela nationalized the iron and oil industry without vigorous objection from the multinationals or the U.S. government.[41]

Ultimately SELA included twenty-five Latin American governments, a few of them — Honduras, El Salvador, and the Dominican Republic — Cold War allies of the United States. Their purpose was not so much political as economic determination to gain control over commodity prices and to break their dependency with vigorous import-substitution measures, in which governments provided domestic producers with a greater share of the consumer market by the expedient of shielding them from foreign competition.

Concurrently the OAS suffered a noticeable decline and with it a loss of U.S. prestige in the inter-American system. In 1969 the OAS had played a minor role in mediating the hundred-hour war between Honduras and El Salvador (known derisively as the Soccer War). Afterward the U.S. delegates began to lose their effectiveness in "guiding" the Latin American nations, especially on economic issues. At OAS economic meetings, the Latin American delegates would often repair to another room, decide among themselves on a series of recommendations, and then casually inform their American colleagues. A few old Alliance for Progress hands from the early 1960s, disillusioned with such scenarios, began calling for American withdrawal from the organization. When Nixon visited China in early 1972, a number of Latin American governments called for a thaw in Cuban-American relations, beginning with a lifting of the embargo. Several outspoken U.S. congressmen visited Cuba, interviewed Castro, and returned to Washington with cautious recommendations for a Cuban-American understanding. At the OAS foreign ministers gathering of 1974 in Quito, Ecuador, Washington was apparently ready to acquiesce in lifting the embargo but was joined in abstention by five states — Haiti, Guatemala, Bolivia, Brazil, and Nicaragua — which meant that the measure failed.

Even the smaller states of the Caribbean, most of them newly independent and vulnerable to European and especially U.S. economic and political power, now dared challenge the colossus to the north. Throughout the region there was a pervasive sense that one imperial master had been exchanged for another and they must now find some common bond, as Michael Manley, the socialist leader of Jamaica, expressed it. In the early 1960s they had tried, but failed, to sustain a West Indian federation. Lacking political unity, they had fashioned the Caribbean Free Trade Association and Caribbean Development Bank, followed in 1973 by the Caribbean Community. The United States had not opposed any of these; the Rockefeller Report, in fact, had encouraged such regional arrangements. But the cumulative effect was to fuel Caribbean determination to deal more forcefully with the multinationals that set up operations in the insular Caribbean and to ignore Washington's strictures about consorting with Castro's Cuba. Jamaica established friendly relations with Havana and imported Cuban advisers. In Guyana, where Kennedy had prevented Cheddi Jagan from taking power, President Forbes Burnham proclaimed a "cooperativist republic" and nationalized the holdings of Reynolds Aluminum. Eric Williams in Trinidad/Tobago launched an economic program modeled on the Puerto Rican example and then joined other Caribbean countries in abandoning it.[42]

Cuba, an outcast in the insular Caribbean in the 1960s, won new admirers — not, as Washington believed, for the revolution's economic appeal but for Castro's symbolic role as a Third World leader. In 1966, still irritated over his treatment by the Soviets in the Missile Crisis, Castro played host to the Tricontinental Conference. Participants espoused anticolonial, procommunist, anti-imperialist, and especially anti-American sentiments. Guevara called for global revolution. Castro elected to take the battle not to Latin America but to Africa, where an anticolonial struggle still raged. To the United States, the

Cuban venture into Africa validated the charge that Castro was a Soviet lackey, and his dispatch of troops to Angola virtually killed efforts at any Cuban-American understanding, but to the black Caribbean, which had been swept by a negritude movement early in the decade, his proclamation of a war against imperialism in Africa had powerful appeal. In the final assessment, Castro had to choose between the opportunity of easing tensions with the United States or reaffirming his revolutionary mandate. He chose the latter. Certainly, without Soviet acquiescence and military aid, the Cubans might not have undertaken such a costly venture, but Castro was not doing so as a Soviet surrogate. He believed in his mission.[43]

None of these events, as the Linowitz Report tried to explain, meant that the United States had "lost" Latin America. More concretely, they signaled that Latin America's priorities had moved beyond the Cold War agenda and that Washington must now adjust its policies accordingly. The United States had awakened from the Pan-American dream to a Latin American reality. Policies of the 1960s — when it had dominated hemispheric affairs, established hemispheric priorities, and largely charted the course of hemispheric economies — ill-served U.S. fundamental interests a decade later. Political and economic diversity now characterized Latin America. Several countries, notably Brazil and Mexico, were part of the New Industrial Economic Order. Strategic concerns still dominated American thinking but not Latin America's. Several countries had opened commercial and diplomatic contacts not only with Cuba but also with Eastern European nations, China, and the Soviet Union. The shift represented less a political than an economic realignment of the hemisphere with the global economy.[44]

The Transformation of Greater North America

In the mid-1970s, in the aftermath of the Watergate crisis and the election of Jimmy Carter, the prevailing mood in the nation about the hemispheric experience of the United States in the 1960s and early 1970s was reflective if not grim. Military governments had returned to power, the Cuban Revolution was more entrenched than ever, and, if anything, the palpable anti-Americanism identified during the 1958 Nixon visit appeared more intense. Kennedy had committed the United States to a Latin American reformation. That quest, it now appeared to some, had faltered if not failed because of his parallel and even greater determination to wage the battle for the hemisphere in the name of the nation's Cold War agenda. Carter, to his credit, pledged to rectify the record yet preserve U.S. security interests. In the election of 1980, the electorate determined that he, too, had failed, not for want of good intentions but for other reasons.

In retrospect, the lesson of the experience proved to be more nuanced: the United States may have failed, but America had not, and in the course of these years of uncertainty — from the heady days of the 1960 presidential campaign to the moral agenda Jimmy Carter pledged to bring to U.S. policy in the hemisphere — Latin America had changed, but North America and especially the United States had changed even more. In several Latin American nations, military men, not those civilian middle-class reformers and parties identified by U.S. leaders, provided the means of social advancement for ordinary, largely male, Latin Americans.

America provided a second route. In a decade in which the United States refused to discard its Cold War globalist strategy in its approach to Latin America, America reinforced the north-south connection. As the United States waged its covert war against Cuba, America began taking in Cubans. It was a political decision, certainly, but one with lasting social, economic, and cultural implications for the future. In the year that United States forces entered Santo Domingo to end a civil war — an intervention that irreparably damaged the Alliance for Progress — America adopted a sweeping new immigration law that conveyed another message to Third World peoples, especially those in Latin America and the Caribbean.

Inspired in large measure by the civil rights movement and its goal of removing racial or ethnic discrimination, the law stipulated that immigrants would be admitted on the basis of skills and professions and not country of origin. The most far-reaching impact of the law, however, lay in its professed goal of family reunification, which dramatically increased the numbers of those legally admitted. There was an ambiguous legacy of this transformation — an undeniable economic benefit but one increasingly measured against the costs of services, loss of jobs to newcomers, social and cultural adjustments, and, most disturbingly, a parallel increase in undocumented immigration. Third

World peoples were the biggest beneficiaries. Fifty percent of the newcomers from the late 1960s to the end of the century came from Latin America and the Caribbean. Of those, by far the largest numbers immigrated from Mexico.[45]

Two other programs also drew their inspiration from the idealism of the 1960s — the Peace Corps and the Partners of the Americas (originally called the Partners of the Alliance). In the beginning, critics derided the first as the "kiddie corps." By the end of the decade, when the early enthusiasm for the Alliance for Progress had waned, radicals denounced the Peace Corps as an imperialist front organization. (In some countries, notably Chile, the CIA did use Peace Corps volunteers to gather information on leftist activities.) Conservatives thought the programs virtually useless, but like its sister program (Partners of the Americas), the Peace Corps represented an effort to bring expertise and technical assistance to many Latin American and Caribbean peoples and to reaffirm the nation's cultural ideals. Ironically, as did the new immigration law, these programs have had a more lasting effect on the transformation of domestic society and culture in what is often regarded as a tumultuous and violent decade scarred by the bitter debates over Vietnam and the civil rights movement.[46]

From this perspective, then, perhaps the most profound political and social consequences of what Kennedy's advisers called the "Battle for the Hemisphere" occurred in the three disparate nations of Greater North America — Canada, the United States, and Mexico. As the relationship between the three grew more intertwined economically, their political encounters on the global and regional stage became more conflicted. Canadians deeply resented U.S. pressures during the Missile Crisis, and as the decade wore on, Canada became the model of the welfare state, a sharp contrast with the warfare created at the expense of the projected War on Poverty. As the social and cultural fabric of the United States split into different patterns, Canadians adopted a two-nation identity — one French, one English. Expo '67 permitted Canadians to model their economic progress and cultural harmony.

Mexico remained at odds with the United States over Cuba and the ending of the *bracero* program and embarked on an ambitious development program of its northern frontier, in large part to reverse what many Mexicans considered a relentless southward push of U.S. economic might. To demonstrate that the country had joined the ranks of the world's modern industrial nations,

the government hosted the 1968 Olympics, only to suffer global embarrassment when a local protest in the capital escalated into a major clash between
embittered city residents and authorities. The confrontation ended in a bloody
spectacle as the government made war on its own people. Decades after the
event, Mexicans remained bitterly divided about its causes and even more embittered over its legacy. In 1973, the Mexican military put down an insurrection
in impoverished Guerrero State. Some attributed its origins to Cubans and the
spread of Marxist ideology among peasants, but it was largely homegrown.
Canadians, too, fell victim to violent politics, although not so severe as what
had happened in Mexico or even the United States. After his election as prime
minister, Pierre Trudeau (a Quebecois) tried vainly to ameliorate the escalating tensions between Anglo and French, only to find his government assailed
from both sides. In the end, as Quebecois nationalists became more violent,
the government cracked down with a War Measures Act to quell it.

In the early 1970s the political relationship between the three governments
seemed more acrimonious than in the late 1950s and early 1960s. Certainly,
anti-Americanism had intensified in both Mexico and Canada. Yet, viewed
more closely, the three nations had a shared experience — a demographic explosion in the numbers of young people in the population, rapid economic
growth, and (except for Mexico) dramatic changes in social legislation. Crises
shook the political system, and in the government's response to each, the
middle classes of each country, the major beneficiaries of post–World War II
expansion, began to doubt the ability of their respective political systems to
meet the challenge. More than these similarities, the economies of the three
countries grew more interdependent. One demographic statistic, however, had
profound implications for the North American future. In 1965, the numbers
of legal Mexican and Canadian immigrants to the United States were almost
equal. A decade later, authorized entries from Mexico stood ten times higher
than those from Canada, and undocumented immigrants from Mexico had
dramatically escalated.[47]

In the mid-1970s, as the U.S. Congress probed more deeply into the activities
of the CIA and other intelligence agencies in Latin America, some Americans
began to question virtually every policy decision made about the region from
the early days of the Kennedy administration, especially the disaster of the Bay

of Pigs and the terrifying prospect of nuclear war with the Soviet Union, to the fall of the Allende government in Chile. They began to doubt the guiding precepts of those who shaped the Alliance for Progress. In the process, as has so often been the case when the American people attempt to affix responsibilities for policies that go astray or turn out badly, their explanations ranged from the models applied to the forceful way in which the United States carried out its professed design for the hemisphere, and to the difficulty of trying to address the pressing social and economic problems in the hemisphere with political solutions of diminishing utility.

Once the Cuban Revolution began to take its leftward turn, the American people and Congress reacted by insisting the administration do something. The response was enough to mollify some of the criticism but not enough to bring down the Cuban regime, at least not at any price the United States was willing to pay or the American people would approve. The revolution survived and by decade's end had strengthened its grip on the island. On the other hand, Cubans were unable to replicate their revolution anywhere else in the Americas. Whether or not that was due to U.S. anticommunist policies or to Alliance for Progress funding ("Fidel's money," as cynics often called it, implying that without the threat from Cuba there would have been no Alliance for Progress), the unwillingness of most Latin Americans to "buy into" the Cuban model, its inappropriateness for specific cases, or some other reason, few of the soothsayers of the mid-1970s could say for sure. For all their talent, those who shaped U.S. policy toward the hemisphere in the 1960s had failed to grasp an essential truth: you cannot get to the left of the left with reformist measures, and to choose the right as an ally is to make a Faustian bargain. In the process those you may hurt the most may very well be those you are professing to save.

In 1976, the year of Jimmy Carter's narrow victory in the presidential race and celebration of the nation's bicentennial, the image of the United States in the Americas stood no higher than it had been on the eve of the Cuban Revolution. Bureaucratic-authoritarian regimes, buttressed by sometimes brute military power, held sway in Brazil, Argentina, Uruguay, and Chile. Elsewhere governments invoked the anti-guerrilla or anticommunist rhetoric favored by Washington to crack down on labor unions, political parties, universities, and other institutions of political pluralism and representative democracy. As criticism of U.S. policies intensified in Congress, Latin America's beleaguered elites found it more and more difficult to use traditional anti-U.S. strategies to persuade the poor that an intrusive and imperialist United States was principally to blame for their condition. At the same time, the leveling influence of American culture — in everything from fast food to Hollywood cinema, the shopping mall, grassroots development projects, language institutes, and missionaries spreading the heresy of evangelical Christianity to the urban and rural dispossessed — began to take hold.

8   The Defiant Hemisphere

More than any president since John Kennedy, Jimmy Carter sensed opportunity in Latin America's more assertive posture toward the United States. He spoke movingly and convincingly about renewed American concerns in the hemisphere: vindication of Panama's just demands for a new canal treaty, a fundamental understanding with Castro's Cuba, human rights (an increasingly important issue to Congress), and Central America's distresses along with their implications for American interests. Eschewing the encompassing slogans of previous American leaders who had promised too much and accomplished too little in treating Latin Americans, Carter (reflecting, perhaps, his engineer's approach to problems) focused on regional and bilateral issues. In the past, he rightly acknowledged, U.S. hemispheric policy had usually floundered because of hard decisions made in specific situations (Castro's revolution, the Dominican crisis, or Guatemala in 1954) requiring a response that inevitably antagonized Latin Americans. In opting for the obverse approach, Carter ultimately found himself condemned for betraying traditional American interests.[1]

Morality, Reason, and Power

The Panama Canal issue befuddled the administration from the beginning. Back in 1973, when the Panamanian economy had begun to slide from the effect of high oil prices, Omar Torrijos, who had seized power in 1968, dramatically announced that the treaties offered by the Johnson administration were unacceptable. He rallied Latin America behind the cause of Panama, and (in a move that embarrassed Washington) invited the UN Security Council to Panama. There he virtually forced the U.S. delegate to exercise a veto to kill a pro-Panamanian resolution. The following year, Kissinger acquiesced in an eight-point agreement to negotiate new canal treaties with the Panamanian minister, Juan Tack. Panama would get a new canal treaty and, by the end of the century, control of the canal. The Canal Zone, a de facto colony in Panamanian eyes, would be terminated. More important, the United States agreed to redefine its security interests on the isthmus.[2]

Perhaps to themselves Americans could admit the justness of Panama's demands, but they deeply believed the canal symbolized American triumph over adversity. Campaigning in 1976, Carter had learned just how attached they were to the waterway, and he responded to their concerns by assuring them that he would not relinquish a vital strategic and commercial lifeline. But retention of U.S. control and Panamanian reconciliation were not compatible, so Carter opted for the latter. He had, frankly, no realistic choice. Among its other recommendations about a new policy with Latin America, the Linowitz Commission had urged the negotiation of a new canal treaty with Panama, and shortly before assuming office Carter had learned from seven Latin American leaders that failure to settle this long-standing issue would align the hemisphere against him. A few weeks after his inauguration, he named Ellsworth Bunker (old but skillful in dealing with Latin Americans) and Sol Linowitz to head his negotiating team. They adopted the Kissinger-Tack formula and by August had produced two agreements: a canal treaty and a neutrality treaty.

Torrijos and Carter signed the treaties in a dignified ceremony in September. In both countries a furious debate ensued. Torrijos had to use his considerable popularity to persuade Panamanians to accept treaties that fell short of Panamanian aspirations. Carter had to convince a coterie of hard-line senators that the neutrality treaty permitted U.S. military action to preserve canal security and then had to reassure the harassed Torrijos that the reservation did not mean "intervention" in Panamanian internal affairs. The narrow victory in the Senate was, Carter believed, the triumph of moral principle and political determination, and he *had* preserved vital American interests. But the cost was diminution of his political prestige. Panama had no constituency in the United States, but the canal did. For both governments, predictably, the symbolic importance of the canal (for Panamanians, a continual reminder of the American economic and military presence; for Americans, a monument to American engineering and determination) overshadowed the more somber analyses about the pressing need for a new treaty.[3]

Torrijos had accomplished something no other Panamanian had been able to do. He had capitalized on Carter's belief that the 1903 treaty and the resentments it had generated among Panamanians were as much moral as strategic issues. The hard-drinking Panamanian military populist succeeded in forging a national coalition through intimidation, coercion, manipulation, bluff, and charisma. For Carter, however, the process of obtaining Senate approval of the treaties and the even more contentious debate in the House of Representatives over implementing legislation proved politically debilitating. From the flag riots of 1959 to the approval of the Panama Canal treaties in 1979, the relationship between the two countries had dramatically altered. Panamanians became more united than ever; with the withdrawal from Vietnam, Americans were less certain about their role in the Third World.[4]

Panama brought Carter plaudits but no victories elsewhere in Latin America, Neither did his abrupt call for a dialogue with Castro work to his benefit. In the 1976 campaign he had voiced caution about altering Cuban policy, citing Cuba's disturbing role in the Angolan civil war, but as president he declared that the United States should have "normal relations" with all countries. The two governments signed a fishing agreement and opened "Interests Sections" in Havana and Washington. Carter lifted restrictions on travel to Cuba. And in a media coup, Barbara Walters interviewed Castro, who promised to release a few American prisoners and hinted that full diplomatic relations might be possible in Carter's second term. But within the year Carter had grown suspicious of Castro's meddling in Angola, a concern that escalated in 1978 when Castro dispatched troops into Ethiopia. By the third year of his presidency, as tales of a Soviet brigade in Cuba swept through Washington cocktail parties, the vaunted Cuban-U.S. reconciliation of 1977 had deteriorated into mutually recriminating exchanges.

In the process, the informal character of the Cuban-U.S. relationship changed, largely through migration. By the end of the 1980s, a million Cubans had emigrated from the island to the mainland, from the ousted exiles and talented, white professionals in the first wave to the more racially mixed and socially heterogeneous migrants of the 1970s and 1980s. The arrivals of the 1960s, many of whom settled in south Florida, had been a privileged group; they were granted subsidies and provided generous benefits by Dade County and the state of Florida. Their imprint on Miami became one of the storied (and controversial) accounts of U.S. immigration — an economic clout of $1 billion in 1985, and a highly visible presence in medicine, law, construction,

and banking. Locals sometimes referred to the city as Havana, U.S.A. Miami's
Cubans did not sever their contact with the island, however. Granted the right
to visit the island in 1977, these transplants brought back consumer goods difficult if not possible to obtain by ordinary Cubans. Pressure for the right to
emigrate to the United States increased dramatically, as the 1980 Mariel boatlift demonstrated. But there would be no normalization of diplomatic relations. Such a move would have been an embarrassment for Washington and
constituted a political victory for Castro. The punitive policy of the United
States, symbolized by the trade embargo, meant not only that Cuba's efforts to
spread the revolutionary message in the Americas would be limited but that
the Soviet Union would have to maintain its $365 million annual subsidy.[5]

Elsewhere, especially in the Southern Cone, Carter's determination to fuse
morality, reason, and power (which can be mixed but rarely blended) in U.S.
policy toward the hemisphere brought not compliance but, increasingly, defiance. In 1976 a military junta in Argentina, declaring that inflation and political disorder threatened the nation, had overthrown the government of Isabel
Perón. Determined to break the Left, the military launched a war against terrorism that ultimately reached gruesome severity. Fifteen thousand, it was estimated, "disappeared" in the Argentina of the junta. They were swept away in
the middle of the night, tortured, killed, and interred without markers. Their
families never learned of their whereabouts. Even if discovered, the torso of
one victim was sometimes buried with the head of a second and the limbs of
a third. Some of the more outspoken, such as the journalist Jacobo Timerman,
survived incarceration and went into exile. Timerman wrote a despairing account of his suffering in *Prisoner without a Name, Cell without a Number*.
Despite the odious character of Argentina's war against terrorism and the ac-
cumulating evidence of the junta's violation of human rights, the Carter team
divided over policy. Cyrus Vance, the secretary of state, argued for sanctions;
Zbigniew Brzezinski, the president's national security adviser, who had already
spoken of ending Washington's hegemonic pretensions in the hemisphere,
viewed a vigorous human rights policy as injurious to American relations not
only with Argentina but also with Chile and Brazil.[6]

The president sided with Vance, a decision that accurately reflected the hostile mood in Congress toward Latin America's authoritarian regimes. Carter
singled out the Argentine junta for its human rights violations and reduced

its foreign aid allotment by 50 percent.[7] Argentina denounced the American move, but Congress wanted to go even farther by cutting off all military assistance to the generals in Buenos Aires. For a few months the president resisted the pressure, then finally acquiesced, citing Argentina's gross violations of human rights. Other financial pressures against the junta followed. But the severity of the Argentine government's internal policies lessened only slightly under these sanctions. In retaliation, the junta singled out U.S. companies, subjecting them to such intense pressures that they inundated Washington with complaints. Carter softened his Argentine policy. The junta promised the restoration of civilian rule in 1979 — a promise it did not keep — and gave Timerman respite from his ordeal in an Argentine torture chamber. A trickle of American aid reentered the country. After the Soviet invasion of Afghanistan in 1979, which brought a grain embargo from Washington, Carter tried to persuade the Argentines not to increase their grain exports to the Soviet Union. As compensation, the Argentines wanted a relaxation of administration pressures, but Pat Derian, assistant secretary of state for human rights, threatened to resign. In the end, the Argentines sold more grain to the Russians, the military sanctions remained in effect, and Derian stayed at her post.

In one of the numerous ironic twists of Cold War politics, the Argentines felt little pressure from communist states, including Cuba. Castro valued the ties he had with the generals in Buenos Aires far more than any presumed ideological affinity with the Argentine revolutionary Left. Indeed, his initial reaction to the stated necessity of the 1976 Argentine military takeover closely resembled that taken by Washington. But the junta's leaders erred when they assumed that U.S. leaders were less concerned about human rights violations in Argentina than in Pinochet's Chile. Nothing so controversial as the assassination of Orlando Letelier occurred in Argentina. Yet the Timerman case and the parallel charges of anti-Semitism brought pressure not only from the American Jewish community but also from its Western European counterpart. As Carter struggled through his last year in office, the junta softened its stand against dissidents. This action coupled with its firmness in challenging Washington on the issue of grain sales to the Soviet Union actually helped to ease tensions.[8]

In Brazil, which Brzezinski called one of the "new influentials" in the Third World, Carter encountered further obstacles to his policy of forceful benevolence. In size, population, and economy, Brazil (together with Mexico) symbolized the New Industrial Economic Order that had come of age in the 1970s. In the last years of the Ford administration, Kissinger had negotiated a memorandum of understanding with the Brazilian government on a number of political and economic issues. Indeed, the U.S. relationship with Brazil was of greater importance to Carter than either Argentina or Chile. Yet, as Carter had declared in the 1976 presidential campaign, however crucial Brazil was to Washington's strategic and economic calculations, the repressiveness of the Brazilian military government warranted American disapproval. Afterward, the Human Rights Office of the Department of State cited Brazil for serious violations of political rights, the first step toward shutting off military aid. Before that occurred, however, the Brazilian government peremptorily canceled its military assistance pact with the United States (which had been in force since 1952) and declared that it would not accept U.S. aid. Carter's protestations over a West German offer to supply the Brazilians with nuclear technology (Brazil had not signed the treaty banning nuclear weapons from Latin America) — followed by Washington putting pressure on Bonn to cancel the arrangement — so infuriated the Brazilians that it took three years for Carter to mollify them.[9]

In retrospect, Latin American hostility overshadowed Carter's occasional but significant small victories. He kept up fairly consistent pressure on Latin America's most egregious violators of human rights. Without such pressure, they doubtless would not have lessened the severity of their rule. The process of Latin American democratization that Ronald Reagan later lauded (and for which he took credit) owed its provenance not to Reagan primarily but to the human rights activism of Carter in Latin America. Carter also criticized his predecessors for neglecting Mexico and used his influence to assure that Mexican laborers in America, even those without proper documentation, were not deprived of their human rights. Yet when he drew attention to the increasing numbers of illegal entries of Mexicans into the United States, Mexico joined the chorus of Latin American critics of his policies.[10]

The Mexican case in the Carter agenda proved especially complicated for a variety of reasons — the rapid development and population growth on the northern border, increasing U.S. concerns over immigration, and dramatic changes in Mexico's economic policy. Carter gave Mexico top priority in his administration, to the point of assembling a special Mexico task force and, according to rumor, doing a daily reading of his Spanish Bible. But he came into the presidency at an inopportune time for improving relations with the nation's southern neighbor. When Carter won his improbable electoral victory, the Mexican economy was in free fall, triggering a peso devaluation that persisted into the 1980s. Fortuitously, the discovery of vast new oil fields in Campeche permitted the new Mexican president, José López Portillo, to undertake ambitious new projects without the restrictions imposed by the International Monetary Fund to concern him. Mexico went on a development spending spree. The government unwisely constructed a 1,350-kilometer gas line from Chiapas to the northern border on the supposition that U.S. companies would pay an inflated price for the gas, only to scuttle the project when the Carter administration opposed the plan as "oil blackmail." Angered, López pursued a more anti-U.S. policy in strife-torn Nicaragua by recognizing and aiding the Sandinista government and expressing ideological identity with the revolutionary movement in El Salvador. But Mexico's dream of becoming a developed economy was shattered when the price of oil dropped sharply as U.S. and British wells began increasing production. The government avoided bankruptcy only by the expediency of a $1.8 billion loan from the United States and another $3.85 billion from the International Monetary Fund.[11]

Latin American governments came to regard Carter as yet another American leader who promised much and delivered too little. He spoke about human rights. They talked of internal security problems and the unavoidability of "dirty wars" against terrorism. He talked of a North-South Dialogue. They responded with renewed pleas for access to markets, technology, and financial assistance from the modern industrial nations. There was a noticeable gap between his rhetoric about what he wanted to do for Latin America and his performance. In all fairness, Carter administration officials concerned with Latin America often fought hard for a policy but lost out to more persuasive advocates of a contradictory policy. And, as Abraham Lowenthal has astutely observed, a surprisingly powerful array of private enterprises and organizations — international banks, labor unions, oil companies — can often frustrate American policy in Latin America, and *their* priorities sometimes get more attention from Congress. Latin American aspirations and needs required more than a new administration whose leader called for a new policy. What Latin

America wanted in the 1970s was the benefits of a modern economic order without the strains it often places on the social order. This ideal was beyond the ability of Carter or any American leader to bring about.[12]

Carter's failure lay not in flawed priorities or the lack of will to achieve them but rather in his unwillingness to recognize that no nation can easily blend morality and power into an effective foreign policy and in his inability to harness those diverse public and private American interests and enterprises with a stake in the hemisphere to carry out his goals. No American leader, however well-intentioned, can readily succeed with policies that are crafted to shape events but instead are shaped by those events. Unlike Nixon, Carter instinctively sensed long-standing Canadian resentments over myriad issues, including the habit of U.S. leaders to voice a "special relationship" between the two nations but accord Canada too little respect. Yet even the goodwill between the president and Prime Minister Pierre Trudeau did not prevent the worsening of relations. Carter saw Latin America as he wanted it to be, not as it is. He expressed the aspirations of America, not the definable hemispheric goals of the United States. In doing so, he had paid a political price, albeit the beneficiary turned out to be his successor. When democracy resurfaced in the Latin America of the 1980s, Americans gave Ronald Reagan much of the credit. But Latin Americans knew better, and Carter joined John F. Kennedy as the most admired modern U.S. presidents in Latin America.

The Central American Crisis

In an era when American hegemony in Latin America declined, Washington's hemispheric strategists took their stand in Central America.

Until the Nicaraguan and Salvadoran upheavals of 1979 sent the isthmian economy downward, Central America had been one of the post–World War II economic successes in Latin America. Even under the strain of a rapidly growing population (growing from 8 million to more than 20 million from 1950 to 1979), its national economies had expanded vigorously. In 1960, before the Alliance for Progress got under way, its often combative governments had fashioned the Central American Common Market. Despite squabblings between competitive states and the inability of isthmian producers to shield themselves against the intrusion of American companies, the isthmian economy grew, and the middle class expanded.[13]

As the expectations of a generation of Central Americans for a better life heightened, those who ruled failed to produce a more democratic political or social order. And in the countryside the demands for land of an expanding agro-export economy sometimes took a heavy toll on traditional peasant cultures. Cattle grazing and cotton growing — twin programs encouraged by U.S. agricultural development policies — took food lands out of production. In the process the expanding state economy drove *campesinos* from their meager holdings. A generation of Salvadoran rural people, pushed off the land to make room for bigger and more powerful growers, migrated into relatively sparsely settled Honduras. The growing hostility to their presence ultimately drove many back into El Salvador and precipitated the confrontation between the two governments in the 1969 Soccer War. The war ended after one hundred hours, but the severity of the agrarian situation worsened. It was especially grim in Guatemala, where a "dirty war" had gone on in the countryside off and on since 1954. Peasants sometimes organized, as in Honduras, and compelled a usually indifferent government to respond to their needs, but in Honduras and elsewhere they were generally too weak or too frightened to fight. They went elsewhere — into more isolated regions or into the crowded national capitals, where their presence and their demands created new problems.[14]

As the decade ended, the "inevitable revolution" Robert Kennedy had warned about came not in Guatemala (where the soothsayers had predicted) but in Nicaragua and El Salvador.

In his first two years Carter had articulated a benign policy for Latin America and tried to apply it to Central America. Despite cynicism about the gap between American professions and actions, especially in human rights diplomacy, he had made converts — even among American conservatives — and his sustained commitments to this cause *had* made a difference. Human rights violations declined noticeably in those nations whose governments denounced American interference in their internal affairs and repudiated their military assistance pacts with Washington.

The revolution in Nicaragua against Somoza posed more difficult choices. In 1970 the Somozas had appeared as secure as ever, but in 1972 Somoza perpetuated his familial rule in a fraudulently unconstitutional manner. When

Managua was devastated by an earthquake in the same year, he committed the government to rebuilding the capital on land he had acquired at a pittance and resold at enormously inflated prices. By the mid-1970s, the corruption of the regime had reached such proportions that it sickened all Nicaraguans. He began moving in on businesses formerly reserved for other Nicaraguan families. The mix of greed and ambition transformed those who had quietly tolerated his excesses into an increasingly vocal protest group. The acknowledged leader of the moderate opposition was Pedro Joaquin Chamorro, editor of *La Prensa*, who put together a coalition of labor organizations and anti-Somoza politicians in the Democratic Union of Liberation.

Chamorro and the union denounced Somoza's misrule, but they fought mostly with words. The Sandinista Liberation Front (FSLN), which in 1974 had perhaps no more than a hundred soldiers, began to challenge the urban opposition for attention. In late 1974 the FSLN kidnapped a dozen prominent Nicaraguans and held them for a million-dollar ransom, release of fourteen of their comrades, and safe-conduct passes to Cuba. Somoza was so outraged by the incident that he began a brutal campaign the following year to eradicate the guerrillas. With American aid, he initiated a counterinsurgency in the northern mountains, where the guard drove *campesinos* from their homes into resettlement areas (a policy, ironically, that the Sandinistas occasionally followed in the war against their enemies, the Contras). The outrages brought down on Somoza the condemnation of the church and eventually of the U.S. government. Somoza's credibility in Washington rapidly diminished. The assassination of Chamorro in January 1978 brought on a general strike in Managua and prompted demands from the moderates for Somoza's resignation. For a few months, the Sandinistas appeared to be losing control of the direction of the revolution, but in August Edén Pastora led a dramatic capture of the National Assembly. He demanded a ransom and safe passage for his men to the sanctuary of Omar Torrijos's Panama. Crowds of Nicaraguans along the route to the airport cheered him. The incident convinced Carter that Somoza might not be able to survive.[15]

Despite his distaste for this man whose father had abetted the marines in the Sandino war a half-century before, Carter astutely perceived the limited choices he confronted in Nicaragua. Perhaps unwittingly, his human rights policies had inspired the Nicaraguan opposition, which grew stronger with every week, into believing that the United States, which, as Nicaraguans argued, had put the Somozas into power, would now remove them. Not only in Nicaragua but elsewhere, especially in Costa Rica, Venezuela, and Panama, the disgust with Somoza reached frenzied levels. Somoza had to go, but for Carter the troublesome matter was his successor. Somoza confronted a popular opposition, it was clear, and if he tried to stay in power, Nicaragua would plunge into civil war. If anything, the United States had to intrude to prevent that, but, more important, it had to find some alternative to the core of Marxists in the FSLN who, if Somoza fell, would doubtless install an anti-American government. In truth, summer 1978 found the Carter administration with no long-term strategy for dealing with the explosive Nicaraguan situation, save for preparing to deal with a weakening middle political movement and a revolutionary FSLN that would accept nothing short of the dictator's removal.[16]

Fifty years before, the solution would have been simple — dispatch the marines and hold an election. But Carter had already made it clear that he would not ask Somoza to resign or, if Somoza refused to quit, forcibly remove him. Given this self-imposed limitation on the use of American power — which Latin Americans should have applauded — he moved quickly to introduce the OAS mechanism into the disturbed Nicaraguan political scene. When the OAS pressed the dictator to hold a plebiscite, Somoza, sensing he might be able to manipulate Washington into giving him enough time to crush the Sandinistas, toughened. Carter showed his displeasure a month later by shutting off aid to the Somoza regime, but by then the dictator had strengthened the guard. It would, he believed, defend the family to the death.[17]

Somoza had rejuvenated the guardians of the dynasty, but his armed enemies had also consolidated. Once split into three factions — each with a different strategy for the war against him — they consolidated into a liberating army. In May and June, a steady flow of supplies from Cuba came through Panama and Costa Rica to sustain them in their final assault. Only toward the end, as Somoza subjected the cities of Nicaragua to a vengeful, destructive bombardment that roused the urban populace against him, did the moderate opposition have an opportunity to put itself in a position to succeed him. In the last week of the civil war, American pressure on Somoza to step down, carried out through the OAS, escalated, but the moderates saw in this no discernible advantage. The Sandinistas realized the American effort would effectively deny them the power they had won by armed struggle and successfully opposed it. Mexico, Panama, Venezuela, and Costa Rica supported them. Shortly afterward, Somoza left the country.

Thus in less than a year Nicaragua's plunge into social and political chaos had reached a point where American pressure, once decisive in the history of the republic, was no longer a determining influence. Rejecting intervention, Carter had tried persuasive and, increasingly, forceful diplomacy in Nicaragua. Throughout he had blended moral concern and reason. But in retrospect his policy had not determined the course of Nicaraguan history in the final year of the Somoza dynasty. Rather, the calamitous events of that year had established a fearful and destructive pattern that made Nicaragua a victim of its tormented history and the United States ultimately a bystander to the exorcism of the demon the Sandinistas believe it had wrongfully imposed on them fifty years before.[18]

In the beginning neither the Sandinistas nor the Carter administration consciously sought a confrontation. With Marxists in the core of their movement, they were presumably committed to a reconstruction of Nicaraguan society, yet they began with a practical course — a mixed economy, nonalignment, and political pluralism. With the first they hoped to absorb the small but influential business and professional class; with the second they professed to keep Nicaragua out of the Cold War; and with the last they offered a stunted political culture the opportunity to create "real democracy" in which elections dominated by narrow political elites are less determining than the participation of popular organizations, labor unions, and *campesinos*. The *comandantes* and the FSLN would mold Nicaragua along socialist lines but would not exclude the private sector from the new Nicaragua, where all labored for the common good. They made the anticipated overtures to the Cubans, who sent teachers and medical personnel to assist in the literacy and health campaigns. Castro advised them not to make Cuba's mistakes by cutting themselves off from the United States. Their approach impressed neighboring Costa Rica and Panama, two countries whose support had been vital to the Sandinista victory, and apparently persuaded Carter that the United States, by using desperately needed foreign aid as a lever, would be able to bolster the Nicaraguan middle class and contain the revolution.

But events now pressed on U.S. policy in Central America. Three months after the Sandinista victory, as the president was putting together a significant aid package for Nicaragua, the military government in El Salvador (which had received Washington's moral disapprobation for its human rights violations) fell to a reformist military cadre that brought civilians into the government and spoke of ending the grip of the military-elite alliance that had been fashioned in the early 1930s. Hard-liners, mostly in the Defense Department, saw the isthmian condition increasingly in a strategic context, and within the foreign policy bureaucracy they harassed those who called for American support for Salvadoran reform with grim scenarios about falling dominoes and threats to America's national interests "in our backyard." As he had done in Nicaragua before Somoza's fall, Carter expressed his commitment to reform, but he was apprehensive about the means, particularly the inclusion of popular organizations in the political process, to obtain them. He hesitated, giving the Salvadoran ruling elite the opportunity to fashion its solution to the leftist challenge — paramilitary vigilantes and death squads, which began a systematic, increasingly grisly campaign to dispose of those who defied the social order.

Carter's strategy in El Salvador revealed one of the basic flaws in his Latin American policy. It was realistic, he believed, to encourage progressive change in a nation rather than rely on an inherently unstable anticommunist regime. To carry out such a policy in a country undergoing revolutionary change, as was the case in Nicaragua, or to sustain a corrupt military by arguing that national security interests warrant it is to encourage perceptions of weakness and indecision, not resolve or determination.[19]

In the months after the October coup, the lasting hope of Washington was the continued participation of the Christian Democrats in the succession of juntas. On this middle-class, reformist political movement the United States had staked its commitment in Chile in the 1960s. In El Salvador, however, it had abruptly allied itself with a Christian Democracy that had already begun to splinter over a fundamental party principle — civilian dominance of the military. Through 1980, as successive months brought new horror stories from El Salvador, the most repulsive were the assassination of Archbishop Oscar Romero and Mario Zamora, a Christian Democratic leader. These were accompanied by announcements of an agrarian reform program, which began in the spring with phase 1, the dividing of estates larger than 1,250 acres. Even here, the elite was able to retain its hold by parceling out the land to relatives or unleashing the death squads on peasants who dared to claim it. By the end of the year, when three American nuns and a Catholic lay worker were raped and murdered near the international airport, the policy of reform and repression had wrought little reform and many deaths. And in this year the Christian Democratic Party and its leftist allies dissolved their momentary political alliance, and then the Christian Democrats — rent by internal disputes, challenged by a rightist coalition, its leaders harassed and murdered — fled to the Left and Right on the political spectrum.

One of them sensed opportunity. José Napoleón Duarte, wrongfully denied power in 1972, made his pact with the generals. They would permit him to rule if he did not tell them how to fight their war.

The Strategic Option

Surprisingly, Americans retained a fleeting belief in a middle course in Central America, but in 1980 their growing estrangement from the world and its troubles (symbolized in the 444-day ordeal of American hostages in Tehran) took its toll. By summer, when the national political conventions took place, they were ready for the reassurance of the more militant voice of Ronald Reagan. Carter had taken limited but visible steps to deal with the deteriorating isthmian situation. He had furthered the cause of democracy in Guatemala and Honduras, but he had not resolved the crisis in El Salvador nor had he brought the Sandinistas to heel with promises of American aid. The Mariel boatlift — the sealift of 125,000 Cubans whom Castro allowed to emigrate, piled on boats hastily dispatched from Miami and sailed for Florida while the U.S. government warned over its radios that they lacked permission to enter the United States — served as a metaphor for American debility in the Caribbean. What had begun as apparent triumph several months before (when Cuban exiles had visited the island with their enthusiastic tales of life in Miami) and continued with Cubans flooding into Latin American embassies demanding asylum, Americans disconsolately argued, had ended with Castro unloading the residue of his mental hospitals and prisons on a United States too embarrassed to refuse them. Most of the Marielitos were soon absorbed into the vigorous Cuban American community, but Castro exploited the episode.

What Reagan proposed was not so much a different strategy to confront the Central American crisis but different tactics to attain American objectives.[20] For inspiration he drew on Truman's resolve in the 1947 Greek crisis, genesis of the containment doctrine, and Theodore Roosevelt's display of American power to show how the United States responded when Latin Americans, as Roosevelt often said, "got in the revolutionary frame of mind." Carter had offered the American people a realistic but complex and therefore disturbing assessment of the hemisphere's problems. Reagan substituted tough talk and new priorities. The United States had slipped in Central America because it had lost its commitment to confront the "evil empire" of the Soviet Union. Détente had been a chimera. It had not diminished Soviet meddling in the Third World, as Americans (though not Russians) had anticipated. The Sandinista victory, the "giveaway of our canal," the Soviet invasion of Afghanistan and its military commitments to Ethiopia, the Salt II treaty, guerrilla war in El Salvador — the list went on, but the story of American weakness was depressingly familiar.

A band of Reagan ideologues had best expressed this presumably unarticulated public disenchantment in a thought-piece entitled the Santa Fe doctrine. Coupled with renegade Democrat Jeane Kirkpatrick's damnation of Carter's tolerance of the excesses of U.S. enemies (in the cause of revolutionary change) and his relentless pressure on our friends (in the cause of human rights), the Santa Fe doctrine made an emotionally persuasive case for drawing the line. Central America offered the most sensible place to take a stand. The Soviets dared not confront U.S. power there, nor would they pay the economic price for sustaining "another Cuba," whatever the psychological or political self-satisfaction it might offer. Containment, which had begun in Europe after World War II, now shifted to Central America, where American power and the will to use it would bring victory.[21]

With Carter gone, the hard-liners were now in the ascendancy in the bureaucracy. Their ideologue was Secretary of State Alexander Haig. The guerrilla war in El Salvador, he averred, was yet another episode in the East-West struggle. Defeat of the insurrection in that country would be symbolically equivalent to "rolling back the communist tide" elsewhere. More concretely, momentum seemed to be on Washington's side. In late 1980 the Salvadoran guerrillas had persuaded the Sandinistas to help them, and early in the following year they had unleashed their urban commandos to bring down the fragile coalition government. The attack proved a disaster: the resurgent Salvadoran military used the occasion to brutalize its urban opposition and make them cower. Although Carter had grown more skeptical of Sandinista professions and had labored to prevent the triumph of the Salvadoran Left by political means, he had not, either in his rhetoric or his actions, drawn those clear divisions that Americans apparently wanted to see. Untroubled by political ambivalence, in Latin America or at home, Reagan did. In the early years of the new administration, the only meaningful debate within the administration lay between those who wanted to contain the Sandinista revolution to Nicaragua and those who wanted to overthrow it.

El Salvador provided a means to reconcile these twin groups. Until the "Resistencia" in Nicaragua in 1982 — what the Nicaraguan government and most Americans called the "Contras" — the latter group was apparently content with an enhanced U.S. military presence in Honduras and support for the Salvadoran military's struggle against the guerrillas in the countryside. The traditionalists who were uneasy with the militarization of the isthmus ultimately found philosophical satisfaction in Reagan's support for Duarte in El Salvador, a commitment that would produce in 1982 a coalition government of rightists and Christian Democrats and, following a "demonstration election" in 1984, a victory for America's "last, best hope" in El Salvador.

Reagan's approach to Central America had stated objectives and, presumably, sufficient American political and military commitment to achieve those objectives, but from the beginning he encountered unanticipated problems. Some could be attributed to his failure to create a bipartisan consensus for his Central American policy, others to the hesitance of Congress to fund an increasingly costly and dangerous enterprise that would ultimately necessitate the use of U.S. troops. Determined to fashion a coalition, Reagan delivered a bracing speech in April 1983 in which he applauded "democratic" El Salvador and castigated "Marxist" Nicaragua. The wallowing moderates in Congress stood forewarned about the perils of remaining on the sidelines in a battle in which the issues seemed so clear. For those who believed he was pursuing a military solution in the isthmus, he rejoined, "Bullets are no answer to economic inequities, social tensions or political disagreements. Democracy is what we want."[22]

But that was the problem. Even if the issues had been clear, the way to resolve them was not. Americans listened to the president, liked what they heard, liked the way he said it, and certainly liked him, but were disturbed and frustrated by Central America and its complexities. Not only was the public uncertain about the issues in Central America, but an embarrassing number of Americans could not have identified the Central American countries or correctly located them without a map. ("Where is Nicaragua?" was not only a query; it became the title of a book.) Geographical and cultural ignorance had proved no impediment to earlier generations of Americans confronted with an isthmian crisis. With determination, power, and economic and political leverage, the United States could resolve the modern predicament of Central America. Ironically, the popular president, who had inspired a generation of born-again Christians to shift their loyalties away from Carter, soon found his Central American strategy under assault from some of these same religious groups. In 1981 the Washington spokesperson for the American Baptist Churches testified in a congressional hearing that "the United States and the right-wing junta are aiding the elimination of the center as a political reality in El Salvador."[23]

The Reagan administration soon lost another potential hemispheric ally. Not surprisingly, the military government of Argentina identified Central America as a security issue and not only approved the Reagan administration's commitment of arms to El Salvador but sent military supplies to the Salvadoran government. But in April 1982, when the Argentine military government invaded the Malvinas (Falkland) Islands, the United States supported its British ally. The Argentine defeat not only brought down the military government but effectively ended U.S.-Argentine cooperation in Central America.[24]

The insular Caribbean, too, found itself snared by the American strategic option. There were renewed efforts to isolate Cuba, which had made some diplomatic headway in the region in the 1970s, and unsubtle reminders to Suriname and especially Grenada, which had opted for alternative development strategies that increasingly displeased Washington. Unlike most other powers with historic interests in the region, which (except for the Conservative government

of Margaret Thatcher in Great Britain) extended their aid largely without political conditions, the U.S. government always extracted a political price for its
benevolence. Strategic considerations, the Caribbean recipients soon learned,
determined American priorities for development assistance. In the first year
of the Reagan watch, Secretary of State Alexander Haig met with Canadian,
Mexican, and Venezuelan representatives in the Bahamas and laid out what
appeared at first to be the basis of a mini–Marshall Plan for the Caribbean.
They were initially heartened by Haig's economic agenda and the subsequent
announcement of the Caribbean Basin Initiative (CBI) but within the year
were embarrassed by its overtly political implications.

To get the money, the Caribbean countries had to distance themselves
from Cuba, Nicaragua, and Grenada, which were excluded, as was Panama.
Although the aid package (with its initial outlay of $350 million) was a sorely
needed boost for devastated economies, only a few — notably the pro-American
government of Edward Seaga in Jamaica — alertly sensed American priorities
and rhapsodized about the benefits of the free market. It took extensive lob-
bying from the administration and concessions to American textile and shoe
manufacturers before Congress finally approved the CBI. In the end, the biggest beneficiaries were American exporters and not the neediest Caribbean
recipients.[25]

The cause of the strategic option improved somewhat — as did public awareness of Central America — after the October 1983 "liberation of Grenada" from
a band of tropical Marxists (who had taken out their leader and shot him), the
Kissinger Commission Report (which undergirded the administration's isthmian policy), Duarte's victory in El Salvador, and Reagan's landslide victory
over Walter Mondale in 1984. Congressional Democrats still warned of the
dangers of another Vietnam but narrowly supported aid to the Nicaraguan
"freedom fighters," whose struggle had begun to weaken the already precarious Nicaraguan economy. American aid became the lifeline to the Duarte government and, ultimately, to the Salvadoran military. But the American public remained skeptical, and virtually every major religious denomination was
divided over U.S. policy. Outspoken critics of U.S. policy in many churches
dispatched support groups to Nicaragua.[26]

Nor was Reagan able to create a hemispheric support group for his Central

American policy. Fearful of U.S. military intervention in Central America, the larger countries pressed Washington to disengage from the isthmian morass by reversing its policy of militarization. When that failed, four regional governments — Panama, Venezuela, Colombia, and Mexico — initiated discussions on the island of Contadora (off Panama) in 1982. Reagan at first ignored their efforts, but Contadora's widespread public appeal compelled him to offer lukewarm support. When the Contadora group pleaded for a cessation of U.S. military buildup in the region, the administration responded with a large military exercise in Honduras. The Contadora group eventually produced a draft proposal in 1984, which at least offered a beginning for a negotiated settlement in Central America, but American pressure on El Salvador, Honduras, and Costa Rica — each beholden to U.S. economic assistance — killed its chances.

Regarding Central America the American people expressed convictions, U.S. business charted markets, American leaders identified "legitimate" strategic interests, and each called for analyses to achieve consensus. The National Bipartisan Commission on Central America (known as the Kissinger Commission) tried to fashion one. Reagan wanted confirmation of Soviet and Cuban involvement in Central America. With some qualification, the commission provided it but observed that the isthmus's profound social and economic inequities were equally persuasive explanations for the political convulsions that had wrought the Sandinista triumph in Nicaragua and guerrilla war in El Salvador. The United States must confront the Marxist challenge in the first, its report concluded, and should address the second.[27]

Too few Americans paid attention to Kissinger's solemn observation in delivering the commission's report in early 1985. In Central America, he said, there is an argument for "doing nothing" and for "doing a great deal more," but worse than "doing nothing" would be "doing too little." Perhaps unintentionally, he provided the president, the Congress, and the American people — few of whom wanted to "do nothing" or "a great deal more," especially if it might mean dispatching U.S. troops to fight in a counterinsurgency campaign — with the rationale for choosing the worst option. Sometime later, when neither increased military commitment nor economic aid had resolved the isthmian crisis, a sardonic Kissinger suggested that the United States bomb Nicaragua with the Kissinger Commission Report. He had failed to perceive that the United

States had chosen a hard-line policy in Central America, but America, with its expressed doubts about the moral and human costs of the strategic option, had elected another course.

After years of U.S. aid, Central America in the mid-1980s appeared no closer to resolution of its inner conflict. Frustrated by eight years of war, the isthmian presidents convened in Guatemala in 1987 and signed the first of several accords, more inspirational than precise in their wording, calling for peace. For his noteworthy efforts in this process, Costa Rican president Oscar Arias was awarded the Nobel Prize for Peace. What he had secured was mitigation of conflict and a dialogue among peoples at war with themselves. Arias ventured to Washington to explain why Central Americans found *their* pact — even with its faith in dialogue between warring political factions and the uncertainty of its future — preferable to *our* plan to resolve their conflict. He eloquently conveyed how Central Americans had suffered since 1979, but he could not explain to an American audience why Central Americans view the uncertainties of political turbulence as a less frightening prospect than the collapse of the social order.

The conflict in Central America from the early 1970s until the 1990s exacted a frightening human toll, including some two million refugees who fled northward into Mexico, the United States, and Canada. Immigration officials in each country manipulated the volatile issue of refugees to serve political interests. Mexican high officials chose to make the ever-growing numbers of Central Americans fleeing into the country into political pawns — even to the point of denying the enormity of the problem of encampments in southern Mexico. But outcries from concerned middle-class Mexicans and local indigenous people compelled the government to re-examine the problem. The U.S. government reacted to the issue in an even more capricious manner. Indirectly committed to right-wing military and paramilitary groups in Nicaragua and El Salvador, the Reagan administration was tardy in its response to the deplorable status of isthmian refugees until it confronted the combined pressures from the United Nations and particularly the unanticipated hostility of more than four hundred religious and social activist groups. Lastly, Canadian officials reacted to the problem less ambivalently, as befitting that nation's historically more benign policy toward refugees, but acknowledged the growing anti-immigrant elements within the country.[28]

The Economic Agenda

In the 1980s Latin American democracy, in part inspired by Carter's human rights policy, changed the form if not the content of hemispheric political culture. For this political sea change from the dismal 1970s, Reagan took undeserved credit. The heroes of the democratic restoration were those Latin Americans who decried the lingering power and influence of dictatorships or military governments. In 1980, when authoritarian politics was the rule, few observers would have anticipated that by 1987 it would be the exception. Even in Central America, the determination of strife-ridden countries and their peoples to prevent the erosion of democratic processes stood as symbolic defiance of those who believed they held real power because they held the guns. And in Panama, strategically vital to the United States, a generation of thugs and thieves who followed Torrijos confronted in summer of 1987 a people divided by economic and social cleavages but united in their disgust for military rule.

As the decade wore on, however, there were recurring questions about the survival of democracy amid economic decline. After World War II, Latin America's economic analysts spoke of "structural problems" — uneven growth, the failure to develop domestic markets, dependence on foreign investment, and bloated state bureaucracies. Latin American governments carried these economic debilities into the modern era, even as their economies registered impressive gains. Some took corrective measures, but in general Latin America entered the 1980s with inadequate economic systems. As in the 1930s, the outside world and its economic pressures plunged the hemisphere into another cycle of debilitating economic downturns. Escalating oil prices severely damaged the oil-poor countries. In a perverse way, because of rapid expansion of the public sector, financed largely by foreign loans, the oil producers, particularly Mexico, found themselves awash in credit, and when the oil glut hit, they were just as quickly adrift in a sea of debt.[29]

By 1988 Latin Americans owed international banks almost $400 billion. Production, real income, and wages had fallen sharply since 1980. The gains of the previous decade dissolved in red ink. With them went much of the promise of economic modernization. In 1982, when the economic crisis struck Mexico, the United States arranged an emergency bailout, but the price for Mexico and especially for its people was high. Mexico had to impose an austerity that caused real wages to decline by almost 50 percent. Elsewhere, the demands of the International Monetary Fund (which largely reflects U.S. international economic policy) proved so severe that *El Fondo* became as despised a symbol of American power as, for example, United Fruit Company had been a generation earlier in Central America. Latin America could not pay its debts or even the interest. From 1981 to 1986, debt interest remittances swallowed $130 billion of Latin America's productivity (relatively twice the size of Germany's reparations obligations to Britain and France after World War I). Capital departed Latin America to finance the escalating budget deficit in the United States. The impact in the hemisphere was withering investment and declining consumption.[30]

Out of economic self-interest if not altruism, the United States responded to Latin America's debt crisis but in a way that Latin Americans increasingly found inadequate. Washington's understandable preoccupation with strategic concerns in Central America diverted its attention from the depths of the economic crisis. And following emergency assistance to Mexico (and Brazil) in 1982, the United States disappointed Latin America's indebted with its reluctance to push World Bank loans for hemispheric development or to press the private international banks to reschedule the Latin American debt in accordance with its priorities. In 1985 the U.S. government put forward the Baker plan, which called for $29 billion in loans over a three-year period, but in return Latin American governments had to adopt market-oriented practices, lower trade barriers, and encourage foreign investment. Naturally, given their statist economic philosophies, most — Mexico proved a notable exception — found these too demanding.

Castro, predictably, entered this debate by suggesting that Latin Americans seriously consider debt repudiation, as most did in the calamitous 1930s, or at least become more aggressive on the issue. For the most part, they were not receptive to such a severe measure as repudiation, but a signal of Latin America's distress was Peruvian president Alán Garcia's declaration that his government would adjust its debt repayment to Peruvian income from exports and the Brazilian moratorium on its debt interest payments. And they have become more defiant of Washington's self-appointed economic leadership in the hemisphere. Meeting in Acapulco in late 1987, eight Latin American presidents called for the reincorporation of Cuba into the inter-American system. This meant, presumably, not only the reentry of Cuba into the OAS but its membership in the Inter-American Development Bank and the Latin American Association for Development and Integration, the successor of the Latin American Free Trade Association. Cuba's profound economic differences apparently posed no severe deterrent to these eight countries—the largest, except for Panama and Uruguay, in Latin America—in their recommendation. The proposal was yet another sign of Washington's diminishing political influence in Latin America.

Despite the demands of seemingly insurmountable external forces, Latin American governments in the 1980s became increasingly more sophisticated in assessing their economic condition. For the Left, of course, the only realistic future lay in planned economies, preferably without the rigidity of the Cuban model but with its emphasis on equity. Most Latin American governments wanted the benefits of both, which proved difficult to achieve. They were at least more conscious of past errors in their economic strategies. Under past industrialization schemes, for example, they inadequately managed the operations of transnationals within their borders. Foreign companies produced goods they needed—farm equipment and electric motors—but were permitted to flood local markets with excessively priced and often inappropriate consumer goods that satisfied only the narrow middle-class market. Protected industries did not have to compete in an international market and thus could turn out shoddy goods for the captive domestic market and received energy at often ridiculously low prices. As the 1980s ended, the prospect of Latin America's economic future appeared to be a variation on old themes but with a sobering reminder that Latin Americans must "stop expecting the solutions to our problems to come from outside."[31]

The Social Agenda

More disturbing was the harmful effect hemispheric debt had on fragile democracies. The downward economic spiral of the decade had increasingly severe social costs and, it was feared, ultimately would have political costs as well. The rural dispossessed of a generation ago became the urban dispossessed and shantytown dwellers of the modern age; the malnourished rural child of 1958 became the underemployed father of 1988, whose children clung to life in one of the endless hillside shanties of every Latin American metropolis. *Campesino* families that once lived precariously on the land now lived on the margin of existence in the city. The "revolution of rising expectations," the political mandate of the 1960s, gave way to more ominous comments about the inability of Latin America to pay much more without disturbing social and political repercussions.

In the 1970s and 1980s, most Latin Americans moved up a notch or two on the economic ladder, but too many shifted sideways in the social order. They appeared better off in the cities, yet often the quality of the social services they received diminished. Education expanded at every level and in some countries became as accessible for ordinary urban Latin Americans as for Americans, but its quality lessened. Health care, too, improved, but the emphasis lay on curative rather than preventive medicine and on large urban hospitals rather than small neighborhood or rural clinics. Efforts to reform the tax structure were often limited by oversized and inefficient state bureaucracies, subsidies, military expenditures, and a widespread sentiment among middle- and upper-class Latin Americans that the vast majority of the poor were properly compensated by relatively inexpensive education and medical services and ridiculously cheap public transportation. In reality, of course, Latin America's poor wind up paying relatively more than their more affluent countrymen through indirect or value-added taxes, which were often double what sales taxes were in the United States. Inequity of income distribution was worse in those countries that showed the most remarkable economic growth since World War II, Mexico and Brazil.

The most revealing statistic was demographic. Within every country an internal migration — inspired by a dream — had begun. The Mexican sociologist Pablo González Casanova, writing in the mid-1960s, described it as the belief that the modern economic miracle in his country, which had begun two decades before, would make the son of a country peasant an urban worker and make *his* son a professional. His analysis might have applied to dozens more Latin American countries, about rural peoples displaced by development. The Mexican case is illustrative. Mexico intended an industrial future and so desperately needed its rural labor force that in 1947 the Mexican government pressed the U.S. government to stop the flow of Mexicans illegally entering the United States. Mexican farm youths did move to the city and did get jobs in factories, but their children did not go on to become professionals. By the time González made his analysis, the ability of Mexican industry to absorb this labor force had leveled off, compelling the government to accommodate the excess in the public sector. When government could no longer provide employment, this vast army of migrants joined Mexico's marginal population. They have settled in the rabbit-warren *colonias* of the poor in Mexico City, alien creatures one generation away from a village back in Oaxaca. They know better than to expect very much, but they expect more than their rural parents did. They learn to make do; some form community organizations, creating "Little Oaxaca" in the midst of misery.[32]

In the past, economic and political concerns occupied a central place in Washington's strategic calculations in Latin America, but the 1980s migration within the hemisphere — once a secondary issue in the history of the Americas — assumed a critical and a more determining place in its international politics. In part this modern migration derives its strength from older patterns, not only in the New World but also in the Old World, of movement into sparsely settled regions or to satisfy the labor demands of modern industrial economies to the north. Since the late nineteenth century, laborers migrated north from Mexico, in peace and wartime, to meet the needs of a dynamic U.S. economy, especially in the Southwest. U.S. companies moved assembly plants southward into Mexico, Central America, and the Caribbean to take advantage of a labor supply that did not migrate northward. An international American economy has spawned an international labor force. Dependency theorists argue, sometimes persuasively, that it has not only fostered economic dependency but has retarded Latin American democracy.

Economic downturns, especially those afflicting Latin America in the 1980s, fueled new migrations, often of desperate people who had lost all hope except the fleeting prospect that they will find "on the other side" a temporary job to sustain them. They became the dispossessed of the Third World. Occasionally their plight generated powerful social concerns and prompted the response of governments or the international community or private voluntary organizations. In Central America, civil war and economic debility pushed them from their country huts into the cities, into neighboring countries, into refugee camps of the United Nations, or, ultimately, into the United States — to New Orleans, Houston, Washington, Los Angeles. The confrontation of Cuba and the United States, sustained for more than twenty-five years by the cynical international posturing of the two governments, had made a generation of Cuban migrants pawns of Washington.[33]

In 1980 the United States expanded political refugee status beyond those fleeing communist systems to admit more peoples with well-founded grounds of political persecution from noncommunist countries as well. For the most part, however, U.S. immigration policy has become increasingly restrictive, reflecting the declining needs of the American economy for immigrant labor and the growing public resentment over the vast numbers of "illegals" who have crossed the two-thousand-mile U.S.-Mexican border into *El Norte*. In 1986, after a decade of debate, a coalition of liberals and conservatives produced a major revision of America's immigration law, making "illegal immigration" truly illegal by establishing fines for American employers who hire anyone without proper documentation to work in this country. In what was properly described as a generous offer, the same law offered "legalization" and ultimately citizenship to those "illegals" who were in the country before 1 January 1982. Southwestern agribusiness, which fought such changes for years on the grounds that it could not depend on a domestic labor force, supported the new law only after Congress stipulated that migrant agricultural workers would come under less restrictive measures.

In the beginning, at least, this ten-year debate over immigration reform reflected largely economic concerns and the increasing social costs of the undocumented. (In the debates over the Caribbean Basin Initiative, for example, supporters of immigration reform argued that Caribbean development would stem illegal entry into the United States by offering employment in the sending country.) Americans became increasingly fearful about the changing social character of the country, particularly in southern Florida and southern California, and became irritated over the rising costs of social services provided for these people. There was an apprehension that the newcomers were "Latinizing" America and a sometimes unarticulated fear of a vanishing Americanness. The "illegals," they believed, were forming a subculture of the dispossessed, people doomed to live in the shadows who lived in America but could never be Americanized. In "Latinized" America the older binding ties of a common public language (English), commonly held political values, and common social priorities were unraveling. Such fears were ordinarily manifestations of regional or local resentments — the furious debate over bilingualism in the schools — but inevitably they led to somber assessments about "what kind of nation do we want to be." Not surprisingly, many Americans with strong feelings of social justice supported immigration reform because they believed the "illegals" were being exploited.

The often heated immigration debate in the 1980s revealed the differing ways in which the United States and America confronted the needs of the American economy for a labor force that stretched beyond our borders. The U.S. economy employed Latin Americans — principally Mexicans, Central Americans, and Caribbean peoples — in U.S. multinationals in their countries and as undocumented or documented workers in the United States. For those who employed them, the understandably critical issues were the cost and reliability of their labor. America, especially concerned religious groups in the nation, looked beyond such calculations to the social status of Latin American workers, addressing their social condition not only in this country but in U.S. multinationals in Latin America. Put another way, the United States and America expressed qualitatively differing measures about the Latin American in the workplace of the Americas. One valued his labor; the other, his person.

The Cold War Balance Sheet

The era that began with the fall of Allende and the sobering and occasional self-accusatory reassessment of U.S. policy in the hemisphere in the mid-1970s ended with the creation of an ambitious plan for the economic integration of North America. In most places, the transition from dictatorship to democracy in the 1980s proved relatively peaceful, commencing with the collapse of the Argentine military's humiliating defeat in the Falklands War and in Chile with the voluntary retirement of Pinochet from power. Most Central Americans, exhausted by the decade-long struggle in Nicaragua and El Salvador, seemed resigned to reconciling their differences with ballots, not bullets.

Such was not the case in Panama, however. A few days before Christmas 1989, President George H. W. Bush ordered a military strike in Panama City

(Operation Just Cause) with the intent of removing Panamanian strongman General Manuel Noriega from power. Less than a decade before, Noriega had been a presumably reliable ally of the CIA and in the covert war against Nicaragua. By the late 1980s, however, as the Reagan administration came under increasing fire for allegedly funding the Nicaraguan resistance by arms sales (the Iran-Contra Affair), Noriega had become a target of criticism in the Congress and the press for a variety of illegal activities — smuggling, gun running, money laundering, and drug trafficking. In response, Reagan tried to push him out through a variety of legal and financial pressures. These failed. Noriega became more defiant and just as abruptly more accommodating when the president agreed to drop the drug indictment if Noriega left Panama. But Noriega would not budge and made matters worse when in May 1989 he brazenly used the Defense Forces to overturn the presidential election when it became clear that his opponent would be the likely winner. The OAS pressured Noriega to hold new elections but did not recommend the use of force if he refused. At that point Bush resolved to act.

The fighting lasted only four days, but the human losses and physical devastation, particularly in the poorer sections of Panama City and its suburbs, was considerable — at least a thousand Panamanian and two hundred U.S. casualties. For a few days, Noriega eluded capture by taking refuge in the papal nunciature. Persuaded to surrender, he was spirited away to Miami to stand trial. (He was subsequently found guilty of money laundering and drug trafficking and sentenced to a forty-year prison term.) The reaction to the entire affair by the new president, Guillermo Endara, was ambivalent, comparing Operation Just Cause to a "kick in the head. . . . I would have been happier without an intervention."[34]

His cynicism reflected older and well-justified views that gunboat diplomacy, revived by President Lyndon Johnson in the 1965 crisis in the Dominican Republic, remained a permanent feature of U.S. policy in the Caribbean. In 1993 the United States joined the United Nations in imposing an economic blockade on the Haitian military in order to secure the return of President Jean-Bertrand Aristide to power. The motive of the Bill Clinton administration for joining this endeavor, however, was not the proverbial "Red Menace" in our Caribbean "backyard," but to deter the mounting numbers of desperate Haitians boarding rickety vessels and heading for U.S. sanctuary. In spite of the

U.S. Senate's overwhelming reaffirmation of the Monroe Doctrine during the 1987 Irangate crisis, neither Operation Just Cause or the restoration of Haitian democracy by fifteen thousand troops occasioned even the mildest references to one of the most hallowed shibboleths in U.S. history.[35]

The overthrow of Noriega served as a reminder of U.S. power and of the fundamental flaws in U.S. drug policies in the hemisphere. Just as the United States bore a direct responsibility for the creation of an independent Panama in 1903, it was equally responsible for the damage done in its anti-drug policies from the early 1970s. President Nixon had declared a war on drugs. His successors, Presidents Ford and Carter, committed themselves to the supply-side of that war. President Reagan proved even more militant than any of his three predecessors when he tripled funding for drug eradication, interdiction, and crop substitution.

But the victories were modest, often embarrassingly so. They were largely achieved by bribing or coercing hemispheric governments to support U.S. policy in order to qualify for assistance yet done in a way that did not jeopardize the moneys these governments received from the drug producers. "Decertification" programs aimed at punishing uncooperative governments in effect angered their peoples and caused peasant growers to look to the narcotraffickers for protection. In the same years, however, the Central Intelligence Agency and other government agencies secretly collaborated to shield drug traffickers in the name of national security and covert operations. Not surprisingly, when the Clinton administration committed itself to Plan Colombia — a much-publicized $7.5 billion aid program with a hefty military anti-drug component — both Latin American and domestic critics of the supply-side war plan voiced skepticism.[36]

As the decade wore on, the hemispheric agenda of the United States shifted noticeably toward promotion of economic integration and summitry. Six months after the Panama invasion, President Bush began a vigorous campaign on behalf of the Enterprise of the Americas Initiative (EAI) and its economic twin, the North American Free Trade Agreement (NAFTA). The latter was the brainchild of Mexican president Carlos Salinas de Gortari, who had desperately sought to deal with Mexico's mounting economic problems through free trade and development of the more prosperous Mexican northern frontier. Canada, which had become a full-fledged member of the Organization of

American States in 1990, signed on principally to avoid losing its share of U.S. trade to Mexico.[37]

Hemispheric free trade made little headway and increasingly encountered resistance, particularly in the Southern Cone, and the "one America" concept of security had little appeal to U.S. leaders, but they did express commitment to common challenges — migration, drugs, trade, debt, nuclear proliferation, and the ageless favorite, democracy. Promotion of cultural bonds between the Americas gained new adherents. In summer of 1993, Vice President Al Gore hosted a hemispheric encounter group to discuss Uruguayan José Enrique Rodó's classic 1900 treatise on the differences between the materialist north (the United States) and the more spiritual south (Latin America) that Rodó had identified in his 1900 book, *Ariel*. Surprisingly, the delegates voiced few of the old animosities about U.S. imperialism or Pan-Americanism. Some spoke fondly of the emergence of an "ecumenical America."[38]

The collapse of the Soviet Union and the end of the Cold War had diminished the appeal of communism and weakened the Left. Democratic governments had replaced dictatorships, and civilian rulers had replaced military regimes. In the inter-American system, the onset of a series of summits not only amplified the labor of the Organization of American States but held out the prospect for a healthy dialogue among hemispheric leaders that would be transnational and encompass broad political and cultural issues. In brief, the hemispheric condition at 1990 looked better than it had at 1960.[39]

For some, undoubtedly, there were bitter memories of Latin America's Cold War experience. Few periods have proved as violent and transformative as the Cold War for successive generations of Latin American and Caribbean peoples since World War II. The West and especially the United States may celebrate victory with the collapse of the Berlin Wall and the dismantling of the Soviet Union, but the parallel record for Latin America and the Caribbean is more ambiguous and the human costs certainly higher. For too many Latin American peoples the official U.S. support for regional democratic movements in the 1980s was inadequate atonement for the indirect backing Washington provided for the internal security forces of Argentina, Chile, Uruguay, Brazil, Bolivia, and Paraguay from the 1960s in Operation Condor, a counterinsurgency program aimed at preventing another Cuba. Under Condor, security forces targeted not only armed terrorists and guerrillas but also political opponents of the regime. In the early 1990s, investigators estimated the number of dead at fifty thousand; incarcerated, four hundred thousand; and "disappeared" at thirty thousand.[40]

Yet in the eight years of the Bill Clinton administration in the 1990s the United States squandered opportunities to reclaim the role President Kennedy had marked out at the beginning of his presidency—a policy incorporating social reform, economic development, and liberal democracy within the framework of hemispheric security. Indeed, despite his support for NAFTA and his professed commitment to strengthening democracy, reducing poverty, and protecting the environment, President Clinton displayed little interest in Latin America. He did not visit a Latin American country until his second term. To be sure, he could claim success in helping the Mexicans weather a serious financial crisis in the mid-1990s and in restoring democracy in Haiti, but his delay in interceding in the Haitian imbroglio may have cost several thousand more lives. In any event, his decision to act in Haiti was in part prompted not by any commitment to democracy but by the public's concern about boatloads of Haitian refugees headed for Florida. And his tolerance of Peruvian violations of democratic processes and human rights in the name of fighting a war on drugs further discredited the United States in the Andean region.[41]

To indict the Clinton administration for the allegedly misdirected hemispheric policies of the 1990s is tantamount to ignoring the unanticipated consequences of decisions made in the 1960s, the role of other agencies of government, especially the Congress, the growing public concerns over immigration, and the choices several Latin American governments made.

The most egregious example of a policy gone hopelessly awry was the manner by which the United States ultimately based its goal of promoting democracy and human rights in Cuba on political pressure and economic sanctions when the real purpose lay in an unalterable policy of regime change. In fairness, had the Bush and Clinton administrations been able to handle Cuban policy in the same manner as, say, relations with Canada or even Mexico, there might have been at least some limited achievements. Increasingly, under pressure from a Congress alert to the political impact of the Cuban émigré community, the willingness of Cubans to aid their countrymen, the growing opposition to the hard-line policy from several hemispheric governments, and the growing pressures from U.S. business to end the boycott, the Clinton administration found itself captive to an unworkable policy.

In the mid-1990s, Castro's abrupt decision to permit Cubans to depart the island had so overwhelmed U.S. officials that Congress rescinded the thirty-five-year-old policy of granting automatic asylum to any Cuban who touched U.S. shores. As long as Cubans had the option of emigrating to the United States, Castro could counter the discontent among the population about the deprivations brought on by the collapse of the Soviet lifeline with charges that the United States was responsible. In the 1996 election year, Clinton reluctantly but obligingly signed the Helms-Burton law, which internationalized the embargo by trying to coerce other countries that invested in Cuba or traded with Cuba. There were new restrictions on travel to Cuba and on remittances by Cubans to family members remaining on the island. Defiance of the laws now came increasingly from within the country. And in the following years, hundreds of U.S. corporations and several states called for the end or at least the relaxation of trade sanctions. Americans began traveling to Cuba in violation of the law as control over Cuban policy effectively passed to the Congress, which tightened restrictions on trade and travel even further. Efforts by President George W. Bush to get tougher with Castro by imposing even more impediments on remittances and travel had minimal effect on the aging (and increasingly ailing) Castro.[42]

In the 1990s, the United States forged ahead with its Washington Consensus, a return to some of the late eighteenth-century economic notions of comparative advantage, whereby each nation found its economic niche in the global economy without cumbersome government restrictions or protectionist measures. Yet it did so as this approach began to lose favor throughout the hemisphere. For most of the decade, U.S. corporations and investors had profited as one Latin American country after another had rid itself of cumbersome and allegedly unprofitable state enterprises. Where the achievements of transnational economies were undeniably impressive, as with NAFTA, the social costs proved devastating, particularly in the Mexican countryside, and escalated the gap between rich and poor. Transnational firms drove out local, more traditional enterprises. The descriptive term is the "Wal-Mart effect," which affected small business in the United States as well. Critics identified two fundamental problems with the "earnest" developmental goals identified with modernization theory. The first lay in the belief that with technology and capital "backward" Third World economies could achieve prosperity and democracy. Second, the goal proved elusive and in places the outcome produced tragic results.[43]

As governments pushed ambitious economic plans from above, the defiance and opposition from below intensified. The inauguration of the NAFTA agreement in early 1994 precipitated an armed uprising of mostly indigenous people in Chiapas State in southern Mexico. In both Venezuela and Colombia, once considered democratic models, traditional political parties accustomed to sharing power and willing to adhere to the "Washington consensus" in economic policy confronted serious threats. Despite a long guerrilla war and the growing threat of drug cartels, the Colombian government managed to hold its own but did so with massive infusions of U.S. assistance. In 1998 Hugo Chávez, who had led an unsuccessful military coup in 1992 in neighboring Venezuela, won power at the ballot box and set about to transform the nation (renamed the Bolivarian Republic of Venezuela) into a socialist nation and rid the government of the pernicious influence of Washington.

The emergence of Chávez as a regional and indeed hemispheric challenger to the United States served not only as a reminder of the persistence of Cold War dynamics in Latin America but also as evidence of the influence of Castro and the Cuban Revolution in Latin America. (In the early 1960s, the Cuban government's support of guerrilla movements in Venezuela was the principal reason for its expulsion from the Organization of American States.) As the opponent of the established political order and with the petroleum wealth of the nation to support his agenda, Chávez possessed the will and the means not only to serve as Cuba's newfound benefactor but a supporter of anti-American governments in Bolivia, Nicaragua, Ecuador, and El Salvador. As in the early 1960s, Latin America identified in Venezuela an alternative developmental model.[44]

That was a disturbing prospect not only for U.S. leaders but for Colombia's as well. A century after Colombia had suffered humiliation with the loss of Panama — a defeat many Colombians attributed to U.S. interference in isthmian affairs — the survival of the Colombian government depended on U.S.

economic and military support. But for those charting the course of a new hemisphere in the final years of the twentieth century, more integrated economically and less conflictive, the future seemed brighter. At the first Summit of the Americas, held in Miami in December 1993, representatives had spoken approvingly about strengthening democracy, eradicating poverty and discrimination, and building a hemispheric free trade area. The summitry cycle continued in 1998 with a meeting in Santiago, Chile, where the ideal of economic integration and democracy had diminished only negligibly in spite of concerns about the retarding effect of neoliberal economies on social and economic conditions. Faith in development persisted. At the third summit in Quebec City in early spring 2001, anti-growth demonstrators outside the convention failed to deter the representatives from endorsing a sweeping proposal "to leave future generations a Hemisphere that is democratic and prosperous, more just and generous [and] where no one is left behind. We are committed to making this the century of the Americas."[45]

Epilogue

History, Mark Twain said, does not repeat itself but often rhymes. Although they differed in many respects, the presidents of the United States inaugurated in 1801, 1901, and 2001 — Thomas Jefferson, William McKinley, and George W. Bush — began their terms with every expectation that both the government and the nation confronted similar opportunities and dangers in the hemisphere.

For Jefferson, who dreamed of extending the "empire of liberty" into the North American heartland, the threat involved the survival of the country in a transatlantic world in which the rivalry of Britain and France in Europe no longer benefited the revolutionary "band of brothers" who had exploited that blood feud to win independence. Looking at the upheaval in French Saint-Domingue, where Toussaint Louverture (the "Black Napoleon") ruled with an arrogance every bit equal to that of his French counterpart, he had morbid thoughts at the implications for his continental design if the French restored the slave regime or if the Haitians won their independence, and their very success at undermining slavery directly and indirectly threatened slavery everywhere in the Americas. In either case, the outcome offered little reassurance: the first scenario meant that French power might be ultimately restored in North America; the second prompted apprehensions about the place and power of the growing numbers of free blacks and coloreds in the republic. The proverbial "sphinx of Monticello" lived long enough to observe how problematic and divisive the issues of race, color, slavery, and national security could be when they converged in the infuriatingly complicated and intertwined issues of Missouri statehood, the acquisition of Florida, the divergent British, European, and U.S. response to the wars in Spanish America, and the way that war was fought in the Bolivarian theater.

A century after Jefferson began his first term, when McKinley took the oath of office for the second time, the ongoing debate over the role of the United States in the hemisphere rested on the issues of security and stability, particularly in the Caribbean, the political relationship with the other nations in the

Americas, and the role of the United States in the Pan-American system. More specifically, the president confronted the immediate issue of how to respond to a revolt in the Philippines that erupted in the aftermath of the decision to annex the islands and how the government intended to deal with the transfer of Cuba and Puerto Rico from one power to another. In the case of the first, the issue was resolved temporarily by the imposition of a protectorate and the denial of a revolution that ultimately triumphed six decades later. In the second, the fundamental issue of relationship of the island to the mainland remained unresolved for a century. In all these cases, the dynamics of race, security, and nation combined to frustrate a president genuinely committed to finding a solution about how to incorporate the people and places in the new insular empire without destroying the essential character of the republic. Had he lived, McKinley might have found a solution. His death at the hands of an assassin brought to the presidency Theodore Roosevelt, a nineteenth-century romantic confounded by the ethnic and racial diversity of his America but determined to leave his mark on both the presidency and the hemisphere. Roosevelt and his political and ideological rival, Woodrow Wilson, crafted designs and policies for the U.S. role in the hemisphere that have persisted ever since.

Bush took office in the year that will remain etched in U.S. memories by the fateful date of 11 September and the attack on the World Trade Center and the Pentagon. Understandably, most Americans riveted their attention on the Islamic world, but the crisis rejuvenated national concerns about border security (especially along the two-thousand-mile southern border) and would prompt reconsideration about Western Hemispheric travel and immigration. The attack would lead directly to the creation of a new department within the executive branch — Homeland Security — and the consolidation of customs and immigration responsibilities into the agency of Immigration and Customs Enforcement (ICE), the major division of Homeland Security. At the same time, the events of 9/11 distracted the public from other hemispheric issues of the 1990s — the deepening Latin American discontent with the neoliberal economic agenda crafted largely by U.S. leaders, the unevenness of economic growth, the resurgence of social inequities, among other concerns. In both Europe and North America, particularly, the strike served as a reminder not only about the threat that secular, liberal democratic states confronted in their role as political entities and guarantors of public safety but also the parallel challenge to their presumptive role as architects of a civilizing vision in the global cultural wars of the post–Cold War years.

Over the next few years, concerns about the growing numbers of undocumented aliens in the country (estimated at 12 million at mid-decade) and the perceived vulnerability to terrorism and criminal activity revived calls for a fortified border. A presidency that began with expressions of cordiality to the newly elected Vicente Fox of the National Action Party and renewed enthusiasm for building a trilateral North American community of Mexico, the United States, and Canada ended with a sobering warning from the U.S. Joint Forces Command that fighting between drug cartels and the government could bring about the collapse of the Mexican state and imperil the security of the United States. The reality, as the notable Mexican journalist Enrique Krauze pointed out in a *New York Times* op-ed, is more complicated. Mexico is a young democratic state: in 2000 it did away with the oligarchic state created in the aftermath of the 1910 revolution, and in the first decade of the twenty-first century its government has coped with the twin crises of a financial downturn and a vicious war between rival drug cartels that threatens civil society and the authority of the state. The United States has provided assistance to Mexico to meet this challenge, but the characterization of Mexico as a "failed state" and the unwillingness of North Americans to admit their complicity in this crisis because of their consumption of drugs and supplying of arms to the combatants smacked of hypocrisy.[1]

As in the past, for every indicator of a more cohesive hemisphere with governments committed to common goals, there is an obverse face of a continent with deep and irreconcilable divisions. The U.S. promotion of the Free Trade Area of the Americas encountered not only the objections of President Chávez of the Bolivarian Republic of Venezuela but the more muted demurrals of the leaders of the Mercosur countries (Brazil, Argentina, Paraguay, and Uruguay). At the same time, the United States demonstrated its commitment to human rights and democracy with its support of the Inter-American Democratic Charter (approved on the fateful 9/11 date), an expansive and idealistic document reaffirmed at the Fourth Summit of the Americas at Mar del Plata, Argentina, in November 2005.[2]

The values expressed in the charter and similar official documents of the Organization of American States reflect the universal values of America, broadly defined, ideals the United States professes to support. A comparison between the charter and the fundamental documents of the European Union illustrate the vastly different character of the two entities. The latter has adopted a common currency (adopted by fifteen of its twenty-seven members) and crafted the structure of a super state. In the process, however, there has been considerable disillusion and grumbling about the remoteness and undemocratic character of the union. The OAS, admittedly, lacks many of the strengths and power of the European Union, and justifiable grumbling about U.S. dominance in the organization has persisted off and on since its creation. But the charter expresses values and goals that set it apart from what Europeans have constructed — a declaration of the right of people to democracy, to the exercise of fundamental freedoms and human rights, to social and economic development, to the reduction of poverty and the elimination of extreme poverty, to quality education, to the promotion of a democratic culture, and to the participation of women in the social process.[3]

Resistance to the transnational economic agenda emanating from Washington came initially from below with the 1994 Zapatista revolt in Chiapas, Mexico. Within a decade, as the United States extended NAFTA to Central America and the Dominican Republic and pushed ahead with the Free Trade Area of the Americas (FTAA), opposition to the power and practices of large financial and trade organizations had escalated dramatically. In early 2001 Brazil hosted the first World Social Forum, an anti-globalization political group opposed to the long-range policies of the World Trade Organization. Four years later, a number of South American leaders with differing political philosophies, ranging from the stridently anti-U.S. Hugo Chávez of Venezuela (now the major benefactor of Cuba) to the moderate Ricardo Lagos of Chile, began to turn to other models, none of which bore much resemblance to those put forward by either the Left or the Right during the Cold War. The effective defeat of FTAA, orchestrated by Brazilian president Luiz "Lula" da Silva, signaled that South American governments looked beyond the United States for their long-range development plans.[4]

A disturbing parallel to the escalating criticism of Washington's economic strategy in the Americas has been the re-militarization of U.S. policy in the region, most notably in Colombia and on the U.S.-Mexican border. Under the much-publicized Plan Colombia, the United States provided $4.7 billion in aid to that country from 2000 to 2006, more than 80 percent of which went to military and police forces in support of the government's war on the drug cartels and leftist guerrilla groups. In February 2008 the National Security Archive published documents obtained under the Freedom of Information Act charging that from 1993 Colombian security forces collaborated with members of the country's drug cartels and paramilitary groups in ways that threatened Colombian national security and proved detrimental to U.S. anti-narcotics endeavors. A variation on this theme holds that the policy the Reagan administration employed in Central America in the 1980s became the model used by President Bush in the Middle East after the 9/11 attacks, an example of the "new imperialism."[5]

The resort to a transnational military policy stemmed indirectly from the tolerance of drug trafficking by key U.S. agencies from the 1960s in return for assistance in countering guerrilla activities. By the 1990s, however, the drug traffickers had begun to form alliances with paramilitary groups, guerrillas, and even high-ranking government officials. The economic stakes were clear: a drug trade with modest beginnings in the mid-nineteenth century had become a $40 billion South American enterprise by the early twenty-first century. Both the Departments of State and Defense supported a military solution. By the end of the Clinton administration, U.S. Special Forces operated in fifteen Latin American countries. The School of the Americas (renamed the Western Hemisphere Institute for Security Cooperation in 2001) focused increasingly on training for the drug war. Yet after more than two hundred military operations and the expenditure of a staggering $3.3 billion under the controversial Plan Colombia, the Office of National Drug Control Policy concluded in 2005 that the massive effort had had a negligible effect on reducing coca production. Colombia's president doggedly remained a U.S. ally, but growing resistance in Ecuador and especially among Bolivia's impoverished indigenes to U.S. drug policy toppled the white president and elevated to the presidency Evo Morales, himself of Indian descent and a staunch critic of the country's powerful social elites.[6]

But there is another legacy of the U.S. presence in the hemisphere that some find unsettling and others celebrate. At the turn of the twentieth century, the pervasive fear of culture shock among old-stock Americans centered on southern and eastern Europeans. After the immigration laws of the 1960s, the focus shifted from European immigration to that from South and East Asia, the western Pacific, and Latin America. One distinctive group, whose numbers have grown from the mid-1980s, is composed of those who believe that multiculturalism, "uncontrolled" immigration, and the country's increasing dependence on an immigrant labor force have combined not only to overburden social services but also to change the face and character of the nation. Here, again, one country stands out as the most visible source in the making of the modern United States — Mexico. In 2008, according to a Pew Research Center estimate, 12.7 million Mexican immigrants resided in the United States, a seventeen-fold increase in the thirty-eight-year span from the 1970 census. Of the 12 million undocumented immigrants in the country, Mexicans accounted for almost 60 percent. Mexicans also represented the largest number of legal immigrants (5.7 million or 21 percent). Of all the foreign born in the United States, Mexicans constitute more than 30 percent, the largest concentration from one country since the nineteenth century, when first the Irish and then the Germans occupied this category.[7]

In the years after the end of the *bracero* program in the mid-1960s, Mexican immigrants, once identified as principally agricultural laborers, have worked in wholesale and retail trades, service industries, manufacturing, agriculture, and construction. Despite widespread public outcries reminiscent of those in the 1970s and 1980s, congressional efforts to thrash out a comprehensive immigration reform bill floundered over concerns about lax federal enforcement of the law and reminders of the disappointments over allegedly lax enforcement of the 1986 Immigration Reform and Control Act. At the same time, the report acknowledged that in 2000 undocumented immigrants from Mexico increased the U.S. gross domestic product by $220 billion. Social Security Administration officials pointed out undocumented immigrants contributed a substantial portion of the billions paid into the system under fraudulent names or numbers, moneys that could not be returned as benefits. In the course of the decade, remittances from Mexicans living or working in the United States to families and kin back home grew from $9 billion in 2001 to approximately $25 billion in 2007, a sum second only to petroleum as a source of income to the nation.[8]

A decade in which Americans deemed Mexico culpable for U.S. ails from drugs and immigration had commenced with a seismic shift in that nation's relationship with its colossus neighbor. In spite of the criticism in both countries, the North American Free Trade Agreement, only six years old, had become a reality neither country could ignore. NAFTA had made Mexico the U.S.'s second largest trading partner and the first export market for Texas and California. *Maquiladoras*, once decried as sweatshops and environmental disasters, spread as far south as Chiapas and had become more and more hi-tech. Immigration from Mexico into the United States was institutionalized, making Mexicans by far the largest Hispanic presence in the country (65 percent) or three out of five of every Spanish-speaking residents in a decade in which Hispanics would surpass African Americans as the largest ethnic minority.

Mexico's vocal anti-American elements decried these economic developments as yet another indicator of the country's increasing subservience to a powerful United States. After the surprising victory of the National Action Party in 2000, Mexican leaders, once supporters of revolutionary movements in Central America and defenders of the Cuban deviance in the hemisphere, voiced more anti-Cuban sentiments. Mexicans reared in the belief that the United States was the ideological and cultural enemy were now persuaded to accept the once heretical notion that the country's future lay in an economic alliance with their powerful neighbor. Perhaps Mexico could be a bridge between the United States and the rest of Latin America. That prospect was fanciful but not the economic and human reality of other ties: in 2009 daily trade between the two countries amounted to $1 billion. A million Americans and Mexicans cross the two-thousand-mile border each day to vacation, shop, visit families, work, or go to school. In the fifteen years after NAFTA took effect, U.S. exports to Mexico rose by almost 200 percent; in the same period, Mexican exports to the United States escalated by more than 300 percent. As millions of Americans call for strengthening border security and building a wall between the nations, the bonds between them grow.[9]

A parallel belief that often defies explanation when set against the historical record is the belief that North America is a powerful region of one superpower and two uneasy neighbors that has more population and more economic might than the European Union. Since 1775, both Canada and later Mexico have persistently rejected the American Revolution and its fundamental credos. Their foreign policies have reflected this ambivalence, even as NAFTA did away with many of the investment and trade barriers to integration. That reality and the security concerns prompted by the attacks of 9/11 led to a meeting between the leaders of the three nations in Texas in March 2005. Their joint statement was ambitiously titled a "Security and Prosperity Partnership," conceptually trilateral but in essence devoid of much vision. The reality, as two eminent Canadian historians have astutely noted, is that however much U.S. leaders speak about a "special relationship" with Canada or a "bond" with Mexico, the disturbing reality is that Washington deals with both countries according to its own interests and the foreign-policy precepts it has historically espoused — liberalism, internationalism, capitalism, and anticolonialism.[10]

At the same time, there is the palpable sense among the critics of North American free trade in both Mexico and Canada that the creation of a North American Union — the presumed objective of the creators of NAFTA — will ultimately erode national sovereignty and even national identity. The European Union, sometimes held up as a model to be emulated, these critics point out, represented largely the joining of equals. (Indeed, the principal idea lay in the belief that the uniting of France and Germany in an economic pact offered the best safeguard against another European war.) But the evolving union of two disparate cultures and weaker economies to an economic and military superpower, they warn, will serve largely to accelerate the Americanization of both our northern and southern neighbors, transforming each into an economic colony. The benefited companies in both are largely American-owned. (Wal-Mart is now the largest transnational employer in Mexico, and in the larger cities Starbucks has become a favorite gathering place for middle- and upper-class Mexicans.) In a variation on this theme, the historian and social commentator Victor Davis Hanson believes that the endangered North American culture is that of the United States. The combination of multiculturalism and mass immigration has transformed California — once considered the model for the American ideal of assimilation and upward mobility — into a society of separatist identities where powerful business interests exploit the cheap immigrant labor and then depend on an overburdened social service and educational system to take on the burden of caring for and educating its people.[11]

Viewed in historical perspective, the contemporary comments about the social and cultural impact of the 45 million people of Latino heritage residing in the United States relate as much to the judgments of early twentieth-century generations as those of the Cold War. Indeed, to look at modern definitions of Americanization in the context of undeniably optimistic views of liberal internationalism in the 1960s is to slight the relevant debates over immigration in the early twentieth century between traditional cultural groups fearful of the waves of Europeans and the economic titans who needed and exploited their labor. Attentive to the political and cultural implications of this increasingly harsh exchange, Theodore Roosevelt condemned the hyphenates resisting assimilation as well as the native who doggedly refused to accept those who tried to fit in. True to his conviction that a new nation would spring forth if the newcomer would assimilate, he was equally assertive in his belief that racism had no place in the nation. Yet he could never reconcile his enduring faith in the process of Americanization with the reality that the modern concept of American nationhood depended on drawing on a color line. The radical Randolph Bourne alertly noted in a seminal 1916 essay that Americanization was not working out as planned by traditional elements who naively believed that assimilation meant — had to mean — abandonment of one's heritage and ways. "We cannot Americanize America worthily by sentimentalizing and moralizing history," Bourne concluded.[12]

The "transnational America" he described a century ago has become a reality, but its human provenance is not European but Asian, Pacific islander, and especially Latin American and Caribbean. The United States is the fifth largest Latin American nation in the world, surpassed only by Argentina, Mexico, Brazil, and Colombia. More than 50 percent of the foreign-born population in this country come from a Latin American country. Hispanics constitute more than 70 percent of the population in three states — Arizona, New Mexico, and Florida. They have created transnational communities, some of which were established before World War II. Others, such as the Cuban community in Miami (depicted by one author as Havana, U.S.A.) or the Dominican enclaves of New York, are more recent. Others seem improbably "out of place" — Mexicans in Gainesville, Georgia, highland Mayans from Guatemala in Morganton, North Carolina. Their impact on music, food, film, television, sports (particularly baseball and boxing), business, and, increasingly, in local, state, and national politics has risen dramatically in the past half century. The dramatic growth of the Latino population has led to the flourishing of a modern dialect — Spanglish — the hybridization of Spanish and English. Critics blame its use on bilingual education, but its roots go back to the encounters between English- and Spanish-speaking peoples in the colonial era.[13]

The hemispheric identity of the United States was reaffirmed in a March 2009 public announcement from the Western Hemisphere Affairs division of the Department of State. In anticipation of the convening of the Fifth Summit of the Americas in Trinidad and Tobago, the statement noted that the meeting would be an "opportunity for the United States to demonstrate that America remains a reliable partner in the hemisphere, committed to working with our neighbors in a spirit of partnership to uphold our shared values and pursue policies that bring direct benefits to all peoples of the Americas."[14]

The statement reiterates shopworn phrases but notably invokes the name "America" to affirm them. That choice, perhaps inadvertent, implies that U.S. leaders recognize they must invoke the name *America* to justify the place and role of the United States in a hemisphere whose governments remain suspicious of its motives, fearful of its power, and resentful of its record in the history of the Americas from the Revolution to the present. In other words, the "America" of Simón Bolívar or José Martí or Fidel Castro or Hugo Chávez possesses a strikingly different memory of the history of the Americas and, more important, of the meaning we Americans give to those words and ideas that we identify with the history of the Americas — *freedom, liberty, democracy, equality, race, nation, sovereignty,* and *self-determination,* among others.

Modern debates over the role of the United States in the Americas, particularly during the Cold War years, generally revolve around these issues, although such terms as *drug trafficking, immigration, environmental deterioration, multiculturalism, grassroots development,* and *anti-Americanism* have joined the list. Indeed, some of these additional items fell directly within the theme of the Fifth Summit of the Americas — "Securing Our Citizens' Future by Promoting Human Prosperity, Energy Security, and Environmental Sustainability" — but the contentious nature of such meetings means that all will be invoked. Certainly, the final statement of the meeting was less inspirational than the statement about summitry in the 2003 document, "The OAS: Its Relevance Today," which proudly noted that in the course of a decade the governments of the Americas had achieved "a general consensus on political and economic principles [grounded] on democracy and market economics [that] enabled unprecedented cooperation and integration throughout the hemisphere."[15]

The Inter-American Dialogue, one of several U.S. think tanks concerned with U.S. policy in the Americas, offered a cautiously optimistic assessment of the meeting, suggesting that the nation had a "second chance" to address key problems, the majority of which were directly related to the Cold War — Cuba, drugs, immigration, trade, the Venezuelan challenge, democracy, and human rights — as well as a reminder that Brazil (one of five hemispheric G20 countries) warrants consideration of a ranking similar to what we profess to accord Canada. (In 2009 Brazil joined Russia, India, and China in the creation of a newcomer economic powerhouse group, BRIC.) The public image of the summit turned out to be less a meeting of the minds over the undeniably common problems confronting a hemisphere of persistently fractious governments and leaders than a series of public statements by President Hugo Chávez of Venezuela about the past transgressions of Europeans and then the United States against Latin Americans. President Barack Obama responded that now may be the time for an easing of U.S.-Cuba relations as well as our troubled relationship with both Venezuela and Bolivia and its indigenous president, Evo Morales. Few of the testimonials at the Summit surpassed the optimism in Secretary of State Hillary Clinton's statement about the infuriatingly more complicated issues in U.S.-Mexican relations: "This is one of the most important relationships that exists between any two countries in the world. We are part of the same family, we share this continent as our common home, and we will inhabit a common future."[16]

Ordinarily, U.S. leaders use such expressions to describe this nation's relationship with Great Britain, a reminder of our transatlantic bond with the mother country. Clinton's words are a sign that perhaps the United States is now willing, whether out of conviction or necessity, to acknowledge the importance and the value of its place in the Western Hemisphere. Skeptics, north and south, could cite the historical record of the United States in the hemisphere, particularly during the Cold War, to question any such notion. But I believe there are other considerations that warrant closer attention.

The most important is a reminder of the intimate connection between the domestic history of the nation, particularly from the Revolution to the Civil

War, and every major issue identified with the role and policy of the United States in the Americas from those earliest years of contact until the present — revolution, slavery, race, expansion, empire, governance, among others. In those formative years, U.S. leaders and the American public developed fundamental ideas and beliefs about the other nations and peoples of the Americas. They developed these beliefs and attitudes from a variety of perspectives — ranging from a belief that because of its revolutionary experience and the creation of the first independent state in the Americas, the United States constituted a model that might be emulated, on the one hand, to the equally arrogant attitude that because of their Iberian heritage of mixed-race peoples, their participation in the wars of independence and the political culture, and the failure to reconcile the bitter divisions among their elites, the future of independent Spanish America was bleak. Put simply, the general attitude of U.S. leaders was that they had been able to control the chaotic forces and passions from below, but their counterparts in Spanish America had not. Alexis de Tocqueville confirmed this judgment in his classic survey of the nation, *Democracy in America*.

The truth of the matter, as the aging Jefferson recognized in following the bitter and intertwined debates over the U.S. response to the Spanish-American wars of independence and the admission of Missouri as a slave state, was the sobering realization that the nation's leaders had not resolved but had essentially delayed resolution of the most fundamental problems of the wars of independence in the Americas — the color question and the fear of the revolution from below, symbolized by the Haitian upheaval. In this era, Americans more and more identified parallel threats to the republic — the expansion of slavery and the slave power and the parallel fear that instability in Mexico and the circum-Caribbean would lead to a revival of European power that would imperil U.S. security. Although the circumstances and the actors varied, those fears persisted into the twentieth century. As much as the imperial or missionary impulse, they explain U.S. expansion in North America and the Caribbean and why doing nothing has never been a realistic option for any U.S. leader.[17]

A second consideration is my belief that such terms as *Latin America* or *Latin American policy of the United States* or *U.S.–Latin American relations* have a diminished utility as a framework for understanding the role and place of the United States in the Americas. The role of Canada as a hemispheric actor, which became more formal with its membership in the Organization of American States, not only brings North America more clearly into focus but also reinforces the argument for a hemispheric perspective. Latin America lacks precise definition. More so than the United States or Canada, the vast region we call Latin America is an amalgam of distinctive and very different states. Colombia is as different from Venezuela as Virginia is from Texas. The revolutionary dynamic in Cuban history has followed a different pattern than that in Saint-Domingue (Haiti). Certainly, there are numerous instances in the history of the hemisphere where the Latin American nations are united in their views about U.S. policy, but just as important are those even more numerous times when the bilateral relationship between the United States and a Latin American nation offers a more useful approach. In brief, the greater attention this edition gives to Canada and North America is a reminder of the need for a truly hemispheric assessment. Just as important, too, is the reminder that in numerous ways the various states and regions of the United States not only bring differing perspectives to national politics but have played significant roles in our relationship with specific Latin American countries and subregions.

Third, the willingness of the United States to acknowledge that our power and influence in the hemisphere has not so much diminished but that other hemispheric countries have notably improved in several critical measures of governance and economic development is a welcome beginning for a "second chance" for the nation in this hemisphere. As the statement from the Western Hemisphere Affairs division of the State Department affirmed, the United States is now willing to be a "reliable partner," not a policeman or even a model in a hemisphere whose governments and people remain ambivalent if not uniformly hostile or resentful about our role. Certainly, there is acceptance if not agreement with our profession that national security is uppermost. But there have to be self-imposed limits and restraints in protecting that security and a recognition of the limits of what we have to offer the other nations of the hemisphere as a guide for political and economic development.

As the first generations of U.S. leaders learned, ours is not the only meaningful or consequential revolution of the revolutionary age. Our patriotic fervor and nationalism are no more intensely felt than those of Cubans or Mexicans or Brazilians or Canadians. The first people to reject the American Revolution were not Spanish Americans but French Canadians. Anti-Americanism among Canadians is far more subtle than that of Mexicans or Venezuelans and has virtually nothing to do with the racial prejudices that are central to our historically negative assessments of Latin American and Caribbean peoples, but it runs just as deep in the national psyche. Canada's experience in the development of political rights, economic growth, territorial expansion, and social policy — each achieved with far less violence and conflict than occurred in the United States — is as compelling a model for hemispheric governments as that of its powerful southern neighbor.

What is too often forgotten in the persistent reminders about the fundamental differences between the United States and the other Americas is a reality equally as meaningful — a shared experience that altered the ways in which the peoples and states of the Americas have perceived one another, occasionally as allies or kindred spirits, more often as adversaries whose differing cultural, political, and ethnic heritages left deep fissures even as the contact between governments and especially peoples grew. Myths and stereotypes of the other peoples of the Americas have played an often negative role in how we Americans look at our hemispheric neighbors, undeniably, and how our neighbors, particularly Mexicans and Canadians, look at us. But there can be no denying the unappreciated bonds of a shared experience from the revolutionary age to the present.

Whether the issue relates to federalist structures of government, the encounter between European, African, and indigenous peoples, the experience of slavery and coercive labor systems, the problem of pacification of the countryside, economic development, nationhood and nationalism, or the treatment of indigenous peoples, the governments and the peoples of the Americas have a shared experience in dealing with these issue if rarely a common solution to them. Theirs may be a symbiotic bond, one without a convergence of values, but it is no less meaningful. Undeniably, the history of the United States cannot be understood without an appreciation of the linkages between this country and Europe, Africa, and even Asia, but more important are the ties we have with the other peoples and nations of the Americas.

The early leaders of the United States sensed this truth, even as French Canadians rejected their revolutionary overtures and, later, as they doubted the worthiness of the Spanish American cause and became alarmed at the way the "George Washington" of Spanish America, the Venezuelan Simón Bolívar, fought the struggle by arming mixed-race and slave troops. But Washington himself acknowledged that his victory depended on the staying power of social marginals, not the minutemen of Revolutionary lore. When we look at what Bolívar or Benito Juárez or José Martí fought for — independence, nationhood, unity — or when we consider how issues of race and color have impacted the political culture, the patterns of nationalism from the age of revolution to modern times, or efforts to reconcile the twin promises of the revolutionary age — human rights and progress — we see not the "other America" but the other face of ourselves.

To accept that is to affirm that the United States is a global power but America is something different — an aspiration and an ideal with an identity inextricably linked to the hemisphere. Although he meant "Spanish America," Simón Bolívar best expressed the sentiment in the Jamaica Letter of September 1815: "More than anyone, I desire to see America fashioned into the greatest nation in the world, greatest not so much by virtue of her area and wealth as by her freedom and glory."[18]

Notes

1. The Revolutionary Age

1. Qtd. in Lester D. Langley, *The Americas in the Age of Revolution, 1750–1850* (New Haven, Conn., 1996), 37.

2. John Herd Thompson and Stephen J. Randall, *Canada and the United States: Ambivalent Allies*, 4th ed. (Athens, Ga., 2008), 9–12.

3. Andrew Shaughnessy, *An Empire Divided: The American Revolution and the British Caribbean* (Philadelphia, 2000), 213–14, 220–21, 230–31, 241–48.

4. Arthur Whitaker, *The Spanish-American Frontier, 1783–1795: The Westward Movement and the Spanish Retreat in the Mississippi Valley* (Lincoln, Neb., 1927), 13; Richard B. Morris, *The Peacemakers: The Great Powers and American Independence* (New York, 1965), 321–22, 419–20.

5. François Furstenberg, "The Significance of the Trans-Appalachian Frontier in Atlantic History," *American Historical Review* 113 (June 2008): 647–77.

6. Qtd. in Arthur P. Whitaker, *The Mississippi Question, 1795–1803: A Study in Trade, Politics and Diplomacy* (Washington, D.C., 1934), 34–35.

7. Ibid., 155–58.

8. Qtd. in Alexander DeConde, *This Affair of Louisiana* (New York, 1976), 100.

9. Qtd. in Winthrop D. Jordan, *White over Black: American Attitudes toward the Negro, 1550–1812* (Chapel Hill, N.C., 1968), 381. Albert Gallatin, a representative from Pennsylvania and early abolitionist, put the case against Haitian independence succinctly: "No more would be more unwilling than I to constitute a whole nation of freed slaves . . . and thus to throw so many wild tigers on society" (qtd. in Gordon S. Brown, *Toussaint's Clause: The Founding Fathers and the Haitian Revolution* [Jackson, Miss., 2005], 141).

10. *Archivo de General Miranda, 1750–1810*, 15 vols. (Caracas, 1929), 15: 207.

11. In January 1811, lower Louisiana experienced a slave revolt so frightening to white residents of New Orleans that in retaliation authorities placed the decapitated heads of executed leaders on poles. A chronicler of the revolt explained: "The people of this territory wished, by this terrible warning, to protect against the repetition of the horrors of the revolt in Santo Domingo" (qtd. in Robert L. Paquette, "Revolutionary Saint Domingue in the Making

of Territorial Louisiana," in *A Turbulent Time: The French Revolution and the Greater Caribbean*, ed. David Barry Gaspar and David Patrick Geggus (Bloomington, Ind., 1997), 219.

12. Qtd. in Furstenberg, " Significance of the Trans-Appalachian Frontier," 671. Laurent Dubois, *Avengers of the New World: The Story of the Haitian Revolution* (Cambridge, Mass., 2004). See also Dubois's companion volume, *A Colony of Citizens: Revolution and Slave Emancipation in the French Caribbean, 1787–1804* (Chapel Hill, N.C., 2004); and David Patrick Geggus and Norman Fiering, eds., *The World of the Haitian Revolution* (Bloomington, Ind., 2009).

13. Arthur P. Whitaker, *The Western Hemisphere Idea: Its Rise and Decline* (Ithaca, N.Y., 1954), 28–29.

14. Karen Racine, *Francisco de Miranda: A Transatlantic Life in the Age of Revolution* (Wilmington, Del., 2003), 141–72.

15. Harry Bernstein, "Las primeras relaciones intelectuales entre New England y el mundo hispánico (1700–1815)," *Revista Hispánica Moderna* 5 (1938): 8.

16. On the role of popular groups see Eric Van Young, *The Other Rebellion: Popular Violence, Ideology, and the Mexican Struggle for Independence, 1810–1821* (Palo Alto, Calif., 2001).

17. Peggy Liss, *Atlantic Empires: The Network of Trade and Revolution, 1713–1826* (Baltimore, 1983), 229, contends that the American and Latin American revolutions represented similar "outgrowths of internal expansion and changing attitudes, international struggles, shifting international economic arrangements, and new outlooks on colonies by the metropolis and the other way around."

18. Arthur P. Whitaker, *The United States and the Independence of Latin America, 1800–1830* (New York, 1964; orig. pub., 1941), 94–99.

19. Thompson and Randall, *Canada and the United States*, 19–23.

20. Qtd in Whitaker, *United States and the Independence*, 126. In the first few years after the exile of Napoleon, thousands of veterans of the armies that had battled for more than two decades commenced a transatlantic migration to the Americas. Some became recruits into Bolívar's reconstituted army for the liberation of northern South America. Others found their way into New Orleans or Saint Louis, where they joined a generation of slaveholding émigrés from Haiti. Among this human invasion into the Gulf Coast states were 30,000 Bonapartists, who settled on a 90,000-acre tract of west Alabama land the U.S. Congress seized from the Creek Indian nation. See Rafe Blauford, *Bonapartists in the Borderlands: French Exiles and Refugees on the Gulf Coast, 1815–1835* (Tuscaloosa, Ala., 2005).

21. March 28, 1818, qtd. in James F. Hopkins, ed., *The Papers of Henry Clay*, vol. 2, *The Rising Statesman, 1815–1820* (Lexington, Ky., 1961), 551. See also Lester D. Langley, *Simón Bolívar: Venezuelan Rebel, American Revolutionary* (Lanham, Md., 2009), 65–70.

22. H. M. Brackenridge, "A Letter on South American Affairs," in *Voyage to South America, Performed by Order of the American Government, in the Years 1817 and 1818, in the Frigate Congress*, 2 vols. (Baltimore, 1819), 1: 346.

23. Adams to George Erving, 28 November 1818, in Worthington C. Ford, ed. *The Writings of John Quincy Adams*, 7 vols. (New York 1913–1917), 6: 487–88.

24. Qtd. in ibid., 336.

25. Whitaker, *United States and the Independence*, 358–63.

26. Ernest R. May, *The Making of the Monroe Doctrine* (Cambridge, Mass., 1975), stresses the domestic political implications of a unilateral statement.

27. Qtd. in Harold Bierck, ed., *Selected Writings of Simón Bolívar*, Vicente Lecuna, comp., Lewis Bertrand, trans. (2 vols., New York, 1951), 2: 458–59.

28. For an assessment of Bolívar from the perspective of contemporary U.S. leaders and, contrastingly, the Liberator's views of the United States, see Lester D. Langley, "The Image of Simón Bolívar in the United States in the Revolutionary Era," and David Bushnell, "The United States as Seen by Simón Bolívar: Too Good a Neighbor," in *Simón Bolívar: Essays on the Life and Legacy of the Liberator*, ed. David Bushnell and Lester D. Langley (Lanham, Md., 2008), 123–45.

29. Qtd. in Johnson, *Hemisphere Apart*, 11.

30. Qtd. in Ron Seckinger, *The Brazilian Monarchy and the South American Republics, 1822–1831* (Baton Rouge, La., 1984), 27–28. For a provocative interpretation of the emerging North American view of Latin America in the early nineteenth century, see Frederick B. Pike, *The United States and Latin America: Myths and Stereotypes of Civilization and Nature* (Austin, Tex., 1992), esp. 1–112. For a suggestive assessment of the changing meanings of the Monroe Doctrine over successive generations, see Gretchen Murphy, *Hemispheric Imaginings: The Monroe Doctrine and Narratives of U.S. Empire* (Durham, N.C., 2005).

31. Many Americans of the mid-nineteenth century shared this negative view of Spanish colonialism. A generation of New England intellectuals from the 1830s to the 1880s — among them, William Hickling Prescott and Washington Irving — created for curious American readers an "enduring view of the Hispanic world's relevance, indeed centrality to the United States." Regrettably, their literary impact did little to change popular associations of Spain and by

implication Spanish Americans with religious bigotry and despotism. Iván Jaksic, *The Hispanic World and American Intellectual Life, 1830-1880* (New York, 2007).

32. Qtd. in Rafe Blaufarb, "The Western Question: The Geopolitics of Latin American Independence," *American Historical Review* 112 (June 2007): 29.

33. See Whitaker, *Western Hemisphere Idea*, 14–16.

34. Robert Remini, *Andrew Jackson and the Course of American Empire, 1767–1821* (New York, 1977), 382.

35. On the contrast in the thinking of U.S. leaders in the 1780s and 1820s on the means to preserve the union and the nation's relationship to the Spanish American revolutions see James E. Lewis Jr., *The American Union and the Problem of Neighborhood: The United States and the Collapse of the Spanish Empire, 1783–1829* (Chapel Hill, N.C., 1998).

2. Manifest Destiny

1. Wallace Stegner, qtd. in Eric Foner, *The Story of American Freedom* (New York, 1988), 50.

2. For a more detailed comparison, see J. H. Elliott, *Empires of the Atlantic World: Britain and Spain in America, 1492–1830* (New Haven, Conn., 2006).

3. Jackson, Annual Message to Congress, 8 December 1830. On the sordid history of Indian removal in the making of continental empire, see Paul VanDeveldeer, *Savages and Scoundrels: The Untold Story of America's Road to Empire Through Indian Territory* (New Haven, Conn., 2009).

4. Qtd. in William Manning, ed., *Diplomatic Correspondence of the United States: Inter-American Affairs*, 12 vols. (Washington, D.C., 1932–1939), 5: 503–4. For a Colombian view of this incident, see Germán Cavelier, *La política internacional de Colombia*, 2nd ed., 4 vols. (Bogotá, 1959).

5. *El Tiempo*, 19 February 1829, in Despatches, Argentina, National Archives (microfilm).

6. John Forbes to Secretary of State, 25 May 1829, ibid.

7. Francis Baylies to Secretary of State, 26 September 1832, in Manning, *Diplomatic Correspondence*, 1: 165.

8. David M. K. Sheinin, *Argentina and the United States: An Alliance Contained* (Athens, Ga., 2006), 14–16.

9. Qtd. in John Herd Thompson and Stephen J. Randall, *Canada and the United States: Ambivalent Allies*, 4th ed. (Athens, Ga., 2008), 30.

10. David Pletcher, *The Diplomacy of Annexation: Texas, Oregon, and the Mexican War* (Columbia, Mo., 1973), is unsurpassed for its balance and objectivity in chronicling U.S. expansionism in the 1830s and 1840s.

11. Timothy J. Henderson, *The Mexican Wars for Independence* (New York, 2009), 219.

12. Qtd. in Eugene C. Barker, *Mexico and Texas, 1821–1835* (New York, 1965; orig. pub., 1928), 148. For a different view of Texan-Mexican relations see Vicente Filósola, *Memorias para la historia de la Guerra de Tejas*, 2 vols. (Mexico City, 1849), 2: 170–71, 222–25.

13. James Hook to Lord Palmerston, 30 April 1841, in Ephraim D. Adams, ed., *British Diplomatic Correspondence Concerning the Republic of Texas* (Austin, Tex., 1918), 38.

14. Buchanan to Slidell, 10 November 1845, in Manning, *Diplomatic Correspondence*, 8: 173.

15. Qtd. in Sean Wilentz, *The Rise of American Democracy: Jefferson to Lincoln* (New York, 2005), 564.

16. The question of responsibility for the coming of the war remains a contentious issue, largely shaped by nationalist sentiments. Timothy J. Henderson, *A Glorious Defeat: Mexico and the United States* (New York, 2007), emphasizes the debilitating impact of Mexican centralist/federalist divisions, the power and influence of the military and the church in Mexican affairs, and U.S. perceptions of Mexican weakness. The older view that militant Mexican leaders unnecessarily provoked the conflict glosses over two pieces of evidence — the exaggerated claims of Texas leaders to the Rio Grande boundary and Texas's refusal to accept Mexico's offer of independence *if* that meant forswearing statehood. No Mexican government could have met Polk's conditions for peace and survived. Brian Delay, "Why Mexico Fought," *Diplomatic History* 33 (January 2009): 125–28.

17. For a succinct and provocative assessment of U.S.-Mexican relations from the 1820s to the 1860s see W. Dirk Raat, *Mexico and the United States: Ambivalent Vistas*, 3rd ed. (Athens, Ga., 2004; orig. pub., 1992), 55–78. Several older but still useful studies are Frederick Merk, *Manifest Destiny and Mission in American History: A Reinterpretation* (New York, 1963); Merk, *The Monroe Doctrine and American Expansionism, 1843–1846* (New York, 1966); Carlos Bosch García, *Historia de las relaciones entre México y los Estados Unidos, 1819–1848* (Mexico City, 1961); and Gene Brack, *Mexico Views Manifest Destiny, 1821–1846* (Albuquerque, N.M., 1975).

18. *New York Herald*, 11 April 1848, qtd. in Robert Johannsen, *To the Halls of the*

Montezumas: The Mexican War in the American Imagination (New York, 1985), 303.

19. Brian DeLay, *War of a Thousand Deserts: How Indians Shaped the Era of the U.S.-Mexican War* (New Haven, Conn., 2008).

20. Thomas Hietala explores this theme in *Manifest Design: Anxious Aggrandizement in Late Jacksonian America* (Ithaca, N.Y., 1985), 255–57.

21. On the racial dynamics of expansionism see Reginald Horsman, *Race and Manifest Destiny: The Origins of American Racial Anglo-Saxonism* (Cambridge, Mass., 1981), 217.

22. Gustave A. Nuermberger, "The Continental Treaties of 1856: An American Union Exclusive of the United States," *Hispanic American Historical Review*, 20 (February 1940): 32–55. John P. Harrison, "Science and Politics: Origins and Objectives of Mid-Nineteenth Century Government Expeditions to Latin America," *Hispanic American Historical Review*, 35 (May 1955): 175–202, shows how the United States used scientific interest and manifest destiny to advance its policies in Latin America.

23. Louis A. Pérez Jr., *Cuba and the United States: Ties of Singular Intimacy*, 3rd ed. (Athens, Ga., 2003; orig. pub., 1990), 42–46.

24. Basil Rauch, *American Interest in Cuba, 1848–1855* (New York, 1948), covers the U.S. urgency in dealing with Cuba but should be supplemented with the monumental work of Herminio Portell Vilá, who argues that López favored independence and was thus not a pawn of the southern "slavocracy."

25. C. Stanley Urban, "The Africanization of Cuba Scare, 1853–1855," *Hispanic American Historical Review* (February 1957), 29–45; Pérez, *Cuba and the United States*, 47–50.

26. Robert E. May, *The Southern Dream of Caribbean Empire, 1854–1861* (Baton Rouge, La., 1961), demonstrates how southerners believed the pursuit of tropical empire would restore the South to its preeminence in the nation.

27. For a discussion of the treaty and the boom years in Panama in the 1850s see Stephen J. Randall, *Colombia and the United States: Hegemony and Interdependence* (Athens, Ga., 1992), 26–34; and Michael L. Conniff, *Panama and the United States: The Forced Alliance*, 2nd ed. (Athens, Ga., 2001; orig. pub., 1992), 33–40.

28. Michael Gobat, review of Aimes McGuinnes, *Path of Empire: Panama and the California Gold Rush* (Ithaca, N.Y., 2008), *Diplomatic History* 32 (November 2008): 981–84.

29. "British Aggression in Central America," *U.S. Magazine and Democratic Review*, n.s., 1 January 1851, 14.

30. Squier to Secretary of State, 12 September 1848, in John Clayton Papers, Library of Congress. The standard biography of Chatfield is Mario Rodríguez, *A Palmerstonian Diplomat in Central America: Frederick Chatfield, Esq.* (Tucson, Ariz., 1964).

31. For a summary of these episodes, see Thomas M. Leonard, *Central America and the United States: The Search for Stability* (Athens, Ga., 1991), 11–30; Charles Brown, *Agents of Manifest Destiny* (Chapel Hill, N.C., 1980); and Comisión Histórico de la Campaña de 1856–1857, *Documentos relativos a la Guerra contra los filibusteros* (San José, Costa Rica, 1956).

32. Gregorio Delgado, "Walker, Nicaragua, y Cuba," *Revista del Archivo y Biblioteca Nacional* 33 (November–December 1954, January–June 1955): 383–93.

33. William Walker, *The War in Nicaragua* (Mobile, Ala., 1860).

34. Qtd. in Comisión Histórico de la Campaña de 1856–1857, *Documentos relativos a la Guerra contra los filibusteros*, 64.

35. Qtd. in Thompson and Randall, *Canada and the United States*, 39.

36. On these themes, see Fredrick Pike, *The United States and Latin America: Myths and Stereotypes of Civilization and Nature* (Austin, Tex., 1992), 13, 19–20, 39, 46–49, 62–63, 67, 183; and Andars Stephanson, *Manifest Destiny: American Expansion and the Empire of Right* (New York, 1996), who spans over three centuries and emphasizes the religious content of manifest destiny.

3. The Imperial Design

1. Qtd. in Germán Arciniegas, *Latin America: A Cultural History* (New York, 1966), 379.

2. Walter Nugent, *Habits of Empire: A History of American Expansion* (New York, 2008), 238–39. See also Kristin Hoganson, *Fighting for American Manhood: How Gender Politics Provoked the Spanish-American and Philippine-American Wars* (New Haven, Conn., 1998); and her equally provocative study *Consumers' Imperium: The Global Production of American Domesticity, 1865–1920* (Chapel Hill, N.C., 2007). For yet another perspective see Walter L. Hixson, *The Myth of American Diplomacy: National Identity and U.S. Foreign Policy* (New Haven, Conn., 2008).

3. Qtd. in Lester D. Langley, *The Americas in the Modern Age* (New Haven, Conn., 2003), 16. For a comparison of military doctrine in the Indian wars in North America, see Bruce Vandervort, *Indian Wars of Canada, Mexico, and the United States* (London, 2006), who attributes success in the U.S. case not

to military strategy but to the ability of whites to curtail their internal disputes and consolidate their power.

4. In truth, Canada could ill afford a "wild west." U.S. expenditures in the Indian wars in 1869 exceeded the entire Canadian budget! See John Herd Thompson and Stephen J. Randall, *Canada and the United States: Ambivalent Allies*, 4th ed. (Athens, Ga., 2008), 49. For a comparison of the methods used by the Texas Rangers and the Mounties in policing their respective "Wests," see Andrew Graybill, *Policing the Great Plains: Rangers and Mounties in the Policing of the North American Frontier, 1875-1910* (Lincoln, Neb. 2007).

5. David Pletcher, *The Diplomacy of Trade and Investment: American Economic Expansion in the Hemisphere, 1865–1900* (Columbia, Mo., 1995); Eric T. L. Love, *Race over Empire: Racism and U.S. Imperialism, 1865–1900* (Chapel Hill, N.C., 2004).

6. Nugent, *Habits of Empire*, 242–44.

7. For a suggestive overview of the character of the late nineteenth-century U.S. economy and how it shaped one group of entrepreneurs in Central America, see chapter 1 (written mostly by Thomas Schoonover) of Langley and Schoonover, *The Banana Men: American Mercenaries and Entrepreneurs in Central America, 1880–1930* (Lexington, Ky., 1995). See also E. Bradford Burns, *Progress and Poverty* (Berkeley, Calif., 1979), which is a severe indictment of the liberal agenda for progress in Latin America in this era. Its message should be measured against Bill Albert, *South America and the World Economy from Independence to 1830* (London, 1983), who argues that dependency did foster some material progress. On the Grace Company see Lawrence A. Clayton, *Grace, W. R. Grace & Co.: The Formative Years, 1850–1930* (Ottawa, Ill., 1985).

8. Leopoldo Zea, *Positivismo y la circumstancia mexicana* (Mexico City, 1985), 187–88. For more discussion of U.S. economic penetration into Mexico in the late nineteenth century, see David Pletcher, *Rails, Mines, and Progress: Some American Promoters in Mexico, 1867–1911* (Ithaca, N.Y., 1958), 307.

9. W. Dirk Raat, *Mexico and the United States: Ambivalent Vistas*, 3rd ed. (Athens, Ga., 2000; orig. pub., 1992), 90–94. For a more critical view of the American presence, see John Mason Hart, *Empire and Revolution: The Americans in Mexico since the Civil War* (Berkeley, Calif., 2002).

10. Walter LaFeber, *The New Empire: An Interpretation of American Expansion, 1860–1898* (Ithaca, N.Y., 1963), 1–61.

11. Qtd. in G. Pope Atkins and Larman C. Wilson, *The Dominican Republic and the United States: From Imperialism to Transnationalism* (Athens, Ga., 1998),

26. See also Sumner Welles, *Naboth's Vineyard: The Dominican Republic, 1844-1924*, 2 vols. (Washington, D.C., 1928), 1: 140-41, 238-39, 324-25; and J. J. Montllor, "Oposición dominicana a la anexión a los Estados Unidos," *Boletín del Archivo Nacional* (Dominican Republic) 4 (Diciembre 1941): 395-407.

12. Ramiro Guerra y Sánchez, *Guerra de los diez años, 1868-1878*, 2 vols. (Havana, 1950), 1: 166. For a general discussion see Pérez, *Cuba and the United States*, 50-54.

13. Conniff, *Panama and the United States*, 51.

14. David Pletcher, *The Awkward Years: American Foreign Relations under Garfield and Arthur* (Columbia, Mo., 1962), 7-8, 23-24, 31-33; William F. Sater, *Chile and the United States: Empires in Conflict* (Athens, Ga., 1990), 33-50.

15. D. C. M. Platt, *Latin America and British Trade, 1860-1914* (London, 1972), 78-86. Joseph Smith, *Illusions of Conflict: Anglo-American Diplomacy, 1865-1896* (Pittsburgh, 1979), argues that the British intended to remain economic but not political competitors with the United States in Latin America.

16. For a scathing Latin American assessment, see Alonso Aguilar, *Pan-Americanism: From Monroe to the Present, A View from the Other Side* (New York, 1968), 36-42.

17. Enrico Mario Santí, "'Our America,'" the Gilded Age, and the Crisis of Latinamericanism," in *José Martí's 'Our America': From National to Hemispheric Cultural Studies*, ed. Jeffrey Belnap and Raúl Fernández (Durham, N.C., 1998), 179, 188-89.

18. Sater, *Chile and the United States*, 68.

19. Charles W. Calhoun, "American Policy toward the Brazilian Naval Revolt of 1893-1894: A Re-examination," *Diplomatic History* 4 (Winter 1980): 39-56.

20. Pérez, *Cuba and the United States*, 65-76. For contrasting accounts of how Martí and other Latino migrants viewed the Gilded Age culture of the United States see Laura Lomas, *Translating Empire: José Martí, Migrant Latino Subjects, and American Modernities* (Durham, N.C., 2008); and Anne Fountain, *José Martí and U.S. Writers* (Gainesville, Fla., 2003).

21. Pérez, *Cuba and the United States*, 90-91. See also his *Cuba between Empires, 1878-1902* (Pittsburgh, 1983). In a perceptive reconsideration of the driving motives behind the war, Kristin L. Hoganson suggests yet another — the belief that support for arbitration of the conflict by several prominent women's organizations served largely to weaken the national resolve and martial spirit. In this configuration of the dynamics of the political culture, to continue the metaphor, Theodore Roosevelt embodied the vindicating warrior and William

McKinley, the weak and compromising leader. See Hoganson, *Fighting for American Manhood: How Gender Politics Provoked the Spanish-American and Philippine-American Wars* (New Haven, Conn., 1998). The addition of honor and manhood to an already crowded list of explanations for this war, however, distracts us even more so from the singularly central fear of Roosevelt's generation—the persistent fear of threats and challenges to political and social order, whether from secessionists, Indians, militant labor, or the uncertainties of what might happen in Cuba if the Spanish proved unable to contain the rebellion. Undeniably, Roosevelt often spoke and wrote in gendered language about the need to confront these threats, but his motive had less to do with any fears about vindicating manliness than in containing the threat. Put differently, he did not ask *why* but *how* best to meet the challenge.

22. Qtd. in Pérez, *Cuba and the United States*, 98–99.
23. Love, *Race over Empire*, passim.
24. See Bartholomew H. Sparrow, *The Insular Cases and the Emergence of American Empire* (Lawrence, Kans., 2006).
25. Thompson and Randall, *Canada and the United States*, 66–70.
26. Roosevelt to Trevelyan, 9 September 1906, Roosevelt Papers (microfilm), reel 413; Allan Millett, *The Politics of Intervention: The Military Occupation of Cuba, 1906–1909* (Columbus, Ohio, 1968), 90–91.
27. Lester D. Langley, *The Banana Wars: United States Intervention in the Caribbean, 1898–1934* (Lexington, Ky., 1983), 20–33.
28. Arthur P. Whitaker, *The Western Hemisphere Idea: Its Rise and Decline* (Ithaca, N.Y., 1954), 86–87. The Latin American position, wrote Alonso Aguilar, was "legally and politically unobjectionable," but The Hague adopted the Porter doctrine, which forbade the use of force to collect debts if the debtor nation agreed to the decision of the arbitrator (Aguilar, *Pan Americanism*, 52).

4. Pax Americana

1. I have pursued this theme in greater detail in *The Banana Wars: United States Intervention in the Caribbean, 1898–1934* (Lexington, Ky., 1983). Louis Pérez Jr. assesses the historiography of U.S. intervention in "Intervention, Hegemony, and Dependency: The United States in the Caribbean, 1878–1980," *Pacific Historical Review* 51 (May 1982): 165–94. On the Brazilian-American "alliance" see E. Bradford Burns, *The Unwritten Alliance: Rio-Branco and Brazilian American Relations* (New York, 1966).

2. Langley, *Banana Wars*, 227–33.

3. Julie Greene, *The Canal Builders: Making American Empire at the Panama Canal* (New York, 2009).

4. Edward P. Kohn, *Canadian-American Relations and the Anglo-Saxon Idea, 1895–1903* (Montreal, 2004); John Herd Thompson and Stephen I. Randall, *Canada and the United States: Ambivalent Allies*, 4th ed. (Athens, Ga., 2008), 80–92.

5. Randolph Bourne, "Transnational America," in *Randolph Bourne: The Radical Will, Selected Writings, 1911, 1918*, ed. Olaf Hanson (New York, 1977), 248–64; Herbert Croly, *The Promise of American Life* (1909; rpt., New Brunswick, N.J., 1996).

6. Efforts to identify and codify a distinctly American international law governing relations between the American republics got underway at the 1902 Mexico City conference and gained strength at the 1906 meeting in Rio de Janeiro. These legal projections clashed with the fundamental proposals requiring arbitration that the Second Hague Convention endorsed in 1907. Most Latin American governments believed strongly in the idea of nonintervention and pressed for the development of an American international law. In October 1912, delegates to a special meeting in Washington, D.C., founded the American Institute of International Law and agreed upon a Declaration of Principles by which foreigners would be governed by the laws of the state in which they resided.

7. For a survey of the impact of the Platt Amendment from its inception to its demise, see Louis A. Pérez, Jr., *Cuba Under the Platt Amendment, 1902–1934* (Pittsburgh, 1986).

8. Aline Helg, *Our Rightful Share: The Afro-Cuban Struggle for Equality, 1886–1912* (Chapel Hill, N.C., 1995), 2, 4–7.

9. Dana G. Munro, *Intervention and Dollar Diplomacy in the Caribbean, 1900–1921* (Princeton, N.J., 1964), 146–74; Pedro Joaquín Chamorro, *Orígenes de la intervención americana en Nicaragua* (Managua, 1951), 13; Scott Nearing and Joseph Freeman, *Dollar Diplomacy: A Study in American Imperialism* (New York, 1925), 151–68.

10. Emily Rosenberg, *Financial Missionaries to the World: The Politics and Culture of Dollar Diplomacy, 1900–1930* (Cambridge, Mass., 1999).

11. Croly, *Promise of American Life*, 302.

12. Langley, *Banana Wars*, 77–165; Berto Ulloa, *La revolución intervenida: Relaciones diplomáticas entre México y los Estados Unidos, 1910–1914* (Mexico City, 1971), 136–56.

13. W. Dirk Raat, *Mexico and the United States: Ambivalent Vistas*, 3rd ed. (Athens, Ga., 2000; orig. pub., 1992), 120–24.

14. Arthur P. Whitaker, *The Western Hemisphere Idea: Its Rise and Decline* (Ithaca, N.Y., 1954), 114–18. Mark Gilderhus elaborates on Wilson's hemispheric "vision" in *Pan American Visions: Woodrow Wilson in the Western Hemisphere, 1913–1921* (Tucson, Ariz., 1986).

15. For a survey of the two occupations, see G. Pope Atkins and Larman C. Wilson, *The Dominican Republic and the United States: From Imperialism to Transnationalism* (Athens, Ga., 1998), 37–64; and Gayle Plummer, *Haiti and the United States*, 101–20.

16. Joseph Tulchin, *Latin America and World War I* (New York, 1971), 10.

17. Qtd. in Frederick C. Luebke, *Germans in Brazil: A Comparative History of Cultural Conflict in World War I* (Baton Rouge, La., 1987), 159.

18. American propaganda efforts against Germany in Latin America were successful; see James Mock, "The Creel Committee in Latin America," *Hispanic American Historical Review* 22 (May 1942): 262–79. Emily Rosenberg explores the Mexican-Argentine "bloc" against the United States in "World War I and 'Continental Solidarity,'" *Americas* 31 (January 1975): 313–34. See also A. Conil Paz, *La neutralidad argentina y la Primera Guerra Mundial* (Buenos Aires, 1976).

19. Qtd. in Thompson and Randall, *Canada and the United States*, 100. As part of its invasion plans, the U.S. War Department requested maps of western Canada from Canadian authorities!

20. Robert Freeman Smith ably catalogs the U.S. confrontation with Mexican revolutionary nationalism in *The United States and Revolutionary Nationalism in México, 1916–1932* (Chicago, 1972).

21. Qtd. in Robert Seidel, *Progressive Pan Americanism: Development and United States Policy toward South America, 1906–1931* (Ithaca, N.Y., 1973), 592.

22. C. H. Haring, *South America Looks at the United States* (New York, 1929), assesses anti-Americanism in the 1920s. Perhaps the most arrogant and certainly the most disastrous effort to export the U.S. economic model along with American culture to Latin America in the twenties was the creation of Fordlandia, Henry Ford's ambitious rubber plantation project in the Brazilian Amazon. The plantation was twice the size of Delaware and featured a company town modeled on a Midwestern industrial city. See Greg Grandin, *Fordlandia: The Rise and Fall of Henry Ford's Forgotten Jungle City* (New York, 2009).

23. Helen Delpar, *The Enormous Vogue of Things Mexican: Cultural Relations between the United States and Mexico, 1920–1935* (Tuscaloosa, Ala., 1992).

24. Jean Franco, *The Modern Culture of Latin America: Society and the Artist* (New York, 1967), 71–72.

25. On the banana business and isthmian politics see Thomas Karnes, *Tropical Enterprise: The Standard Fruit and Steamship Co. in Latin America* (Baton Rouge, La., 1978), 70–88. On the political and "moral" imprint of U.S. enterprise, see Thomas F. O'Brien, *The Revolutionary Mission: American Enterprise in Latin America, 1900–1945* (New York, 1996).

26. On the role of the banana companies in Central America, see Lester D. Langley and Thomas Schoonover, *The Banana Men: American Mercenaries and Entrepreneurs in Central America, 1880–1930* (Lexington, Ky., 1995).

27. On these two occupations see Mary A. Renda, *Taking Haiti: Military Occupation and the Culture of U.S. Imperialism, 1915–1940* (Chapel Hill, N.C., 2001); Hans Schmidt, *The United States Occupation of Haiti, 1916–1934* (New Brunswick, N.J., 1971); and Bruce Calder, *The Impact of Intervention: The Dominican Republic during the U.S. Occupation of 1916–1924* (Austin, Tex., 1984).

28. Samuel G. Inman, *Inter-American Conferences, 1826–1954* (Washington, D.C., 1965), 86–104.

29. Langley, *Banana Wars*, 181–223. On Sandino see the classic biography by Neill Macaulay, *The Sandino Affair* (Chicago, 1967; rpt. Durham, N.C., 1986); and Gustavo Alemán Bolaños, *Sandino: El libertador* (Mexico City, 1952).

30. Robert Ferrell, "Repudiation of a Repudiation," *Journal of American History* 51 (March 1965): 669–73.

31. For an assessment of the legacy of U.S. identity with dictatorships see David Schmitz, *Thank God They're on Our Side: The United States and Right-Wing Dictatorships, 1921–1965* (Chapel Hill, N.C., 1999). Of the triumvirate of despots who came to power in the early 1930s with tacit U.S. approval — Fulgencio Batista in Cuba, Anastasio Somoza García in Nicaragua, and Rafael Leonidas Trujillo in the Dominican Republic — the most devious, sinister, and manipulative was the last. See Eric Paul Roorda, *The Dictator Next Door: The Good Neighbor Policy and the Trujillo Regime in the Dominican Republic, 1930-1945* (Durham, N.C., 1998); and Lauren Derby, *The Dictator's Seduction: Politics and the Popular Imagination in the Era of Trujillo* (Durham, N.C., 2009).

32. Qtd. in Donald Dozer, *Are We Good Neighbors? Three Decades of Inter-American Relations, 1939–1960* (Gainesville, Fla., 1959), 4.

33. On the role of U.S. economic advisers in Latin America, see Paul W. Drake, ed., *Money Doctors, Foreign Debts, and Economic Reforms in Latin America from the 1890s to the Present* (Wilmington, Del., 1994).

34. Doubtless Roosevelt bore at least some responsibility for acquiescing in these despotic regimes. "Somoza may be an s.o.b., but at least he's *our* s.o.b.," a remark often attributed to Roosevelt, served as metaphor for the new political reality. Ironically, one researcher thoroughly scoured the Roosevelt papers at Hyde Park in a vain search for this quotation. See Robert Pastor, *Condemned to Repetition: The United States and Nicaragua* (Princeton, N.J., 1987), 3.

35. Dick Steward, *Trade and Hemisphere: The Good Neighbor Policy and Reciprocal Trade* (Columbia, Mo., 1975), 1–12, 100–122. For an assessment of the politics of the Good Neighbor policy see Irwin F. Gellman, *Good Neighbor Diplomacy: United States Policies in Latin America, 1933–1945* (Baltimore, 1979).

36. Fredrick B. Pike, *The United States and Latin America: Myths and Stereotypes of Civilization and Nature* (Austin, Tex., 1992), 222–25, 241–42, 245–48, 249–57, 261.

5. A Hemisphere at War

1. David Haglund, *Latin America and the Transformation of U.S. Strategic Thought, 1936–1940* (Albuquerque, N.Mex., 1984), 85–95; Lester D. Langley, *The United States and the Caribbean in the Twentieth Century*, rev. ed. (Athens, Ga., 1985), 163–71.

2. On the differing positions of each government see Kenneth D. Lehman, *Bolivia and the United States: A Limited Partnership* (Athens, Ga., 1999), 70–72; and Frank O. Mora and Jerry W. Cooney, *Paraguay and the United States: Distant Allies* (Athens, Ga., 2007), 69–74.

3. Qtd. in Glen Barclay, *Struggle for a Continent: A Diplomatic History of South America, 1919–1945* (New York, 1972), 51–52.

4. The final settlement required another three years to achieve. Although not impartial, it did bring peace to the Chaco. See Leslie Rout, *Politics of the Chaco Peace Conference, 1935–39* (Austin, Tex., 1970).

5. Stanley E. Hilton, *Brazil and the Great Powers, 1930–1939: The Politics of Trade Rivalry* (Austin, Tex., 1975), 51.

6. David M. K. Sheinin, *Argentina and the United States: An Alliance Contained* (Athens, Ga., 2006), 72.

7. Tulio Halperín Donghi, *Historia contemporánea de América Latina* (Madrid, 1969), 356–75.

8. Sheinin, *Argentina and the United States*, 73.

9. R. A. Humphreys, *Latin America and the Second World War*, 2 vols. (London, 1981), 1: 4–38. On the character of the Estado Novo see Leslie Bethell, "Politics in Brazil under Vargas, 1930–1945," in *The Cambridge History of Latin America*, vol. 9, *Brazil since 1930*, ed. Bethell (New York, 2008).

10. On Beals, see the largely sympathetic account by John A. Britton, *Carleton Beals: A Radical Journalist in Latin America* (Albuquerque, N.M., 1987).

11. William F. Sater, *Chile and the United States: Empires in Conflict* (Athens, Ga., 1990), 109–110.

12. Michael L. Conniff, *Panama and the United States: The Forced Alliance* (Athens, Ga., 1992), 91.

13. W. Dirk Raat, *Mexico and the United States: Ambivalent Vistas*, 3rd ed. (Athens, Ga., 2000; orig. pub., 1992), 145–47. See also Friedrich E. Schuler, *Mexico between Hitler and Roosevelt: Mexican Relations in the Age of Lázaro Cárdenas, 1934–1940* (Albuquerque, N.Mex., 1998).

14. Holger Herwig, *The Politics of Frustration: The United States in German Naval Planning, 1889–1941* (Boston, 1976), 187.

15. Qtd. in Haglund, *Latin America*, 105.

16. Qtd. in ibid., 108.

17. Steward, *Trade and Hemisphere*, 273–75; David Green, *The Containment of Latin America: A History of the Myths and Realities of the Good Neighbor Policy* (Chicago, 1971), 60–74.

18. Stetson Conn, Rose C. Engelman, and Byron Fairchild, *Guarding the United States and Its Outposts* (Washington, D.C., 1964), 328.

19. John A. Logan, *No Transfer: An American Security Principle* (New Haven, Conn., 1961), 309–45.

20. John Herd Thompson and Stephen J. Randall, *Canada and the United States: Ambivalent Allies*, 4th ed. (Athens, Ga., 2008), 142–46.

21. Gerald Haines, "Under the Eagle's Wings: The Franklin Roosevelt Administration Forges an American Hemisphere," *Diplomatic History* 1 (Fall 1977): 373–88; J. Manuel Espinosa, *Inter-American Beginnings of U.S. Cultural Diplomacy, 1936–1948* (Washington, D.C., 1976).

22. Max Paul Friedman, *Nazis and Good Neighbors: The United States Campaign against the Germans of Latin America in World War II* (Cambridge, U.K., 2003).

23. Qtd. in Rosemary Thorp, "The Latin American Economies in the 1940s," in *Latin America in the 1940s: War and Postwar Transitions*, ed. David Rock (Berkeley, Calif., 1994), 45.

24. Blanca Torres Ramírez, *México en la segunda guerra mundial* (Mexico City, 1979; E. Cárdenas de la Peña, *Gesta en el Golfo: La segunda Guerra mundial y México* (Mexico City, 1966).

25. In the process, the "alliance" and its debilitating connotation of dependence laid the basis for anti-Americanism in Brazil. See Frank McCann, "Brazil, the United States, and World War II," *Diplomatic History* 3 (Summer 1979): 57–76; and McCann, *The Brazilian-American Alliance, 1937–1945* (Princeton, N.J., 1974).

26. Thompson and Randall, *Canada and the United States*, 146–65.

27. Stephen J. Randall, *Colombia and the United States: Hegemony and Interdependence* (Athens, Ga., 1992), 163–73; Judith Ewell, *Venezuela and the United States: From Monroe's Hemisphere to Petroleum's Empire* (Athens, Ga., 1996), 147–48.

28. Lehman, *Bolivia and the United States*, 93–94.

29. Michael Grow, *The Good Neighbor Policy and Authoritarianism in Paraguay* (Lawrence, Kans., 1981), 59–113.

30. Michael Francis, *The Limits of Hegemony: United States Relations with Argentina and Chile in World War II* (Notre Dame, Ind., 1977); and Randall Woods, *The Roosevelt Foreign Policy Establishment and the Good Neighbor: The United States and Argentina, 1941–1945* (Lawrence, Kans., 1979).

31. Qtd. in Humphreys, *Latin America and the Second World War*, 2: 177.

32. Randall Woods, "Conflict or Community? The United States and Argentina's Admission to the United Nations," *Pacific Historical Review* 46 (August 1977): 361–86, argues that the United States was persuaded to support Argentina's claim out of commitment to the principle of sovereignty and nonintervention.

33. Sheinin, *Argentina and the United States*, 84-86.

34. Demetrio Boersner, *Relaciones internacionales de América Latina* (San José, C.R., 1982), 249, observes: "The Second World War had a stimulating impact on economic and social development in Latin America and contributed to future standard changes or the impetus to achieve such changes."

35. Fredrick Pike, "Latin America and United States Stereotypes in the 1920s and 1930s," *Americas* 42 (October 1985): 131–62.

36. Qtd. in Samuel Baily, *The United States and the Development of South America, 1945–1975* (New York, 1976), 44.

37. On the Argentine affair see Sheinin, *Argentina and the United States*, 87–89; and the more critical account in Green, *Containment of Latin America*, 25–54.

38. Qtd. in Baily, *United States and the Development*, 60.

39. Qtd. in Roger Trask, "The Impact of the Cold War on United States–Latin American Relations, 1945–1949," *Diplomatic History* 1 (Summer 1977): 281. See also Herbert Braun, *The Assassination of Gaitán: Public Life and Urban Violence in Colombia* (Madison, Wis., 1985), 190.

40. Qtd. in Trask, "Impact of the Cold War," 278.

41. Qtd. in Randall, *Colombia and the United States*, 193.

42. Fredrick B. Pike, *The United States and Latin America: Myths and Stereotypes of Civilization and Nature* (Austin, Tex., 1992), 294–96.

43. Randall and Thompson, *Canada and the United States*, 160–66.

6. The Cold War

1. Final Act, XXX, qtd. in Graham H. Stuart and James L. Tigner, *Latin America and the United States*, 6th ed. (Englewood Cliffs, N.J., 1975), 72; Stephen J. Randall, *Colombia and the United States*, 188–96.

2. Raúl Prebisch, "El desarrollo económico de la América Latin y sus principales problems, *Revista de Economía Argentina* 48 (1949): 211–21, 254–66.

3. Y [Louis Halle], "On a Certain Impatience with Latin America," *Foreign Affairs* 27 (July 1950): 568.

4. Qtd. in Thomas Bohlin, "United States–Latin American Relations and the Cold War" (Ph.D. diss., University of Notre Dame, 1973), 67. Kennan recommended an end to "moralizing" about Latin America, writing, "It seems to me unlikely that there could be any other region of the earth in which nature and human behavior could have combined to produce a more unhappy and hopeless background for the conduct of human life" (Department of State, *Foreign Relations of the United States, 1950* [Washington, D.C., 1861–], 2: 600).

5. Department of State, *Foreign Relations, 1950*, 2: 319; F. Parkinson, *Latin America, the Cold War, and the World Powers* (Beverly Hills, Calif., 1973), 26–30. See also Bryce Wood, *The Dismantling of the Good Neighbor Policy* (Austin, Tex., 1985).

6. Cosío Villegas (Américo Paredes, trans.) *American Extremes* (Austin, Tex., 1964), 52.

7. David M. K. Sheinin, *Argentina and the United States: An Alliance Contained* (Athens, Ga., 2006), 100; William F. Sater, *Chile and the United States: Empires in Conflict* (Athens, Ga., 1990), 126–27.

8. W. Dirk Raat, *Mexico and the United States: Ambivalent Vistas*, 3rd ed. (Athens,

Ga., 2000), 158; Mario Ojeda, *Política exterior de México* (Mexico City, 1976), 50–51, 57.

9. John Herd Thompson and Stephen J. Randall, *Canada and the United States: Ambivalent Allies*, 4th ed. (Athens, Ga., 2008), 175; see also pp. 181–214; Randall, *Colombia and the United States*, 204.

10. For an analysis of this critical year in Costa Rica see John P. Bell, *Crisis in Costa Rica: The 1948 Revolution* (Austin, Tex., 1971).

11. Kyle Longley, *The Sparrow and the Hawk: Costa Rica and the United States during the Rise of José Figueres* (Tuscaloosa, Ala., 1997).

12. For a statistical analysis of U.S. aid see J. W. Wilkie, *The Bolivian Revolution and U.S. Aid since 1952* (Los Angeles, 1969).

13. Kenneth D. Lehman, *Bolivia and the United States: A Limited Partnership* (Athens, Ga., 1999), 117–23.

14. Much of this section relies on Richard Immerman, *The CIA in Guatemala* (Austin, Tex., 1982), which should be read alongside Piero Gleijesis, *Shattered Hope: The Guatemalan Revolution and the United States, 1944–1954* (Princeton, N.J., 1992). For a perceptive overview of the Eisenhower administration's policy toward Latin America, see Stephen Rabe, *Eisenhower and Latin America: The Foreign Policy of Anti-Communism* (Chapel Hill, N.C., 1988).

15. The role of UFCo in the overthrow of Arbenz is candidly retold in Thomas McCann, *An American Company: The Tragedy of United Fruit* (New York, 1976). See also Guillermo Toriello, *La batalla de Guaemala* (Mexico City, 1955), 161–91.

16. Qtd. in Cole Blasier, *The Hovering Giant: U.S. Responses to Revolutionary Change in Latin America, 1910–1955*, rev. ed. (Pittsburgh, 1985), 168.

17. Nick Cullather, *Secret History: The CIA's Classified Account of Its Operations in Guatemala, 1952–1954* (Stanford, Calif., 2006).

18. Thomas Zoumaras, "Containing Castro: Promoting Homeownership in Peru, 1956–1961," *Diplomatic History* 10 (Spring 1986): 161–82.

19. As R. Harrison Wagner observed, those who decried the inadequacies of Eisenhower's policies toward Latin America in the 1950s exaggerated the impact of peacetime economic assistance by drawing on the unusual wartime experience as an example of what was possible. See *United States Policy toward Latin America: A Study in Domestic and International Politics* (Stanford, Calif., 1970), 161.

20. Gerald K. Haines, *The Americanization of Brazil: A Study of U.S. Cold War Diplomacy in the Third World, 1945–1954* (Wilmington, Del., 1989); Elizabeth

A. Cobbs, *The Rich Neighbor Policy: Rockefeller and Kaiser in Brazil* (New Haven, Conn., 1992); Stanley E. Hilton, "The United States, Brazil, and the Cold War: End of the Special Relationship," *Journal of American History* 68 (December 1981): 599–624.

21. *El Tiempo* (Bogotá), 15 February 1948, qtd. in Donald Dozer, *Are We Good Neighbors? Three Decades of Inter-American Relations, 1930–1960* (Gainesville, Fla., 1959), 305.

22. For this section I have relied heavily on Raymond Carr, *Puerto Rico: A Colonial Experiment* (New York, 1948).

23. Juan Ángel Silen, *Historia de la nación puertorriqueña* (Río Piedras, P.R., 1973), 326–28; Gordon Lewis, *Puerto Rico: Freedom and Power in the Caribbean* (New York, 1968), 113–33.

24. Jason C. Parker, *Brother's Keeper: The United States, Race, and Empire in the British Caribbean, 1937–1962* (New York, 2008). For a suggestive account of how local workers, businesses, and governments engaged U.S. tourists in the cultural encounters of empire, see Dennis Merrill, *Negotiating Paradise: U.S. Tourism and Empire in Twentieth-Century Latin America* (Chapel Hill, N.C., 2009).

25. The classic statement about the fall of an era of dictators, still relevant, is Tad Szulc, *Twilight of the Tyrants* (New York, 1959).

26. Judith Ewell, *Venezuela and the United States: From Monroe's Hemisphere to Petroleum's Empire* (Athens, Ga., 1996), 154–61, 165–98. See also Darlene Rivas, *Missionary Capitalist: Nelson Rockefeller in Venezuela* (Chapel Hill, N.C., 2002).

27. Louis A. Pérez Jr., *Cuba and the United States: Ties of Singular Intimacy*, 3rd ed. (Athens, Ga., 2003), 210–37.

28. On Castro's "conversion" to Marxism see Richard Welch Jr., *Response to Revolution: The United States and the Cuban Revolution, 1959–1961* (Chapel Hill, N.C., 1985), 9–14. For an assessment of the intellectual origins of the Cuban Revolution see Sheldon Liss, *Radical Thought in Cuba* (Lincoln, Neb., 1987).

29. Philip Bonsal, "Cuba, Castro, and the United States," *Foreign Affairs* 45 (January 1967): 260–76; and his book, *Cuba, Castro, and the United States* (Pittsburgh, 1971), 108–9.

30. Michael Francis, "The U.S. Press and Castro: A Study in Declining Relations," *Journalism Quarterly* 44 (Summer 1967): 257–66. The role of Herbert Matthews in the portrayal of Castro and his revolution to the U.S. public is retold in

Anthony DePalma, *The Man Who Invented Fidel: Castro, Cuba, and Herbert L. Matthews* (New York, 2006).

31. For a chronicle of the efforts to overthrow Castro, see Dan Bohning, *The Castro Obsession: U.S. Covert Operations against Cuba, 1959–1965* (Washington, D.C., 1965).

32. Arthur Schlesinger Jr., *A Thousand Days: John F. Kennedy in the White House* (Boston, 1965), 226–56. See also Karl Meyer and Tad Szulc, *The Cuban Invasion: The Chronicle of a Disaster* (New York, 1962); and *The Bay of Pigs: The Leaders' Story of Brigade 2506* (New York, 1964).

33. The official Cuban account can be found in *Playa Girón, derrota del imperialismo* (Havana, 1961).

34. Jerome Levinson and Juan de Onis, *The Alliance That Lost Its Way: A Critical Report on the Alliance for Progress* (Chicago, 1970), 46–49.

35. Qtd. in *Time* (16 February 1962); E. V. Corominas, *Cuba en Punta del Este* (Buenos Aires, 1962).

36. Michael Dobbs, *One Minute to Midnight: Kennedy, Khrushchev, and Castro on the Brink of Nuclear War* (New York, 2008), 6–18, 335–36, 340, 346–51.

37. Robert Divine, ed., *The Cuban Missile Crisis* (Chicago, 1971), 7–57, offers a summary and follows with selections that debate the issues. Herbert Dinerstein, *The Making of the Missile Crisis, October 1962* (Baltimore, 1976), concludes that neither the United States nor the USSR wanted a confrontation.

38. Thompson and Randall, *Canada and the United States*, 209.

39. Aleksandr Fursenko and Timothy Naftali, *"One Hell of a Gamble": Khruschev, Castro, and Kennedy, 1958–1964* (New York, 1997).

40. Qtd. in Jorge I. Domínguez, *To Make a World Safe for Revolution: Cuba's Foreign Policy* (Cambridge, Mass., 1989), 29. Although not a member of the OAS, Canada also refused to break diplomatic relations.

7. Years of Uncertainty

1. Qtd. in Stephen G. Rabe, *The Most Dangerous Area in the World: John F. Kennedy Confronts Communist Revolution in Latin America* (Chapel Hill, N.C., 1999), 98.

2. On these themes, see Lars Schoultz, *That Infernal Little Cuban Republic: The United States and the Cuban Revolution* (Chapel Hill, N.C., 2009); Louis A. Pérez Jr., *Cuba in the American Imagination: Metaphor and the Imperial Ethos* (Chapel Hill, N.C., 2008).

3. U.S. Congress, House of Representatives, Committee on Foreign Affairs, Subcommittee on Inter-American Affairs, *New Directions for the 1970s: Toward a New Strategy of Inter-American Development: Hearings* (Washington, D.C., 1969), 699, 715.

4. *Report on the Alliance for Progress* (Washington, D.C., 1963), v–x; Rabe, *Most Dangerous Area*. On modernization theory and its adherents, see Michael E. Latham, *Modernization as Ideology: American Social Science and "Nation Building" in the Kennedy Era* (Chapel Hill, N.C., 2000).

5. Lawrence A. Clayton, *Peru and the United States: The Condor and the Eagle* (Athens, Ga., 1999), 235. Belaunde won the presidency the following year. On the convoluted Dominican power struggle in the post-Trujillo years, see G. Pope Atkins and Larman C. Wilson, *The Dominican Republic and the United States: From Imperialism to Transnationalism* (Athens, Ga., 1998), 125–26.

6. Stephen G. Rabe, *United States Intervention in British Guiana: A Cold War Story* (Chapel Hill, N.C., 2005).

7. Edwin Lieuwen, *Generals vs. Presidents: Neo-Militarism in Latin America* (New York, 1964), 63–68.

8. Jerome Levinson and Juan de Onis, *Alliance That Lost Its Way: A Critical Report on the Alliance for Progress* (Chicago, 1970), 86–87. The most optimistic statement in the 1950s on the role of the middle class in Latin America's future is John J. Johnson, *Political Change in Latin America: The Emergence of the Middle Sectors* (Stanford, Calif., 1958).

9. Robert A. Packenham, *Liberal America and the Third World: Political Development Ideas in Foreign Aid and Social Service* (Princeton, N.J., 1973), 100.

10. Alan McPherson, *Yankee No! Anti-Americanism in U.S.–Latin American Relations* (Cambridge, Mass., 2003), 6–8.

11. Thomas Mann and Lyndon Johnson, record of telephone conversation, 11 June 1964, in *Foreign Relations of the United States, 1964–1968*, vol. 31, *South and Central America, Mexico* (Washington, D.C., 2004), 45. Johnson's pledge about the "living memorial" to Kennedy was made four days after the president was shot (1).

12. McPherson, *Yankee No! Anti-Americanism in U.S.–Latin American Relations* 88–89.

13. Michael L. Conniff, *Panama and the United States: The Forced Alliance* (Athens, Ga., 1992), 118–21; Lester D. Langley, "U.S.–Panamanian Relations since 1941," *Journal of Inter-American Studies and World Affairs* 12 (July 1970): 339–66; Víctor F. Goytía, *La tragedia del Canal* (Panama City, 1966), 5.

14. *New York Times*, 3, 4 April 1964; Levinson and de Onis, *Alliance That Lost Its Way*, 90–91; "Brazil Marks 40th Anniversary of Military Coup," National Security Archive Document.

15. Qtd. in Samuel Shapiro, ed., *Cultural Factors in Inter-American Relations* (Notre Dame, Ind., 1968), 101–2; see also Jan Knippers Black, *United States Penetration of Brazil* (Philadelphia, 1977), 260; and Leslie Bethell, "Politics in Brazil under the Liberal Republic, 1945-1964," in *Cambridge History of Latin America*, ed. Bethell, vol. 9, *History of Brazil* (New York, 2008), 146, 161.

16. Kenneth D. Lehman, *Bolivia and the United States: A Limited Partnership* (Athens, Ga., 1999), 155–57.

17. The speech is reprinted in Martin Needler, *The U.S. and the Latin American Revolution* (Boston, 1972), 145–53.

18. John Bartlow Martin, *Overtaken by Events: The Dominican Crisis from the Fall of Trujillo to the Civil War* (New York, 1966), 547–90, 637–45.

19. McPherson, *Yankee No!* 129–30.

20. Atkins and Wilson, *Dominican Republic and the United States*, 128–33.

21. Abraham Lowenthal, *The Dominican Intervention* (Cambridge, Mass., 1972), 42–61; Tad Szulc, *Dominican Diary* (New York, 1965), 65–77.

22. Lyndon Johnson, "The Dominican Republic: A Target of Tyranny," *Vital Speeches* 31 (15 May 1965): 450–52.

23. Theodore Draper, *The Dominican Revolt: A Case Study in American Policy* (New York, 1968), 183–200. For Juan Bosch's view on the crisis see his book, *Pentagonism: A Substitution for Imperialism* (New York, 1968), 20–22, 106–7, 108–22.

24. Randall B. Woods, "Conflicted Hegemon: LBJ and the Dominican Republic," *Diplomatic History* 32 (November 2008): 749–66.

25. *New York Times*, 26 January 1970.

26. Clayton, *Peru and the United States*, 234–50.

27. Sater, *Chile and the United States*, 148–58. On Project Camelot, see Irving Louis Horowitz, ed., *The Rise and Fall of Project Camelot: Studies in the Relationship between Social Science and Practical Politics* (Cambridge, Mass., 1967). On Colombia and Venezuela, see Stephen J. Randall, *Colombia and the United States: Hegemony and Interdependence* (Athens, Ga., 1992), 240; and Judith Ewell, *Venezuela and the United States: From Monroe's Hemisphere to Petroleum's Empire* (Athens, Ga., 1996), 213–18.

28. John C. Dreier, "New Wine in Old Bottles: The Changing Inter-American System," *International Organization* 22 (1968): 477–93. In the last years of

the decade — in spite of Washington's disapproval — Latin American governments expanded their economic and political ties with communist governments.

29. Qtd. in Samuel Baily, *The United States and the Development of South America, 1945–1975* (New York, 1976), 118.

30. Nelson Rockefeller, *The Rockefeller Report on the Americas* (Chicago, 1969), esp. ch. 1.

31. For a disturbing survey of the impact of U.S. training of Latin American police, see Martha K. Huggins, *Political Policing: The United States and Latin America* (Durham, N.C., 1998).

32. Eric Baklanoff, "The Expropriation of United States Investments in Latin America," *SECOLAS Annals* 8 (1977): 48–60.

33. Margaret Power, "The Engendering of Anticommunism and Fear in Chile's 1964 Presidential Election," *Diplomatic History* 32 (November 2008): 931–53; Leonard Gross, *The Last Best Hope: Eduardo Frei and Chilean Democracy* (New York, 1967).

34. U.S. Congress, Senate, Committee on Foreign Relations, *Hearings on the International Telephone and Telegraph Co. in Chile, 1970–1971*, 2 vols. (Washington, D.C., 1973).

35. Richard Feinberg, *The Triumph of Allende: Chile's Legal Revolution* (New York, 1972), is largely sympathetic.

36. U.S. Congress, House of Representatives, Committee On Foreign Affairs, *Hearings: The U.S. and Chile during the Allende Years, 1970–1973* (Washington, D.C., 1973), offers assessments from varying positions.

37. For Allende's account of these years, see *La conspiración contra Chile* (Buenos Aires, 1973); and for the role of foreign companies in his downfall, see James Petras and Morris Morley, *The United States and Chile* (New York, 1975).

38. *New York Times*, 13 January 1971.

39. Sater, *Chile and the United States*, 186. For differing views, see Robert J. Alexander, *The Tragedy of Chile* (Westport, Conn., 1978); and James Petras and Morris H. Morley, *The United States and Chile: Imperialism and the Overthrow of the Allende Government* (New York, 1975).

40. On Latin America's economic defiance, see R. H. Swansborough, *The Embattled Colossus: Economic Nationalism and the United States Investors in Latin America* (Gainesville, Fla., 1976).

41. Ewell, *Venezuela and the United States*, 204–8.

42. Gérard Pierre-Charles, *El Caribe contemporánea* (Mexico City, 1981), 292–332.

43. Piero Gleijesis, "Moscow's Proxy? Cuba and Africa, 1975–1988," *Journal of Cold War Studies* 8.4 (Fall 2006): 98–146.

44. Commission on United States–Latin American Relations (the Linowitz Commission), *The Americas in a Changing World* (New York, 1975), esp. 11–61.

45. David Reimers, *Still the Golden Door: The Third World Comes to America* (New York, 1985).

46. Elizabeth Cobbs Hoffman, *All You Need Is Love: The Peace Corps and the Spirit of the 1960s* (Cambridge, Mass., 1998).

47. Langley, *The Americas in the Modern Age*, 218–23.

8. The Defiant Hemisphere

1. On Carter's policies, see Gaddis Smith, *Morality, Reason and Power: American Diplomacy during the Carter Years* (New York, 1986), 109–32.

2. Walter LaFeber, *The Panama Canal: The Crisis in Historical Perspective* (New York, 1978), 160–227.

3. Kissinger correctly perceived that the canal issue might give Ronald Reagan an effective issue in challenging Gerald Ford for the 1976 Republican nomination. See Adam Clymer, *Drawing the Line at the Big Ditch: The Panama Canal Treaties and the Rise of the Right* (Lawrence, Kan., 2008).

4. Michael L. Conniff, *Panama and the United States: The Forced Alliance* (Athens, Ga., 1992), 134–39.

5. Louis A. Pérez Jr., *Cuba and the United States: Ties of Singular Intimacy*, 3rd ed. (Athens, Ga., 2003), 252–63. Ironically, as some critics of the country's Cuban policy observed, that amount virtually equaled the annual federal costs of the U.S. presence in Puerto Rico.

6. Arthur Schlesinger Jr., "Human Rights and the American Tradition," *Foreign Affairs* 57 (1979): 503–26.

7. U.S. Congress, House of Representatives, Committee on Foreign Affairs, *Report: Human Rights in the International Community and in United States Foreign Policy, 1945–1976* (Washington, D.C., 1977), is a compilation of documents.

8. David M. K. Sheinin, *Argentina and the United States: An Alliance Contained* (Athens, Ga., 2006), 166–73.

9. Leslie Bethell and Celso Castro, "Politics in Brazil under Military Rule, 1964–

1985," in *Cambridge History of Latin America*, ed. Bethell, vol. 9, *Brazil since 1930* (New York, 2008), 208–9.

10. Cynthia Brown, *With Friends Like These: The Americas Watch on Human Rights and U.S. Policy in Latin America* (New York, 1985).

11. W. Dirk Raat, *Mexico and the United States: Ambivalent Vistas*, 3rd ed. (Athens, Ga., 2000), 159–62.

12. Abraham Lowenthal, "Latin America: A Not-so-Special Relationship," in *Foreign Policy on Latin America, 1970–1980* (Boulder, CO, 1983), 128–38.

13. Henry Kissinger et al., *Report of the National Bipartisan Commission on Central America* and *Supplement* (Washington, D.C., 1984), is required reading. For a variety of perspectives, see Lester D. Langley, *Central America: The Real Stakes* (New York, 1985); Walter LaFeber, *Inevitable Revolutions: The United States in Central America* (New York, 1983); and Daniel Camacho and Manuel Rojas, ed., *La crisis centroamericana* (San José, C.R., 1984).

14. Robert Williams, *Export Agriculture and the Crisis in Central America* (Chapel Hill, N.C., 1986).

15. For a detailed analysis, written by a member of the Carter administration's NSC staff, see Robert Pastor, *Condemned to Repetition: The United States and Nicaragua* (Princeton, N.J., 1987).

16. Pastor, *Condemned to Repetition*, 70.

17. Richard Millett, *Guardians of the Dynasty* (New York, 1977), critically assesses the role of the National Guard in Nicaraguan politics.

18. For a general discussion of Carter's policy in Central America, see Thomas M. Leonard, *Central America and the United States: The Search for Stability* (Athens, Ga., 1991), 168–78.

19. LaFeber, *Inevitable Revolutions*, 255.

20. José Miguel Insulza, La crisis en centroamérica y el caribe y la seguridad de los Estados Unidos," in Jaime Bastida et al., *Centroamérica: Crisis y política internacional* (Mexico City, 1984), 193–226.

21. For the impressions of the Latin American Left of the "Reagan Doctrine," see Luis Maira, ed., *La política de Reagan y la crisis centroamericana* (San José, C.R., 1982).

22. Qtd. in Thomas Carothers, *In the Name of Democracy: U.S. Policy toward Latin America in the Reagan Years* (Berkeley, Calif., 1991), 28.

23. Qtd. in Lars Schoultz, *National Security and United States Policy toward Latin America* (Princeton, N.J., 1987), 4–5.

24. Sheinin, *Argentina and the United States*, 174–77.

25. Anthony Payne, *The International Crisis in the Caribbean* (Baltimore, 1984), 62.

26. Nicaragua's economic problems stemmed from more than the Contra war. See Carlos Vila, *The Sandinista Revolution: National Liberation and Social Transformation in Central America* (New York, 1986). For an account of the widespread concern over human rights violations in Central America, see Cynthia Brown, *With Friends Like These: The Americas Watch on Human Rights and U.S. Policy in Latin America* (New York, 1985), 235–36.

27. *The Report of the President's Bipartisan Commission on Central America* (New York, 1984).

28. On the Central American refugee issue in North America, see María Cristina García, *Seeking Refuge: Central American Migration to Mexico, the United States, and Canada* (Berkeley, Calif., 2006).

29. Marcelo Serrato, "Las dificultades financieras de México y la política petrolera hacia el exterior," in *La política exterior de México: Desafíos de los ochenta*, ed. Olga Pellecer (Mexico City, 1983), 287–303.

30. Rosemary Thorpe and Laurence Whiteheads, ed., *Latin American Debt and the Adjustment Crisis* (Pittsburgh, 1987).

31. Víctor Urquidi, "The World Crisis and the Outlook for Latin America," in *Politics and Economics of External Debt Crisis: The Latin American Experience*, ed. Miguel Wionczck (Boulder, Colo., 1985), 51. For a mid-1980s view of the Latin American condition in 2000, see Gonzalo Martner, ed., *América Latina hacia el 2000* (Caracas, 1986).

32. Pablo González Casanova, *La democracia en México* (Mexico City, 1965).

33. For a mid-1980s assessment of the impact of immigration on development see Robert Pastor, ed., *Migration and Development in the Caribbean: The Unexpected Connection* (Boulder, Colo., 1985).

34. Qtd. in Conniff, *Panama and the United States*, 167.

35. Gaddis Smith, *The Last Years of the Monroe Doctrine, 1945–1993* (New York, 1994), 224–25.

36. For a depressing assessment of U.S. drug policy in the late twentieth century, see Ted Galen Carpenter, *Bad Neighbor Policy: Washington's Futile War on Drugs in Latin America* (New York, 2003); and Peter Dale Scott and Jonathan Marshall, *Cocaine Politics: Drugs, Armies, and the CIA in Central America* (Berkeley, Calif., 1998).

37. Raat, *Mexico and the United States*, 190–95. Two symbiotic legacies of the growing human and economic integration of the United States and Mexico are the creation of a consumer culture fashioned on necessity and desire and

the militarization of the border. See Alexis McCressen, ed., *Land of Necessity: Consumer Culture in the United States–Mexican Borderlands* (Durham, N.C., 2009); and Timothy J. Dunn, *Blockading the Border and Human Rights: The El Paso Operation That Remade Immigration Enforcement* (Austin, Tex., 2009).

38. Robert S. Leiken, Introduction to *A New Moment in the Americas* (Miami, 1994), x. Rodó took the character "Ariel" from William Shakespeare's "The Tempest" and portrayed him as the "good spirit" that would overcome the evil "Caliban," a shallow "monster." Latin Americans should adopt North American positivist values, Rodó believed, but dignify them with the spiritual and poetic qualities North Americans lacked in their pursuit of material well-being. Germán Arciniegas, *Latin America: A Cultural History*, trans. Joan MacLean (New York, 1967), 488.

39. Ironically, as the power of the state diminished in the resurgence of democracy, the Latin American left proved less able to mobilize workers, peasants, and the urban poor for a return to the developmental strategies of earlier years. Jorge Castañeda, *Utopia Unarmed: The Latin American Left after the Cold War* (New York, 1993).

40. J. Patrice McSherry, *Predatory States: Operation Condor and Covert War in Latin America* (Lanham, Md., 2006); Gilbert M. Joseph and Daniela Spenser, eds., *In from the Cold: Latin America's New Encounter with the Cold War* (Durham, N.C., 2009).

41. David Scott Palmer, *U.S. Relations with Latin America during the Carter Years* (Gainesville, Fla., 2006).

42. Pérez, *Cuba and the United States*, 265–81.

43. On this theme see Arturo Escobar, *Encountering Development: The Making and Unmaking of the Third World* (Princeton, N.J., 1995).

44. On the modern "Castro connection" in Venezuela see Brian Nelson, *The Silence and the Scorpion: The Coup against Chávez and the Making of Modern Venezuela* (New York 2009).

45. Summit of the Americas, Final Declarations, April 22, 2001.

Epilogue

1. World War 4 Report in *Weekly News Update on the Americas*, 11 January 2009; Enrique Krauze, *New York Times*, 24 March 2009. See also the Special Report sponsored by the Council of Foreign Relations, *Building a North American Community*, Task Force Report no. 53 (2005).

2. "Timely Demise for Free Trade Area of the Americas," *Global Politician*, 25 November 2005.

3. For a text of the Inter-American Democratic Charter, see the Organization of American States website: http://www.oas.org.

4. Alan McPherson, *Intimate Ties, Bitter Struggles: The United States and Latin America since 1945* (Washington, D.C., 2006), 111–39. Amaury Souza assesses Brazil's goals in international affairs since the mid-1990s in *A agenda internacional do Brasil: A política externa brasileira de FHC a Lula* (Rio de Janeiro, 2009).

5. Adam Isacson, "Did Plan Colombia Work? A Look at the Numbers," *Latin America/Permalink* 18 January 2006; "Colombian Paramilitaries and the United States," *National Security Archive Update*, 16 February 2008; Greg Grandin, *Empire's Workshop: Latin America, the United States, and the Rise of the New Imperialism* (New York, 2006).

6. Paul Gootenberg, *Andean Cocaine: The Making of a Global Drug* (Chapel Hill, N.C., 2009), 4–5.

7. Pew Research Center for the People and the Press, *Mexican Immigrants in the United States, 2008* (Washington, D.C., 2009).

8. Walter A. Ewing, "The Cost of Doing Nothing: The Need for Comprehensive Immigration Reform," *Immigration Policy Brief*, January 2004.

9. Robert S. Leiken, "With a Friend Like Fox," *Foreign Affairs* 80 (March/April 2001), 46–61; Department of State, Bureau of Public Affairs, "The United States and Mexico: A Multifaceted Partnership," 13 April 2009.

10. Robert A. Pastor, "A North American Community," *Norteamérica* 1.1 (January–June 2006): 209–13; John Herd Thompson and Stephen J. Randall, *Canada and the United States: Ambivalent Allies*, 4th ed. (Athens, Ga., 2008), 338–39. For a contrasting view, see Anthony DePalma, *Here: A Biography of the New American Continent* (New York, 2001).

11. Susan Thompson, *Vive le Canada* (31 August 2006); Joseph Contreras, *In the Shadow of the Giant: the Americanization of Modern Mexico* (New Brunswick, N.J., 2009); Victor Davis Hanson, *Mexifornia: A State of Becoming* (San Francisco, 2003).

12. Randolph Bourne, "Trans-National America," in Bourne, *The Radical Will: Selected Writings, 1911–1918*, ed. Olaf Hansen (New York, 1977), 264.

13. Ilan Stevens, *Spanglish: The Making of a New American Language* (New York, 2003).

14. Under Secretary for Political Affairs, Bureau of Western Hemisphere Affairs, "Summit of the Americas," 12 April 2009.

15. Mission of Chile, "The OAS: Its Relevance Today," June 2003.
16. Department of State, Bureau of Public Affairs, "The United States and Mexico: A Multifaceted Partnership," 13 April 2009.
17. See David Patrick Geggus and Norman Fiering, eds. *The World of the Haitian Revolution* (Bloomington, Ind., 2009).
18. *Selected Writings of Bolívar*, 2 vols., ed. Harold Bierck Jr., trans. Lewis Bertrand, comp. Vicente Lecuna (New York, 1951), 1: 115.

Bibliographical Essay

With the completion of the "United States and the Americas" series, a detailed bibliographical essay identifying U.S. relations with individual countries or regions would be superfluous. With a few exceptions, this essay identifies general works related to broad themes in the U.S. experience in the Western Hemisphere from the American Revolution to the present.

The most comprehensive bibliography of United States–Latin American relations is David Trask, Michael C. Meyer, and Roger Trask, *A Bibliography of United States–Latin American Relations since 1810* (Lincoln, Neb., 1968), with a *Supplement* (Lincoln, Neb., 1979). For those interested in related items that may have been excluded from these volumes, the *Handbook of Latin American Studies* (Cambridge, Mass., Gainesville, Fla., and Austin, Tex., 1936–present, now available on a single compact disk) provides a virtually exhaustive bibliography in all fields of Latin American studies. The Latin American Network Information Center (LANIC) provides academics, scholars, teachers, and the general public access to information about Latin America today. The one-volume *Guide to American Foreign Relations since 1700* (Santa Barbara, Calif., 1983) is now available in an expanded two-volume edition under the general editorship of Robert Beisner: *American Foreign Relations since 1600: A Guide to the Literature* (Santa Barbara, Calif., 2003). Two works that fall under a broad definition of bibliographical guide and essay are Helen Delpar, *Looking South: The Evolution of Latin Americanist Scholarship in the United States, 1850–1975* (Tuscaloosa, Ala., 2008), a balanced assessment; and Mark T. Berger, *Under Northern Eyes: Latin American Studies and U.S. Hegemony in the Americas* (Bloomington, Ind., 1995), which is more detailed but more critical of U.S. policy. For Canadian–United States relations see the superb bibliographical essay in John Herd Thompson and Stephen J. Randall, *Canada and the United States: Ambivalent Allies*, 4th ed. (Athens, Ga., 2008).

General works on United States–Latin American relations, in English and Spanish, fall generally into three categories—those designed essentially as texts, lacking an overarching theme; those more attentive to the dynamics of the relationship in the twentieth century, particularly during the Cold War; and those offering either a defense or, more likely, critique of U.S. policy. Mark Gilderhus,

The Second Century: U.S.-Latin American Relations since 1889 (Wilmington, Del., 1999), skillfully blends the insights of all three approaches.

In the first category, texts, the most notable work is Graham Stuart and James L. Tigner, *Latin America and the United States*, 6th ed. (Englewood Cliffs, N.J., 1975), which is immensely detailed but lacks thematic unity. For those looking for a more concise summary, J. Lloyd Mecham, *A Survey of United States–Latin American Relations* (Boston, 1965), focuses largely on U.S. strategic concerns; and Federico Gil, *Latin American–United States Relations* (New York, 1971), identifies the cycles of U.S. interest. Wilfrid Hardy Callcott, *The Western Hemisphere: Its Influence on United States Policies to the End of World War II* (Austin, Tex., 1968); and J. Lloyd Mecham, *The United States and Inter-American Security, 1889–1960* (Austin, Tex., 1961), maintain that U.S. policy has been consistent. Excellent parallel texts from the Latin American view are G. Pope Atkins, *Latin America in the International Political System* (New York, 1977); Harold Davis et al., *Latin American Diplomatic History: An Introduction* (Baton Rouge, La., 1977); and Harold Davis and Larman Wilson, eds., *Latin American Foreign Policies: An Analysis* (Baltimore, 1975). Demetrio Boersner, *Relaciones internacionales de América Latina* (San José, C.R., 1986), is socialist in tone but often displays balance in its assessments.

In the second category, those focusing on the Cold War era, some of the most useful works are by political scientists: Abraham Lowenthal, *Partners in Conflict: The United States and Latin America* (Baltimore, 1987), which makes the case for Latin America's "transformation" since 1961; Harold Molineau, *U.S. Policy toward Latin America: From Regionalism to Globalism* (Boulder, Colo., 1986), which makes an eloquent argument for a policy of nonintervention; and Michael Kryzanek, *U.S.-Latin American Relations* (New York, 1985), which examines the internal forces, official and private, that act on hemispheric policy. Cole Blasier, *The Hovering Giant: United States Responses to Revolutionary Change in Latin America* (Pittsburgh, 1985), which focuses on Mexico, Bolivia, Cuba, Guatemala, Grenada, and Central America, is a model study. Richard Newfarmer, ed., *From Gunboats to Diplomacy: New U.S. Policies for Latin America* (Baltimore, 1984), is especially good on specific countries and alertly incorporates essays on current economic questions and the often unmeasured impact of immigration. Of the recent texts, two of the most provocative are Peter Smith, *Talons of the Eagle: Latin America, the United States, and the World* (New York, 2007); and *Intimate Ties, Bitter Struggles: The United States and Latin America since 1945* (Washington, D.C., 2006).

In the third category, those evaluating U.S. policy, the essential starting point is Samuel Flagg Bemis, *The Latin American Policy of the United States: An Historical*

Interpretation (New York, 1943), which is less an interpretation than a defense of U.S. policy and a response to the geopolitical thesis of Nicholas Spykman, *America's Strategy in World Politics* (New York, 1942). Gordon Connell-Smith, *The United States and Latin America: An Historical Analysis of Inter-American Relations* (New York, 1974), is a mild critique. Juan José Arévalo, *The Shark and the Sardines* (New York, 1961), may be the most widely read polemic on U.S. policy in the Western Hemisphere. Other writers have followed parallel themes in Spanish: Genaro Carnero Checo, *El Aguila Rampante: El imperialismo Yanqui sobre América Latina* (Mexico, 1956); Ramón Oliveres, *El Imperialismo Yanqui en América: La dominación política y económica del Continente* (Buenos Aires, 1952); and Pablo Franco, *La influencia de los Estados Unidos* (Montevideo, 1967), which emphasize economic themes. Alonso Aguilar, *Pan Americanism from Monroe to the Present: A View from the Other Side* (New York, 1969), argues that the United States has historically exploited Latin America. Jules Benjamin, "The Framework of U.S. Relations with Latin America in the Twentieth Century: An Interpretive Essay," *Diplomatic History* 11 (Spring 1987): 91–112, is essential reading.

This "United States and the Americas" series of the University of Georgia Press is dedicated to the belief that U.S. relations with individual countries and regions in the Western Hemisphere, expanded beyond the traditional government-to-government focus, remains a relevant issue, not only for those who make policy but as a reminder of the diversity of the Americas. To that end, the individual volumes in the series are designed to "stand alone" in the literature yet reflect the broad themes I set forth for them. The main titles convey the uniformity of the series, but the authors chose the subtitles, which in their minds reflect the particularity of the bilateral relationship. The individual volumes are G. Pope Atkins and Larman C. Wilson, *The Dominican Republic and the United States: From Imperialism to Nationalism* (1998); Lawrence A. Clayton, *Peru and the United States: The Condor and the Eagle* (1999); Michael L. Conniff, *Panama and the United States: The Forced Alliance* (1992, 2001); Judith Ewell, *Venezuela and the United States: From Monroe's Hemisphere to Petroleum's Empire* (1996); Thomas M. Leonard, *Central America and the United States: The Search for Stability* (1991); Kenneth D. Lehman, *Bolivia and the United States: A Limited Partnership* (1999); Frank O. Mora and Jerry Cooney, *Paraguay and the United States: Distant Allies* (2007); Louis A Pérez Jr., *Cuba and the United States: Ties of Singular Intimacy* (1990, 1997, 2003); Ronn Pineo, *Ecuador and the United States: Useful Strangers* (2007); Brenda Gayle Plummer, *Haiti and the United States: The Psychological Moment* (1992); W. Dirk Raat, *Mexico and the United States: Ambivalent Vistas* (1994, 1996, 2004); Stephen J. Randall, *Colombia and the United States: Hegemony and Interdependence* (1992); William F. Sater, *Chile and the United States: Empires in Conflict* (1990); Joseph Smith, *Brazil and the United States: Convergence and Divergence* (forthcoming); David M. K. Sheinen, *Argentina and the United States: An Alliance Contained* (2006); and John Herd Thompson and Stephen J. Randall, *Canada and the United States: Ambivalent Allies* (1994, 1997, 2002, 2008).

In both Latin America and the United States a few writers have attempted exploratory and interpretive essays on comparative cultures of the Americas or coped with the unanswerable question: Do the Americas have a common history? A convenient summary of the latter is contained in Lewis Hanke, ed., *Do the Americas Have a Common History?: A Critique of the Bolton Theory* (New York, 1964). Of those who have explored "culture" (defined in its broadest sense) to find some explanation for the political and economic differences between the United States and Latin America, a few of the older but still useful accounts are Glen Dealy, *The Public Man: An Interpretation of Latin American and Other Catholic Countries* (Amherst, Mass., 1977); E. Lawrence Harrison, *Underdevelopment Is a State of Mind: The Latin American Case* (Cambridge, Mass., 1985), which lays the blame for Latin America's economic debilities on its cultural priorities and relies heavily on Carlos Rangel, *The Latin Americans: Their Love-Hate Relationship with the United States* (New York, 1977). Jacques Maritain, *Reflections on America* (New York, 1958); Luis Alberto Sánchez, *Existe América Latina?* (Mexico City, 1945); and Mariano Baptista Gumucio, *Latinoamericanos y Norteamericanos: Cinco siglos de dos culturas* (La Paz, Bolivia, n.d.) are generally favorable to the United States.

Eduardo Galeano attempts in a trilogy, *Memory of Fire* (New York, 1986–1988), to make a statement through historical vignettes on the experience of Latin America over five centuries. Samuel Shapiro, ed., *Cultural Factors in Inter-American Relations* (Notre Dame, Ind., 1968), explores in twenty-four essays the varied imprint of culture on the hemispheric relationship. Germán Arciniegas, *Latin America: A Cultural History* (New York, 1967), esp. the introduction and pp. 487–522, deftly integrates cultural and literary themes. Akira Iriye, "Culture and Power: International Relations as Inter-Cultural Relations," *Diplomatic History* 3 (Spring 1979): 115–28, suggests that diplomatic relations between nations often derive their character from the interactions between differing cultures. Two strikingly different works contrasting the cultural and political traditions of Latin America and the United States are Fredrick B. Pike, *The United States and Latin America: Myths and Stereotypes of Civilization and Nature* (Austin, Tex., 1992); and Howard J. Wiarda, *The Soul of Latin America: The Cultural and Political Tradition* (New Haven, Conn.,

2001). On the cultural dynamics of inter-American relations in the context of empire, see Gilbert M. Joseph, Catherine LeGrand, and Ricardo D. Salvatore, eds., *Close Encounters of Empire: Writing the Cultural History of U.S.-Latin American Relations* (Durham, N.C., 1998).

Despite the diminished appeal of the older concept of a Western Hemispheric idea in the post–World War II era, some modern scholars have begun to revisit the theme, broadly defined. Arthur P. Whitaker, *The Western Hemisphere Idea: Its Rise and Decline* (Ithaca, N.Y., 1954), explores the impact of an idea on generations of American and Latin American leaders from Jefferson to Franklin Roosevelt, arguing that its utility diminished noticeably in the 1950s. For later assessments of hemispheric "connections," see Benedict Anderson, *Imagined Communities: Reflections on the Origin and Spread of Nationalism*, rev. ed. (London, 1991); Don H. Doyle and Marco Antonio Pamplona, eds., *Nationalism in the New World* (Athens, Ga., 2006); Felipe Fernández-Armesto, *The Americas: A Hemispheric History* (New York, 2003); David Sheinin, ed., *Beyond the Ideal: Pan Americanism in Inter-American Affairs* (New York, 2000); Richard M. Morse, *New World Soundings: Culture and Ideology in the Americas* (Baltimore, 1988); and the nuanced definition of hemispheric civilization explored in Charles A. Jones, *American Civilization* (London, 2007). Two works that combine both comparative and the relatively recent genre of "hemispheric" history are Lester D. Langley, *The Americas in the Age of Revolution, 1750–1850* (New Haven, Conn., 1996); and *The Americas in the Modern Age* (New Haven, Conn., 2003). For a broader perspective on the place of the Western Hemisphere in the Atlantic World, see the highly praised text by Thomas Benjamin, *The Atlantic World: Europeans, Africans, Indians, and Their Shared History, 1400–1900* (New York, 2009).

Throughout this account, I have emphasized or certainly implied that the fundamental character of the U.S. relationship with the other Americas can best be understood by looking more closely at the formative first century described in part 1, "Genesis." For a detailed comparison of the new world empires of Britain and Spain, see the magisterial account of J. H. Elliott, *Empires of the Atlantic World: Britain and Spain in the Americas, 1492–1830* (New Haven, Conn., 2006). Peggy Liss, *Atlantic Empires: The Network of Trade and Revolution, 1713–1826* (Baltimore, 1983), effectively demonstrates that theories of empire or economic models often fail to explain the realities of transatlantic rivalries in the eighteenth century. No one did more to explore the private and personal actors in the United States–Latin American experience from 1783 to 1830 (when the hemispheric relationship took on its fundamental character) than Arthur P. Whitaker. In *The Spanish American*

Frontier, 1783–1795 (Cambridge, Mass., 1927), *The Mississippi Question, 1795–1803: A Study in Trade, Politics, and Diplomacy* (Washington, D.C., 1934), and, especially, *The United States and the Independence of Latin America, 1800–1830* (Baltimore, 1941), Whitaker traced two parallel stories, one of rival governments and nations, the other, more consequential, of conflicts and agreements between their peoples that often influenced political decisions. The first two volumes in this trilogy have been largely superseded by more recent scholarship, but the last remains as fresh as it was when first published. As the title suggests, John J. Johnson, *A Hemisphere Apart: The Foundations of United States Policy toward Latin America* (Baltimore, 1990), argues that domestic and international issues reinforced rather than overcame the differences between the two Americas in the critical fifteen years after the War of 1812. Iván Jaksic, *The Hispanic World and American Intellectual Life, 1820–1880* (New York, 2007) ably details the history of a generation of mid-nineteenth-century New England intellectuals who became fascinated with Spain and the Hispanic world and their relevance. For a more nuanced approach to this era, framed in an account of the life of the most controversial Spanish American revolutionary leader, see Lester D. Langley, *Simón Bolívar: Venezuelan Rebel, American Revolutionary* (Lanham, Md., 2009).

For the era of manifest destiny, Albert K. Weinberg, *Manifest Destiny: A Study of Nationalist Expansion in American History* (Baltimore, 1935), retains its authoritativeness, as does Frederick Merk, *Manifest Destiny and Mission in American History: A Reinterpretation* (New York, 1963). Both should be supplemented with the recent appraisal of Anders Stephanson, *Manifest Destiny: American Expansionism and the Empire of Right* (New York, 1996). In two works Harry Bernstein assesses inter-American intellectual links: *Origins of Inter-American Interest, 1700–1812* (Philadelphia, 1945); and *Making an Inter-American Mind* (Gainesville, Fla., 1961). The first explores how tentative commercial ties inspired individuals in differing cultures to learn more about one another. David Pletcher, *The Diplomacy of Annexation: Texas, Oregon, and the Mexican War* (Columbia, Mo., 1973), bears the mark of careful research, balanced judgments, and authoritativeness. The same can be said for his companion volume, *The Diplomacy of Trade and Investment: American Economic Expansionism in the Hemisphere, 1865–1900* (Columbia, Mo., 1998). For the late nineteenth century, Walter LaFeber, *The New Empire: An Interpretation of American Expansion, 1860–1898* (Ithaca, N.Y., 1963), often finds in Latin American policy evidence to sustain his economic theme. Often critiqued, the work has yet to be effectively rebutted. Lester D. Langley, *Struggle for the American Mediterranean: United States–European Rivalry in the Gulf-Caribbean,*

1776–1904 (Athens, Ga., 1976), is a convenient summary. For an elegantly written account of the making of American empire, see Walter Nugent, *Habits of Empire: A History of American Expansion* (New York, 2008).

Inevitably, the idea of manifest destiny would be conflated with race as a dynamic factor in the making of both American continental and especially insular empire. For various interpretations of this theme, see Eric Love, *Race over Empire: Racism and U.S. Imperialism, 1865–1900* (Chapel Hill, N.C., 2004); Reginald Horsman, *Race and Manifest Destiny: The Origins of American Racial Anglo-Saxonism* (Cambridge, Mass., 1981); Michael Krenn, *The Color of Empire: Race and American Foreign Relations* (Washington, D.C., 2006); and Brenda Gayle Plummer, ed., *Window On Freedom: Race, Civil Rights, and Foreign Affairs, 1945–1988* (Chapel Hill, N.C., 2003). For two different approaches to the history and legacy of the black diaspora, see Michael L. Conniff and Thomas J. Davis, et al., *Africans in the Americas: A History of the Black Diaspora* (New York, 1994); and George Reid Andrews, *Afro–Latin America, 1800–2000* (New York, 2004).

Yet another topic of current inquiry into the state of the Americas is Latin American economic development and dependency. The succinct study by Stanley Stein and Barbara Stein, *The Colonial Heritage of Latin America: Essays on Economic Dependence in Perspective* (New York, 1970), offers a depressing assessment of Latin America in the twentieth century as the lamentable outcome of a colonial economy that has not achieved modernity. From there the reader can move to the more turgid (and more detailed) analyses in C. F. H. Cardoso and Hector Pérez Brignoli, *Historia económica de América Latina*, 2 vols. (Barcelona, 1979); F. H. Cardoso and E. Faletto, *Dependency and Development in Latin America* (London, 1979); Andre Gunder Frank, *Capitalism and Under-development in Latin America: Historical Studies of Chile and Brazil* (New York, 1967); Celso Furtado, *Economic Development of Latin America: Historical Background and Contemporary Problems* (Cambridge, Eng., 1977); William Glade, *The Latin American Economies: A Study of Their Institutional Evolution* (New York, 1969); Albert O. Hirschman, *The Strategy of Economic Development* (New Haven, Conn., 1959); the works of D. C. M. Platt, especially *Trade, Finance, and Politics in British Foreign Policy, 1815–1914* (Oxford, 1968), and *Latin America and British Trade, 1806–1914* (London, 1972); and Raúl Prebisch, *The Economic Development of Latin America* (New York, 1950).

A useful summary, with appropriate case studies and an excellent bibliography, is Christopher Abel and Colin Lewis, eds., *Latin America, Economic Imperialism and the State: The Political Economy of the External Connection from Independence to the Present* (London, 1985). On the impact of the debt crisis see Jonathan Hartlyn and Samuel Morley, eds., *Latin American Political Economy: Financial Crisis and Political Change* (Boulder, Colo., 1986). Thomas McCann, *An American Company: The Tragedy of United Fruit* (New York, 1976), provides a casebook example, written by a longtime publicist for the company, of a multinational enterprise in Central America and the Caribbean. Two important special studies on American investors and companies in Latin America are Robert Swansbrough, *The Embattled Colossus: Economic Nationalism and the United States Investors in Latin America* (Gainesville, Fla., 1976); and Paul Sigmund, *Multinationals in Latin America: The Politics of Nationalization* (Madison, Wis., 1980).

In assessing the Monroe Doctrine and Pan-Americanism most scholars have focused largely on political, economic, and security issues. A handy collection of essays is Donald M. Dozer, ed., *The Monroe Doctrine: Its Modern Significance* (New York, 1965), which contains representative American and Latin American views. Isidro Fabela, in *Intervención* (Mexico City, 1959), covering the legal ramifications of the subject from 1865 to 1954, reinforces the anti-U.S. Mexican view and thus should be judged alongside Ann Van Wynen and A. J. Thomas Jr., *Intervention: The Law and Its Import in the Americas* (Dallas, 1956). John A. Logan, *No Transfer: An American Security Principle* (New Haven, Conn., 1961), traces the history of a corollary of the doctrine. Dexter Perkins, *A History of the Monroe Doctrine*, rev. ed. (Boston, 1963), sums up his three-volume account from 1823 to 1907 and concludes with an assessment of the doctrine in the twentieth century. Gaddis Smith, *The Last Years of the Monroe Doctrine, 1945–1993* (New York, 1993), catalogs the decline and perhaps even the irrelevance of the doctrine since the 1950s. Two opposing interpretations of the inter-American system are Gordon Connell-Smith, *The Inter-American System* (New York, 1966), who is critical; and J. Lloyd Mecham, *The United States and Inter-American Security, 1889–1960* (Austin, Tex., 1961), who is generally favorable to U.S. policies.

For a general survey of U.S. policy toward the circum-Caribbean, see Lester D. Langley, *The United States and the Caribbean in the Twentieth Century*, 4th ed. (Athens, Ga., 1989). The early twentieth-century interventions are detailed in Lester D. Langley, *The Banana Wars: United States Intervention in the Caribbean, 1898–1934*, rev. ed. (Wilmington, Del., 2001), which details the military's involvement; and especially the two-volume account of Dana Gardner Munro, *Intervention and Dollar Diplomacy in the Caribbean, 1900–1921* (Princeton, N.J., 1964), and *The United States and the Caribbean Republics, 1921–1933* (Princeton, N.J., 1973). For the Good Neighbor era and after, I have relied on Donald Dozer, *Are We Good Neighbors? Three Decades of Inter-American Relations* (Gainesville, Fla., 1961), which incorporates considerable Latin American disenchantment with postwar U.S. policy to show how the wartime unity deteriorated. Irwin Gellman, *Good Neighbor Diplomacy: United States Policy in Latin America, 1933–45* (Baltimore, 1979), provides a balance to the hostile account in David Green, *The Containment of Latin America: A History of the Myths and Realities of the Good Neighbor Policy* (Chicago, 1971). Bryce Wood gives a meticulous analysis in *The Making of the Good Neighbor Policy* (New York, 1961) and in *The Dismantling of the Good Neighbor Policy* (Austin, Tex., 1985), which focuses on Argentina, Bolivia, and Chile to explain the collapse of the policy.

In an indictment of U.S. policy, Samuel Baily, *The United States and the Development of South America, 1945–1975* (New York, 1975), demonstrates how American planners foiled hemispheric aspirations for economic integration. Stephen Rabe, *Eisenhower and Latin America* (Chapel Hill, N.C., 1988), shows the president's activist role in shaping hemispheric policy. The companion volume, *The Most Dangerous Area in the World: John F. Kennedy Confronts Communist Revolution in Latin America* (Chapel Hill, N.C., 1999), offers a sobering reappraisal of the policy of a president who remains very much admired in Latin America. For the Alliance for Progress, Jerome Levinson and Juan de Onis, *The Alliance That Lost Its Way* (Chicago, 1970), retains its freshness and sense of immediacy. Two important collections of essays are Richard Gray, ed., *Latin America and the United States in the 1970s* (Itasca, Il., 1971); and Kevin Middlebrook and Carlos Rico, eds., *The United States and Latin America in the 1980s* (Pittsburgh, 1986), which ranges over political, economic, social, and security issues in its essays.

For those who see U.S. policy in Central America as metaphorical explanation for the essential character of U.S.–Latin American relations, a good beginning (among the seven hundred or so books on Central America published since 1979), is Walter LaFeber, *Inevitable Revolutions: The United States in Central America*, rev. ed. (New York, 1984), a book that had enormous influence among American religious groups disillusioned with "Reagan's War" in Central America. John H. Coatsworth, *Central America and the United States: The Clients and the Colossus* (New York, 1994), is more analytical. A less damning indictment of U.S. policy, with more sensitivity to the legacy of isthmian culture and history, is Lester D. Langley, *Central America: The Real Stakes* (New York, 1985).

Margaret Daly Hayes, *Latin America and the U.S. National Interest: A Basis for U.S. Foreign Policy* (Boulder, Colo., 1984), should be read alongside Lars Schoultz, *National Security and United States Policy toward Latin America* (Princeton, N.J., 1987). Tom Farer, *The Grand Strategy of the United States in Latin America* (New

Brunswick, N.J., 1988); and Lars Schoultz, *Human Rights and United States Policy toward Latin America* (Princeton, N.J., 1981), are indicative of the often unbridgeable chasm between those who debate the conflicting goals of the *United States* and *America* in the Americas. A companion volume is Lars Schoultz, *Beneath the United States: A History of U.S. Policy toward Latin America* (Cambridge, Mass., 1998).

Europeans and Americans may believe that the Cold War is over, but many Latin Americans retain a bitter memory of its often violent impact on their lives and nations. For this perspective see Greg Grandin, *Empire's Workshop: Latin America, the United States, and the Rise of the New Imperialism* (New York, 2006); and Gilbert Joseph and Daniela Spenser, eds., *In From the Cold: Latin America's New Encounter with the Cold War* (Durham, N.C., 2008). Robert A. Pastor, *Exiting the Whirlpool: U.S. Foreign Policy toward Latin America and the Caribbean* (New York, 2001), offers a balanced account that conveys both the author's knowledge of the region and his experience in the policy process.

The reader interested in the "new hemisphere" should look to the publications and Internet websites of the myriad official and private social, educational, environmental, health, business, and especially religious organizations that have a deepening reach among hemispheric peoples. Among the most helpful are those of the Inter-American Dialogue, Americas.org, Pew Hispanic Center, Inter-American Development Bank, Summit of the Americas, Institute of the Americas, the Organization of American States, the Washington Office on Latin America (WOLA), and the North American Congress on Latin America (NACLA).

Index